Continuous/Discrete-Time Fractional Systems: Modelling, Design and Estimation

Continuous/Discrete-Time Fractional Systems: Modelling, Design and Estimation

Guest Editors

Gabriel Bengochea

Manuel Duarte Ortigueira

MDPI

Basel • Beijing • Wuhan • Barcelona • Belgrade • Novi Sad • Cluj • Manchester

Guest Editors

Gabriel Bengochea
Academia de Matemática
Universidad Autónoma
de la Ciudad de México
Ciudad de México
México

Manuel Duarte Ortigueira
Centre of Technology
and Systems
NOVA University of Lisbon
Caparica
Portugal

Editorial Office
MDPI AG
Grosspeteranlage 5
4052 Basel, Switzerland

This is a reprint of the Special Issue, published open access by the journal *Fractal and Fractional* (ISSN 2504-3110), freely accessible at: https://www.mdpi.com/journal/fractalfract/special_issues/62W7D075N9.

For citation purposes, cite each article independently as indicated on the article page online and as indicated below:

Lastname, A.A.; Lastname, B.B. Article Title. *Journal Name* **Year**, *Volume Number*, Page Range.

ISBN 978-3-7258-6238-2 (Hbk)
ISBN 978-3-7258-6239-9 (PDF)
https://doi.org/10.3390/books978-3-7258-6239-9

Contents

About the Editors

Gabriel Bengochea

Gabriel Bengochea received a Mathematics degree at Metropolitan Autonomous University in April 2000 and master's and doctoral degrees at the same institution in 2006 and 2013, respectively. Now, he is an Associate Professor at the Autonomous University of Mexico City. He has published over 26 papers in journals and conferences with revisions. He is a regular reviewer of international journals. His main scientific interests are Fractional Calculus, Operational Calculus, and Fractional Systems.

Manuel Duarte Ortigueira

Manuel Duarte Ortigueira received an Electrical Engineering degree at Instituto Superior Técnico, Universidade Técnica de Lisboa, in April 1975 and PhD and Habilitation degrees at the same institution in 1984 and 1991, respectively. Now, he is an Associate Professor with Habilitation (retired) at the Electrical Engineering Department of the NOVA School of Science and Technology of NOVA University of Lisbon. He has also been a professor at Instituto Superior Técnico and Escola Náutica Infante D. Henrique. He has published 3 books on Digital Signal Processing, Fractional Calculus, and Fractional Signals and Systems and over 200 papers in journals and conferences with revisions, and has 2 registered patents. His research activity started in 1977 at Centro de Análise e Processamento de Sinais, and continued at Instituto de Engenharia de Sistemas e Computadores (INESC), where he worked with the Digital Signal Processing and Signal Processing Systems groups. Since 1997, he has worked at Instituto de Novas Tecnologias (UNINOVA), where he collaborates with the Signal Processing group of the Center of Technology and Systems. He is a regular reviewer of international journals and a member of the scientific committee of several journals and conferences. His main scientific interests are Fractional Signal Processing, Digital Signal Processing, and Biomedical Signal Processing.

Preface

This Reprint is the result of an attempt to go beyond the usual applications of Fractional Calculus. Originally, the underlying idea was to avoid being limited by what could be considered a constraint: the RL/C environment. Although we cannot say that we were successful, we are happy with the truly innovative applications. Physics is a vast field where fractional models can expand and evolve.

Dr. Bengochea dedicates this work to his beloved wife, M.A. Alma Erazo Ordaz, without whom none of this would have been possible. Dr. Ortigueira dedicates this work to his granddaughter, Luisa. Finally, we would like to thank Diana Lu for all her efforts in bringing this work to fruition.

Gabriel Bengochea and Manuel Duarte Ortigueira
Guest Editors

fractal and fractional

MDPI

Article

Discrete-Time Fractional Difference Calculus: Origins, Evolutions, and New Formalisms

Manuel Duarte Ortigueira

NOVA School of Science and Technology, UNINOVA-CTS and LASI, NOVA University of Lisbon, Quinta da Torre, 2829-516 Caparica, Portugal; mdo@fct.unl.pt

Abstract: Differences are introduced as outputs of linear systems called differencers, being considered two classes: shift and scale-invariant. Several types are presented, namely: nabla and delta, bilateral, tempered, bilinear, stretching, and shrinking. Both continuous and discrete-time differences are described. ARMA-type systems based on differencers are introduced and exemplified. In passing, the incorrectness of the usual delta difference is shown.

Keywords: nabla difference; delta difference; ARMA; ARFIMA; bilateral difference; tempered; bilinear; stretching difference

MSC: 26A33

1. Introduction

All everyday human activities give rise to signals that carry a certain type of information about the systems that generated them. These signals are bounded functions that are collected to be studied, transmitted and manipulated in order to extract the information they carry. Discrete-Time Signal Processing (DTSP), also called Digital Signal Processing, is a set of mathematical and engineering techniques that allow the processing (collection, study, analysis, synthesis, transformation, storage, etc.) of signals performed mainly on digital devices.

Combining ideas, theories, algorithms and technologies from different quadrants, the DTSP has not stopped continuously evolving and increasing its already vast field of applications. This evolution was motivated by the enormous progress of digital technologies that allow the construction of processors, in general, more reliable and robust than analog ones and, above all, more flexible. The on-chip implementation of specialized processors (e.g., FFT) has facilitated the application of mathematical techniques that would be difficult (or impossible) to perform analogically. The DTSP plays an important role in communication systems where its mission is to handle signals, both at transmission and reception, in order to achieve an efficient and reliable flow of information between source and receiver. However, it is not only in communication systems that we find DTSP applications. In fact, its field of action has widened and includes areas such as speech, radar and sonar, seismology, bio-medicine, economics, astronomy, etc. In mathematics, it has been very useful in the study of functions and in solving differential equations. The well-known Newton series is very famous.

Mathematically, the DTSP relied on several important tools such as real and complex analysis, difference equations, discrete-time Fourier and Z transforms, algebra, etc. It benefited from the enormous development of signal theory in the 2nd half of the 20th century when signal processing techniques reached a sufficiently high degree of development. However, its origins are much earlier.

In general, we can "date" the beginning of the study of signals to the discovery of periodic phenomena that led to the introduction of the notions of year, week, day, hour, etc. With an equal degree of importance, we can consider the theory and representation of music made by the Pythagoreans as the first spectral analysis. It is important to note that they actually made a discrete time-frequency formulation. More recently, we refer to the discovery and study of the spectrum of sunlight by Newton (1666) and the works of mathematicians such as Euler, Gauss (who devised the first algorithm for the fast Fourier transform in 1805), Fourier (who created the basis for spectral analysis), Sturm and Liouville. These works had direct implications on the way of studying signals in the frequency domain, which did not cease to evolve and gain importance from the 1940s thanks to the works of the theoretical field of stochastic processes (Wiener and Kolmogorov): correlation, adapted filter, Wiener filter, etc. [1,2], which are notions that would become the basis of modern developments in spectral analysis (Tukey, Parzen, Akaike, Papoulis, and Burg). It was also Tukey who, with Cooley, rediscovered the algorithm that allowed the implementation of the FFT in 1965, which was a milestone in signal analysis.

The difference equations, taking the form of the ARMA (autoregressive-moving average) model, had a rapid increase in importance due to the works of Box, Jenkins, Oppenheim, Kailath, Kalman, Robinson, Rabiner, and many others in the 1980s of the 20th century [3–8]. We can place here the real beginning and affirmation of DTSP. Nevertheless, the discovery of computers was perhaps the biggest impulse given to the DTSP by the possibility of discrete implementation of processor devices, which was previously made exclusively with analog technology and to perform simulations that allow to predict, with great accuracy, the behavior of a given system. This led to an autonomization of the theory of "Discrete Signals and Systems" that became an independent branch, leading to alternative technological solutions based on digital design and realization devices [3,4,8–15]. Although the main developments were based on difference equations, the true origins were not forgotten and motivated some attempts to model and identify systems based on the delta difference [16–20].

The emergence of fractional tools has opened new doors to the modeling and estimation of everyday systems that were known to be best described by fractional systems. However, this does not mean that there was a coherent theory of fractional systems in discrete time. Probably the first attempt was made in [21], but the systems described are not really fractional, although they use fractional delays. In the last 20 years, many texts have been published on fractional differences and derivatives in discrete time, leading to different views of what fractional systems in discrete time are and how they are characterized [22–28]. The purpose of this paper is exactly to describe the mathematical basis underlying the main formulations. We introduce differences through a system approach to highlight the fact that the required definition must be valid for any function regardless of its support. This allows for a broader scope. On the other hand, it is important to make a clear distinction between time flow from left to right (causal case) or the other way around (anti-causal). Under normal conditions, they should not be mixed. To this end, we define "time sequence" as an alternative to "time scale", avoiding the confusion that the latter might introduce. We will proceed with the definitions of nabla (causal) and delta (anti-causal) differences and enumerate their main properties. We proceed with the introduction of other formulations, such as discrete-time, bilateral, tempered differences, and the completely new bilinear differences. These differences are "invariant under translations". We propose new "scale-invariant differences" that are connected to Hadamard derivatives. For all the presented differences, ARMA-type difference equations are proposed.

Given the importance of discrete signals inherent in this work, we review the classical sampling theorem valid for the case of shift-invariant systems [14,29–32] and another one suitable for scale-invariant systems, but they different from similar studies in the literature [33,34].

The paper is outlined as follows. In Section 2, we present several mathematical tools useful in the paper and clarify some notions. The sampling theorems are introduced here. Section 3 is used to make a historical overview of the difference evolutions, both continuous and discrete-time. The different approaches are described. The problems created by some definitions are criticized in Section 4. The main contributions in this paper are presented in Section 5 where several shift-invariant differencers and accumulators, say: nabla, delta, two-sided, tempered, and bilinear, are introduced. For all the definitions, continuous-time and discrete-time versions are presented. The scale-invariant differences are introduced and studied in Section 6. All the described differences are suitable for defining ARMA-type linear systems. This is exemplified in Section 7. Finally, we present a brief discusion.

2. Preliminaries

2.1. Glossary and Assumptions

In the evolution of the DTSP, several notions have been introduced without retaining a clear meaning. In fractional calculus, there is considerable confusion in the terminology adopted having, in some cases, the same name for different operators. Here, we try to clarify the meaning of some terms in order to avoid confusion. Therefore, we start with some fundamental terms. Later, we will introduce others, which are needed in the rest of the document [35].

- Anti-causal [36]
  An anti-causal system is causal under reverse time flow. A system is *anti-causal* if the output at any instant depends only on values of the input and/or output at the present and future time instants. The delta derivative is an example of an anti-causal system.
- Anti-difference
  The operator that is simultaneously the left and right inverse of the difference will be called *anti-difference*.
- Backward
  Reverse time flow—from future to past.
- Causal operator or system [37–39]
  A system is *causal* if the output at any instant depends only on the values of the input and/or output at the present and past instants. The nabla derivative is an example of a causal system.
- Forward
  Normal time flow—from past to future.
- Fractional
  Fractional will have the meaning of a non-integer real number.
- Scale-invariant system
  A system is scale-invariant if a stretching or shrinking in the input produces the same stretching/shrinking in the output. It is described by the Mellin convolution [33,40]

$$y(\tau) = x(\tau) \star g(\tau) = \int_0^\infty x\left(\frac{\tau}{\eta}\right) g(\eta) \frac{d\eta}{\eta}.$$

- Signal
  Bounded function that conveys some kind of information.
- Shift-invariant system
  A system is shift-invariant if a delay or lead in the input produces the same delay/lead in the output. It is described by the usual convolution [37]

$$y(t) = x(t) * g(t) = \int_{-\infty}^{+\infty} x(t-\eta) g(\eta) \mathrm{d}\eta.$$

- System [37,38]
  Any operator that transforms signals into signals. We will often use the terms system and operator interchangeably.

2.2. Some Mathematical Tools

Traditionally, the delta symbol is used for the so-called "forward difference" and it comes from a long time ago [41], while nabla is attached to the "backward difference" [42], in contradiction with the time flow. However, they are generalized for any order through the same way: the binomial theorem [43]. Let $\alpha \in \mathbb{R} - \mathbb{Z}^-$. Then,

$$(1-z)^\alpha = \sum_{k=0}^{\infty} (-1)^k \binom{\alpha}{k} z^k, \quad |z| < 1. \tag{1}$$

We can extend it for negative integer values of α through the Pochhammer symbol. The binomial coefficients

$$\binom{\alpha}{\beta} = \frac{\Gamma(\alpha+1)}{\Gamma(\alpha-\beta+1)\Gamma(\beta+1)}$$

assume a central role in the theory we will develop in the following. They enjoy interesting properties [36,44]:

- $$\left|\binom{\alpha}{\beta}\right| \leq \frac{A}{\beta^{\alpha+1}}, \text{ for } \beta \to \infty,$$

  with $A > 0$.

- $$\binom{\alpha}{n} = \frac{\Gamma(\alpha+1)}{\Gamma(\alpha-n+1)n!} = (-1)^n \frac{(-\alpha)_n}{n!}, \quad n \in \mathbb{N},$$

  where $(a)_n$ is the Pochhammer symbol for the rising factorial

  $$(a)_n = \prod_{k=0}^{n-1} (a+k) = \frac{\Gamma(a+n)}{\Gamma(a)}, \text{ with } (a)_0 = 1,$$

  generalized as

  $$(a)_\beta = \frac{\Gamma(a+\beta)}{\Gamma(a)}, \text{ with } (a)_0 = 1.$$

- $$\binom{\alpha}{n} = (-1)^n \binom{n-\alpha-1}{n}.$$

- $$\binom{\alpha+n}{n} = \binom{\alpha+n}{\alpha}.$$

- $$\sum_{m=0}^{\infty} \binom{\alpha}{m}\binom{\beta}{n-m} = \binom{\alpha+\beta}{n}.$$

- The falling factorial is represented by [42]

  $$(a)^{(n)} = \prod_{k=0}^{n-1} (a-k) = \frac{\Gamma(a+1)}{\Gamma(a+1-n)}, \text{ with } (a)_0 = 1,$$

  so that

  $$\binom{\alpha}{n} = \frac{(\alpha)^{(n)}}{n!}, \quad n \in \mathbb{N},$$

  and

  $$(a)^{(n)} = (-1)^n (-a)_n.$$

  It is generalized by

  $$(a)^{(\beta)} = \frac{\Gamma(a+1)}{\Gamma(a+1-\beta)}, \text{ with } (a)_0 = 1,$$

and

$$(a)^{(\beta)} = (a - \beta + 1)_\beta.$$

The (bilateral) Laplace transform (LT) is given [45]:

$$\mathcal{L}[h(t)] = H(s) = \int_{-\infty}^{\infty} h(t)e^{-st}\,\mathrm{d}t,\ s \in \mathbb{C}, \tag{2}$$

that is assumed to converge in some non-void region (region of convergence—ROC) which may degenerate into the imaginary axis, givig rise to the Fourier transform (with $s = i\omega$.) We define the inverse LT by the Bromwich integral

$$h(t) = \mathcal{L}^{-1}F(s) = \frac{1}{2\pi i}\int_{a-i\infty}^{a+i\infty} H(s)e^{st}\,\mathrm{d}s,\ t \in \mathbb{R}, \tag{3}$$

where $a \in \mathbb{R}$ is called abscissa of convergence. Frequently, we denote by γ the integration path.

In a similar way, we define the Mellin transform (MT) by [40]

$$\mathcal{M}[h(t)] = H(v) = \int_{0}^{\infty} h(t)t^{-v-1}\,\mathrm{d}t,\ v \in \mathbb{C}, \tag{4}$$

with an inverse similar to (3)

$$h(t) = \mathcal{M}^{-1}H(v) = \frac{1}{2\pi i}\int_{\gamma} H(v)t^{v}\,\mathrm{d}v,\ t \in \mathbb{R}^+. \tag{5}$$

For the discrete-time case, we define the Z transform [14,36] by

$$\mathcal{Z}[f(n)] = F(z) = \sum_{n=-\infty}^{+\infty} f(n)z^{-n}, \quad z \in \mathbb{C}, \tag{6}$$

with the inverse given by the Cauchy integral

$$f(n) = \frac{1}{2\pi\, i}\oint_c F(z)z^{n-1}\mathrm{d}z, \tag{7}$$

where c is the unit circle. With the change of variable $z = e^{i\omega},\ -\pi < \omega \leq \pi$, we obtain the discrete-time Fourier transform.

2.3. On Time Sequences

A powerful approach to the continuous/discrete unification and generalization was introduced by Aulbach and Hilger through the calculus on *time scales* [46,47]. These are non-empty closed subsets $\mathbb{T}$ of the set $\mathbb{R}$ of real numbers. Let t be the current instant. Using the language of the time-scale calculus, the previous next instant is denoted by $\rho(t)$. Similarly, the next following point on the time scale $\mathbb{T}$ is denoted by $\sigma(t)$. One has

$$\rho(t) = t - \nu(t), \quad \sigma(t) = t + \mu(t),$$

where $\nu(t)$ and $\mu(t)$ are called the *graininess* functions. These functions can be used to construct any time sequences. However, we will not continue this way.

Remark 1. *The designation "time scale" is misleading, since the word "scale" is associated to a notion of stretching or shrinking, frequently having a relation to a speed or a rate. For example, consider a function $f(t)$ defined on $\mathbb{R}$ and a parameter $a > 0$, which allow us to define a new function $g(t) = f(at)$. We modified the way that the flux of information is delivered. An interesting* *example is given by the classic turntables where we are able to switch from a rotation speed to another one. This parameter is usually called scale. Therefore, we propose here the use of the designation time sequence.*

In this work, we will consider time sequences $\mathbb{T}$ defined by a set of discrete instants t_n, $n \in \mathbb{Z}$, and by the corresponding *graininess* functions. We define a direct graininess [48,49]

$$t_n = t_{n-1} + \nu_n, \quad n \in \mathbb{Z},$$

and reverse graininess

$$t_n = t_{n+1} - \mu_n, \quad n \in \mathbb{Z},$$

where we avoid representing any reference instant t_0. These definitions of "irregular" sequences are suitable for dealing with some of the most interesting time sequences we find in practice. However, we have some difficulties in doing some kind of manipulations that are also very common. Let us consider a time sequence defined on $\mathbb{R}$ and unbounded when $t \to \pm\infty$. For example, a time sequence defined by

$$t_n = nT + \tau_n, \quad n \in \mathbb{Z}, \quad T > 0, \quad |\tau_n| < \frac{T}{2},$$

which we can call an "almost linear sequence" [50]. However, in the most interesting engineering applications, we consider regular (uniform) sequences

$$\mathbb{T} = h\mathbb{Z} = \{\ldots, -3h, -2h, -h, 0, h, 2h, 3h, \ldots\},$$

with $h \in \mathbb{R}^+$.

Remark 2. *We can consider a slided time sequence by a given value, $a + h\mathbb{Z}$, $a < h$, but this corresponds to introducing another parameter that we cannot determine due to the relativistic character of any time sequence. In other words, we need another time sequence not depending on a to fix it. However, this may be an acceptable procedure for studying continuous-time functions.*

Now, consider a power transformation of a time sequence:

$$\theta = q^t.$$

We generate a new (scale)–sequence which is in $\mathbb{R}^+$. In particular, we will obtain sequences such as

$$\theta_n = \theta^n, \quad n \in \mathbb{Z}, \quad \theta > 0,$$

or

$$\theta_n = \theta_{n-1} \cdot \tau_n, \quad n \in \mathbb{Z}, \quad \tau_n > 0.$$

We will use these sequences when dealing with scale-invariant differences.

2.4. On the Sampling

Let $f(t)$, $t \in \mathbb{R}$ be a continuous-time bounded function. The discrete-time function obtained from $f(t)$ by retaining the values at a set of pre-specified instants is the sampled function, $f(t_n)$, $n \in \mathbb{Z}$. The procedure for obtaining such a function is called *ideal sampling*. From an operator (system) point of view, this is obtained with the help of the comb distribution. Although we can consider irregular combs, we will not do it here [50]. We intend to use uniform time sequences that lead us to the usual comb. This is a periodic repetition of the Dirac delta function [51–54]. Here, we state it in the following format.

$$c(t) = \sum_{n=-\infty}^{+\infty} \delta(\frac{t}{T} - n), \tag{8}$$

where T is the sampling interval. The Fourier transform (FT) of this function is also a periodic comb.

$$FT\left[\sum_{n=-\infty}^{+\infty} \delta(t-nT)\right] = \frac{2\pi}{T}\sum_{m=-\infty}^{+\infty} \delta(\omega - m\frac{2\pi}{T}). \tag{9}$$

The comb is called the ideal sampler because, when multiplying a given function, $x(t)$, by a comb, $c(t)$, it retains the samples of the original function, giving rise to a modulated comb:

$$x_s(t) = x(t)\cdot c(t) = \sum_{n=-\infty}^{+\infty} x(t)\delta(\frac{t}{T}-n) = T\sum_{n=-\infty}^{+\infty} x(nT)\delta(t-nT). \tag{10}$$

If $x(t)$ has a jump at $t = n_0 T$, we use the half sum of the lateral limits $x(n_0 T) = \frac{x(n_0T^+)+x(n_0T^-)}{2}$, which is in agreement with the inverse Laplace and Fourier integrals. Let $X(s)$ be the LT of $x(t)$. Then, the LT of $x_s(t)$ is given by [28]

$$X_s(s) = FT[x(t)\cdot c(t)] = \sum_{m=-\infty}^{+\infty} X(s - im\frac{2\pi}{T}), \tag{11}$$

stating the well-known phenomenon: sampling in a given domain implies a repetition in the transform domain, meaning that the sampling operation produces a repetition of the transform in parallel to the real axis in strips of width $\frac{2\pi}{T}$. We observe here the reason for including T in (11): the term corresponding to $m = 0$ is $X(s)$. The study we performed was based on the Laplace transform, but it can be performed also with the Fourier transform.

The choice of T depends on the objectives of the work at hand. In general, we can choose any value except if we have in mind the recovery of $X(s)$ from $X_s(s)$. In such a case, we can impose that $X(s)$ and $X_s(s)$ have the same poles in the strip defined by $|Im(s)| < \frac{\pi}{T}$. However, the most known approach is the *Whittaker–Kotel'nikov–Shannon sampling theorem* [12,14,29–32]

Theorem 1. *If a function is bandlimited to $[-\frac{\pi}{T}, \frac{\pi}{T}]$, it is completely determined by giving its ordinates at a series of points spaced T seconds apart [29–31]:*

$$f(t) = \sum_{k=-\infty}^{\infty} f(kT)\ \mathrm{sinc}(\frac{t}{T}-k), \tag{12}$$

where

$$\mathrm{sinc}(t) = \frac{\sin(\pi t)}{\pi t},$$

with $\mathrm{sinc}(0) = 1$ *being the so-called sinc function that is the impulse response of the ideal lowpass filter [14].*

Consider the instant $a + nT,\ n \in \mathbb{Z},\ \gamma = a/T < 1$ and denote $f(nT)$ by f_n. We obtain

$$f(a+nT) = \sum_{k=-\infty}^{\infty} f(kT)\ \mathrm{sinc}(\frac{a}{T}+n-k)$$

and

$$f_{n+\gamma} = \sum_{k=-\infty}^{\infty} f(kT)\ \mathrm{sinc}(\gamma+n-k),$$

that states what we can call fractional translation, which allows expressing unknown intermediate values in terms of the uniformly spaced samples. The reverse can also be performed [21].

The Whittaker–Kotel'nikov–Shannon sampling theorem is based on the usual Fourier transform that has a relation with the shift-invariant systems, since it is defined in terms of the eigenfunctions of such systems: the exponentials. To obtain a similar theorem for scale-invariant systems, we start from the Fourier–Mellin transform that we define by:

$$F(iv) = \int_0^\infty f(\tau)\tau^{-iv-1}d\tau, \tag{13}$$

with inverse

$$f(\tau) = \frac{1}{2\pi}\int_{-\infty}^\infty F(iv)\tau^{iv}dv, \tag{14}$$

obtained from (4) and (5) by letting $v = iv$.

Let $Q \in \mathbb{R}^+$. As above, consider a bandlimited scale function as the one verifying

$$F(iv) = 0, \quad |v| > \frac{\pi}{Q},$$

that has an associated Fourier series

$$F(iv) = \sum_{k=-\infty}^{\infty} F_k e^{-ikQv},$$

with

$$F_k = \frac{Q}{2\pi}\int_{-\frac{\pi}{Q}}^{\frac{\pi}{Q}} F(iu)e^{ikQu}\mathrm{d}u = Qf(e^{kQ}), \;\; k \in \mathbb{Z}.$$

We have successively

$$\begin{aligned} f(\tau) &= \frac{1}{2\pi}\int_{-\frac{\pi}{Q}}^{\frac{\pi}{Q}} \sum_{k=-\infty}^{\infty} F_k e^{-ikQv}\tau^{iv}dv, \\ &= \sum_{k=-\infty}^{\infty} F_k \frac{1}{2\pi}\int_{-\frac{\pi}{Q}}^{\frac{\pi}{Q}} e^{iv(\ln(\tau)-kQ)}\tau^{iv}dv, \\ &= \sum_{k=-\infty}^{\infty} F_k \frac{\sin\left[\frac{\pi}{Q}(\ln(\tau)-kQ)\right]}{\pi(\ln(\tau)-kQ)}, \\ &= \sum_{k=-\infty}^{\infty} F_k \frac{\sin\left[\pi\left(\frac{\ln(\tau)}{Q}-k\right)\right]}{Q\pi(\frac{\ln(\tau)}{Q}-k)}. \end{aligned}$$

Therefore, the scale-invariant sampling theorem reads

Theorem 2. *Let $f(\tau)$, $\tau \in \mathbb{R}^+$ be a bandlimited scale function. It is completely determined by giving its ordinates at a series of exponentialy spaced points*

$$f(\tau) = \sum_{k=-\infty}^{\infty} f(e^{kQ})\,\mathrm{sinc}\left(\frac{\ln(\tau)}{Q} - k\right). \tag{15}$$

From this and through a comparison with Theorem 1, we conclude that the scale-invariant comb is given by:

$$s(\tau) = \sum_{k=-\infty}^{\infty} \delta\left(\frac{\ln(\tau)}{Q} - k\right), \tag{16}$$

that represents a sequence of impulses located at the points in the set $\mathcal{Q} : \tau = e^{kQ}$, $k \in \mathbb{Z}$. These results, slightly different from similar results existing in the literature [33,34], will be used later in the corresponding difference definitions.

These two sampling theorems require that the functions have Fourier transforms with bounded support. However, this may not happen in practice, originating what is known by "aliasing", and several procedures exist to alleviate its effect [14,29–31]. If we do not want to recover the continuous-time function, the sampling theorems give us a chance to reduce the losses in the continuous-to-discrete conversion.

Remark 3. *Traditionally, we simplify the notation by writing* $f_n = f(nT)$ *and* $f_{n+\gamma} = f((n+\gamma)T)$*. We will adopt this procedure. For the case stated in (15), we set* $q = e^Q$ *and* $f_{q^n} = f(e^{nQ})$*.*

3. Historical Overview

3.1. Euler Procedure

Newton and Leibniz introduced their (different) approaches to infinitesimal calculus in the 17th century. Leibniz's approach was based on generalizations of sums and differences. In particular, his definition of derivative was formulated in terms of limits of increments

$$f'(t) = \frac{df}{dt} = \lim_{h\to 0} \frac{f(t) - f(t-h)}{h} \quad f'(t) = \frac{df}{dt} = \lim_{h\to 0} \frac{f(t+h) - f(t)}{h}. \tag{17}$$

Euler (1768) took these formulae, removed the limit operation and used the "incremental quotients" as approximations of the derivative in solving differential equations on a set, $\mathbb{T}$, of pre-defined values of t, $\mathbb{T} = t_n$, $n = 0, 1, 2, \cdots$. With this procedure, he was led to discrete functions, $f(t_n)$. It was the birth of the "difference equations", and the procedure is the currently known Euler method. So, the difference equations gained the protagonism that belonged to the differential equations. This procedure originated the "numerical analysis" in mathematics and, in the 20th century, the discrete-time signal processing [13–15,36,37,55,56] that is a well established scientific area being responsible for important realizations in our daily life.

The former procedure, retaining the incremental ratio, was not completely abandoned; it continued being important as an intermediate step to obtain difference equations [14], and it was used in some applications [17,18]. The modern approach to differential discrete equations dates back to Hilger's works on looking for a continuous/discrete unification [46,47,57].

To give a more precise idea and clarify the nomenclature, consider the differential equation

$$\frac{df(t)}{dt} + af(t) = \frac{dg(t)}{dt} + bg(t),$$

where $f(t)$ and $g(t)$ are real functions of real variables and $a, b \in \mathbb{R}$. Using the first incremental ratio

$$\nabla f(t) = \frac{f(t) - f(t-h)}{h}, \tag{18}$$

in the equation, we obtain

$$\nabla f(t) + af(t) = \nabla g(t) + bg(t), \tag{19}$$

that leads to

$$(1 + ah)f(t) - f(t-h) = (1 + bh)g(t) - g(t-h), \tag{20}$$

that is a difference equation. Note that only present and past values are involved: it represents a causal system. With a similar procedure for the other derivative

$$\Delta f(t) = \frac{f(t+h) - f(t)}{h}, \tag{21}$$

we obtain

$$\Delta f(t) + af(t) = \Delta g(t) + bg(t), \tag{22}$$

that gives

$$f(t+h) - (1+ah)f(t) = g(t+h) - (1+ah)g(t), \quad (23)$$

that is again a difference equation but involving only present and future values: anti-causal.

If we sample the function at a given discrete time grid $\mathbb{T}: t_n,\ n \in \mathbb{Z}$, (19) and (22) become discrete-time differential equations, while (20) and (23) transform into discrete-time difference equations.

3.2. Differences and Fractional Calculus

A fractional difference was introduced for the first time in 1832 by Liouville [58,59] who used it for defining a fractional derivative. His first formula, derived directly to be a generalization of the delta derivative, assumed the form:

$$\bar{\Delta}_L^{\alpha} f(t) = h^{-\alpha} \sum_{k=0}^{\infty} (-1)^k \binom{\alpha}{k} f(t + (\alpha - k)h). \quad (24)$$

This formula constituted a second step into defining fractional-order derivatives. However, Liouville recognized that such a formula was not exactly what he was looking for and introduced also another one, much more interesting, that we can write as

$$\nabla^{\alpha} f(t) = h^{-\alpha} \sum_{k=0}^{\infty} (-1)^k \binom{\alpha}{k} f(t - kh). \quad (25)$$

He observed that if $f(t) = e^{st},\ t \in \mathbb{R}$, the summation was convergent if $Re(s) > 0$. This formula was the base of the fractional derivative definition used by Grünwald [60] and Letnikov [61,62]. It is important to note that the Liouville definition was assumed to be valid for functions of exponential type and defined on $\mathbb{R}$ or $\mathbb{C}$, while Grünwald and Letnikov worked on $[t_0, t] \in \mathbb{R}$.

In the study of operators based on his operational methods, Heaviside obtained the same result and made a study of the binomial series which he generalized [43,63,64]. This approach was retaken later by E. Post (1930) [65] and by P. Butzer and U. Westphal (1974) [66]. In addition, in 1974, J. Diaz and T. Osier obtained a particular case of (24) with $h = 1$ [67]. In a later section, we will perform the analysis of such a definition.

It is important to highlight that while searching for a definition convergent for $Re(s) < 0$, Liouville arrived at the delta-type difference

$$\Delta_L^{\alpha} f(t) = (-h)^{-\alpha} \sum_{k=0}^{\infty} (-1)^k \binom{\alpha}{k} f(t + kh). \quad (26)$$

However, this route to fractional calculus never gained the favor of the vast majority of researchers, so it was basically considered as an approximation and used in numerical methods. Very interesting are the integral representations for (25) and (26) [25,67] and the two-sided differences [68,69]. The approach and applications introduced by V. Tarasov are also very important [23,24].

Due to its (bad) influence, we are going to study the "difference" (24) that states the first attempt Liouville made to define a fractional derivative using an infinite summation. It seems that in an independent way, Diaz and Osler proposed as a delta difference the expression [67]

$$\Delta_{D+O}^{\alpha} f(t) = \sum_{k=0}^{\infty} (-1)^k \binom{\alpha}{k} f(t + \alpha - k). \quad (27)$$

As it is easy to observe, this formula, while agreeing with the requests in the positive integer order, fails in the fractional order, since it uses simultaneously past and future values. This fact has implications in the discrete-time differences deduced from it.

To make a fair analysis, let us apply the LT to (24). We obtain

$$F_{\Delta^{\alpha}_{D+O}}(s) = e^{\alpha s} \sum_{k=0}^{\infty} (-1)^k \binom{\alpha}{k} e^{-ks} F(s). \tag{28}$$

The series converges only for $Re(s) > 0$, which implies causality, contrarily to what we were expecting, since the delta difference should be anti-causal. Therefore, the formula (24) does not make sense, and not good consequences should be expected from it.

3.3. Discrete-Time Differences

A less likely appearance of a discrete difference happened in a different context, the summation of series using Cesàro's method [43,70,71], where S. Chapman introduced a fractional delta discrete difference as being given by

$$\Delta^{\alpha}_{C} v_n = \lim_{p \to \infty} \sum_{k=0}^{p-n+1} (-1)^k \binom{\alpha}{k} v_{n+k}, \quad n \in \mathbb{N}, \tag{29}$$

that was considered by G. Isaacs as an alternative to Diaz and Osler's approach, which was mainly due to the validity of the associativity of orders [72]. However, in 1962, Isaacs proposed another formulation reading

$$\Delta^{N}_{I} v_n = \sum_{k=n}^{\infty} \binom{k-n-N-1}{k-n} v_k, \quad n \in \mathbb{N}. \tag{30}$$

It is important to highlight that Isaacs' formulae express anti-causal differences as we should expect. Among several interesting results, he presented what can be considered a discrete Leibniz rule

$$\Delta^{N}_{I}(v_n w_n) = \sum_{k=N}^{\infty} \binom{N}{k} \Delta^{k}_{I} v_n \Delta^{N-k}_{I} w_{n+k}.$$

Meanwhile, discrete signal (time-series) analysis, which has benefited from major developments since World War II, received a spectacular boost with the publication of the landmark book *Time Series Analysis: Forecasting and Control* by George E. P. Box and Gwilym M. Jenkins [4]. Here, the authors presented a coherent and mathematically well-founded study of the ARMA models and their evolution, the Autoregressive-Moving Integrated Average models (ARIMA) [10,73]. The "integrated" factor pointed already to what was going to happen next: the insertion of a "fractionally integrated" term, leading to the ARFIMA models [74–80]. To the formalization of this new model, the concept of fractional differencing was introduced through (1) [74,75]

$$(1 - z^{-1})^{\alpha} = \sum_{k=0}^{\infty} (-1)^k \binom{\alpha}{k} z^{-k} = \sum_{k=0}^{\infty} \frac{(-\alpha)_k}{k!} z^{-k},$$

for $|z| > 1$, meaning that

$$\nabla^{\alpha} v_n = \sum_{k=0}^{\infty} \frac{(-\alpha)_k}{k!} v_{n-k}, \quad n \in \mathbb{Z}, \tag{31}$$

that corresponds to make $h = 1$ in the nabla (Liouville–)Grünwald–Letnikov difference. These two formulae were also introduced earlier by Cargo and Shisha in the study of the zeros of polynomials [81]. The fractionally differenced and integrated models have gained roots and continue being used today [10,15,82]. In engineering, namely in signal processing, a fractional generalization of the ARMA model has been proposed [25,27].

A brief glance at (31) may give us an impression of repulsion due to the summation to infinity. However, such an impression is incorrect, because if the function is null for $n < n_0 \in \mathbb{Z}$, the summation becomes finite. For example, if $v_n = 0,\ n < 0$,

$$\nabla^\alpha v_n = \sum_{k=0}^{n} (-1)^k \frac{(-\alpha)_n}{n!} v_{n-k}, \quad n \in \mathbb{N}. \tag{32}$$

However, H. Gray and N. Zhang did not notice this fact and, in 1988, proposed an alternative through a new definition of the fractional difference. They had in mind to preserve many properties of fractional derivative definitions, namely the exponent law and the important Leibniz rule. To obtain it, they started from the summation formula that they repeated using the Cauchy procedure to obtained the n-fold summation

$$\nabla^{-N} f(t) = \frac{1}{\Gamma(N)} \sum_{k=k_0}^{t} (t-k+1)_{N-1} f(k).$$

This definition can be extended to $N \in \mathbb{Z}_0^-$. It is important to refer that such a formula was already known from the theory of Z transform [9], since it corresponds to the inverse of a multiple pole at the point $z = 1$ in the complex plane (discrete integrator or accumulator). Gray and Zhang were led to the following definition:

Let $\alpha \in \mathbb{R}$ and $f(t)$ are defined over the set $\mathbb{T} = k_0 - N, k_0 - N + 1, \cdots, 0, 1, \cdots, t \in \mathbb{Z}$. The α-order summation over $\mathbb{T}_0 = k_0, k_0 + 1, \cdots, t \in \mathbb{Z}$ is defined by

$$\nabla^{-\alpha} f(t) = \frac{\nabla^N}{\Gamma(\alpha+N)} \sum_{k=k_0}^{t} (t-k+1)_{N+\alpha-1} f(k), \tag{33}$$

where $N = \max 0, N_0 \in \mathbb{Z}$ such that $0 < \alpha + N < 1$. The α-order derivative is defined by the substitution $-\alpha \to \alpha$. This definition is coherent with the usual integer-order difference. It is interesting to note that the above definition mimics the Riemann–Liouville definition of fractional derivative [36,44,83]. It can be shown that, setting $N - 1 < \alpha \leq N \in \mathbb{Z}_0^+$, we obtain

$$\begin{aligned} \nabla^\alpha f(t) &= \frac{\nabla^N}{\Gamma(N-\alpha)} \sum_{k=k_0}^{t} (t-k+1)_{N-\alpha-1} f(k) \\ &= \frac{\nabla^N}{\Gamma(N-\alpha)} \sum_{k=0}^{t-k_0} (k+1)_{N-\alpha-1} f(t-k). \end{aligned} \tag{34}$$

Consider the $N = 0$ case and note that

$$(k+1)_{-\alpha-1} = \frac{\Gamma(-\alpha+k)}{\Gamma(k+1)} = (-1)^k \binom{\alpha}{k}$$

meaning that (33) coincides with (26), provided that we remove the constraint on the domain of $f(t)$ and let it be defined over $\mathbb{Z}$. On the other hand, we can prove that if $N > 0$,

$$\nabla^N \binom{\alpha}{k} = \binom{\alpha+N}{k}.$$

In such a case, we can write, for any α

$$\begin{aligned} \nabla^\alpha f(t) &= \frac{\nabla^N}{\Gamma(N-\alpha)} \sum_{k=0}^{\infty} (k+1)_{-\alpha-1} f(t-k) \\ &= \sum_{k=0}^{\infty} (-1)^k \binom{\alpha}{k} f(t-k). \end{aligned} \tag{35}$$

This last expression coincides with (26) when $h = 1$. We can conclude that the work of H. Gray and N. Zhang shows a different but equivalent to Liouville's and Chapman's way to introduce fractional differences. They presented the causal (nabla) version, but it is not very difficult to obtain the corresponding anti-causal (delta). It is important to remark that they introduced, for the first time, the discrete-time Riemann–Liouville-type difference. The Caputo-type difference was introduced later for both nabla and delta cases [84–86]. Meanwhile, K. Miller and B. Ross [87] presented an approach to delta difference that we will consider next. After these publications, it seems there existed a time gap of almost 11 years without any novelty on the subject excepting the revision of the difference concepts having in consideration the notions and unification introduced by Hilger [46,47] and the discrete-time approximations to continuous-time derivatives by I. Podlubny [88]. In [57], Bohner and Peterson revised the concepts of differences and derivatives in terms of the notion of *time scale*.

4. A Critical View of Some Aspects Related to Differences

4.1. A "Fractional Delta Difference" that Is Not a Delta Difference

Concerning the fractional difference, only in 2007, F. Atici and P. Eloe returned to the subject by considering the delta difference first [89,90] and the nabla later [91]. Although they introduce a similar formulation to Gray and Zhang's, it seems they were unaware of it, at least initially. They intended to follow closely the continuous-time fractional derivative definitions. The starting point was the definition of Miller and Ross, which [87] they recovered [89,90]. However, this definition was based off the continuous-time difference of Diaz and Osler that we studied above. These works were followed by many others in the last 15 years. This had, as a consequence, a parallel introduction of several similar but different formalizations, even from the same author, of both nabla and delta differences, as the Riemann–Liouville-like and Caputo-like formulations, their compositions, and difference equations [22,84,85,89,90,92–103].

As referred, the approach of Atici and Eloe started by using the definition of Miller and Ross for the fractional discrete delta sum given by

$$\left(\Delta_a^{-\alpha} f\right)(t) = \frac{1}{\Gamma(\alpha)} \sum_{u=a}^{t-\alpha} (t - \sigma(u))^{(\alpha-1)} f(u) \tag{36}$$

where $\alpha > 0$, $\sigma(t) = t + 1$, and $t = a + \alpha + k, k = 0, 1, 2, \cdots, N - 1$. The function $f(t)$ was defined in $\mathbb{T}_a = a, a + 1, a + 2, \cdots$. As shown by D. Mozyrska [99], it can assume the form

$$\Delta^{-\alpha} f(t) = \sum_{m=0}^{k} \binom{k - m + \alpha - 1}{k - m} f(a + m) \tag{37}$$

For the nabla difference, again in disagreement with Gray and Zhang, they proposed [90,91,104]

$$\nabla^{-\alpha} f(t) = \frac{1}{\Gamma(\alpha)} \sum_{u=a}^{t} \frac{\Gamma(t - u + \alpha - 1)}{\Gamma(t - u)} f(u)$$

As above, set $u = a + m$ and $t = a + 1 + k$ to obtain

$$\nabla^{-\alpha} f(t) = \frac{1}{\Gamma(\alpha)} \sum_{n=0}^{k} \frac{\Gamma(k - m + \alpha - 1)}{\Gamma(k - m + 1)} f(a + m) = \frac{1}{\Gamma(\alpha)} \sum_{n=0}^{k} \frac{\Gamma(n + \alpha - 1)}{\Gamma(n + 1)} f(a + k - m).$$

For other versions, see [84,92,95,98,104,105].

Remark 4. *Strangely, the domain of the above delta sum is not $\mathbb{T}_a$ but $\mathbb{T}_{a+\alpha}$. This means that the value at a given instant depends on past values, which is a causal behavior contrary to what we where expecting, since it is assumed to be a delta difference, which is anti-causal. In addition, most applications to engineering, economics, or statistics involve discrete-time systems where* *all the components, expressed in terms of sums and differences, are defined on the same time sequence. However, a lot of people accepted the formulation of Miller and Ross as correct for the delta difference with corresponding results. In fact, similar situations are repeated in other formulations [84,92,95,98,104,106]. This has a very important consequence: it is impossible to define ARMA-type equations using these differences.*

Example 1. *To have an idea of the incorrectness of the delta difference definition, assume that* $a = 0$ *and* $f(t) = e^{-t}$, $t \in \mathbb{Z}$. *Let us compute three cases:*

1. *Order 1 difference*
$$\Delta f(t) = e^{-t-1} - e^{-t} = (e^{-1} - 1)e^{-t}.$$
For a given t*, the difference depends on the present and future values.*
2. *Order* -1 *difference*
$$\Delta^{-1} f(t) = -e^{-t} - e^{-t-1} - e^{-t-2} \dots = -e^{-t} \sum_{n=0}^{\infty} e^{-n} = (e^{-1} - 1)^{-1} e^{-t}.$$
Again, for a given t*, the* -1*-order difference (sum) depends on the present and future values.*
3. *Order* $-1/2$ *difference*
with $t = 1/2 + k$*, we have*
$$\begin{aligned}\Delta^{-1/2} f(t) &= \sum_{m=0}^{k} \binom{k-m-1/2}{k-m} e^{-m} \\ &= e^{-k} \sum_{m=0}^{k} \binom{n-1/2}{n} e^{n} \\ &= e^{-t+1/2} \sum_{m=0}^{k} (-1)^m \binom{-1/2}{m} e^{m} \\ &= e^{-(t+1/2)} + 1/2 e^{-(t-1/2)} - \frac{1}{8} e^{-(t-3/2)} \dots\end{aligned}$$
Contrarily to the above examples, the $-1/2$*-order derivative depends on one future value and infinite past values. Therefore, an operator that we were expected to be anti-causal is essentially causal.*

4.2. One for All or One for Each

In some discrete-time formulations, as well as in the usual continuous-time fractional calculus, it is current to attach to a given difference/derivative definition the support of the function at hand. This means that for any function, there is a particular difference/derivative definition. It is a one to one case. This was the procedure used by Gray and Zhang. However, it creates difficulties, since we cannot add functions and differences/derivatives with different durations. This is strange because it is assumed that the differences/derivatives are linear operators.

Alternatively, we can define general differences/derivatives over the whole possible domain ($\mathbb{R}$ or $\mathbb{Z}$) and only particularize at the moment of the computation. To understand the situation, consider two functions

$$f(n) = \begin{cases} 0 & n > a \\ n & a \le n \le b \\ 0 & n > b. \end{cases}$$

$$g(n) = n, \quad a \le n \le b.$$

At first glance, it looks like they are the same. However, they express different situations:

1. $f(n)$ expresses a situation where there is a past and a future. It is like some system that exists, is in stand-by first, acts for some time, and returns to the previous state. It is the situation corresponding to many physical, biological, and social systems.
2. $g(n)$, on the contrary, has no past and will have no future: something is born, lives for some time and disappears.

Assume that we want to define and compute a Z transform of such functions. In the first, we use the usual definition

$$F(z) = \sum_{n=-\infty}^{\infty} f(n)z^{-n}, \tag{38}$$

that gives

$$F(z) = \sum_{n=a}^{b} nz^{-n}.$$

On the other hand, for $g(n)$, we have to make a new definition

$${}_aG_b(z) = \sum_{n=a}^{b} nz^{-n}, \tag{39}$$

valid only for all the functions defined in the interval $a \leq n \leq b$. However, $F(z)$ and ${}_aG_b(z)$ are complex variable functions analytic in the same region and to which corresponds the same inversion integral that leads to the same inverse. In fact, the Cauchy integral

$$h(n) = \frac{1}{2\pi i} \oint_c H(z)z^{n-1}dz$$

defines a function $h(n)$ on $\mathbb{Z}$. This is interesting: the inverse transform imposes an extrapolation of $g(t)$ so that its domain is $\mathbb{Z}$, although its support is $a \leq n \leq b$. This means that we should use (38) as a definition of Z transform and consider functions of the type $f(n)$, even if its support is finite. Therefore, we do not need to specify the support in defining differences, derivatives, and transforms.

4.3. The Riemann–Liouvile and Caputo-like Procedures

In many works and due to the influence of traditional fractional calculus, it has become commonplace to use Riemann–Liouvile and Caputo-type procedures. These, instead of doing a direct difference computation, use a convolution between an integer-order difference and a fractional sum. However, while being mathematically correct, it is not a suitable way of doing computations, since

1. We are increasing unnecessarily the number of operations; this is very important in computational implementations, because we are increasing the numerical error [14,107];
2. We throw most of the computational burden on negative-order binomial coefficients that behave asymptotically like $\frac{1}{n^{-\alpha+1}}$, so decreasing very slowly or even increasing.

In continuous fractional calculus, the Riemann–Liouville integral becomes singular when the order is positive (derivative case), as Liouville recognized in his first paper [108], having proposed both procedures that transfer the singular behavior to the derivative of integer order. However, such a difficulty does not appear in discrete-time formulations, since the computational burden falls heavily on the binomial coefficients, directly or otherwise, which can be computed through the Pochhammer symbol that is always non-singular. Therefore, there is neither particular reason nor advantage in using those procedures.

5. Shift-Invariant Differencers and Accumulators

5.1. Causal

Consider two bounded piecewise continuous functions $f(t), g(t),\ t \in \mathbb{R}$ with $f(-\infty) = g(-\infty) = 0$. For simplicity, assume they are of exponential order so that we assure they have Laplace transforms, $F(s), G(s),\ s \in \mathbb{C}$, analytic over suitable ROC.

Definition 1. *Let us define a nabla or causal differencer as a linear system whose output, at a given instant, is the difference between the input at that instant and at a previous one:*

$$g(t) = f(t) - f(t-h), \tag{40}$$

where $h > 0$ is the delay.

The output will be called *nabla difference* and represented by $\nabla f(t)$. From this definition, we can draw some conclusions:

1. It is a moving-average system, which is sometimes called a "feedforward" system;
2. Its impulse response is given by:

   $$\phi(t) = \delta(t) - \delta(t-h),$$

   so that

   $$g(t) = \phi(t) * f(t),$$

   implying that

   $$G(s) = (1 - e^{-sh})F(s). \tag{41}$$

3. The transfer function is

   $$H(s) = 1 - e^{-sh}, \tag{42}$$

   having $\mathbb{C}$ as the ROC.
4. We can associate in series as many systems as we can in such a way that the output of the $(n-1)$-th system is the input of the next one, n-th

   $$f_n(t) = g_{n-1}(t),\ \ g_0(t) = f(t)$$

   and

   $$g_n(t) = f_n(t) - f_n(t-h) = g_{n-1}(t) - g_{n-1}(t-h).$$

   The transfer function of the association is given by

   $$G(s) = \left[1 - e^{-sh}\right]^n F(s),$$

   that inverted gives the n-th order nabla difference

   $$\nabla^n f(t) = \sum_{k=0}^{n} (-1)^k \binom{n}{k} f(t-kh). \tag{43}$$

Now, let us return back to (40) and invert the role of the functions: assume that the input is $g(t)$ and the output is $f(t)$ (feedback system)

$$f(t) = f(t-h) + g(t)$$

that can be reused to give:

$$f(t) = g(t) + g(t-h) + f(t-2h) = g(t) + g(t-h) + g(t-2h) + f(t-3h) = \cdots$$

It is not hard to see that

$$f(t) = \nabla^{-1}g(t) = \sum_{n=0}^{\infty} g(t-nh), \tag{44}$$

with LT

$$F(s) = G(s)\sum_{n=0}^{\infty} e^{-nsh} = \left[1-e^{-sh}\right]^{-1} G(s), \quad Re(s) > 0. \tag{45}$$

Relation (44) shows why this operator is called an accumulator or sum. The series association of n equal accumulators gives the n-th order nabla sum:

$$\nabla^{-n}g(t) = \sum_{k=0}^{\infty}(-1)^k\binom{-n}{k}g(t-kh). \tag{46}$$

Definition 2. *This result together with (43) suggests that the α-order nabla differencer/accumulator be given by*

$$\nabla^{\alpha}f(t) = \sum_{k=0}^{\infty}(-1)^k\binom{\alpha}{k}f(t-kh), \tag{47}$$

where α is any real number.

The corresponding LT is

$$\mathcal{L}[\nabla^{\alpha}f(t)] = \left[1-e^{-sh}\right]^{\alpha}F(s), \quad Re(s) > 0. \tag{48}$$

Therefore, there are some facts that we must emphasize:

1. A difference/sum is the output of a system: differencer/accumulator;
2. The system structure is independent of the inputs;
3. If the order is not a positive integer, even if the input function has finite support, the output has infinite support; in particular, if $f(t)$ has support $[a,b] \subset \mathbb{R}$, $g(t)$ is not identically null above any real value: the support is $[a,\infty]$. This is a very important fact that is frequently forgotten or dismissed.
4. If the input is a right-hand function, so is the output; in particular, if $f(t) = 0,\ t < 0$, then $\nabla^{\alpha}f(t) = 0$, for negative t and for $t \geq 0$, we have

$$\nabla^{\alpha}f(t) = \sum_{k=0}^{n}(-1)^k\binom{\alpha}{k}f(t-kh), \tag{49}$$

   where $n = \lfloor t/h \rfloor$ is the the great integer such that $n \leq t/h$.
5. The ROC of the transfer function is defined by $Re(s) > 0$, as expected, since we are dealing with a causal system.

5.2. Anti-Causal

Consider the conditions of the previous subsection, but now with with $f(\infty) = g(\infty) = 0$.

Definition 3. *We define delta or anti-causal differencer as a linear system whose output, at a given instant, is the difference between the input at that instant and at a future one:*

$$g(t) = f(t) - f(t+h), \tag{50}$$

where $h > 0$ is the lead.

The output will be called the *delta difference* and represented by $\Delta f(t)$. Note that it is the symmetric of the current definition (21). Traditionally, the symmetric of (50) is considered: $g(t) = f(t+h) - f(t)$. To simplify and highlight the similarity to the nabla difference, we found it preferable to omit the – sign.

From this definition and the previous results, we conclude that:

1. It is also a moving-average system;
2. The LT gives
$$G(s) = (1 - e^{+sh})F(s). \tag{51}$$
3. The transfer function is
$$H(s) = 1 - e^{+sh}, \tag{52}$$
having $\mathbb{C}$ as ROC.
4. The association in a series of n systems as above has a transfer function given by
$$G(s) = \left[1 - e^{sh}\right]^n F(s),$$
that inverted gives the n-th-order delta difference
$$\Delta^n f(t) = \sum_{k=0}^{n} (-1)^k \binom{n}{k} f(t + kh). \tag{53}$$
5. In a similar way, the delta accumulator is
$$\Delta^{-1} g(t) = \sum_{n=0}^{\infty} g(t + nh). \tag{54}$$

The series association of n accumulators is expressed by
$$\nabla^{-n} g(t) = \sum_{k=0}^{\infty} (-1)^k \binom{-n}{k} g(t - kh) \tag{55}$$
and has LT
$$\mathcal{L}[\Delta^{-n} g(t)] = \left[1 - e^{sh}\right]^{-n} G(s), \quad Re(s) < 0. \tag{56}$$

Definition 4. *This result, together with (43), suggests that the α-order delta differencer/accumulator be defined by*
$$\Delta^{\alpha} f(t) = \sum_{k=0}^{\infty} (-1)^k \binom{\alpha}{k} f(t + kh), \tag{57}$$
where α is any real number.

The corresponding LT is
$$\mathcal{L}[\Delta^{\alpha} f(t)] = \left[1 - e^{sh}\right]^{\alpha} F(s), \quad Re(s) < 0. \tag{58}$$

This and the nabla differences have similar characteristics. Therefore, and in particular, we can say relatively to the delta difference:

1. If the order is not a positive integer, even if the input function has finite support, the output has infinite support; in particular, if $f(t)$ has support $[a, b] \subset \mathbb{R}$, $g(t)$ is not identically null below any real value; the support is $[-\infty, b]$.
2. If the input is a left-hand function, so is the output; in particular, if $f(t) = 0,\ t > 0$, then $\Delta^{\alpha} f(t) = 0$, for positive t and for $t \leq 0$, we have
$$\Delta^{\alpha} f(t) = \sum_{k=0}^{n} (-1)^k \binom{\alpha}{k} f(kh - |t|), \tag{59}$$
where $n = \lfloor -t/h \rfloor$ is the the great integer such that $n \leq -t/h$.

3. The ROC of the transfer function is defined by $Re(s) < 0$, as expected, since we are dealing with an anti-causal system.
4. We can account for the $(-)$ sign we removed above by inserting the factor $(-1)^\alpha$ into (57).

5.3. Properties

The nabla and delta differencers have similar properties that we will describe for the first. The most important are [25]

- *Additivity and commutativity of the orders*
  $\nabla^\alpha[\nabla^\beta f(t)] = \nabla^\beta[\nabla^\alpha f(t)] = \nabla^{\alpha+\beta} f(t)$.
- *Neutral element*
  This comes from the last property by putting $\beta = -\alpha$, $\nabla^\alpha[\nabla^{-\alpha} f(t)] = \nabla^0 f(t) = f(t)$. This is very important because it states the existence of the inverse, which is in coherence with the previous sub-sections.
- *Inverse element*
  From the last result, we conclude that there is always an inverse element: for every α-order difference, there is always a $-\alpha$-order difference given by the same formula.
- *Associativity of the orders*

$$\nabla^\gamma\left[\nabla^\alpha\nabla^\beta\right] f(t) = \nabla^{\gamma+\alpha+\beta} f(t) = \nabla^{\alpha+\beta+\gamma} f(t) = \nabla^\alpha\left[\nabla^{\beta+\gamma}\right] f(t).$$

  It is a consequence of the additivity.
- *Derivative of the product*

$$\nabla^\alpha[f(t)g(t)] = \sum_{m=0}^{\infty} \binom{\alpha}{m} \nabla^m f(t) \nabla^{\alpha-n} g(t - mh). \tag{60}$$

  The delta case is slightly different as expected

$$\Delta^\alpha[f(t)g(t)] = \sum_{m=0}^{\infty} \binom{\alpha}{m} \Delta^m f(t) \Delta^{\alpha-m} g(t + mh).$$

5.4. Discrete-Time Differences

In the Introduction, we mentioned the importance of discrete-time signals. In Section 2.4, we showed how to obtain them by sampling continuous-time signals. However, we must highlight an important fact: discrete-time signals exist by themselves, without there needing to be a continuous-time signal from which they resulted. There are many signals that are inherently discrete. This means that in each case, there is necessarily a clock that defines the time sequence in which we work. Therefore, the delay/lead, h, must be equal or a multiple of the sampling interval used to obtain the discrete-time formulation for differences. For simplicity, we choose the sampling interval equal to h so that $\mathbb{T} = \{t = nh,\ n \in \mathbb{Z}\}$, giving

$$\nabla^\alpha f_k = \sum_{n=0}^{\infty} \frac{(-\alpha)_n}{n!} f_{k-n}, \quad k \in \mathbb{Z}, \tag{61}$$

and

$$\Delta^\alpha f_k = \sum_{n=0}^{\infty} \frac{(-\alpha)_n}{n!} f_{k+n}. \quad k \in \mathbb{Z}, \tag{62}$$

that can assume different forms:

$$\nabla^\alpha f_k = \sum_{n=-\infty}^{k} \frac{(-\alpha)_{k-n}}{(k-n)!} f_n, \quad k \in \mathbb{Z} \tag{63}$$

and

$$\Delta^\alpha f_k = \sum_{n=k}^{\infty} \frac{(-\alpha)_{n-k}}{(n-k)!} f_n, \quad k \in \mathbb{Z}. \tag{64}$$

As it is obvious, the Formulae (61)–(64) express input/output relations that are discrete-time convolutions between the input f_n and the binomial coefficients (impulse responses) to produce the outputs that are the differences. Such relations are mediated by the called impulse responses that are the outputs, h_n, when the input is the Kroneckker delta defined by

$$\delta_n = \begin{cases} 1 & n = 0 \\ 0 & n \neq 0. \end{cases}$$

In passing, we define the discrete-time step by

$$\varepsilon_n = \begin{cases} 1 & n \geq 0 \\ 0 & n < 0. \end{cases}$$

Therefore, the impulse responses of the nabla and delta differences are, respectively,

$$h_n = \frac{(-\alpha)_n}{n!}\varepsilon_n$$

and

$$g_n = \frac{(-\alpha)_{-n}}{(-n)!}\varepsilon_{-n},$$

where $n \in \mathbb{Z}$, which is in agreement with the causality. It is important to remark that

1. Both responses have finite duration if $\alpha \in \mathbb{N}$, and the systems are called FIRs (finite impulse systems) [14].
2. If $\alpha \notin \mathbb{N}$, both responses extend to infinite, and the corresponding systems are IIR (infinite impulse response).
3. If $f_k = 0,\ k < 0$, then $\nabla^\alpha f_k = 0$, for negative k, and for $k \geq 0$, we have

$$\nabla^\alpha f_k = \sum_{n=0}^{k} \frac{(-\alpha)_n}{n!} f_{k-n}, \quad k \in \mathbb{Z} \tag{65}$$

or,

$$\nabla^\alpha f_k = \sum_{n=0}^{k} \frac{(-\alpha)_{k-n}}{(k-n)!} f_n, \quad k \in \mathbb{Z}. \tag{66}$$

4. Similarly, if $f_k = 0,\ k > 0$, then $\Delta^\alpha f_k = 0$ for positive k and we obtain for $k \leq 0$

$$\Delta^\alpha f_k = \sum_{n=0}^{|k|} \frac{(-\alpha)_n}{n!} f_{n-|k|}. \quad k \in \mathbb{Z} \tag{67}$$

or

$$\Delta^\alpha f_k = \sum_{n=0}^{|k|} \frac{(-\alpha)_{n-k}}{(n-k)!} f_n, \quad k \in \mathbb{Z}. \tag{68}$$

5. It is a simple task to obtain formulae for functions with other supports.
6. The Z transforms of the above discrete-time differences can be obtained from the corresponding LT by setting $z = e^{sh}$. For example, the Z transform of the nabla difference (61) is

$$\mathcal{Z}[\nabla^\alpha f_k] = (1 - z^{-1})^\alpha F(z), \tag{69}$$

in the suitable ROC in the region defined by $|z| > 1$.
7. If, in any particular application, a time sequence with the form $\mathbb{T} = a + nh, ; n \in \mathbb{Z}$, $a \in \mathbb{R}$ is used, we can make a substitution $f(a + nh)$ for $f(nh)$.

5.5. Two-Sided Differences

There is another differencer, two-sided (bilateral), which is given by

$$\Theta_0^1 f(t) = f(t+h/2) - f(t-h/2), \tag{70}$$

that originates two bilateral fractional differences, but we will not study both here [68,69,109]. We can easily obtain one of them by combining a delta with a nabla difference.

Definition 5. *Let $t = kh,\ k \in \mathbb{Z}$. We define a bilateral differencer through*

$$\Theta_\theta^\beta f_k = \nabla^a \Delta^b f_k = \sum_{n=-\infty}^{+\infty} \frac{(-1)^n \Gamma(\beta+1)}{\Gamma\left(\frac{\beta+\theta}{2} - n + 1\right)\Gamma\left(\frac{\beta-\theta}{2} + n + 1\right)} f_{k-n}, \tag{71}$$

with $\beta = a + b$ (difference order) and $\theta = a - b$ (asymmetry parameter).

For $\beta \in \mathbb{Z}^-$, we obtain singular cases that were treated in [69]. Suitable choices of these paramters allow us to recover the above introduced differences:

- With $\theta = \beta$, we obtain (47);
- Similarly, with $\theta = -\beta$ and variable change, we obtain (57);

Some particular cases of (71) are very interesting:

1. Riesz-type difference, $\theta = 0$,

$$\Theta_0^\beta f_k = \sum_{n=-\infty}^{+\infty} \frac{(-1)^n \Gamma(\beta+1)}{\Gamma(\frac{\beta}{2} - n + 1)\Gamma(\frac{\beta}{2} + n + 1)} f_{k-n}. \tag{72}$$

2. Feller-type difference, $\theta = \pm 1$,

$$\Theta_1^\beta f_k = \sum_{n=-\infty}^{+\infty} \frac{(-1)^n \Gamma(\beta+1)}{\Gamma(\frac{\beta+1}{2} - n + 1)\Gamma(\frac{\beta-1}{2} + n + 1)} f_{k-n}. \tag{73}$$

3. Two-sided discrete Hilbert transform, $\beta = 0$,

$$\Theta_\theta^0 f_k = \sum_{n=-\infty}^{+\infty} (-1)^n \cdot \frac{1}{\Gamma\left(\frac{\theta}{2} - n + 1\right)\Gamma\left(\frac{-\theta}{2} + n + 1\right)} f_{k-n}. \tag{74}$$

With $\theta = 1$, we obtain the usual discrete-time formulation of the Hilbert transform [14].

Remark 5. *It must be noticed that in the general case stated in (71), the difference $\Theta_\theta^\beta f_k$ does not have Z transform, since the ROC degenerates in the unit circle ($z = e^{i\omega}$), meaning that it has discrete-time Fourier transform, $F(e^{i\omega})$ [68,109]:*

$$\mathcal{F}\left[\Theta_\theta^\beta f_k\right] = |2\sin(\omega/2)|^\beta e^{-i\omega\theta} e^{i\,\mathrm{sgn}(\omega)\theta\pi/2} F(e^{i\omega}), \quad |\omega| < \pi, \tag{75}$$

where sgn(.) *is the signum function.*

5.6. The Tempered Differences

We introduced above the three standard definitions for the differences of order one (40), (50) and (70). With a slight modification, we obtain their tempered versions. We only need to make adaptations of the results described in [110]. The concept of a tempered fractional difference was introduced, for the first time, by Sabzikar et al. [111], starting from the Grünwald–Letnikov derivative. Their results are similar to those that we are going to present.

Definition 6. *Let $\lambda \in \mathbb{R}$. We can define three tempered differences (TDs):*

- *Nabla TD*

$$\nabla_{\lambda,f} f(t) = f(t) - e^{-\lambda h} f(t-h), \tag{76}$$

that has LT

$$\mathcal{L}[\nabla_\lambda f(t)] = \left[1 - e^{-\lambda h} e^{-sh}\right] F(s), \tag{77}$$

for any $s \in \mathbb{C}$.

- *Delta TD*

$$\Delta_\lambda f(t) = f(t) - e^{\lambda h} f(t+h). \tag{78}$$

Its LT is valid for any $s \in \mathbb{C}$ and given by

$$\mathcal{L}[\Delta_\lambda f(t)] = \left[1 - e^{\lambda h} e^{sh}\right] F(s), \tag{79}$$

As above, we removed a $(-)$ sign.

- *Two-sided TD*

$$\Theta_{\theta,\lambda} f(t) = \left[e^{\lambda \frac{h}{2}} f(t + \frac{h}{2}) - e^{-\lambda \frac{h}{2}} f(t - \frac{h}{2}).\right] \tag{80}$$

It is straightforward to invert the relations (76) and (78), and so, we obtain the first-order anti-differences

$$\nabla_\lambda^{-1} f(t) = \sum_{n=0}^{\infty} e^{-n\lambda h} f(t - nh) \tag{81}$$

and

$$\Delta_\lambda^{-1} f(t) = \sum_{n=0}^{\infty} e^{n\lambda h} f(t + nh) \tag{82}$$

that can be generalized for any real order.

Definition 7. *For $\alpha \in \mathbb{R}$, we can write [110]*

$$\nabla_\lambda^\alpha f(t) = \sum_{n=0}^{\infty} \frac{(-\alpha)_n}{n!} e^{-n\lambda h} f(t - nh), \tag{83}$$

and

$$\Delta_\lambda^\alpha f(t) = \sum_{n=0}^{\infty} \frac{(-\alpha)_n}{n!} e^{n\lambda h} f(t + nh). \tag{84}$$

Definition 8. *To obtain the discrete-time versions, we set $t = nh$ and $\mu = e^{\lambda h}$ so that we can write [110]*

$$\nabla_\lambda^\alpha f_k = \sum_{n=0}^{\infty} \frac{(-\alpha)_n}{n!} \mu^{-n} f_{k-n}, \tag{85}$$

and

$$\Delta_\lambda^\alpha f_k = \sum_{n=0}^{\infty} \frac{(-\alpha)_n}{n!} \mu^{n} f_{k+n}, \tag{86}$$

valid for any $\alpha \in \mathbb{R}$.

The bilateral tempered fractional differences are somehow more involved. They can be obtained from the results introduced in [112]. We will not do it here.

5.7. Bilinear Differences

One of the most interesting methods of obtaining discrete-time systems from continuous-time templates is through the conformal transformations, so that we pass from the LT context, (s), to the one of Z transform, (z) [28]. The traditional procedures can be described by

$$s = 1 - z^{-1},$$

for the nabla case and

$$s = z - 1,$$

for the delta case. Basically, z^{-1} and z correspond to delay and lead, respectively. This procedure is equivalent to the one described in Section 5.4. It has a great drawback: the imaginary axis in the s plane is transformed into the Hilger circles $|z-1| = 1$ and $|z+1| = 1$ [25]. This fact brings some inconvenience [28].

Another alternative to obtain continuous to discrete conversion is through the bilinear (Tustin) transformation [28,113]

$$s = \frac{2}{h}\frac{1-z^{-1}}{1+z^{-1}},$$

which leads to discrete-time formulations similar to the GL-like above obtained. In [114], new discrete-time fractional derivatives based on the bilinear transformation were introduced and studied. In agreemennt with such a theory, we propose new differences here.

Definition 9. *Let us define a bilinear nabla differencer as a linear system whose output, at a given instant, is given by*

$$g(t) + g(t-h) = f(t) - f(t-h) \tag{87}$$

and the bilinear delta differencer by

$$g(t) + g(t+h) = f(t) - f(t+h). \tag{88}$$

In terms of the LT, we can write, respectively,

$$G(s) = \frac{1-e^{-sh}}{1+e^{-sh}}F(s) \tag{89}$$

and

$$G(s) = \frac{1-e^{sh}}{1+e^{sh}}F(s). \tag{90}$$

It is obvious that we can formulate symmetric bilinear differences from the LT

$$G(s) = \frac{e^{sh/2} - e^{-sh/2}}{e^{sh/2} + e^{-sh/2}}F(s). \tag{91}$$

To avoid any repetition of concepts, we will consider the nabla case only. The above formulae suggest immediately how we make a continuous-to-discrete conversion by using the substitution $e^{sh} \to z$.

Definition 10. *We define the bilinear nabla fractional difference through*

$$\mathcal{Z}[\nabla_b^\alpha f_k] = \left[\frac{1-z^{-1}}{1+z^{-1}}\right]^\alpha F(z), \quad |z| > 1. \tag{92}$$

Attending to the results in [114], we can write

$$\nabla_b^\alpha f_n = \sum_{k=0}^{\infty} \psi_k^\alpha f_{n-k}, \quad n \in \mathbb{Z}, \tag{93}$$

where [114]

$$\psi_k^\alpha = \sum_{m=0}^{k} \frac{(-\alpha)_m}{m!} \frac{(-1)^{k-m}(\alpha)_{k-m}}{(k-m)!}, k \in \mathbb{Z}_0^+ \tag{94}$$

In particular, for $\alpha = \pm 1$, we have

- $\psi_k^1 = \begin{cases} 0 & k<0 \\ 1 & k=0 \\ 2(-1)^k & k>0 \end{cases}$
- $\psi_k^{-1} = \begin{cases} 0 & k<0 \\ 1 & k=0 \\ 2 & k>0 \end{cases}$

Although these new differences seem to be rather involved, they are easily implemented with the help of the fast Fourier transform (FFT) [114].

We can also obtain two-sided bilinear differences, but the procedure is rather involved and not very useful. However, the frequency domain representation is easily obtained from (91).

6. Scale-Invariant Differences

In previous sections, we dealt preferably with the shift-invariant differences. Here, we will consider others that have deep relations with the scale-invariant derivatives [40].

Consider two bounded piecewise continuous functions $f(t), g(t),\ t \in \mathbb{R}^+$ with $f(0), g(0) = 0$. For simplicity, assume they are of polynomial order, so that we assure they have Mellin transforms, $F(v), G(v),\ v \in \mathbb{C}$, analytic over suitable ROC.

Definition 11. *Let $q > 1$. We define a stretching differencer as a linear system whose output, at a given scale, is the difference between the input at different scales:*

$$g(\tau) = f(\tau) - f(\tau q^{-1}), \quad \tau \in \mathbb{R}^+, \tag{95}$$

where q is the scale constant.

The output will be called the *stretching difference* and represented by $\triangleleft f(t)$. Letting $q < 1$, we obtain the *shrinking difference*, $\triangleright f(t)$. Therefore, their properties are similar. We will study the first only, because the other is easy to obtain. From this definition, we can draw some conclusions:

1. Its impulse response is given by:

$$\phi(\tau) = \delta(\tau - 1) - \delta(\tau/q - 1),$$

so that

$$g(\tau) = \phi(\tau) \star f(\tau),$$

implying that

$$G(v) = (1 - q^{-v})F(v). \tag{96}$$

2. The transfer function is

$$H(v) = 1 - q^{-v}, \tag{97}$$

having $\mathbb{C}$ as the ROC.

3. As in the shift-invariant case, if associated in series n systems, the resulting system defines the n-th order stretching difference that has a transfer function given by

$$H(v) = \left[1 - q^{-v}\right]^n,$$

from which we obtain the n-th order stretching difference

$$\lhd^n f(\tau) = \sum_{k=0}^{n} (-1)^k \binom{n}{k} f(\tau q^{-k}). \tag{98}$$

Now, let us return back to (40) and invert the role of the functions: assume that the input is $g(\tau)$ and the output is $f(\tau)$

$$f(\tau) = f(\tau q^{-1}) + g(\tau),$$

that can be reused to give:

$$f(\tau) = g(\tau) + g(\tau q^{-1}) + f(\tau q^{-2}) = g(\tau) + g(\tau q^{-1}) + g(\tau q^{-2}) + f(\tau q^{-3} = \cdots$$

It is not hard to see that

$$f(\tau) = \lhd^{-1} g(\tau) = \sum_{n=0}^{\infty} g(\tau q^{-n}), \tag{99}$$

with MT

$$F(v) = G(v) \sum_{n=0}^{\infty} q^{-nv} = \left[1 - q^{-v}\right]^{-1} G(s), \quad \textit{for } Re(v) > 0. \tag{100}$$

Relation (99) shows why this operator is again an accumulator. The series association of n equal accumulators gives the n-th order stretching sum:

$$\lhd^{-n} g(\tau) = \sum_{k=0}^{\infty} (-1)^k \binom{-n}{k} g(\tau q^{-k}). \tag{101}$$

Definition 12. *This result together with (98) suggests that the α-order stretching differencer/accumulator must be given by*

$$\lhd^{\alpha} f(\tau) = \sum_{k=0}^{\infty} (-1)^k \binom{\alpha}{k} f(\tau q^{-k}), \tag{102}$$

where α is any real number.

As we observe, this difference uses an exponential domain in agreement with our considerations above (Section 2.3). The corresponding MT is

$$\mathcal{M}[\lhd^{\alpha} f(\tau)] = \left[1 - q^{-v}\right]^{\alpha} F(v), \quad \textit{for } Re(v) > 0. \tag{103}$$

Therefore, the shrinking difference is defined by

$$\rhd^{\alpha} f(\tau) = \sum_{k=0}^{\infty} (-1)^k \binom{\alpha}{k} f(\tau q^{k}), \tag{104}$$

having MT

$$\mathcal{M}[\rhd^{\alpha} f(\tau)] = \left[1 - q^{v}\right]^{\alpha} F(v), \quad \textit{for } Re(v) < 0. \tag{105}$$

Remark 6. *The relations (100) and (105) show that there is a scale-invariant system that produces the difference as an output.*

To obtain the discrete-scale versions, we only need to make a sampling in agreement with Theorem 2. Let $\tau = q^n$. For the stretching difference, we obtain

$$\lhd^{\alpha} f_{q^n} = \sum_{k=0}^{\infty} (-1)^k \binom{\alpha}{k} f_{q^{n-k}}, \tag{106}$$

while for the shrinking one, it is

$$\triangleright^{\alpha} f_{q^n} = \sum_{k=0}^{\infty} (-1)^k \binom{\alpha}{k} f_{q^{n+k}}. \tag{107}$$

As we can see, they are formally similar to the nabla and delta differences; they only differ in the sampling sequence used: linear or exponential. Thus, from a purely discrete point of view, we have no way of making any distinction between linearly or exponentially sampled functions. This means that if we want to define stretching and shrinking differences in discrete time, we have to break the continuous connection: we have to work exclusively with the sequences defined in $\mathbb{Z}$. So, having a sequence $f_n,\ n \in \mathbb{Z}$, we wonder how to define stretched and shrunk sequences so that we can introduce differences. In [115], ways to produce stretched and shrunk sequences were presented. In principle, we could use them to define differences, but this procedure has difficulties, since the operations of stretching and shrinking involve all knowledge of the underlying sequence, and the scale transformation system is two-sided.

However, we can use the traditional "decimation" operation used in signal processing to define a stretching difference [5,8,14].

Definition 13. *Let N be a positive integer (decimation parameter). We define a stretching difference through*

$$\triangleleft_N f_n = f_n - f_{Nn}. \tag{108}$$

We can show immediately that if M is a positive integer, then

$$\triangleleft_N^M f_n = \sum_{m=0}^{M} (-1)^m \binom{M}{m} f_{N^m n}. \tag{109}$$

If $f_n = n^a,\ n \in \mathbb{N}, a \in \mathbb{R}$, then

$$\triangleleft_N^M n^a = \sum_{m=0}^{M} (-1)^m \binom{M}{m} N^{am} n^a = [1 - N^a]^M n^a. \tag{110}$$

Proceeding as above, we obtain

$$\triangleleft_N^{-M} f_n = \sum_{m=0}^{M} \frac{(M)_m}{m!} f_{N^m n}, \tag{111}$$

that allows us to write

$$\triangleleft_N^M n^a = \sum_{m=0}^{M} (-1)^m \frac{(M)_m}{m!} N^{am} n^a = [1 - N^a]^{-M} n^a. \tag{112}$$

Definition 14. *These relations suggest we write*

$$\triangleleft_N^{\alpha} f_n = \sum_{m=0}^{\infty} \frac{(-\alpha)_m}{m!} f_{N^m n}, \tag{113}$$

so that

$$\triangleleft_N^{\alpha} n^a = \sum_{m=0}^{\infty} \frac{(-\alpha)_m}{m!} N^{am} n^a = [1 - N^a]^{\alpha} n^a. \tag{114}$$

This last relation seems to point to a definition of a "discrete Mellin transform", as

$$F(v) = \sum_{k=1}^{\infty} f_k k^v, \quad v \in \mathbb{C},$$

which is different from other proposed in the past [33,34]. We do not go further in this way.

The properties of the stretching discrete difference just proposed are readily deduced from the results in Section 5.3. From such a definition, the reason for not defining a shrinking difference is evident.

7. The ARMA-Type Difference Linear Systems

Definition 15. *We define an ARMA-type difference linear system through the following equation [25,28]*

$$\sum_{k=0}^{N} a_k \mathcal{D}^{\alpha_k} y(t) = \sum_{k=0}^{M} b_k \mathcal{D}^{\beta_k} x(t), \tag{115}$$

where a_k and b_k ($k = 0, 1, \cdots$,) with $a_N = 1$ are real numbers. The operator $\mathcal{D}$ is any difference defined previously. The orders N and M are any positive integers. The positive real numbers α_k and β_k with $k = 0, 1, \cdots$, form strictly increasing sequences.

The most interesting systems are those with commensurate orders:

$$\sum_{k=0}^{N} a_k \mathcal{D}^{k\alpha} y(t) = \sum_{k=0}^{M} b_k \mathcal{D}^{k\alpha} x(t). \tag{116}$$

In the shift-invariant cases, the exponentials are the eigenfunctions and the eigenvalues are the transfer functions [27,36,116]. In the scale-invariant system, such a role is played by the powers [40]. The corresponding (Laplace, Z, Mellin) transforms give the *impulse response* or Green function of the system.

Example 2. *Consider the ARMA(1,1) system:*

$$\nabla^\alpha y(t) + a y(t) = b_1 \nabla^\alpha x(t) + b_0 x(t)$$

and let $x(t) = e^{st}$, $t \in \mathbb{R}$. The output will be $y(t) = H(s)e^{st}$, $t \in \mathbb{R}, c \in \mathbb{C}$, with

$$H(s) = \frac{b_1(1-e^{-sh})^\alpha + b_0}{(1-e^{-sh})^\alpha + a}, \qquad Re(s) > 0.$$

The impulse response is not easily obtained. From

$$\begin{aligned} H(s) &= \frac{b_1(1-e^{-sh})^\alpha + b_0 + b_1 a - b_1 a}{(1-e^{-sh})^\alpha + a} \\ &= b_1 + \frac{b_0 - b_1 a}{(1-e^{-sh})^\alpha + a} = b_1 + (b_0 - b_1 a)\sum_{m=0}^{\infty} a^m (1-e^{-sh})^{-(m+1)\alpha}, \\ &= b_1 + (b_0 - b_1 a)\sum_{m=0}^{\infty} a^m \sum_{k=0}^{\infty} \frac{((m+1)\alpha)_k}{k!} e^{-ksh}. \end{aligned}$$

we get

$$h(t) = b_1\delta(t) + (b_0 - b_1 a)\sum_{m=0}^{\infty} a^m \sum_{k=0}^{\infty} \frac{((m+1)\alpha)_k}{k!}\delta(t-kh).$$

The output for any $x(t)$ is given by the usual convolution

$$y(t) = b_1 x(t) + (b_0 - b_1 a)\sum_{m=0}^{\infty} a^m \sum_{k=0}^{\infty} \frac{((m+1)\alpha)_k}{k!} x(t-kh).$$

In the discrete-time case, we set $t = nh$, $n \in \mathbb{Z}$ to give

$$\nabla^\alpha y_n + a y_n = b_1 \nabla^\alpha x_n + b_0 x_n.$$

If the input is the exponential $z^n, n \in \mathbb{Z}, z \in \mathbb{C}$*, the output is* $y_n = H(z)z^n, n \in \mathbb{Z}, z \in \mathbb{C}$*, where*

$$H(z) = \frac{b_1(1-z^{-1})^\alpha + b_0}{(1-z^{-1})^\alpha + a}, \quad |z| > 1.$$

We can obtain the Z transform inverse of this function approximately through the FFT. However, proceeding as above, we obtain

$$h_n = b_1\delta_n + (b_0 - b_1 a)\sum_{m=0}^{\infty} a^m \sum_{k=0}^{\infty} \frac{((m+1)\alpha)_k}{k!}\delta_{n-k}.$$

As in the continuous-time case, the output corresponding to a given input is obtained through the discrete convolution

$$y_n = b_1 x_n + (b_0 - b_1 a)\sum_{m=0}^{\infty} a^m \sum_{k=0}^{\infty} \frac{((m+1)\alpha)_k}{k!}x_{n-k}.$$

Example 3. *Consider the scale-invariant AR(1) difference system defined by the equation*

$$\rhd_3^{1/2} y_n = \rhd_3^{1/2} x_n - x_n$$

and let $x_n = n^{-2},\ n \in \mathbb{Z}_0^-$.

Accordingly to what we wrote in the last section, the solution is, for $n \in \mathbb{N}$,

$$y_n = x_n - \sum_{m=0}^{\infty} \frac{(1/2)_m}{m!} x_{3^m n}.$$

So,

$$y_n = n^{-2} - \sum_{m=0}^{\infty} \frac{(1/2)_m}{m!} 3^{-2m} n^{-2} = n^{-2}\left[1 - (1 - 1/9)^{-1/2}\right] = \frac{2\sqrt{2} - 3}{2\sqrt{2}} n^{-2}.$$

8. Which Difference?

We described the most interesting differences. We ask ourselves which one should be used in a particular application. In some uses, there is doubt. For example, in most engineering applications, such as digital signal processing, which is the basis of many electrical, mechanical, or biomedical systems, the nabla derivative is the appropriate one. In fact, these systems are causal.The bilinear nabla systems are similar, but they have one important advantage: they are suitable for frequency domain implementations with the fast Fourier transform. The reduction in the number of operations should be a goal in applications. If the independent variable is not time, but any other, such as space, the delta or bilateral derivative can also be used. Although often employed, the delta difference is not suitable for most applications; its anti-causal characteristic gives rise to unstable systems.

In dealing with stochastic processes, such as the fractional Brownian motion or other generalized discrete fractional processes, the nabla or the two-sided can be used [117–119].

The integer-order differences and systems are characterized by having short memory and an exponentially decreasing impulse response, which is unsuitable for many applications. On the other hand, the fractional systems have long memory, since they have power decrease impulse responses, which brings too big of an influence of the past into the present. The tempered systems offer an intermediate solution. In engineering, the frequency domain analysis helps in deciding which system is more suitable. This fact makes the area of filter design one of the most important in applications.

The scale-invariant differences and systems, considered separately from the shift-invariant analogues, only recently were introduced. The corresponding discrete versions were proposed above for the first time. Therefore, there are no prescribed applications.

9. Discussion

Differences are basic building blocks for defining derivatives, but they can be used in many applications to solve differential equations and model many systems. In most situations, shift-invariant differences are used, although scale-invariant versions are also useful. Here, they have been studied separately. General continuous-time cases have been introduced, although the main interest has been placed on the discrete versions.

When looking for a discrete-time equivalent to continuous-time differential systems, there is a difference system that works as an intermediate [28]. Normally, such a system is not used for anything else. Discrete differences and systems are fundamental in computational applications that are the primary means for practical implementations. For this reason, when introducing differences, we adopted a system point of view to emphasize that differences are outputs of linear systems, which implies that they are defined independently of the inputs, notably their duration. Moreover, outputs are generally of infinite duration, even if the input support is finite. In addition to the classic differences, we introduce new ones such as bilateral and tempered differences.

The option by system approach for introducing differences allowed us to define ARMA-type linear systems, enlarging the classic procedure used in time-series analysis and processing which supported many important applications in engineering, economics, statistics, and so on. It is important to remark that many interesting functions we find in applications are acquired under a discrete-time form without having any analytical formula. This implies that we have to deal with functions (signals) defined in the set of integers. Anyway, implicit in any application, there is a time sequence imposed by an underlying clock which imposes a working domain that we cannot change. This aspect was frequently dismissed in the past, which is a fact that led to some "abnormalities" such as the loss of (anti-)causality. This happened, for example, with the assumed "delta difference" that is not really a delta difference, since it should be anti-causal, but it is bilateral. This fact is expected to make a review of some associated concepts and tools.

The theory we have just described leaves open issues that deserve consideration in future research. In fact, we have not considered the modeling/identification problems [16–20]. To do so, the frequency-domain approach will certainly be a safe way forward. This can be applied by adapting and extending the studies in [25,114] by defining suitable transforms. It is important to highlight the fact that such transforms use the eigenfunctions of the differences as kernels. Another open issue is the interaction between the ARMA difference systems above introduced and the stochastic processes, as referred above. This will imply the search for estimation methods that may involve spectral estimation.

Funding: The author was partially funded by National Funds through the Foundation for Science and Technology of Portugal under the projects UIDB/00066/2020.

Conflicts of Interest: The author declares no conflict of interest.

References

1. Kolmogoroff, A. Interpolation und Extrapolation von stationären zufälligen Folgen. *Bull. Acad. Sci. URSS Math. [Izvestia Akad. Nauk. SSSR]* **1941**, 5, 3–14.
2. Wiener, N. *Extrapolation, Interpolation, and Smoothing of Stationary Time Series: With Engineering Applications*; MIT Press: Cambridge, MA, USA, 1949; Volume 113.
3. Jenkins, G.M.; Priestley, M. The spectral analysis of time-series. *J. R. Stat. Soc. Ser. B (Methodol.)* **1957**, 19, 1–12. [CrossRef]
4. Box, G.; Jenkins, G. *Time Series Analysis: Forecasting and Control*; Holdan-Day: San Francisco, CA, USA, 1970.
5. Oppenheim, A.V.; Schafer, R.W. *Discrete-Time Signal Processing*, 3rd ed.; Prentice Hall Press: Upper Saddle River, NJ, USA, 2009.
6. Kailath, T. *Linear Systems*; Information and System Sciences Series; Prentice-Hall: Upper Saddle River, NJ, USA,1980.
7. Kailath, T. Lectures on Wiener and Kalman filtering. In *Lectures on Wiener and Kalman Filtering*; Springer: Vienna, Austria, 1981; pp. 1–143.
8. Rabiner, L.R.; Gold, B. *Theory and Application of Digital Signal Processing*; Prentice-Hall: Englewood Cliffs, NJ, USA, 1975.
9. Jury, E.I. *Analysis and Synthesis of Sampled-Data Control Systems*; Columbia University: New York, NY, USA, 1953.
10. Pollock, D.S.G.; Green, R.C.; Nguyen, T. *Handbook of Time Series Analysis, Signal Processing, and Dynamics*; Elsevier: Amsterdam, The Netherlands, 1999.

11. Robinson, E.A.; Treitel, S. *Geophysical Signal Analysis*; Society of Exploration Geophysicists: Tulsa, OK, USA, 2000.
12. Papoulis, A. *Signal Analysis*; McGraw-Hill: New York, NY, USA, 1977; pp. 1–435.
13. Ifeachor, E.C.; Jervis, B.W. *Digital Signal Processing: A Practical Approach*; Pearson Education: Harlow, Essex, England, 2002.
14. Proakis, J.G.; Manolakis, D.G. *Digital Signal Processing: Principles, Algorithms, and Applications*; Prentice Hall: Upper Saddle River, NJ, USA, 2007.
15. Brockwell, P.J.; Davis, R.A. *Time Series: Theory and Methods*; Springer Science & Business Media: Berlin/Heidelberg, Germany, 2009.
16. Neuman, C.P. Properties of the delta operator model of dynamic physical systems. *IEEE Trans. Syst. Man Cybern.* **1993**, *23*, 296–301. [CrossRef]
17. Premaratne, K.; Salvi, R.; Habib, N.; LeGall, J. Delta-operator formulated discrete-time approximations of continuous-time systems. *IEEE Trans. Autom. Control* **1994**, *39*, 581–585. [CrossRef]
18. Poor, H.V. Delta-operator based signal processing: Fast algorithms for rapidly sampled data. In Proceedings of the 36th IEEE Conference on Decision and Control, San Diego, CA, USA, 10–12 December 1997; Volume 1, pp. 872–877.
19. Gessing, R. Identification of shift and delta operator models for small sampling periods. In Proceedings of the 1999 IEEE American Control Conference (Cat. No. 99CH36251), San Diego, CA, USA, 2–4 June 1999; Volume 1, pp. 346–350.
20. Fan, H.; Liu, X. Delta Levinson and Schur-type RLS algorithms for adaptive signal processing. *IEEE Trans. Signal Process.* **1994**, *42*, 1629–1639. [CrossRef]
21. Ortigueira, M.D. Introduction to fractional linear systems. Part 2. Discrete-time case. *IEE Proc. Vis. Image Signal Process.* **2000**, *147*, 71–78. .:20000273. [CrossRef]
22. Goodrich, C.; Peterson, A.C. *Discrete Fractional Calculus*; Springer International Publishing AG: Cham, Switzerland, 2015.
23. Tarasov, V.E. Exact discrete analogs of derivatives of integer orders: Differences as infinite series. *J. Math.* **2015**, *2015*, 134842. [CrossRef]
24. Tarasov, V.E. Lattice fractional calculus. *Appl. Math. Comput.* **2015**, *257*, 12–33. [CrossRef]
25. Ortigueira, M.D.; Coito, F.J.V.; Trujillo, J.J. Discrete-time differential systems. *Signal Process.* **2015**, *107*, 198–217. [CrossRef]
26. El-Khazali, R.; Machado, J.T. Closed-Form Discretization of Fractional-Order Differential and Integral Operators. In Proceedings of the Fractional Calculus: ICFDA 2018, Amman, Jordan, 16–18 July 2018; Springer: Singapore, 2019; pp. 1–17.
27. Ortigueira, M.D.; Machado, J.T. The 21st century systems: An updated vision of discrete-time fractional models. *IEEE Circuits Syst. Mag.* **2022**, *22*, 6–21. [CrossRef]
28. Ortigueira, M.D.; Magin, R.L. On the Equivalence between Integer-and Fractional Order-Models of Continuous-Time and Discrete-Time ARMA Systems. *Fractal Fract.* **2022**, *6*, 242. [CrossRef]
29. Butzer, P.; Engels, W.; Ries, S.; Stens, R. The Shannon sampling series and the reconstruction of signals in terms of linear, quadratic and cubic splines. *SIAM J. Appl. Math.* **1986**, *46*, 299–323. [CrossRef]
30. Gensun, F. Whittaker–Kotel'nikov–Shannon sampling theorem and aliasing error. *J. Approx. Theory* **1996**, *85*, 115–131. [CrossRef]
31. Unser, M. Sampling-50 years after Shannon. *Proc. IEEE* **2000**, *88*, 569–587. [CrossRef]
32. Marvasti, F. *Nonuniform Sampling: Theory and Practice*; Springer Science & Business Media: New York, NY, USA, 2012.
33. Bertrand, J.; Bertrand, P.; Ovarlez, J. The Mellin Transform. In *The Transforms and Applications Handbook*, 2nd ed.; Poularikas, A.D., Ed.; CRC Press: Boca Raton, FL, USA, 2000.
34. De Sena, A.; Rocchesso, D. A fast Mellin and scale transform. *EURASIP J. Adv. Signal Process.* **2007**, *2007*, 89170. [CrossRef]
35. Ortigueira, M.D.; Machado, J.A.T. Fractional Derivatives: The Perspective of System Theory. *Mathematics* **2019**, *7*, 150. [CrossRef]
36. Ortigueira, M.D.; Valério, D. *Fractional Signals and Systems*; De Gruyter: Berlin, Germany; Boston, MA, USA, 2020.
37. Oppenheim, A.V.; Willsky, A.S.; Hamid, S. *Signals and Systems*, 2nd ed.; Prentice-Hall: Upper Saddle River, NJ, USA, 1997.
38. Shmaliy, Y. *Continuous-Time Systems*; Springer: Dordrecht, The Netherlands, 2007.
39. Gulgowski, J.; Stefański, T.P. Generalization of Kramers-Krönig relations for evaluation of causality in power-law media. *Commun. Nonlinear Sci. Numer. Simul.* **2021**, *95*, 105664. [CrossRef]
40. Ortigueira, M.D.; Bohannan, G.W. Fractional Scale Calculus: Hadamard vs. Liouville. *Fractal Fract.* **2023**, *7*, 296. [CrossRef]
41. Lacroix, S.F. *Traité des Differénces et des Séries*; Duprat: Paris, France, 1800.
42. Householder, A.S. *Principles of Numerical Analysis*; McGraw-Hill Book Company: New York, NY, USA, 1953.
43. Hardy, G.H. *Divergent Series*; American Mathematical Soc.: Ann Arbor, MI, USA, 2000; Volume 334.
44. Samko, S.G.; Kilbas, A.A.; Marichev, O.I. *Fractional Integrals and Derivatives*; Gordon and Breach: Yverdon, Switzerland, 1993.
45. Ortigueira, M.D.; Machado, J.T. Revisiting the 1D and 2D Laplace transforms. *Mathematics* **2020**, *8*, 1330. [CrossRef]
46. Aulbach, B.; Hilger, S. A unified approach to continuous and discrete dynamics. Qualitative Theory of Differential Equations. In *Colloquia Mathematica Sociefatis János Bolyai*; North-Holland: Amsterdam, The Netherlands, 1990; Volume 53, pp. 37–56.
47. Hilger, S. Analysis on Measure Chains—A Unified Approach to Continuous and Discrete Calculus. *Results Math.* **1990**, *18*, 18–56. [CrossRef]
48. Ortigueira, M.D.; Torres, D.F.; Trujillo, J.J. Exponentials and Laplace transforms on nonuniform time scales. *Commun. Nonlinear Sci. Numer. Simul.* **2016**, *39*, 252–270. [CrossRef]
49. Şan, M.; Ortigueira, M.D. Unilateral Laplace Transforms on Time Scales. *Mathematics* **2022**, *10*, 4552. [CrossRef]
50. Ortigueira, M.D. The comb signal and its Fourier transform. *Signal Process.* **2001**, *81*, 581–592. [CrossRef]
51. Ferreira, J. *Introduction to the Theory of Distributions*; Pitman Monographs and Surveys in Pure and Applied Mathematics; Pitman: London, UK, 1997.

52. Gelfand, I.M.; Shilov, G.P. *Generalized Functions*; Academic Press: New York, NY, USA, 1964; Volume 3, English translation.
53. Hoskins, R.; Pinto, J. *Theories of Generalised Functions: Distributions, Ultradistributions and Other Generalised Functions*; Woodhead Publishing Limited: Cambridge, UK, 2010.
54. Hoskins, R. *Delta Functions: An Introduction to Generalised Functions*; Woodhead Publishing Limited: Cambridge, UK, 2009.
55. Roberts, M. *Signals and Systems: Analysis Using Transform Methods and Matlab*, 2nd ed.; McGraw-Hill: New York, NY, USA, 2003.
56. Vaidyanathan, P.P. The theory of linear prediction. *Synth. Lect. Signal Process.* **2007**, *2*, 1–184.
57. Bohner, M.; Peterson, A. *Dynamic Equations on Time Scales: An Introduction with Applications*; Springer Science & Business Media: Berlin/Heidelberg, Germany, 2001.
58. Liouville, J. Memóire sur le calcul des différentielles à indices quelconques. *J. l'École Polytech. Paris* **1832**, *13*, 71–162.
59. Dugowson, S. Les Différentielles Métaphysiques (Histoire et Philosophie de la Généralisation de L'ordre de Dérivation). Ph.D. Thesis, Université Paris Nord, Villetaneuse, France, 1994.
60. Grünwald, A.K. Ueber "begrentz" Derivationen und deren Anwendung. *Z. Math. Phys.* **1867**, *12*, 441–480.
61. Letnikov, A. Note relative à l'explication des principes fondamentaux de la théorie de la différentiation à indice quelconque (A propos d'un mémoire). *Mat. Sb.* **1873**, *6*, 413–445.
62. Rogosin, S.; Dubatovskaya, M. Fractional Calculus in Russia at the End of XIX Century. *Mathematics* **2021**, *9*, 1736. [CrossRef]
63. Heaviside, O., III. On Operators in Physical Mathematics. Part I. *Proc. R. Soc. Lond.* **1893**, *52*, 504–529.
64. Heaviside, O., VIII. On operations in physical mathematics. Part II. *Proc. R. Soc. Lond.* **1894**, *54*, 105–143.
65. Post, E.L. Generalized differentiation. *Trans. Am. Math. Soc.* **1930**, *32*, 723–781. [CrossRef]
66. Butzer, P.L.; Westphal, U. An access to fractional differentiation via fractional difference quotients. In *Fractional Calculus and Its Applications: Proceedings of the International Conference Held at the University of New Haven, June 1974*; Springer: Berlin/Heidelberg, Germany, 2006; pp. 116–145.
67. Diaz, J.; Osler, T. Differences of fractional order. *Math. Comput.* **1974**, *28*, 185–202. [CrossRef]
68. Ortigueira, M.D. Fractional central differences and derivatives. *J. Vib. Control* **2008**, *14*, 1255–1266. [CrossRef]
69. Ortigueira, M.D. Two-sided and regularised Riesz-Feller derivatives. *Math. Methods Appl. Sci.* **2021**, *44*, 8057–8069. [CrossRef]
70. Chapman, S. On non-integral orders of summability of series and integrals. *Proc. Lond. Math. Soc.* **1911**, *2*, 369–409. [CrossRef]
71. Kuttner, B. On Differences of Fractional Order. *Proc. Lond. Math. Soc.* **1957**, *s3-7*, 453–466. [CrossRef]
72. Isaacs, G.L. Exponential laws for fractional differences. *Math. Comput.* **1980**, *35*, 933–936. [CrossRef]
73. Granger, C. New classes of time series models. *J. R. Stat. Soc. Ser. D (Stat.)* **1978**, *27*, 237–253. [CrossRef]
74. Granger, C.W.; Joyeux, R. An introduction to long-memory time series models and fractional differencing. *J. Time Ser. Anal.* **1980**, *1*, 15–29. [CrossRef]
75. Hosking, J.R.M. Fractional differencing. *Biometrika* **1981**, *68*, 165–176. [CrossRef]
76. Gonçalves, E. Une généralisation des processus ARMA. *Ann. d'Ećonomie Stat.* **1987**, 109–145. [CrossRef]
77. Elder, J.; Elliott, R.J.; Miao, H. Fractional differencing in discrete time. *Quant. Financ.* **2013**, *13*, 195–204. [CrossRef]
78. Graves, T.; Gramacy, R.; Watkins, N.; Franzke, C. A brief history of long memory: Hurst, Mandelbrot and the road to ARFIMA, 1951–1980. *Entropy* **2017**, *19*, 437. [CrossRef]
79. Dingari, M.; Reddy, D.M.; Sumalatha, V. Time series analysis for long memory process of air traffic using arfima. *Int. J. Sci. Technol. Res.* **2019**, *8*, 395–400.
80. Monge, M.; Infante, J. A Fractional ARIMA (ARFIMA) Model in the Analysis of Historical Crude Oil Prices. *Energy Res. Lett.* **2022**, *4*. [CrossRef]
81. Cargo, G.; Shisha, O. Zeros of polynomials and fractional order differences of their coefficients. *J. Math. Anal. Appl.* **1963**, *7*, 176–182. [CrossRef]
82. Burnecki, K.; Weron, A. Algorithms for testing of fractional dynamics: A practical guide to ARFIMA modelling. *J. Stat. Mech. Theory Exp.* **2014**, *2014*, P10036. [CrossRef]
83. Kilbas, A.A.; Srivastava, H.M.; Trujillo, J.J. *Theory and Applications of Fractional Differential Equations*; Elsevier: Amsterdam, The Netherlands, 2006.
84. Abdeljawad, T. On Riemann and Caputo fractional differences. *Comput. Math. Appl.* **2011**, *62*, 1602–1611. [CrossRef]
85. Abdeljawad, T. Dual identities in fractional difference calculus within Riemann. *Adv. Differ. Equ.* **2013**, *2013*, 36. [CrossRef]
86. Ostalczyk, P. Remarks on five equivalent forms of the fractional–order backward–difference. *Bull. Pol. Acad. Sci. Tech. Sci.* **2014**, *62*, 271–278. [CrossRef]
87. Miller, K.; Ross, B. Fractional difference calculus. In *Proceedings of the International Symposium on Univalent Functions, Fractional Calculus and Their Applications, Nihon University, Koriyama, Japan, May 1988*; Ellis Horwood: Chichester, West Sussex, England, UK, 1989; pp. 139–152.
88. Podlubny, I. Matrix approach to discrete fractional calculus. *Fract. Calc. Appl. Anal.* **2000**, *3*, 359–386.
89. Atici, F.M.; Eloe, P.W. A transform method in discrete fractional calculus. *Int. J. Differ. Equ.* **2007**, *2*, 165–176.
90. Atici, F.; Eloe, P. Initial value problems in discrete fractional calculus. *Proc. Am. Math. Soc.* **2009**, *137*, 981–989. [CrossRef]
91. Atici, F.M.; Eloe, P. Discrete fractional calculus with the nabla operator. *Electron. J. Qual. Theory Differ. Equ. [Electron. Only]* **2009**, *2009*, 1–12. [CrossRef]
92. Bastos, N.R.; Torres, D.F. Combined Delta-Nabla Sum Operator in Discrete Fractional Calculus. *arXiv* **2010**, arXiv:1009.3883.

93. Bastos, N.R.; Ferreira, R.A.; Torres, D.F. Necessary optimality conditions for fractional difference problems of the calculus of variations. *arXiv* **2010**, arXiv:1007.0594.
94. Ferreira, R.A.; Torres, D.F. Fractional h-difference equations arising from the calculus of variations. *Appl. Anal. Discret. Math.* **2011**, *5*, 110–121. [CrossRef]
95. Holm, M. Sum and difference compositions in discrete fractional calculus. *Cubo* **2011**, *13*, 153–184. [CrossRef]
96. Bastos, N.R. Fractional calculus on time scales. *arXiv* **2012**, arXiv:1202.2960.
97. Mohan, J.J.; Deekshitulu, G. Fractional order difference equations. *Int. J. Differ. Equ.* **2012**, *2012*, 780619. [CrossRef]
98. Mozyrska, D.; Girejko, E. Overview of fractional h-difference operators. In *Proceedings of the Advances in Harmonic Analysis and Operator Theory: The Stefan Samko Anniversary, Lisbon and Aveiro, Portugal, in June–July, 2011*; Operator Theory: Advances and Applications; Springer: Basel, Swizerland, 2013; Volume 229, pp. 253–268.
99. Mozyrska, D. Multiparameter fractional difference linear control systems. *Discret. Dyn. Nat. Soc.* **2014**, *2014*, 183782. [CrossRef]
100. Atıcı, F.M.; Dadashova, K.; Jonnalagadda, J. Linear fractional order h-difference equations. *Int. J. Differ. Equ. (Spec. Issue Honor. Profr. Johnny Henderson)* **2020**, *15*, 281–300.
101. Wang, Q.; Xu, R. A review of definitions of fractional differences and sums. *Math. Found. Comput.* **2023**, 6, 136–160. [CrossRef]
102. Wei, Y.; Zhao, L.; Zhao, X.; Cao, J. Enhancing the Mathematical Theory of Nabla Tempered Fractional Calculus: Several Useful Equations. *Fractal Fract.* **2023**, *7*, 330. [CrossRef]
103. Joshi, D.D.; Bhalekar, S.; Gade, P.M. Controlling fractional difference equations using feedback. *Chaos Solitons Fractals* **2023**, *170*, 113401. [CrossRef]
104. Abdeljawad, T.; Atici, F.M. On the definitions of nabla fractional operators. In *Abstract and Applied Analysis*; Hindawi Publishing Corporation: New York, NY, USA, 2012; Volume 2012, p. 406757.
105. Bastos, N.R.; Ferreira, R.A.; Torres, D.F. Discrete-time fractional variational problems. *Signal Process.* **2011**, *91*, 513–524. [CrossRef]
106. Alzabut, J.; Grace, S.R.; Jonnalagadda, J.M.; Santra, S.S.; Abdalla, B. Higher-Order Nabla Difference Equations of Arbitrary Order with Forcing, Positive and Negative Terms: Non-Oscillatory Solutions. *Axioms* **2023**, *12*, 325. . [CrossRef]
107. Graham, R.L.; Knuth, D.E.; Patashnik, O.; Liu, S. Concrete mathematics: A foundation for computer science. *Comput. Phys.* **1989**, *3*, 106–107. [CrossRef]
108. Liouville, J. Memóire sur quelques questions de Géométrie et de Méchanique, et sur un nouveau genre de calcul pour résoudre ces questions. *J. l'École Polytech. Paris* **1832**, *13*, 1–69.
109. Ortigueira, M.D. Riesz potential operators and inverses via fractional centred derivatives. *Int. J. Math. Math. Sci.* **2006**, *2006*, 48391:1–48391:12. [CrossRef]
110. Ortigueira, M.D.; Bengochea, G.; Machado, J.A.T. Substantial, tempered, and shifted fractional derivatives: Three faces of a tetrahedron. *Math. Methods Appl. Sci.* **2021**, *44*, 9191–9209. [CrossRef]
111. Sabzikar, F.; Meerschaert, M.M.; Chen, J. Tempered fractional calculus. *J. Comput. Phys.* **2015**, *293*, 14–28. [CrossRef]
112. Ortigueira, M.D.; Bengochea, G. Bilateral tempered fractional derivatives. *Symmetry* **2021**, *13*, 823. [CrossRef]
113. Tustin, A. A method of analysing the behaviour of linear systems in terms of time series. *J. Inst. Electr. Eng.—Part IIA Autom. Regul. Servo Mech.* **1947**, *94*, 130–142. [CrossRef]
114. Ortigueira, M.D.; Machado, J.T. New discrete-time fractional derivatives based on the bilinear transformation: Definitions and properties. *J. Adv. Res.* **2020**, *25*, 1–10. [CrossRef]
115. Ortigueira, M.D.; Matos, C.J.; Piedade, M.S. Fractional discrete-time signal processing: Scale conversion and linear prediction. *Nonlinear Dyn.* **2002**, *29*, 173–190. [CrossRef]
116. Ortigueira, M.D.; Machado, J.A.T. The 21st Century Systems: An updated vision of Continuous-Time Fractional Models. *Circuits Syst. Mag.* **2022**, *22*, 36–56. [CrossRef]
117. Ortigueira, M.D.; Batista, A.G. A fractional linear system view of the fractional Brownian motion. *Nonlinear Dyn.* **2004**, *38*, 295–303. [CrossRef]
118. Ortigueira, M.D.; Batista, A.G. On the relation between the fractional Brownian motion and the fractional derivatives. *Phys. Lett. A* **2008**, *372*, 958–968. [CrossRef]
119. Dissanayake, G.S.; Peiris, M.S.; Proietti, T. Fractionally Differenced Gegenbauer Processes with Long Memory: A Review. *Stat. Sci.* **2018**, *33*, 413–426. [CrossRef]

fractal and fractional

MDPI

Article

Periodically Kicked Rotator with Power-Law Memory: Exact Solution and Discrete Maps †

Vasily E. Tarasov [1,2]

[1] Skobeltsyn Institute of Nuclear Physics, Lomonosov Moscow State University, Moscow 119991, Russia; tarasov@theory.sinp.msu.ru; Tel.: +7-495-939-59-89

[2] Department of Physics, 915, Moscow Aviation Institute (National Research University), Moscow 125993, Russia

† In memory of Professor George M. Zaslavsky (1935–2008) who made a huge contribution to the physics of dynamical chaos and application of fractional calculus, on the 90th anniversary.

Abstract

This article discusses the transformation of a continuous-time model of the fractional system into a discrete-time model of the fractional system. For the continuous-time model, the exact solution of the nonlinear equation with fractional derivatives (FDs) that has the form of the damped rotator type with power non-locality in time is obtained.This equation with two FDs and periodic kicks is solved in the general case for the arbitrary orders of FDs without any approximations. A three-stage method for solving a nonlinear equation with two FDs and deriving discrete maps with memory (DMMs) is proposed. The exact solutions of the nonlinear equation with two FDs are obtained for arbitrary values of the orders of these derivatives. In this article, the orders of two FDs are not related to each other, unlike in previous works. The exact solution of nonlinear equation with two FDs of different orders and periodic kicks are proposed. Using this exact solution, we derive DMMs that describe a kicked damped rotator with power-law non-localities in time. For the discrete-time model, these damped DMMs are described by the exact solution of nonlinear equations with FDs at discrete time points as the functions of all past discrete moments of time. An example of the application, the exact solution and DMMs are proposed for the economic growth model with two-parameter power-law memory and price kicks. It should be emphasized that the manuscript proposes exact analytical solutions to nonlinear equations with FDs, which are derived without any approximations. Therefore, it does not require any numerical proofs, justifications, or numerical validation. The proposed method gives exact analytical solutions, where approximations are not used at all.

Keywords: fractional differential equation; nonlinear differential equations; fractional calculus; fractional dynamics; discrete map with memory; processes with memory

PACS: 45.10.Hj

MSC: 26A33; 34A08

1. Introduction

Integro-differential and integral operators, which satisfy some generalizations of the fundamental theorems of calculus, are called fractional integrals (FIs) and fractional derivatives (FDs) and form the fractional calculus (FC) (see fundamental books [1–5], the

Handbook reviews [6,7], and numerical methods seen in [8–10]). There are many types of FDs and FIs [11–14]. The history of the FC was first described in the 1868 paper [15] and then in a book [1] and papers [16–18], including the history of the application of the FC [19–21]. Equations with FDs with respect to time can be used to describe processes and systems with memory and non-locality in time in the various fields of physics [22–25], including continuum mechanics [26–28], physical kinetics [29,30], thermoelasticity, and diffusion [31,32], and in other sciences, including economics [33,34], biology [35], and engineering [36].

In physics, mechanics, and nonlinear dynamics, the discrete maps are usually derived from differential equations of integer order with periodic kicks (for example, see the books about the nonlinear dynamics [37–39] and the work on physics [22,40–42]). This approach allows us to derive the exact solutions of these nonlinear differential equations without any approximations. Therefore, it is important to have a similar approach to solve nonlinear equations with FDs. Some scientists have tried to generalize this approach to nonlinear equations with FDs to derive the discrete maps with memory (DMMs) and nonlocality in time. Until 2008, nonlinear DMMs were simply postulated in some form (for example, see the papers of Fulinski, Kleczkowski [43], Fick with coauthors [44,45], Giona [46], Gallas [47], and Stanislavsky [48]) and are not exact solutions of any integro-differential equations. Some scientists even proposed a justification that periodic "blows" and kicks knock out the memory of dynamic systems. From this, it was concluded that discrete maps associated with equations with FDs cannot have memory. To solve the problem of finding exact solutions to nonlinear equations with FDs and periodic kicks, deriving the corresponding DMM was proposed by Zaslavsky to various scientists who collaborated with him.The author of this article also offered to solve this problem in 2006. This Zaslavsky problem was successfully solved by the author and then published in 2008 [49]. For the first time, DMMs were obtained from nonlinear equations with FDs without approximations in [49]. Then, this approach was developed in [22,50,51] and then in works [34,52–63] in which the following results were derived:

- The DMMs were derived from the equations with the Caputo and Riemann–Liouville FDs in [22,49–51], including the generalization of the Henon, dissipative, and Zaslavsky maps with memory [22,52,63].
- The DMMs were also derived from equations with FDs describing economic [34,53], population dynamics [54], and quantum dynamic systems [55].
- For the first time, the DMMs were obtained from the equations with FIs in [56].
- The DMMs were obtained from the equations with the Erdelyi-Kober FDs in [57], the Hadamard-type FDs in [58], and the Hilfer FDs in [59].
- For the first time, the DMMs were derived from the equations with the general FDs and FIs in [60,62].
- The DMMs were obtained from the equations with the distributed-order FDs in [61].
- The first computer simulations of some such DMMs, which are obtained from nonlinear equations with FDs, are proposed in papers [63–65].
- New types of the chaotic behavior of systems with nonlocality in time were discovered in these papers [63,64], the 2013 papers [66–68], and the 2014 works [69,70].
- Note also the new works of Mendez-Bermudez and Aguilar-Sanchez [71] about tunable subdiffusion in the DDM; Borin [72] about scaling invariance analyses for DDM; Orinaite, Telksniene, Telksnys, and Ragulskis [73] about the changes of the complexity of DMM; Orinaite, Smidtaite, and Ragulskis [74] about Arnold tongues of divergence in the Caputo DMM.

Note some works about the derivation of exact solutions and the DMMs from equations with FDs and FIs without approximations. The importance of this approach to obtaining DMMs is that these maps are derived from the exact solutions of nonlinear equations with FDs and FIs for a very wide class of nonlinearities without any approximations.

For physics, mechanics, and applied sciences, the DMMs are primarily important due to the connection of these maps with fractional differential and integral equations. Therefore, it is important to obtain DMMs from various equations with FDs and FIs without approximations.

Note that the DMMs were considered before the publication of the 2008 article [49], and their maps were proposed without any connection with equations with FDs or any differential equations at all. It should be also noted that, recently, some DMMs are suggested by using the discrete fractional calculus [75–77] and discrete general fractional calculus [78–80]. Such maps, which are called "fractional difference" maps, were considered by Wu, Baleanu, and Zeng in [81–84], by Edelman in the 2015 works [85–88], in 2018 papers [89,90], in the reviews [91,92], and in the paper of Edelman, Helman, and Smidtaite [93–97]. Unfortunately, such fractional discrete maps are not related with the exact solutions of equations with FDs, and such maps were not obtained from equations with FDs without approximations. In addition, there are no well-founded models in physics, biology, or economics that were described by the equation of the discrete fractional calculus. Unfortunately, there are currently no studies of the relationship between discrete FC, described in [75–77], and classical FC [1–7]. However, the description of the new chaotic type of behavior of nonlinear systems with memory and new types of attractors of "fractional difference" maps is important. This gives hope that similar attractors and similar chaotic behavior are realized in discrete maps obtained from equations with FDs without approximations.

One of the interesting systems with memory that is described by two FDs is the periodically kicked damped rotator. This system with memory is a fractional generalization of the system without memory that is described by the second-order differential equation

$$D_t^2 X(t) + \lambda D_t^1 X(t) = K \mathcal{N}[X(t)] \sum_{k=1}^{\infty} \delta\Big(\frac{t}{T} - k\Big), \tag{1}$$

where $D_t^k = d^k/dt^k$ are the derivatives of integer order $k > 0$, λ is a damping constant, T is a kick period, K is an amplitude of these kicks, $\mathcal{N}[X]$ is a real-valued function, and $\delta(t)$ is the Dirac delta-function. Equation (1) gives [37], pp. 16–17, the memoryless discrete map

$$X_{n+1} - X_n = \frac{1 - e^{-\lambda T}}{\lambda} \Big(P_n + K\, T\, \mathcal{N}[X_n]\Big), \tag{2}$$

$$P_{n+1} = e^{-\lambda T} \Big(P_n + K\, T\, \mathcal{N}[X_n]\Big). \tag{3}$$

These equations are proved in Section 1.2 of [37], pp. 16–17. This map, (2), is known as the kicked damped rotator map.

We should note that such universal DMMs were first obtained and described by the authors in works [22,52,63] for the case $\alpha \in (1, 2)$ and $\beta = \alpha - 1$ in Section 1.3.4 of [52] and Sections 18.11–18.13 in [22]. The first computer simulation of the dissipative standard map with memory ($\mathcal{N}[X_n] = \sin(X_n)$) is realized by Edelman in [63] for $\alpha = 1.9975$.

In this paper, we proposed the generalization of Equation (1) in the form

$$(D_t^\alpha X)(t) + \lambda\, (D_t^\beta X)(t) \;=\; K \mathcal{N}[X(t)] \sum_{k=1}^{\infty} \delta\Big(\frac{t}{T} - k\Big), \tag{4}$$

where D_t^α and D_t^α are the FDs of the arbitrary orders $\alpha > \beta > 0$ [4]; λ is a damping constant; T is a period of the kicks; K is an amplitude of these kicks; $\mathcal{N}[X]$ is a real-valued function; $\delta(t)$ is the Dirac delta-function. Equation (4) can be interpreted as the equation of periodically kicked rotator with power-law memory. The structure of the original equation is of significant importance: its left-hand side is linear and has constant coefficients, the right-hand side is generally nonlinear, but due to delta functions, only the function values at discrete time moments are used.

The following results are proposed in this paper.

- For the first time, the exact solution of the equation of the damped rotator with power-law memory is obtained in the general case for the arbitrary orders of two FDs in this paper.
- The exact solutions of the nonlinear Equation (4) with two FDs for the orders $\alpha > \beta > 0$ are obtained for arbitrary values of the orders of these FDs. In this article, the orders of two FDs are not related to each other, unlike in previous works [22,52,63], where $\alpha \in (1,2]$ and $\beta = \alpha - 1$.
- It should be emphasized that the manuscript proposed exact analytical solutions to nonlinear equations with FDs, which are derived without any approximations. The proposed method gives exact analytical solutions, where approximations are not used at all.
- Using these solutions, we derived the DMMs that describe kicked damped rotator with power-law memory.
- As a simple illustration of the possible directions of the application of the proposed method, the model of economic growth was considered in addition to the well-known model of the fractional damped oscillator with friction, memory, and external kicks.

2. Equation with Two FDs and Periodic Kicks

In this section, the equation of the dynamic systems with periodic kicks and power-law nonlocality in time is proposed as the generalization of the periodically kicked rotator without memory. This equation is an equation with two FDs of the orders α and β ($\alpha > \beta > 0$), which describe nonlocality in time. The search for an explicit exact solution to this nonlinear equation with two derivatives consists of three stages:

(1) At the first stage, the second fundamental theorem of fractional calculus and the properties of FDs and FIs are used to obtain linear non-homogeneous equation with one FD of the order $\alpha - \beta$.

(2) At the second stage, the exact solution of the non-homogeneous linear equation with one FD is derived using Theorem 4.3 of [4].

(3) At the third stage, using the exact solution, which is written for the discrete moments of time, the difference between these solutions at neighboring time points is found as a function of all past discrete moments of time.

2.1. Fractional Differential Equation with Periodic Kicks

Let us consider the equation with two FDs with the periodic kicks

$$\left(D^{\alpha}_{C;0+}X\right)(t) + \lambda\left(D^{\beta}_{C;0+}X\right)(t) = K\mathcal{N}[X(t)]\sum_{k=1}^{\infty}\delta\left(\frac{t}{T} - k\right), \tag{5}$$

where T is a period, K is an amplitude of these kicks, $\mathcal{N}[X]$ is a real-valued function, and $D^{\alpha}_{C;0+}$ and $D^{\beta}_{C;0+}$ are the Caputo FDs of the orders $N-1 < \alpha < N$, $M - 1 < \beta < M$, with $N, M \in \mathbb{N}$ and $\alpha > \beta > 0$, such that

$$\left(D^{\alpha}_{C;0+}X\right)(t) := \left(I^{N-\alpha}_{0+}X^{(N)}\right)(t) = \int_0^t h_{N-\alpha}(t-\tau)\,X^{(N)}(\tau)\,d\tau, \tag{6}$$

$$\left(D^{\beta}_{C;0+}X\right)(t) := \left(I^{M-\beta}_{0+}X^{(M)}\right)(t) = \int_0^t h_{M-\beta}(t-\tau)\,X^{(M)}(\tau)\,d\tau, \tag{7}$$

where $h_\omega(t) = t^{\omega-1}/\Gamma(\omega)$ with $\omega > 0$, $\Gamma(\omega)$ is the gamma function, $X^{(N)}(t) = d^N X(t)/dt^N$, and $X^{(M)}(t) = d^M X(t)/dt^M$ with $N, M \in \mathbb{N}$ [4].

The Dirac delta-functions are the generalized functions [98,99]. In order for the left side of Equation (5) to make sense, the function $\mathcal{N}[X(t)]$ must be continuous at $t = kT$. In Equation (5) with two FDs, we can use $\mathcal{N}[X(t)]$ if $\mathcal{N}[X]$ is continuous since this situation is analogous to the case of an equation with one FD of the order greater than one.

Let us note well-known terms that are used in the discrete maps [22,37,39–42].

- If $\mathcal{N}[t, X(t)] = \mathcal{N}[X(t)]$, then the map is called the universal DMM.
- If $\mathcal{N}[X(t)] = -X(t)$, then the map is the Anosov DMM.
- If $-\eta\,\mathcal{N}[X(t)] = (r-1)\,X(t) - r\,X^2(t)$, then the map is the logistic DMM.
- For $\mathcal{N}[X(t)] = \sin(X(t))$, the map is called the standard or Chirikov–Taylor DMM [41].

Applying the Riemann–Liouville FI $I^{\beta}_{RL;0+}$ of the order β to Equation (5) and using the second fundamental theorem for the FDs and FIs, we obtain the equation

$$\left(I^{\beta}_{RL;0+}D^{\alpha}_{C;0+}X\right)(t) + \lambda\left(I^{\beta}_{RL;0+}D^{\beta}_{C;0+}X\right)(t) - K\left(I^{\beta}_{RL;0+}\mathcal{N}[X(\tau)]\sum_{k=1}^{\infty}\delta\left(\frac{\tau}{T}-k\right)\right)(t) = 0, \tag{8}$$

where

$$\left(I^{\beta}_{RL;0+}f\right)(t) := \int_0^t h_\beta(t-\tau)\,f(\tau)\,d\tau \tag{9}$$

is the Riemann–Liouville FI of the order $\beta > 0$ [1,4].

Equation (8) can be written as the sum of three terms:

$$T_1(t) = \left(I^{\beta}_{RL;0+}D^{\alpha}_{C;0+}X\right)(t), \tag{10}$$

$$T_2(t) = \lambda\left(I^{\beta}_{RL;0+}D^{\beta}_{C;0+}X\right)(t), \tag{11}$$

$$T_3(t) = -K\left(I^{\beta}_{RL;0+}\mathcal{N}[X(\tau)]\sum_{k=1}^{\infty}\delta\left(\frac{\tau}{T}-k\right)\right)(t), \tag{12}$$

where $M-1 < \beta < M$ and $N-1 < \alpha < N$, with $N, M \in \mathbb{N}$ and $\alpha > \beta > 0$.

Let us consider the transformation of these terms of Equation (8).

2.2. *Transformation of First Term of Equation with FDs*

Using the definition of the Caputo FD of the order $\alpha \in (N-1, N]$ with $N \in \mathbb{N}$ and the semigroup property of the Riemann–Liouville FIs, we obtain

$$\left(I^{\beta}_{RL;0+}D^{\alpha}_{C;0+}X\right)(t) = \left(I^{\beta}_{RL;0+}I^{N-\alpha}_{RL;0+}D^N X\right)(t) = \left(I^{N-(\alpha-\beta)}_{RL;0+}D^N X\right)(t), \tag{13}$$

where $\alpha > \beta > 0$, $D^N X(t) := d^N X(t)/dt^N = X^{(N)}(t)$.

Let us consider the following two cases.

(1) If $N-1 < \alpha-\beta < N$ and $X(t) \in AC^N[a,b]$ with $(0,(n+1)T] \subset [a,b]$ and $-\infty < a < b < +\infty$, then we obtain

$$\left(I^{N-(\alpha-\beta)}_{RL;0+}D^N X\right)(t) = \left(D^{\alpha-\beta}X\right)(t) \tag{14}$$

and

$$\left(I^{\beta}_{RL;0+}D^{\alpha}_{C;0+}X\right)(t) = \left(D^{\alpha-\beta}_{C;0+}X\right)(t). \tag{15}$$

In this case, we obtain

$$T_1(t) = \left(D^{\alpha-\beta}_{C;0+}X\right)(t). \tag{16}$$

(2) Let us consider the general case

$$M-1<\beta<M, \quad N-1<\alpha<N, \quad \alpha>\beta>0. \tag{17}$$

Using that

$$\alpha-\beta = (N-1+\{\alpha\}) - (M-1+\{\beta\}) = N-M+\{\alpha\}-\{\beta\}, \tag{18}$$

where $\{x\} = x-[x]$ and $[x]$ is the integer value of the number $x \in \mathbb{R}$, we obtain

$$L-1<\alpha-\beta \leqslant L, \tag{19}$$

where

$$L := \begin{cases} N-M+1 & \{\alpha\} > \{\beta\} \text{ if } N \geqslant M \geqslant 1, \\ N-M & \{\alpha\} < \{\beta\} \text{ if } N > M \geqslant 1, \\ N-M & \{\alpha\} = \{\beta\} \text{ if } N > M, \end{cases} \tag{20}$$

where $\alpha \in (N-1,N]$, $\beta \in (M-1,M]$, and $N, M \in \mathbb{N}$.

For the case $N-L=0$, we obtain $N-1<\alpha-\beta<N$ and Equation (16).

For the case $1 \leqslant N-L \leqslant N$, we have the equalities

$$(I^{\beta}_{RL;0+}D^{\alpha}_{C;0+}X)(t) = (I^{\beta}_{RL;0+}I^{N-\alpha}_{RL;0+}D^N X)(t) =$$

$$(I^{N-(\alpha-\beta)}_{RL;0+}D^N X)(t) = (I^{L-(\alpha-\beta)}_{RL;0+}I^{N-L}D^{N-L}D^L X)(t), \tag{21}$$

if $X(t) \in AC^N[a,b]$ with $(0,(n+1)T] \subset [a,b]$ and $-\infty<a<b<+\infty$, $D^L X(t) := X^{(L)}(t)$, and $D^N X(t) := X^{(N)}(t)$.

Using the second fundamental theorem of the calculus for $(N-L) \in \mathbb{N}$ as

$$(I^{N-L}D^{N-L}f)(t) = f(t) - \sum_{m=0}^{N-L-1} \frac{f^{(m)}(0+)}{m!}t^m, \tag{22}$$

where $1 \leqslant N-L \leqslant N-1$ and $f(t) = X^{(L)}(t)$. Equation (21) gives

$$(I^{L-(\alpha-\beta)}_{RL;0+}I^{N-L}D^{N-L}D^L X)(t) = (I^{L-(\alpha-\beta)}_{RL;0+}I^{N-L}D^{N-L}X^{(L)})(t) =$$

$$(I^{L-(\alpha-\beta)}_{RL;0+}X^{(L)})(t) - \sum_{m=0}^{N-L-1}\frac{X^{(L+m)}(0+)}{m!}(I^{L-(\alpha-\beta)}_{RL;0+}t^m)(t) =$$

$$(D^{\alpha-\beta}_{C;0+}X)(t) - \sum_{m=0}^{N-L-1}\frac{X^{(L+m)}(0+)}{\Gamma(m+L-(\alpha-\beta)+1)}t^{m+L-(\alpha-\beta)}, \tag{23}$$

where we use $m! = \Gamma(m+1)$ and Equation 2.1.16 of [4], p. 71, in the form

$$(I^{L-(\alpha-\beta)}_{RL;0+}t^m)(t) = \frac{\Gamma(m+1)}{\Gamma(m+L-(\alpha-\beta)+1)}t^{m+L-(\alpha-\beta)}, \tag{24}$$

and $\Gamma(z)$ is the gamma function.

As a result, we obtain

$$T_1(t) = \left(D^{\alpha-\beta}_{C;0+}X\right)(t) - \sum_{m=0}^{N-L-1}\frac{X^{(L+m)}(0+)}{\Gamma(m+L-(\alpha-\beta)+1)}t^{m+L-(\alpha-\beta)} \tag{25}$$

for the case (17), where $L \in \mathbb{N}$, $1 \leqslant L \leqslant N-1$, and we obtain

$$T_1(t) = \left(D^{\alpha-\beta}_{C;0+} X\right)(t) \tag{26}$$

for $L = N$, which means $N-1 < \alpha - \beta < N$.

2.3. Transformation of Second Term of Equation with FDs

The second fundamental theorem of FC for the Riemann–Liouville FIs integral and the Caputo FDs is described by Lemma 2.22 of [4], p. 96, in the following form: if $X(t) \in AC^M[a,b]$ with $(0,(n+1)T] \subset [a,b]$ and $-\infty < a < b < +\infty$, and $M-1 < \beta < M$, then the equation

$$\left(I^{\beta}_{RL;a+} D^{\beta}_{C;a+} X\right)(t) = X(t) - \sum_{k=0}^{M-1} \Sigma^C_k(a+)\,(t-a)^k, \tag{27}$$

holds for all $t > a$, where

$$\Sigma^C_k(a) = \lim_{t \to a+} \frac{X^{(k)}(t)}{k!}, \quad \Sigma^C_0(a) = \lim_{t \to a+} X(t). \tag{28}$$

For example, if $0 < \beta < 1$ $(M = 1)$, then

$$\left(I^{\beta}_{RL;a+} D^{\beta}_{C;a+} X\right)(t) = X(t) - X(a) \tag{29}$$

holds $X(t) \in AC^1[a,b]$.

As a result, we obtain

$$T_2(t) = \lambda\, X(t) - \lambda \sum_{k=0}^{M-1} \Sigma^C_k(0+)\, t^k \tag{30}$$

for $\beta \in (M-1, m]$ with $M \in \mathbb{N}$, and

$$T_2(t) = \lambda\, X(t) - \lambda\, X(0+) \tag{31}$$

for $\beta \in (0,1]$.

2.4. Transformation of Third Term of Equation with FDs

Using the Riemann–Liouville FI (9), the third term is represented as

$$T_3(t) = -K \left(I^{\beta}_{RL;0+} \left(\mathcal{N}[X(\tau)] \sum_{k=1}^{\infty} \delta\left(\frac{\tau}{T} - k\right)\right)\right)(t) = \tag{32}$$

$$-\frac{K}{\Gamma(\beta)} \int_0^t (t-\tau)^{\beta-1} \left(\mathcal{N}[X(\tau)] \sum_{k=1}^{\infty} \delta\left(\frac{\tau}{T} - k\right)\right) d\tau. \tag{33}$$

For $nT < t < (n+1)T$, we obtain

$$T_3(t) = -\frac{K}{\Gamma(\beta)} \sum_{k=1}^{n} \int_0^t (t-\tau)^{\beta-1} \left(\mathcal{N}[X(\tau)] \delta\left(\frac{\tau}{T} - k\right)\right) d\tau. \tag{34}$$

Using the equation

$$\int_0^t f(\tau)\, \delta\left(\frac{\tau}{T} - k\right) d\tau = T\, f(kT)\, \theta(t - kT), \tag{35}$$

where $f(\tau)$ is continuous function at $\tau = kT$ and $0 < kT < t$, the term $T_3(t)$ for $nT < t < (n+1)T$ takes the form

$$T_3(t) = -\frac{KT}{\Gamma(\beta)} \sum_{k=1}^{n} (t-kT)^{\beta-1} \mathcal{N}[X(kT)] \, \theta(t-kT), \tag{36}$$

where $\theta(t-kT)$ is the Heaviside step function.

2.5. Equation with One FD

The integration of Equation (5) with two FDs gives the equation with one FD of the order $\alpha - \beta > 0$. Substitution of Equations (26) and (31), or (26), (30), and (36), into equation

$$T_1(t) \; + \; T_2(t) \; + \; T_3(t) \; = \; 0 \tag{37}$$

gives the following linear equations with FD.

(1) Let us consider $\beta \in (0,1)$ such that $N-1 < \alpha < N$ and $N-1 < \alpha-\beta < N$. Substitution of Equations (26), (31), and (36) into Equation (37) gives the linear equation with one FD

$$\left(D^{\alpha-\beta} X\right)(t) + \lambda (X(t) - X(0+)) \; = \; \frac{KT}{\Gamma(\beta)} \sum_{k=1}^{n} (t-kT)^{\beta-1} \mathcal{N}[X(kT)] \, \theta(t-kT). \tag{38}$$

Equation (38) can be represented as the linear equation with FD

$$\left(D^{\alpha-\beta}_{C;0+} X\right)(t) \; = \; -\lambda \, X(t) + F_1(t), \tag{39}$$

where $t \in (nT, (n+1)T)$, $n \in \mathbb{N}$, $\lambda \in \mathbb{R}$, and

$$F_1(t) \; := \; \lambda \, X(0+) - T_3(t) \; =$$

$$\lambda \, X(0+) + \frac{KT}{\Gamma(\beta)} \sum_{k=1}^{n} (t-kT)^{\beta-1} \mathcal{N}[X(kT)] \, \theta(t-kT). \tag{40}$$

(2) Let us consider the case $M-1 < \beta < M$, $N-1 < \alpha < N$, $\alpha > \beta > 0$. Substitution of Equations (25), (30), and (36) into Equation (37) gives the linear equation with the FD

$$\left(D^{\alpha-\beta}_{C;0+} X\right)(t) \; = \; -\lambda \, X(t) + F_2(t), \tag{41}$$

where the function $F_2(t)$ can be written as

$$F_2(t) \; = \; A(t) \; + \; B(t) \; - \; T_3(t) \; =$$

$$A(t) \; + \; B(t) \; + \; \frac{KT}{\Gamma(\beta)} \sum_{k=1}^{n} (t-kT)^{\beta-1} \mathcal{N}[X(kT)] \, \theta(t-kT), \tag{42}$$

where

$$A(t) \; := \; \lambda \sum_{k=0}^{M-1} \Sigma^C_k(0+) \, t^k, \tag{43}$$

$$B(t) \; := \; \sum_{m=0}^{N-L-1} \frac{X^{(L+m)}(0+)}{\Gamma(m+L-(\alpha-\beta)+1)} \, t^{m+L-(\alpha-\beta)}, \tag{44}$$

where L is defined by Equation (20), $\alpha \in (N-1, N]$ and $\beta \in (M-1, M]$.

(3) Let us note a simple particular case of Equations (39) and (41), where $\alpha - \beta$ is a positive integer. If $\{\alpha\} = \{\beta\}$, then

$$\alpha - \beta = N - M = L \in \mathbb{N}, \tag{45}$$

and the FD is the integer-order derivative

$$\left(D^{\alpha-\beta}_{C;0+} X\right)(t) = \frac{d^L X(t)}{dt^L}. \tag{46}$$

Then, in the case $\{\alpha\} = \{\beta\}$, Equations (39) and (41) are differential equations of the integer orders

$$\frac{d^L X(t)}{dt^L} = -\lambda\, X(t) + F_1(t). \tag{47}$$

$$\frac{d^L X(t)}{dt^L} = = -\lambda\, X(t) + F_2(t). \tag{48}$$

If $\alpha = \beta + 1$, then $L = 1$, and we obtain a differential equation of the first order.

Remark 1. *Let us note that Equations* (39) *and* (41) *are linear non-homogeneous equation with one FD of the order* $\alpha - \beta > 0$.

3. Exact Solution of Equation with One FD

3.1. Exact Solution of Equation with One FD

To solve Equations (39) and (41) with FDs, we can use the theorem that was proved in [4], pp. 230–231, as Theorem 4.3. This theorem states that if $F(t) \in C_\gamma[a,b]$ with $(0,(n+1)T] \subset [a,b]$ and $-\infty < a < b < +\infty$, then the Cauchy problem in the form of the equation

$$(D^{\alpha}_{C;a+} X)(t) + \lambda X(t) = F(t), \tag{49}$$

where $\lambda \in \mathbb{R}$ and the initial conditions

$$X^{(k)}(a+) = b_k \in \mathbb{R}, \quad (k = 0, 1, ..., N-1) \tag{50}$$

has a unique solution $X(t) \in C^{\alpha, N-1}_{\gamma}[a,b]$, such that

$$X(t) = \sum_{k=0}^{N-1} b_k\, (t-a)^k\, E_{\alpha,k+1}[-\lambda\,(t-a)^\alpha] + \int_a^t (t-\tau)^{\alpha-1}\, E_{\alpha,\alpha}[-\lambda\,(t-\tau)^\alpha]\, F(\tau)\, d\tau, \tag{51}$$

where $E_{\alpha,\beta}[z]$ is the two-parameter Mittag–Leffler function [4,100]. If $\gamma = 0$ and $F(t) \in C[a,b]$, then the solution belongs to the space $X(t) \in C^{\alpha,N-1}[a,b]$. The two-parameter Mittag–Leffler function $E_{\alpha,\beta}[z]$ is defined [100] by the expression

$$E_{\alpha,\beta}[z] = \sum_{k=0}^{\infty} \frac{z^k}{\Gamma(\alpha k + \beta)}, \tag{52}$$

where $\alpha > 0$, and β are arbitrary real or complex numbers. Note that $E_{1,1}(z) = e^z$.

Here, $C_\gamma[a,b]$ is the weighted space [4], p. 4, of functions $f(t)$ given on finite interval $(a,b]$ such that the function $(t-a)^\gamma f(t) \in C[a,b]$. The space $C^{N-1}_\gamma[a,b]$ is the weighted space [4], p. 4, of the continuously differentiable functions $f(t)$ up to order $N-1$ given on finite interval $(a,b]$ such that $f^{(N)}(t) \in C_\gamma[a,b]$

To solve Equations (39) and (41) for $t \in (nT,(n+1)T)$, $n \in \mathbb{N}$, we will use Theorem 4.3 of [4], where α should be $\alpha - \beta$ and N should be L, $a = 0$. Let $N-1 < \alpha < N$, $0 \leq \gamma < 1$, $\gamma \leqslant \alpha$, $\lambda \in \mathbb{R}$.

As a result, Equations (39) and (41) have the solutions

$$X(t) = \sum_{k=0}^{L-1} b_k\, t^k\, E_{\alpha-\beta,k+1}[-\lambda\, t^{\alpha-\beta}] + \int_0^t (t-\tau)^{\alpha-\beta-1}\, E_{\alpha-\beta,\alpha-\beta}[-\lambda\,(t-\tau)^{\alpha-\beta}]\, F_j(\tau)\, d\tau, \quad (53)$$

where $j = 1$ and $j = 2$ for Equations (39) and (41), respectively.

3.2. Calculating Fractional Integrals in Solution

Let us note that the FIs of the functions $A(t)$ and $B(t)$ for $t \in (nT(n+1)T)$can be reduced to the integral

$$\int_0^t (t-\tau)^{\alpha-\beta-1}\, E_{\alpha-\beta,\alpha-\beta}[-\lambda\,(t-\tau)^{\alpha-\beta}]\, \tau^{\mu-1}\, d\tau. \quad (54)$$

For integration (54) of the function $A(t)$, $B(t)$, we can use Equation (4.4.5) from [100], p. 70, which without tmisprint $\Gamma(\alpha)$ is

$$\int_0^t (t-\tau)^{\beta-1}\, E_{\alpha,\beta}[\lambda\,(t-\tau)^{\alpha}]\, \tau^{\mu-1}\, d\tau = \Gamma(\mu)\, t^{\beta+\mu-1}\, E_{\alpha,\beta+\mu}[\lambda\, t^{\alpha}], \quad (55)$$

where $\beta > 0$ and $\mu > 0$. Note that in Equation (55) the parameter μ can be considered as a positive integer, or as a real positive number.

For our case, in Equation (55), we must use $\alpha - \beta$ instead of α and β in the form

$$\int_0^t (t-\tau)^{\alpha-\beta-1}\, E_{\alpha-\beta,\alpha-\beta}\left[-\lambda\,(t-\tau)^{\alpha-\beta}\right] \tau^{\mu-1} d\tau = \Gamma(\mu)\, t^{\alpha-\beta+\mu-1}\, E_{\alpha-\beta,\alpha-\beta+\mu}\left[-\lambda\, t^{\alpha-\beta}\right] \quad (56)$$

with $\mu = k+1$ for $A(t)$ and $\mu = m + L - (\alpha-\beta) + 1$ for $B(t)$.

Then, the integral of the function $A(t)$ for $t \in (nT, (n+1)T)$ can be written as

$$\int_0^t (t-\tau)^{\alpha-\beta-1}\, E_{\alpha-\beta,\alpha-\beta}[-\lambda\,(t-\tau)^{\alpha-\beta}]\, A(\tau)\, d\tau =$$

$$\lambda \sum_{k=0}^{M-1} \Sigma_k^C(0+) \int_0^t (t-\tau)^{\alpha-\beta-1}\, E_{\alpha-\beta,\alpha-\beta}[-\lambda\,(t-\tau)^{\alpha-\beta}]\, \tau^k\, d\tau =$$

$$\lambda \sum_{k=0}^{M-1} \Sigma_k^C(0+)\, \Gamma(k+1)\, t^{\alpha-\beta+k}\, E_{\alpha-\beta,\alpha-\beta+k+1}\left[-\lambda\, t^{\alpha-\beta}\right]. \quad (57)$$

Using Equation (57) with $k = 0$, we can obtain the integral of the term $\lambda\, X(0+)$ in the function $F_1(t)$ in the form

$$\int_0^t (t-\tau)^{\alpha-\beta-1}\, E_{\alpha-\beta,\alpha-\beta}[-\lambda\,(t-\tau)^{\alpha-\beta}]\, \lambda\, X(0+)\, d\tau =$$

$$\lambda\, X(0+) \int_0^t (t-\tau)^{\alpha-\beta-1}\, E_{\alpha-\beta,\alpha-\beta}[-\lambda\,(t-\tau)^{\alpha-\beta}]\, \tau^0\, d\tau =$$

$$\lambda\, X(0+)\, t^{\alpha-\beta}\, E_{\alpha-\beta,\alpha-\beta+1}\left[-\lambda\, t^{\alpha-\beta}\right]. \quad (58)$$

The integral of the function $B(t)$ for $t \in (nT, (n+1)T)$ can be written as

$$\int_0^t (t-\tau)^{\alpha-1}\, E_{\alpha,\alpha}[-\lambda\,(t-\tau)^{\alpha}]\, B(\tau)\, d\tau =$$

$$\sum_{m=0}^{N-L-1} \frac{X^{(L+m)}(0+)}{\Gamma(m+L-(\alpha-\beta)+1)} \int_0^t (t-\tau)^{\alpha-1}\, E_{\alpha,\alpha}[-\lambda\,(t-\tau)^{\alpha}]\, t^{m+L-(\alpha-\beta)}\, d\tau =$$

$$\sum_{m=0}^{N-L-1} X^{(L+m)}(0+)\, t^{m+L}\, E_{\alpha-\beta,m+L+1}\Big[-\lambda\, t^{\alpha-\beta}\Big]. \tag{59}$$

For the integration of the function $T_3(t)$ $t \in (nT,(n+1)T)$, let us define the function $R_{\alpha,\beta}(t,kT)$ for $t \in (nT,(n+1)T)$, with $n \in \mathbb{N}$ by the equation

$$R_{\alpha,\beta}(t,kT) := \int_0^t (t-\tau)^{\alpha-\beta-1}\, E_{\alpha-\beta,\alpha-\beta}[-\lambda\,(t-\tau)^{\alpha-\beta}]\, \frac{(\tau-kT)^{\beta-1}}{\Gamma(\beta)}\, \theta(\tau-kT)\, d\tau =$$

$$\int_{kT}^t (t-\tau)^{\alpha-\beta-1}\, E_{\alpha-\beta,\alpha-\beta}[-\lambda\,(t-\tau)^{\alpha-\beta}]\, \frac{(\tau-kT)^{\beta-1}}{\Gamma(\beta)}\, d\tau, \tag{60}$$

where we use

$$\int_0^t f(\tau)\,\theta(\tau-kT)\,d\tau = \int_{kT}^t f(\tau)\,d\tau. \tag{61}$$

Using the variable $s = \tau - kT$ and Equation (55) with $\mu = \beta$ in the form

$$R_{\alpha,\beta}(t,kT) = \int_0^{t-kT} ((t-kT)-s)^{\alpha-\beta-1}\, E_{\alpha-\beta,\alpha-\beta}\Big[\lambda\,((t-kT)-s)^{\alpha-\beta}\Big]\, \frac{s^{\mu-1}}{\Gamma(\mu)}\, ds =$$

$$(t-kT)^{\alpha-\beta+\mu-1}\, E_{\alpha-\beta,\alpha-\beta+\mu}\Big[-\lambda\,(t-kT)^{\alpha-\beta}\Big] =$$

$$(t-kT)^{\alpha-1}\, E_{\alpha-\beta,\alpha}\Big[-\lambda\,(t-kT)^{\alpha-\beta}\Big], \tag{62}$$

we obtain that the function $R_{\alpha,\beta}(t,kT)$ has the form

$$R_{\alpha,\beta}(t,kT) = (t-kT)^{\alpha-1}\, E_{\alpha-\beta,\alpha}\Big[-\lambda\,(t-kT)^{\alpha-\beta}\Big], \tag{63}$$

where $\alpha > \beta > 0$. Note that function (63) is defined for $t > kT$, where $k \in \mathbb{N}$, $(k = 1,2,3,\ldots)$.

Remark 2. *We can extend the function* (63) *to values* $t \leqslant kT$, *by*

$$R_{\alpha,\beta}(t,kT) = 0 \qquad \text{if} \quad t \leqslant kT. \tag{64}$$

This is due to the fact that at $t \in (0,T)$, *Equation* (5) *contains the sum of the Dirac delta function from* $k = 1$. *In other words, there is no kick at* $t = 0$. *Using the fact that function* (63) *describes the system response to periodic kicks, one can use* (64).

Example 1. *For the case* $\{\alpha\} = \{\beta\}$, *then* $\alpha - \beta = N - M = L \in \mathbb{N}$, *and function* (60) *can be written as*

$$R_{\alpha,\beta}(t,kT) := \int_0^{t-kT} s^{L-1}\, E_{L,L}[-\lambda\, s^L]\, \frac{(t-kT-s)^{\beta-1}}{\Gamma(\beta)}\, ds =$$

$$(t-kT)^{\alpha-1}\, E_{L,\alpha}\Big[-\lambda\,(t-kT)^L\Big], \tag{65}$$

where $t > kT$ *and* $k \in \mathbb{N}$. *Using the examples of the Mittag–Leffler function* $E_{L,L}[z]$ *with* $L = 1$ *and* $L = 2$ *in the form*

$$E_{1,1}[z] = \exp(z), \qquad E_{2,2}[z] = \frac{\sinh(\sqrt{z})}{\sqrt{z}}, \tag{66}$$

we can obtain examples of function (60) in the form

$$R_{\alpha,\beta}(t,kT) = R_{\beta+1,\beta}(t,kT) := \int_0^{t-kT} \exp(-\lambda\, s)\, \frac{(t-kT-s)^{\beta-1}}{\Gamma(\beta)}\, ds, \tag{67}$$

which is the Riemann–Liouville FI of the order $\beta > 0$ of the function $\exp(-\lambda\, s)$, and

$$R_{\alpha,\beta}(t,kT) = R_{\beta+2,\beta}(t,kT) := \int_0^{t-kT} \frac{\sin(\sqrt{\lambda\, s})}{\sqrt{\lambda\, s}}\, \frac{(t-kT-s)^{\beta-1}}{\Gamma(\beta)}\, s\, ds, \tag{68}$$

where $t > kT$ and $k \in \mathbb{N}$, and we use $\sinh(ix) = i\, \sin(x)$.

Using function (60), the integral of the function $T_3(t)$ for $t \in (nT,(n+1)T)$ with $n \in \mathbb{N}$ can be written as

$$\int_0^t (t-\tau)^{\alpha-\beta-1}\, E_{\alpha-\beta,\alpha-\beta}[-\lambda\,(t-\tau)^{\alpha-\beta}]\, T_3(\tau)\, d\tau =$$

$$-\frac{K\,T}{\Gamma(\beta)} \sum_{k=1}^{n} \mathcal{N}[X(kT)] \int_0^t (t-\tau)^{\alpha-\beta-1}\, E_{\alpha-\beta,\alpha-\beta}[-\lambda\,(t-\tau)^{\alpha-\beta}]\, (\tau-kT)^{\beta-1}\, \theta(\tau-kT)\, d\tau =$$

$$-\,K\,T \sum_{k=1}^{n} \mathcal{N}[X(kT)]\, R_{\alpha,\beta}(t,kT). \tag{69}$$

As a result, Equations (39) and (41) have the following solutions for $t \in (nT,(n+1)T)$. Equation (39), where $L = N$, has the solution

$$X(t) = \sum_{k=0}^{L-1} b_k\, t^k\, E_{\alpha-\beta,k+1}[-\lambda\, t^{\alpha-\beta}] + \int_0^t (t-\tau)^{\alpha-\beta-1}\, E_{\alpha-\beta,\alpha-\beta}[-\lambda\,(t-\tau)^{\alpha-\beta}]\, F_1(\tau)\, d\tau =$$

$$\sum_{k=0}^{N-1} b_k\, t^k\, E_{\alpha-\beta,k+1}[-\lambda\, t^{\alpha-\beta}] + \lambda\, X(0+)\, t^{\alpha-\beta}\, E_{\alpha-\beta,\alpha-\beta+1}\left[-\lambda\, t^{\alpha-\beta}\right] +$$

$$K\,T \sum_{k=1}^{n} \mathcal{N}[X(kT)]\, R_{\alpha,\beta}(t,kT), \tag{70}$$

where $t \in (nT,(n+1)T)$ with $n \in \mathbb{N}$.

Equation (41) has the solution

$$X(t) = \sum_{k=0}^{L-1} b_k\, t^k\, E_{\alpha-\beta,k+1}[-\lambda\, t^{\alpha-\beta}] + \int_0^t (t-\tau)^{\alpha-\beta-1}\, E_{\alpha-\beta,\alpha-\beta}[-\lambda\,(t-\tau)^{\alpha-\beta}]\, F_2(\tau)\, d\tau =$$

$$\sum_{k=0}^{L-1} b_k\, t^k\, E_{\alpha-\beta,k+1}[-\lambda\, t^{\alpha-\beta}] + \lambda \sum_{k=0}^{M-1} \Sigma_k^C(0+)\, \Gamma(k+1)\, t^{\alpha-\beta+k}\, E_{\alpha-\beta,\alpha-\beta+k+1}\left[-\lambda\, t^{\alpha-\beta}\right] +$$

$$\sum_{m=0}^{N-L-1} X^{(L+m)}(0+)\, t^{m+L}\, E_{\alpha-\beta,m+L+1}\left[-\lambda\, t^{\alpha-\beta}\right] + K\,T \sum_{k=1}^{n} \mathcal{N}[X(kT)]\, R_{\alpha,\beta}(t,kT), \tag{71}$$

where $t \in (nT,(n+1)T)$ with $n \in \mathbb{N}$.

Note that all terms of the solutions contain the Mittag–Leffler function $E_{\alpha-\beta,\gamma}[-\lambda(t-kT)^{\alpha-\beta}]$ with different values of the parameter γ ($\gamma = \alpha$, $\gamma = \alpha-\beta$, $\gamma = \alpha-\beta+1$, $\gamma = k+1$, $\gamma = \alpha-\beta+k+1$, $\gamma = m+L+1$).

Example 2. *For the case $\{\alpha\} = \{\beta\}$, then $\alpha - \beta = N - M = L \in \mathbb{N}$, and solution (70) has the form*

$$X(t) = \sum_{k=0}^{L-1} X^{(k)}(0+)\, t^k\, E_{L,k+1}[-\lambda\, t^L] + \lambda\, X(0+)\, t^L\, E_{L,L+1}\Big[-\lambda\, t^L\Big] +$$

$$K\,T \sum_{k=1}^{n} \mathcal{N}[X(kT)]\, R_{\alpha,\beta}(t,kT). \tag{72}$$

and solution (71) is

$$X(t) = \sum_{k=0}^{L-1} X^{(k)}(0+)\, t^k\, E_{L,k+1}[-\lambda\, t^L] + \lambda \sum_{k=0}^{M-1} \Sigma_k^C(0+)\, \Gamma(k+1)\, t^{L+k}\, E_{L,L+k+1}\Big[-\lambda\, t^L\Big] +$$

$$\sum_{m=0}^{M-1} X^{(L+m)}(0+)\, t^{m+L}\, E_{L,m+L+1}\Big[-\lambda\, t^L\Big] + K\,T \sum_{k=1}^{n} \mathcal{N}[X(kT)]\, R_{\alpha,\beta}(t,kT), \tag{73}$$

where $t \in (nT,(n+1)T)$ with $n \in \mathbb{N}$.

For the case $\alpha = \beta + 1$, we have $L = 1$, and solution (72) has the form

$$X(t) = X(0+) + K\,T \sum_{k=1}^{n} \mathcal{N}[X(kT)]\, R_{\beta}(t-kT), \tag{74}$$

where $t \in (nT,(n+1)T)$ with $n \in \mathbb{N}$ and the function

$$R_{\beta}(t) := \frac{1}{\Gamma(\beta)} \int_0^t e^{-\lambda s}\, (t-s)^{\beta-1}\, ds = t^{\beta}\, E_{1,\beta+1}[-\lambda\, t] \tag{75}$$

with $T > 0$. Equation (74) is the Riemann–Liouville FI of the function $e^{-\lambda t}$. Equation (74) for $t \in (nT,(n+1)T)$ describes the solution for all positive α and β, such that $\alpha = \beta + 1$, for example, for $\alpha = 1.2$ and $\beta = 0.2$ or $\alpha = 3.8$ and $\beta = 2.8$, and so on.

To simplify the derivation of the discrete map with memory, we will use the function

$$Q_{\alpha-\beta,L}(t) := \sum_{k=0}^{L-1} X^{(k)}(0+)\, t^k\, E_{\alpha-\beta,k+1}[-\lambda\, t^{\alpha-\beta}] +$$

$$\lambda \sum_{k=0}^{M-1} \Sigma_k^C(0+)\, \Gamma(k+1)\, t^{\alpha-\beta+k}\, E_{\alpha-\beta,\alpha-\beta+k+1}\Big[-\lambda\, t^{\alpha-\beta}\Big] +$$

$$\sum_{j=0}^{N-L-1} X^{(L+j)}(0+)\, t^{j+L}\, E_{\alpha-\beta,j+L+1}\Big[-\lambda\, t^{\alpha-\beta}\Big], \tag{76}$$

if $L \in [1, N-1]$ with $N \in \mathbb{N}$. For $L = N$, the function is defined as

$$Q_{\alpha-\beta,N}(t) := \sum_{k=0}^{N-1} X^{(k)}(0+)\, t^k\, E_{\alpha-\beta,k+1}[-\lambda\, t^{\alpha-\beta}] + \lambda\, X(0+)\, t^{\alpha-\beta}\, E_{\alpha-\beta,\alpha-\beta+1}\Big[-\lambda\, t^{\alpha-\beta}\Big]. \tag{77}$$

Using Equations (76) and (77), solutions (70) and (71) can be represented as

$$X(t) = Q_{\alpha-\beta,L}(t) + K\,T \sum_{k=1}^{n} \mathcal{N}[X(kT)]\, R_{\alpha,\beta}(t,kT) \tag{78}$$

for $t \in (nT, (n+1)T)$ with $n \in \mathbb{N}$ and $L \in [1, N]$ with $N \in \mathbb{N}$. Note the function $R_{\alpha,\beta}(t, kT)$ is defined for $t \in (0, T)$, and we have

$$X(t) = Q_{\alpha-\beta,L}(t), \tag{79}$$

since $R_{\alpha,\beta}(t, kT) = 0$ for $t \leqslant kT$. Note that there are no kicks at $t < T$ since the sum of the delta-function in Equation (5) starts at $k = 1$, i.e., st $t = T$. To reflect this fact in one equation, both Equations (79) and (79) can be written by using the Heaviside step function

$$X(t) = Q_{\alpha-\beta,L}(t) + KT \sum_{k=1}^{n} \mathcal{N}[X(kT)]\, R_{\alpha,\beta}(t, kT)\theta(t - kT), \tag{80}$$

where the step function $\theta(x) = 1$ for $x > 0$ and $\theta(x) = 0$ for $x \leqslant 0$.

To consider the DMMs, we must use the function

$$P_m(t) := X^{(m)}(t), \quad m = 0, \ldots, L. \tag{81}$$

Using the functions (78) and (81), we obtain the equations

$$P_m(t) = Q^{(m)}_{\alpha-\beta,L}(t) + KT \sum_{k=1}^{n} \mathcal{N}[X(kT)]\, R^{(m)}_{\alpha,\beta}(t, kT), \tag{82}$$

where $m = 0, \ldots, L$, $Q^{(m)}_{\alpha-\beta,L}(t)$, and $R^{(m)}_{\alpha,\beta}(t, kT)$ are integer-order derivatives of the functions $Q_{\alpha-\beta,L}(t)$ and $R_{\alpha,\beta}(t, kT)$.

Remark 3. *Note that the derivatives $Q^{(m)}_{\alpha-\beta,L}(t)$ of the integer order m can be calculated explicitly.*

Using Equation (52), which defines the Mittag–Leffler function, we obtain

$$t^{\beta-1} E_{\alpha,\beta}[-\lambda t^{\alpha}] = \sum_{k=0}^{\infty} \frac{(-\lambda)^k\, t^{\alpha k+\beta-1}}{\Gamma(\alpha k + \beta)}. \tag{83}$$

Then, the derivative of the integer order $m \in \mathbb{N}$ has the form

$$\begin{gathered}
\frac{d^m}{dt^m}\left(t^{\beta-1} E_{\alpha,\beta}[-\lambda t^{\alpha}]\right) = \frac{d^m}{dt^m}\left(\sum_{k=0}^{\infty} \frac{(-\lambda)^k\, t^{\alpha k+\beta-1}}{\Gamma(\alpha k + \beta)}\right) = \\
\sum_{k=0}^{\infty} \frac{(-\lambda)^k}{\Gamma(\alpha k + \beta)} \frac{d^m t^{\alpha k+\beta-1}}{dt^m} = \sum_{k=0}^{\infty} \frac{(-\lambda)^k}{\Gamma(\alpha k + \beta)} \frac{\Gamma(\alpha k + \beta)}{\Gamma(\alpha k + \beta - m)}\, t^{\alpha k+\beta-m-1} = \\
\sum_{k=0}^{\infty} \frac{(-\lambda)^k t^{\alpha k+\beta-m-1}}{\Gamma(\alpha k + (\beta - m))} = t^{\beta-m-1} \sum_{k=0}^{\infty} \frac{(-\lambda t^{\alpha})^k}{\Gamma(\alpha k + (\beta - m))} = \\
t^{\beta-m-1} E_{\alpha,\beta-m}[-\lambda t^{\alpha}].
\end{gathered} \tag{84}$$

As a result, we proved the equation

$$\frac{d^m}{dt^m}\left(t^{\beta-1} E_{\alpha,\beta}[-\lambda t^{\alpha}]\right) = t^{\beta-m-1} E_{\alpha,\beta-m}[-\lambda t^{\alpha}] \tag{85}$$

for $m \in \mathbb{N}$. Using Equation (85), we obtain

$$Q^{(m)}_{\alpha-\beta,L}(t) = \frac{d^m}{dt^m} Q_{\alpha-\beta,L}(t) =$$

$$\sum_{k=0}^{L-1} X^{(k)}(0+)\, t^{k-m}\, E_{\alpha-\beta,k-m+1}[-\lambda\, t^{\alpha-\beta}] +$$

$$\lambda \sum_{k=0}^{M-1} \Sigma_k^C(0+)\, \Gamma(k+1)\, t^{\alpha-\beta+k-m}\, E_{\alpha-\beta,\alpha-\beta+k+1}\left[-\lambda\, t^{\alpha-\beta}\right] + \tag{86}$$

$$\sum_{j=0}^{N-L-1} X^{(L+j)}(0+)\, t^{j+L-m}\, E_{\alpha-\beta,j+L-m+1}\left[-\lambda\, t^{\alpha-\beta}\right], \tag{87}$$

where $\alpha - \beta > 0$.

Using Equation (85), *we also obtain the m-order derivative of the function* $R_{\alpha,\beta}(t, kT)$ *in the form*

$$R^{(m)}_{\alpha,\beta}(t, kT) = R_{\alpha-m,\beta-m}(t, kT) = (t - kT)^{\alpha-1-m}\, E_{\alpha-\beta,\alpha-m}\left[-\lambda\,(t - kT)^{\alpha-\beta}\right], \tag{88}$$

where $t \in (nT, (n+1)T)$ *with* $n \in \mathbb{N}$, *and* $\alpha > \beta > 0$. *One can use that*

$$R^{(m)}_{\alpha,\beta}(t, kT) = 0 \tag{89}$$

for $t \leqslant kT$.

The short representation of exact solutions (78) and (82) of the equation with FD allows us to obtain the desired DMMs in the next section.

4. Dissipative Discrete Maps with Memory

Using the exact solutions (78) and (82) of the equation with FDs, we obtain the DMMs a with power-law memory function.

To derive DMMs, we should use discrete moments in time $t = nT$ and $t = (n+1)T$, where $n \in \mathbb{N}$. Using the functions

$$X_j = \lim_{\epsilon \to 0+} X(jT - \epsilon), \tag{90}$$

$$P_{m,j} = \lim_{\epsilon \to 0+} P_m(jT - \epsilon), \quad (j = 1, \ldots, n+1), \tag{91}$$

solutions (78) and (82) at the limit $\epsilon \to 0+$ can be derived in the following forms.

For $nT < t < (n+1)T$ with $n \in \mathbb{N}$, using the solutions for $t = (n+1)T - \epsilon \in (nT, (n+1)T)$, we obtain

$$P_{m,n+1} = Q^{(m)}_{\alpha-\beta,L}((n+1)T) + KT \sum_{j=1}^{n} \mathcal{N}[X_j]\, R^{(m)}_{\alpha,\beta}((n+1)T, jT). \tag{92}$$

For $(n-1)T < t < nT$ with $n \in \mathbb{N}$,, using $t = nT - \epsilon \in ((n-1)T, nT)$, we obtain

$$P_{m,n} = Q^{(m)}_{\alpha-\beta,L}(nT) + KT \sum_{j=1}^{n-1} \mathcal{N}[X_j]\, R^{(m)}_{\alpha,\beta}(nT, jT). \tag{93}$$

Note that

$$P_{m,1} = Q^{(m)}_{\alpha-\beta,L}(nT), \tag{94}$$

since $R^{(m)}_{\alpha,\beta}(t, kT) = 0$ for $t \leqslant kT$.

Subtracting Equation (93) from Equation (92), we obtain

$$P_{m,n+1} - P_{k,n} = Q^{(m)}_{\alpha-\beta,L}((n+1)T) - Q^{(m)}_{\alpha-\beta,L}(nT) +$$

$$K\,T\,\mathcal{N}[X_n]\,R^{(m)}_{\alpha,\beta}((n+1)T,nT)+$$

$$K\,T\sum_{j=1}^{n-1}\mathcal{N}[X_j]\left(R^{(m)}_{\alpha,\beta}((n+1)T,jT)\;-\;R^{(m)}_{\alpha,\beta}(nT,jT)\right), \tag{95}$$

for $n = 2, 3, \ldots$, and for $n = 1$, we have

$$P_{m,2}\;-\;P_{k,1}\;=\;Q^{(m)}_{\alpha-\beta,L}(2T)\;-\;Q^{(m)}_{\alpha-\beta,L}(T)+$$

$$K\,T\,\mathcal{N}[X_1]\,R^{(m)}_{\alpha,\beta}(2T,T), \tag{96}$$

where $m = 0, 1, \ldots, L$.

For $m = 0$, we have $P_{m,n+1} = X_{n+1}$ and $P_{0,n} = X_n$, and the DMMs are

$$X_{n+1}\;-\;X_n\;=\;Q_{\alpha-\beta,L}((n+1)T)\;-\;Q_{\alpha-\beta,L}(nT)+$$

$$K\,T\,\mathcal{N}[X_n]\,R_{\alpha,\beta}((n+1)T,nT)+$$

$$K\,T\sum_{j=1}^{n-1}\mathcal{N}[X_j]\left(R_{\alpha,\beta}((n+1)T,jT)\;-\;R_{\alpha,\beta}(nT,jT)\right) \tag{97}$$

for $n = 2, 3, \ldots$ and for $n = 1$, we have

$$X_2\;-\;X_1\;=\;Q_{\alpha-\beta,L}(2T)\;-\;Q_{\alpha-\beta,L}(T)+$$

$$K\,T\,\mathcal{N}[X_1]\,R_{\alpha,\beta}(2T,T). \tag{98}$$

These discrete maps are the exact solution of the equations with two FDs at the discrete moments in time.

Example 3. *For the case $\alpha = \beta + 1$, the DMM (97) is described as*

$$X_{n+1}\;-\;X_n\;=\;K\,T\,\mathcal{N}[X_n]\,R_{\alpha,\beta}((n+1)T,nT)\;+\;K\,T\sum_{j=1}^{n-1}\mathcal{N}[X_j]\,\mathcal{R}_{\alpha,\beta}(n,j), \tag{99}$$

with the function

$$\mathcal{R}_\beta(n,j)\;:=\;R_\beta((n-j+1)T)\;-\;R_\beta((n-j)T)\;=$$

$$((n-j+1)T)^\beta\,E_{1,\beta+1}[-\lambda\,((n-j+1)T)]\;-\;((n-j)T)^\beta\,E_{1,\beta+1}[-\lambda\,((n-j)T)], \tag{100}$$

where $R_\beta(t)$ is defined by Equation (75).

The DMM (100) describes the exact solutions of equations with FDs at discrete moments of time for all possitive α and β, such that $\alpha = \beta + 1$, for example, for $\alpha = 1.5$ and $\beta = 0.5$ or $\alpha = 1.8$ and $\beta = 0.8$ or $\alpha = 8.2$ and $\beta = 7.1$, and so on.

Note that such univeral DMMs were first obtained and described by the author in works [22,52,63] for the case $\alpha \in (1,2]$ and $\beta = \alpha - 1$ in Section 1.3.4 of [52] and Sections 18.11–18.13 in [22]. The first computer simulation of the dissipative standard map with memory is realized by Edelman in [63] for $\alpha = 1.9975$.

5. Economic Model of Growth with Two-Parameter Memory and Price Kicks

As an example of the application of the proposed DMMs, let us consider an economic growth model (EGM) instead of the usual physical model of the rotator.

The following assumptions are used in the economic model of growth.

(1) Let the price P be a function of released product $Y(t)$, i.e., $P = P(Y(t))$. In the logistic growth model, it is assumed that $P(Y(t)) = b - aY(t)$, where a is the marginal price, and b is the price that is independent of the output.

In economics, we can consider the sudden changes of price in the form of price splashes. Let us assume that the price splashes are periodic with period $\theta > 0$, and we will describe them by the Dirac delta function. In this case, we obtain the economic model with the periodic price kicks. This assumption assumes that the price function $P_s(Y(t))$ with the periodic sharp splashes of the price (periodic price kicks) is

$$P_s(Y(t)) = P(Y(t)) \sum_{k=1}^{\infty} \delta\left(\frac{t}{T} - k\right), \tag{101}$$

where $P(Y)$ is the continuous function of the output Y.

(2) The amount of net investment is assumed to be the fixed part of the income $P(Y(t))\,Y(t)$, such that

$$I(t) = \mu\, P_s(Y(t))\, Y(t), \tag{102}$$

where μ is the norm of net investment ($0 < \mu < 1$), specifying the share of income, which is spent on the net investment.

(3) In the EGM without memory and lag, it is assumed that the rate of change of the output ($dY(t)/dt$) is directly proportional to the value of the net investment $I(t)$ that is described by the accelerator equation

$$I(t) = v\, Y^{(1)}(t), \tag{103}$$

where $v > 0$ is the investment coefficient (the power of the accelerator), and $1/v$ is the marginal productivity of capital (the rate of acceleration).

The standard accelerator equation (103) is generalized in [34] by taking into account the memory effects. The equation of the accelerator with power-law memory [34] can be described as

$$I(t) = v(\alpha)\, (D^{\alpha}_{C;0+} Y)(t), \tag{104}$$

which allows us to take into account the influence of the history of changes in output $Y(\tau)$ on net investment $I(t)$.

This allows us a description that takes into account the impact of the history of changes in the dynamics of output $Y(\tau)$ on the net investment $I(t)$. As a result, we obtain a growth model in a competitive environment with power-law memory, which is considered in [34,53].

In Section 10.5 of book [34], pp. 210–212, the economic growth model with two parameter memories has been proposed and investigated. This model is based on the accelerator with two memory functions

$$I(t) = v_1(\alpha)\, (D^{\alpha}_{C;0+} Y)(t) + v_2(\beta) \left(D^{\beta}_{C;0+} Y\right)(t), \tag{105}$$

where $\alpha > \beta > 0$.

The substitution of Equations (101) and (105) into Equation (102) gives

$$(D^{\alpha}_{C;0+} Y)(t) + \frac{v_2(\beta)}{v_1(\alpha)} \left(D^{\beta}_{C;0+} Y\right)(t) = \frac{\mu}{v_1(\alpha)} \mathcal{N}[X(t)] \sum_{k=1}^{\infty} \delta\left(\frac{t}{T} - k\right). \tag{106}$$

Equation (106) is the equation that describes the EGM growth in a competitive environment with two parameter memory and sharp splashes (price kicks). For price linearity

$P(Y(t)) = b - aY(t)$, the nonlinear equation describes the logistic-type EGM with the two parameter memories.

Equation (106) is Equation (5), where $X(t) = Y(t)$ and

$$\mathcal{N}[X(t)] = Y(t)\, P(Y(t)), \quad \lambda = \frac{v_2(\beta)}{v_1(\alpha)}, \quad K = \frac{\mu}{v_1(\alpha)}. \tag{107}$$

This fact allows us to write the exact solution of the nonlinear Equation (78) with two FDs as

$$Y(t) = \mathcal{Q}_{\alpha-\beta,L}(t) + \frac{\mu\, T}{v_1(\alpha)} \sum_{k=1}^{n} P(Y(kT))\, Y(kT)\, R_{\alpha,\beta}(t, kT), \tag{108}$$

and discrete maps (97) as

$$\begin{aligned} Y_{n+1} - Y_n = \mathcal{Q}_{\alpha-\beta,L}((n+1)T) - \mathcal{Q}_{\alpha-\beta,L}(nT) + \\ \frac{\mu\, T}{v_1(\alpha)} P(Y_n)\, Y_n\, R_{\alpha,\beta}((n+1)T, nT) + \\ \frac{\mu\, T}{v_1(\alpha)} \sum_{j=1}^{n-1} P(Y_j)\, Y_j \Big(R_{\alpha,\beta}((n+1)T, jT) - R_{\alpha,\beta}(nT, jT) \Big), \end{aligned} \tag{109}$$

where $R_{\alpha,\beta}(t, jT)$ and $\mathcal{Q}_{\alpha-\beta,L}(t)$ are defined by Equations (60) and (76) with $\lambda = v_2(\beta)/v_1(\alpha)$.

Dependence on initial conditions is an important issue. Note that the initial conditions will determine whether the economy will grow or fall. This issue is discussed in detail in the book. In this article, the economic model is simply an example of the application. The dependence of economic dynamics on initial conditions is discussed in detail in the book [34].

6. Conclusions

In this paper, the fractional generalization of periodically kicked damped rotator is proposed. This dynamical system is described by the nonlinear equation with two FDs of the arbitrary positive orders α and β, where $\alpha > \beta$ and periodic kicks occur. These FDs allow us to describe power-law non-locality in time. The exact solution of the equation with FDs is obtained in the general case for the arbitrary orders of FGDs in this paper. Using the exact solutions, we derived DMMs that describe a kicked damped rotator with power-law non-localities in time. These maps, described as the exact solution of nonlinear equations with FDs, are at the same discrete time points as the function of all past discrete moments of time. Let us emphasize that these nonlinear dissipative DMMs are derived from the equations with two FDs without any approximations.

Let us note the following possible developments, generalizations, and applications of the proposed methods and results.

- One of the most important continuations of the development of the proposed exact solutions and discrete mappings is computer modeling. It can be assumed that the new type of attractors and the new type of chaotic behavior can be demonstrated in the proposed DMMs obtained from nonlinear equations with FDs. This is an important and very interesting direction of research, namely, the search for new types of chaotic behavior and a new type of attractors in dynamic maps with memory, which are exact solutions of equations with FDs. This is especially important due to the fundamental nature of these new types of the chaotic behavior and a new type of attractors. Unfortunately, such research is only developing, and new types of behavior and attractors have been found only for the simplest maps. A computer simulation of the proposed DMMs will allow us to discover and describe new types of chaotic behavior and new types of attractors with memory. However, such computer simulations are open questions at the present time and require new research to make possible great discoveries in the future.

- Another of the most important continuations of the development of the proposed approach to obtaining exact solutions and discrete mappings is the generalization of the approach to nonlinear equations with power memory to a general form of memory. The proposed model and the three-stage method, which is proposed for solving the nonlinear equation with two FDs and deriving DMMs, can be generalized from the power-law type to the wide class of time nonlocalities by using general FDs (for example, see the basic articles by Luchko [101–103], subsequent articles by Luchko and co-authors [104–106], Ortigueira's paper [107], and Al-Refai and Fernandez's papers [108,109]). These generalized DDMs will be generalizations from equations with the one general FD [60,62] to the equations with two general FDs.
- It is very important to generalize the proposed method and to derive the exact solutions of nonlinear equations with FDs from the one-dimensional case to the multidimensional case. Let us emphasize that the first fractional generalization of the proposed method of obtaining exact analytical solutions and DMMs was suggested in the 2010 works [22,52]. In these works, the fractional generalization of the Henon and Zaslavsky maps, which are the two-dimensional dissipative quadratic maps given by the two coupled equations, is proposed. In paper [63], the computer simulation of the fractional Zaslavsky maps is realized. Then, recently in works [110–113], some multidimensional DMMs are suggested by using the discrete fractional calculus [75–77]. Unfortunately, these fractional discrete maps were proposed without any connection with equations with FDs or any differential equations at all. Therefore, these multidimensional DMMs cannot be considered as the exact analytical solutions of nonlinear equations at discrete time points. Let us note that Orinaite, Smidtaite, and Ragulsk in the 2025 paper [74] proposed to derive the multidimensional DMMs as maps of matrices from the exact analytical solutions of nonlinear fractional differential equations with matrices. This OSR approach to the multidimensional maps, which are exact solutions of equation with FDs, is very promising.
- Applications of the proposed method and the exact solutions of nonlinear equations with two FDs can be realized in various studies, for example, in the following areas: (1) in physics and mechanics to describe systems with dissipation (or friction) and memory [55]; (2) in economics and finance to derive various economic and financial models with memory [34,53]; (3) in describing the chemical kinetics and population dynamics [54]; (4) to describe the behavior of engineering systems involving adaptive memory and path losses due to power-law frequency dispersion [114–116] since the erasure and loss of information can be interpreted as a fading memory; (5) a very interesting and important application can be found for describing self-organization with memory in complex systems and processes [117].

All these possible developments, generalizations, and applications of the proposed methods and results are open questions at the present time and require new research in the future.

Funding: This research received no external funding.

Institutional Review Board Statement: Not applicable.

Informed Consent Statement: Not applicable.

Data Availability Statement: The original contributions presented in this study are included in the article. Further inquiries can be directed to the corresponding author.

Acknowledgments: The work of V.E.T. was conducted under the state assignment of Lomonosov Moscow State University.

Conflicts of Interest: The authors declare no conflicts of interest.

References

1. Samko, S.G.; Kilbas, A.A.; Marichev, O.I. *Fractional Integrals and Derivatives: Theory and Applications*; Gordon and Breach: New York, NY, USA, 1993; 1006p.
2. Kiryakova, V. *Generalized Fractional Calculus and Applications*; Longman and J. Wiley: New York, NY, USA, 1994; 360p, ISBN 9780582219779.
3. Podlubny, I. *Fractional Differential Equations*; Academic Press: San Diego, CA, USA, 1998; 340p, ISBN 978-0-12-558840-9.
4. Kilbas, A.A.; Srivastava, H.M.; Trujillo, J.J. *Theory and Applications of Fractional Differential Equations*; Elsevier: Amsterdam, The Netherlands, 2006; 523p, ISBN 978-0-444-51832-3.
5. Diethelm, K. *The Analysis of Fractional Differential Equations. An Application-Oriented Exposition Using Differential Operators of Caputo Type*; Springer: Berlin/Heidelberg, Germany, 2010. [CrossRef]
6. Kochubei, A.; Luchko, Y. *Handbook of Fractional Calculus with Applications. Volume 1. Basic Theory*; Walter de Gruyter GmbH: Berlin, Germany; Boston, MA, USA, 2019; 481p, ISBN 978-3-11-057081-6. [CrossRef]
7. Kochubei, A.; Luchko, Y. *Handbook of Fractional Calculus with Applications. Volume 2. Fractional Differential Equations*; Walter de Gruyter GmbH: Berlin, Germany; Boston, MA, USA, 2019; 519p, ISBN 978-3-11-057082-3. [CrossRef]
8. Karniadakis, G.E. *Handbook of Fractional Calculus with Applications. Volume 3. Numerical Methods*; Walter de Gruyter GmbH: Berlin, Germany; Boston, MA, USA, 2019; 519p, ISBN 978-3-11-057082-3. [CrossRef]
9. Baleanu, D.; Diethelm, K.; Scalas, E.; Trujillo, J.J. *Fractional Calculus: Models and Numerical Methods*; World Scientific Publ.: Singapore, 2012. [CrossRef]
10. Li, C.; Zeng, C. *Numerical Methods for Fractional Calculus*; Chapman and Hall/CRC: New York, NY, USA, 2015. [CrossRef] . [CrossRef]
11. Ortigueira, M.D. *Fractional Calculus for Scientists and Engineers*; Springer Science and Business Media: Berlin, Germany, 2011. [CrossRef]
12. Ortigueira, M.D.; Tenreiro Machado, J.A. What is a fractional derivative? *J. Comput. Phys.* **2015**, *293*, 4–13. [CrossRef]
13. Ortigueira, M.D.; Tenreiro Machado, J. Which Derivative? *Fractal Fract.* **2017**, *1*, 3. [CrossRef]
14. Valerio, D.; Ortigueira, M.D.; Lopes, A.M. How Many Fractional Derivatives Are There? *Mathematics* **2022**, *10*, 737. [CrossRef]
15. Letnikov, A.V. On the historical development of the theory of differentiation with arbitrary index. *Sb. Math. (Matematicheskii Sb.)* **1868**, *3*, 85–112. Available online: http://mi.mathnet.ru/eng/msb8048 (accessed on 13 July 2025).
16. Ross, B. A brief history and exposition of the fundamental theory of fractional calculus. In *Fractional Calculus and Its Applications. Proceedings of the International Conference Held at the University of New Haven, June 1974*; Series: Lecture Notes in Mathematics; Springer: Berlin/Heidelberg, Germany, 1975; Volume 457, pp. 1–36. [CrossRef]
17. Kiryakova, V. A brief story about the operators of the generalized fractional calculus. *Fract. Calc. Appl. Anal.* **2008**, *11*, 203–220.
18. Machado, J.A.T.; Kiryakova, V.; Mainardi, F. Recent history of fractional calculus. *Commun. Nonlinear Sci. Numer. Simul.* **2011**, *16*, 1140–1153. [CrossRef]
19. Valerio, D.J.; Tenreiro Machado, J.A.; Kiryakova, V. Some pioneers of the applications of fractional calculus. *Fract. Calc. Appl. Anal.* **2014**, *17*, 552–578. [CrossRef]
20. Tarasov, V.E. On history of mathematical economics: Application of fractional calculus. *Mathematics* **2019**, *7*, 509. [CrossRef]
21. Rogosin, S.; Dubatovskaya, M. Fractional calculus in Russia at the end of XIX century. *Mathematics* **2021**, *9*, 1736. [CrossRef]
22. Tarasov, V.E. *Fractional Dynamics: Applications of Fractional Calculus to Dynamics of Particles, Fields and Media*; Springer: New York, NY, USA, 2010; 505p. [CrossRef]
23. Klafter, J.; Lim, S.C.; Metzler, R. (Eds.) *Fractional Dynamics. Recent Advances*; World Scientific: Singapore, 2011. [CrossRef]
24. Tarasov, V.E. (Ed.) *Handbook of Fractional Calculus with Applications. Volume 4. Application in Physics. Part A*; Walter de Gruyter GmbH: Berlin, Germany; Boston, MA, USA, 2019; 306p, ISBN 978-3-11-057088-5. [CrossRef]
25. Tarasov, V.E. (Ed.) *Handbook of Fractional Calculus with Applications. Volume 5. Application in Physics. Part B*; Walter de Gruyter GmbH: Berlin, Germany; Boston, MA, USA, 2019; 319p, ISBN 978-3-11-057089-2. [CrossRef]
26. Mainardi, F. *Fractional Calculus and Waves in Linear Viscoelasticity: An Introduction to Mathematical Models*; World Scientific: Singapore, 2010. [CrossRef]
27. Atanackovic, T.; Pilipovic, S.; Stankovic, B.; Zorica, D. *Fractional Calculus with Applications in Mechanics: Wave Propagation, Impact and Variational Principles*; Wiley-ISTE: London, UK; Hoboken, NJ, USA, 2014. [CrossRef]

28. Atanackovic, T.; Pilipovic, S.; Stankovic, B.; Zorica, D. *Fractional Calculus with Applications in Mechanics: Vibrations and Diffusion Processes*; Wiley-ISTE: London, UK; Hoboken, NJ, USA, 2014. [CrossRef]
29. Uchaikin, V.; Sibatov, R. *Fractional Kinetics in Solids: Anomalous Probability Transport in Semiconductors, Dielectrics and Nanosystems*; World Scientific: Singapore, 2013. [CrossRef]
30. Uchaikin, V.; Sibatov, R. *Fractional Kinetics in Space. Anomalous Transport Models*; Worls Scientific: Singapore, 2018; 300p. [CrossRef]
31. Povstenko, Y. *Fractional Thermoelasticity*; Springer International Publishing: Cham, Switzerland; Heidelberg, Germany; New York, NY, USA; Dordrecht, The Netherlands; London, UK, 2015. [CrossRef]
32. Povstenko, Y. *Linear Fractional Diffusion-Wave Equation for Scientists and Engineers*; Springer: Cham, Switzerland; Heidelberg, Germany; New York, NY, USA; Dordrecht, The Netherlands; London, UK, 2015. [CrossRef]
33. Tarasov, V.E. (Ed.) *Mathematical Economics: Application of Fractional Calculus*; MDPI: Basel, Switzerland; Beijing, China, 2020; 278p, ISBN 978-3-03936-118-2/978-3-03936-119-9. [CrossRef]
34. Tarasov, V.E.; Tarasova, V.V. *Economic Dynamics with Memory: Fractional Calculus Approach*; De Gruyter: Berlin, Germany; Boston, MA, USA, 2021; 602p, ISBN 978-3-11-062460-1. [CrossRef]
35. Ionescu, C.; Lopes, A.; Copot, D.; Tenreiro Machado, J.; Bates, J. The role of fractional calculus in modeling biological phenomena: A review. *Commun. Nonlinear Sci. Numer. Simul.* **2017**, *51*, 141–159. [CrossRef]
36. Ortigueira, M.D. An introduction to the fractional continuous-time linear systems: The 21st century systems. *J. IEEE Circuits Syst. Mag.* **2008**, *8*, 19–26. [CrossRef]
37. Schuster, H.G. *Deterministic Chaos. An Introduction*, 3rd ed.; Wiley-VCH: Weinheim, Germany, 1995; 320p, ISBN 978-3527293155.
38. Collet, P.; Eckman, J.P. *Iterated Maps on the Interval as Dynamical System*; Birkhuser Boston: Basel, Switzerland, 2009. [CrossRef]
39. Lichtenberg, A.J.; Lieberman, M.A. *Regular and Chaotic Dynamics*; Springer: Berlin, Germany, 1992. [CrossRef]
40. Sagdeev, R.Z.; Usikov, D.A.; Zaslavsky, G.M. *Nonlinear Physics. From the Pendulum to Turbulence and Chaos*; Harwood Academic: New York, NY, USA, 1988; 656p, ISBN 3718648326/9783718648320. Available online: https://archive.org/details/nonlinearphysics0000sagd (accessed on 13 July 2025).
41. Chirikov, B.V. A universal instability of many dimensional oscillator systems. *Phys. Rep.* **1979**, *52*, 263–379. [CrossRef]
42. Zaslavsky, G.M. *Hamiltonian Chaos and Fractional Dynamics*; Oxford University Press: Oxford, UK; New York, NY, USA, 2005; 421p. [CrossRef]
43. Fulinski, A.; Kleczkowski, A.S. Nonlinear maps with memory. *Phys. Scr.* **1987**, *35*, 119–122. [CrossRef]
44. Fick, E.; Fick, M.; Hausmann, G. Logistic equation with memory. *Phys. Rev. A* **1991**, *44*, 2469–2473. [CrossRef] [PubMed]
45. Hartwich, K.; Fick, E. Hopf bifurcations in the logistic map with oscillating memory. *Phys. Lett. A* **1993**, *177*, 305–310. [CrossRef]
46. Giona, M. Dynamics and relaxation properties of complex systems with memory. *Nonlinearity* **1991**, *4*, 911–925. [CrossRef]
47. Gallas, J.A.C. Simulating memory effects with discrete dynamical systems. *Phys. A Stat. Mech. Its Appl.* **1993**, *195*, 417–430; Erratum in *Phys. A Stat. Mech. Its Appl.* **1993**, *198*, 339. [CrossRef]
48. Stanislavsky, A.A. Long-term memory contribution as applied to the motion of discrete dynamical system. *Chaos Interdiscip. J. Nonlinear Sci.* **2006**, *16*, 043105. [CrossRef] [PubMed]
49. Tarasov, V.E.; Zaslavsky G.M. Fractional equations of kicked systems and discrete maps. *J. Phys. A* **2008**, *41*, 435101. [CrossRef]
50. Tarasov, V.E. Differential equations with fractional derivative and universal map with memory. *J. Phys. A* **2009**, *42*, 465102. [CrossRef]
51. Tarasov, V.E. Discrete map with memory from fractional differential equation of arbitrary positive order. *J. Math. Phys.* **2009**, *50*, 122703. [CrossRef]
52. Tarasov, V.E. Fractional Zaslavsky and Henon discrete maps. In *Long-Range Interactions, Stochasticity and Fractional Dynamics*; Luo, A.C.J., Afraimovich, V., Eds.; Springer and HEP: New York, NY, USA, 2010; 275p, pp. 1–26. [CrossRef]
53. Tarasova, V.V.; Tarasov, V.E. Logistic map with memory from economic model. *Chaos Solitons Fractals* **2017**, *95*, 84–91. [CrossRef]
54. Tarasov, V.E. Predator-prey models with memory and kicks: Exact solution and discrete maps with memory. *Math. Methods Appl. Sci.* **2021**, *44*, 11514–11525. [CrossRef]
55. Tarasov, V.E. Quantum maps with memory from generalized Lindblad equation. *Entropy* **2021**, *23*, 544. [CrossRef] [PubMed]
56. Tarasov, V.E. Integral equations of non-integer orders and discrete maps with memory. *Mathematics* **2021**, *9*, 1177. [CrossRef]
57. Tarasov, V.E. Nonlinear fractional dynamics with kicks. *Chaos Solitons Fractals* **2021**, *151*, 111259. [CrossRef]
58. Tarasov, V.E. Fractional dynamics with non-local scaling. *Commun. Nonlinear Sci. Numer. Simul.* **2021**, *102*, 105947. [CrossRef]
59. Tarasov, V.E. From fractional differential equations with Hilfer derivatives. *Comput. Appl. Math.* **2021**, *40*, 296. [CrossRef]
60. Tarasov, V.E. General fractional dynamics. *Mathematics* **2021**, *9*, 1464. [CrossRef]
61. Tarasov, V.E. Discrete maps with distributed memory fading parameter. *Comput. Appl. Math.* **2024**, *43*, 113. [CrossRef]
62. Tarasov, V.E. Multi-kernel discrete maps with memory from general fractional differential and integral equations. *Nonlinear Dyn.* 2025, *Accepted for publication*. [CrossRef]
63. Tarasov, V.E.; Edelman, M. Fractional dissipative standard map. *Chaos Interdiscip. J. Nonlinear Sci.* **2010**, *20*, 023127. [CrossRef] [PubMed]

64. Edelman, M.; Tarasov, V.E. Fractional standard map. *Phys. Lett. A* **2009**, *374*, 279–285. [CrossRef]
65. Edelman, M. Fractional standard map: Riemann-Liouville vs. Caputo. *Commun. Nonlinear Sci. Numer. Simul.* **2011**, *16*, 4573–4580. [CrossRef]
66. Edelman, M. ractional maps and fractional attractors. Part I: Alpha-families of maps. *Discontin. Nonlinearity Complex.* **2013**, *1*, 305–324. [CrossRef]
67. Edelman, M. Universal fractional map and cascade of bifurcations type attractors. *Chaos Interdiscip. J. Nonlinear Sci.* **2013**, *23*, 033127. [CrossRef] [PubMed]
68. Edelman, M.; Taieb L. New types of solutions of non-Linear fractional differential equations. In *Advances in Harmonic Analysis and Operator Theory; Series: Operator Theory: Advances and Applications*; Almeida, A., Castro, L., Speck, F.-O., Eds.; Springer: Basel, Switzerland, 2013; Volume 229, pp. 139–155. [CrossRef]
69. Edelman, M. Fractional maps as maps with power-law memory. In *Nonlinear Dynamics and Complexity*; Afraimovich, A., Luo, A.C.J., Fu, X., Eds.; Springer: New York, NY, USA, 2014; Volume 8, pp. 79–120. [CrossRef]
70. Edelman, M. On universality in fractional dynamics. In Proceedings of the International Conference on Fractional Differentiation and Its Applications (ICFDA), Catania, Italy, 23–25 June 2014; 6p. [CrossRef]
71. Mendez-Bermudez, J.A.; Aguilar-Sanchez, R. Tunable subdiffusion in the Caputo fractional standard map. *Commun. Nonlinear Sci. Numer. Simul.* **2024**, *135*, 108075. [CrossRef]
72. Borin, D. Caputo fractional standard map: Scaling invariance analyses. *Chaos Solitons Fractals* **2024**, *181*, 11597. [CrossRef]
73. Orinaite, U.; Telksniene, I.; Telksnys, T.; Ragulskis, M. How does the fractional derivative change the complexity of the Caputo standard fractional map. *Int. J. Bifurc. Chaos* **2024**, *34*, 2450085. [CrossRef]
74. Orinaite, U.; Smidtaite, R.; Ragulskis, M. Arnold tongues of divergence in the Caputo fractional standard map of nilpotent matrices. *Nonlinear Anal. Model. Control* 2025, *Accepted for publications.*
75. Goodrich, C.; Peterson, A.C. *Discrete Fractional Calculus*; Springer: Heidelberg, Germany; New York, NY, USA; Dordrecht, The Netherlands; London, UK, 2015; ISBN 978-3-319-25560-6. [CrossRef]
76. Ferreira, R.A.C. *Discrete Fractional Calculus and Fractional Difference Equations*; Springer: Cham, Switzerland, 2022. [CrossRef]
77. Ortigueira, M.D. Discrete-time fractional difference calculus: Origins, evolutions, and new formalisms. *Fractal Fract.* **2023**, *7*, 502. [CrossRef]
78. Ferreira, R.A.C.; Rocha, C.D.A. Discrete convolution operators and equations. *Fract. Calc. Appl. Anal.* **2024**, *27*, 757–771. [CrossRef]
79. Antoniouk, A.V.; Kochubei, A. Discrete-time general fractional calculus. *Fract. Calc. Appl. Anal.* **2024**, *27*, 2948–2963. [CrossRef]
80. Kochubei, A.N. Chaotic property in general fractional calculus. *Chaos Interdiscip. J. Nonlinear Sci.* **2024**, *34*, 123165. [CrossRef] [PubMed]
81. Wu, G.-C.; Baleanu, D. Discrete fractional logistic map and its chaos. *Nonlinear Dyn.* **2014**, *75*, 283–287. [CrossRef]
82. Wu, G.-C.; Baleanu, D. Jacobian matrix algorithm for Lyapunov exponents of the discrete fractional maps. *Commun. Nonlinear Sci. Numer. Simul.* **2015**, *22*, 95–100. [CrossRef]
83. Wu, G.-C.; Baleanu, D. Stability analysis of impulsive fractional difference equations. *Fract. Calc. Appl. Anal.* **2018**, *21*, 354–375. [CrossRef]
84. Wu, G.-C.; Baleanu, D.; Zeng, S.D. Several fractional differences and their applications to discrete maps. *J. Appl. Nonlinear Dyn.* **2015**, *4*, 339–348. [CrossRef]
85. Edelman, M. Caputo standard alpha-family of maps: Fractional difference vs. fractional. *Chaos Interdiscip. J. Nonlinear Sci.* **2014**, *24*, 023137. [CrossRef] [PubMed]
86. Edelman, M. Fractional maps and fractional attractors. Part II: Fractional difference α-families of maps. *Discontin. Nonlinearity Complex.* **2015**, *4*, 391–402. [CrossRef]
87. Edelman, M. On the fractional Eulerian numbers and equivalence of maps with long term power-law memory (integral Volterra equations of the second kind) to Grunvald-Letnikov fractional difference (differential) equations. *Chaos Interdiscip. J. Nonlinear Sci.* **2015**, *25*, 073103. [CrossRef] [PubMed]
88. Edelman, M. On nonlinear fractional maps: Nonlinear maps with power-law memory. In *Proceedings of the International Conference CCT15—Chaos, Complexity and Transport 2015, Marseilles, France, 1–5 June 2015*; Leoncini, X., Eloy, C., Boedec, G., Eds.; World Scientific: Singapore, 2017; pp. 119–130, ISBN 978-981-3202-74-0. [CrossRef]
89. Edelman, M. On stability of fixed points and chaos in fractional systems. *Chaos Interdiscip. J. Nonlinear Sci.* **2018**, *28*, 023112. [CrossRef] [PubMed]
90. Edelman, M. Universality in systems with power-law memory and fractional dynamics. In *Chaotic, Fractional, and Complex Dynamics: New Insights and Perspectives*; Edelman, M., Macau, E.E.N., Sanjuan, M.A.F., Eds.; Springer International Publishing AG: Cham, Switzerland, 2018; pp. 147–171. [CrossRef]
91. Edelman, M. Maps with power-law memory: Direct introduction and Eulerian numbers, fractional maps, and fractional difference maps. In *Handbook of Fractional Calculus with Applications. Volume 2. Fractional Differential Equations*; Walter de Gruyter GmbH: Berlin, Germany; Boston, MA, USA, 2019; pp. 47–63, ISBN 978-3-11-057082-3. [CrossRef]

92. Edelman, M. Dynamics of nonlinear systems with power-law memory. In *Handbook of Fractional Calculus with Applications. Volume 4. Application in Physics. Part A*; Walter de Gruyter GmbH: Berlin, Germany; Boston, MA, USA, 2019; 306p, pp. 103–132, ISBN 978-3-11-057088-5. [CrossRef]
93. Edelman, M. Cycles in asymptotically stable and chaotic fractional maps. *Nonlinear Dyn.* **2021**, *104*, 2829–2841. [CrossRef]
94. Edelman, M.; Helman, A.B. Asymptotic cycles in fractional maps of arbitrary positive orders. *Fract. Calc. Appl. Anal.* **2022**, *25*, 181–206. [CrossRef]
95. Edelman, M.; Helman, A.B.; Smidtaite, R. Bifurcations and transition to chaos in generalized fractional maps of the orders $0 < \alpha < 1$. *Chaos Interdiscip. J. Nonlinear Sci.* **2023**, *33*, 063123. [CrossRef]
96. Edelman, M. Stability of fixed points in generalized fractional maps of the orders $0 < \alpha < 1$. *Nonlinear Dyn.* **2023**, *111*, 10247–10254. [CrossRef]
97. Edelman, M. Asymptotically periodic and bifurcation points in fractional difference maps. *Fractal Fract.* **2025**, *9*, 231. [CrossRef]
98. Lighthill, M.J. *An Introduction to Fourier Analysis and Generalised Functions*; Cambridge University Press: Cambridge, UK, 1958; 79p, ISBN 9781139171427. [CrossRef]
99. Gel'fand, I.M.; Shilov, G.E. *Generalized Functions. Vol. I: Properties and Operations*; Academic Press: Boston, MA, USA, 1964; and Reprint by American Mathematical Society: Providence, RI, USA, 2016; 423p, ISBN 1-4704-2658-7/978-1-4704-2658-3.
100. Gorenflo, R.; Kilbas, A.A.; Mainardi, F.; Rogosin, S.V. *Mittag-Leffler Functions, Related Topics and Applications*, 2nd ed.; Springer: Berlin, Germany, 2020; 540p. [CrossRef]
101. Luchko, Y. General fractional integrals and derivatives with the Sonine kernels. *Mathematics* **2021**, *9*, 594. [CrossRef]
102. Luchko, Y. General fractional integrals and derivatives of arbitrary order. *Symmetry* **2021**, *13*, 755. [CrossRef]
103. Luchko, Y. Operational calculus for the general fractional derivatives with the Sonine kernels. *Fract. Calc. Appl. Anal.* **2021**, *24*, 338–375. [CrossRef]
104. Al-Kandari, M.; Hanna, L.A.M.; Luchko, Y. Operational calculus for the general fractional derivatives of arbitrary order. *Mathematics* **2022**, *10*, 1590. [CrossRef]
105. Luchko, Y. Fractional differential equations with the general fractional derivatives of arbitrary order in the Riemann-Liouville sense. *Mathematics* **2022**, *10*, 849. [CrossRef]
106. Al-Refai, M.; Luchko, Y. The general fractional integrals and derivatives on a finite interval. *Mathematics* **2023**, *11*, 1031. [CrossRef]
107. Ortigueira, M.D. Searching for Sonin kernels. *Fract. Calc. Appl. Anal.* **2024**, *27*, 2219–2247. [CrossRef]
108. Al-Refai, M.; Fernandez, A. Generalising the fractional calculus with Sonine kernels via conjugations. *J. Comput. Appl. Math.* **2023**, *427*, 115159. [CrossRef]
109. Fernandez, A. Extending Sonine kernels to arbitrary dimensions. *Banach J. Math. Anal.* **2025**, *19*, 25. [CrossRef]
110. Hu, T. Discrete chaos in fractional Henon map. *Appl. Math.* **2014**, *5*, 2243–2248. [CrossRef]
111. Jouini, L.; Ouannas, A.; Khennaoui, A.A.; Wang, X.; Grassi, G.; Pham, V.-T. The fractional form of a new three-dimensional generalized Hénon map. *Adv. Differ. Equ.* **2019**, *2019*, 122. [CrossRef]
112. Khennaoui, A.-A.; Ouannas, A.; Bendoukha, S.; Grassi, G.; Lozi R.P.; Pham, V.-T. On fractional-order discrete-time systems: Chaos, stabilization and synchronization. *Chaos Solitons Fractals* **2019**, *119*, 150–162. [CrossRef]
113. Edelman, M. Asymptotic cycles in fractional generalizations of multidimensional maps. *Fract. Calc. Appl. Anal.* **2025**, *28*, 24–37. [CrossRef]
114. Ding, F.; Zhu, K.; Liu, J.; Peng, C.; Wang, Y.; Lu, J. Adaptive memory event-triggered output feedback finite-time lane-keeping control for autonomous heavy truck with roll prevention. *IEEE Trans. Fuzzy Syst.* **2024**, *32*, 6607–6621. [CrossRef]
115. Jiang, F.; Li, T.; Lv, X.; Rui, H.; Jin, D. Physics-informed neural networks for path loss estimation by solving electromagnetic integral equations. *IEEE Trans. Wirel. Commun.* **2024**, *23*, 15380–15393. [CrossRef]
116. Yang, Y.; Li, H. Neural ordinary differential equations for robust parameter estimation in dynamic systems with physical priors. *Appl. Soft Comput.* **2025**, *169*, 112649. [CrossRef]
117. Tarasoov, V.E. Self-organization with memory. *Commun. Nonlinear Sci. Numer. Simul.* **2019**, *72*, 240–271. [CrossRef]

fractal and fractional

Article

An Operational Approach to Fractional Scale-Invariant Linear Systems

Gabriel Bengochea [1,*] and Manuel Duarte Ortigueira [2]

1 Academia de Matemáticas, Universidad Autónoma de la Ciudad de México, Prolongación San Isidro 151, Col. San Lorenzo Tezonco, Alc. Iztapalapa, Ciudad de México 09790, Mexico
2 NOVA School of Science and Technology, UNINOVA-CTS and LASI, NOVA University of Lisbon, Quinta da Torre, 2829-516 Caparica, Portugal; mdo@fct.unl.pt
* Correspondence: gabriel.bengochea@uacm.edu.mx

Abstract: The fractional scale-invariant systems are introduced and studied, using an operational formalism. It is shown that the impulse and step responses of such systems belong to the vector space generated by some special functions here introduced. For these functions, the fractional scale derivative is a decremental index operator, allowing the construction of an algebraic framework that enables to compute the impulse and step responses of such systems. The effectiveness and accuracy of the method are demonstrated through various numerical simulations.

Keywords: operational calculus; Mellin transform; fractional scale-invariant; fractional scale derivative; stretching derivative; hadamard derivative

MSC: 26A33; 44A40

1. Introduction

The mathematical framework often used to define systems is based on shift-invariant derivatives [1,2], resulting from the works of Leibniz, Euler, Lagrange, and Liouville. However, a different concept was introduced by C. Braccini and G. Gambardella: the form-invariant linear filtering. It was a new kind of processing that was applied to several different fields such as optical pattern recognition, image restoration and reconstruction from projections [3]. This was the first step into the introduction of the scale-invariant linear systems, really done by B. Yazici and R. L. Kashyap for analysis and modelling $1/f$ phenomena and in general the self-similar processes, namely the scale stationary processes [4,5]. In parallel, physicists started studying the importance of scale in several physical systems [6–13]. Although the concept of scale is not very well defined, since it is a parameter expressing relative relations [6], the concept of scale-invariant system is well defined. While the shift-invariant systems are related and use in their definition the usual convolution [14] (D'Alembert's) and corresponding derivatives, the scale-invariant systems are based on the Mellin's convolution [15]. To fully define these systems the fractional scale-derivatives were introduced and studied [16], generalizing the classic Hadamard definitions [17]. These derivatives allow the formalization of linear scale-invariant systems of the autoregressive-moving average (ARMA) type [16,18]. With the use of the Mellin transform, the transfer functions of these systems assume a form identical to the one got from the shift-invariant systems through the use of the Laplace transform [19].

The objective of this paper is the study and search for the impulse and step responses of these systems. For this purpose, we first find a sequence of functions for which the fractional scale derivative behaves as a decremental index operator and then develop an algebraic framework similar to the one we used in the shift-invariant systems [20]. This approach allows us to closed forms for both the impulse and step responses of the systems.

The paper is organized as follows. Section 2 contains some preliminary results [16]. In Section 3 the sequence of functions $\{u_k(\tau)\}_k$ for which Hadamard right (left) derivative and fractional scale derivatives of type Grünwald-Letnikov are decremental index operators is founded. Section 3.2 contains the algebraic framework needed to solve fractional scale-invariant systems. In Section 4 we present an operational method based on algebraic framework introduced in Section 3. Numerical examples are solved in Section 5. Finally, Section 6 contains the main conclusions.

2. Scale–Invariant Systems and Derivatives

2.1. The Mellin Convolution

Definition 1. *We call a linear system scale-invariant or dilation-invariant (DI) if its input–output relation is given by the Mellin convolution [16]*

$$y(\tau) = x(\tau) \star g(\tau) = \int_0^\infty x\left(\frac{\tau}{\eta}\right) g(\eta) \frac{d\eta}{\eta},$$

where $\tau \in \mathbb{R}^+$, and $g(\tau)$ is the impulse response: the response to $x(\tau) = \delta(\tau - 1)$.

We demand that the impulse response, $g(t)$, be at least

- piecewise continuous,
- with bounded variation.

Similarly to the shift-invariant case, where the exponentials are the eigenfunctions, the powers $x(\tau) = \tau^v$, $\tau \in \mathbb{R}^+, v \in \mathbb{C}$, are the eigenfunctions of the dilation-invariant systems. In fact, if the input is $x(\tau) = \tau^v$, then the output is

$$y(\tau) = x(\tau) \star g(\tau) = G(v)\tau^v,$$

where $G(v)$ is the transfer function given by

$$G(v) = \int_0^\infty g(u) u^{-v-1} du, \tag{1}$$

which is a modifed version of the Mellin transform (MT) of the impulse response. The Mellin transform in (1), denoted by $\mathcal{M}[g(\tau)](v)$, has a parameter sign change $-v \to v$ relatively to the usual Mellin transform [15,21,22].

Suppose that $\mathcal{M}[f(\tau)](v)$ and $\mathcal{M}[g(\tau)](v)$ exist in the regions of convergence (ROC) $a_1 < Re(v) < b_1$ and $a_2 < Re(v) < b_2$, respectively. An important property of Mellin convolution is

$$\mathcal{M}[f(\tau) \star g(\tau)](v) = F(v)G(v), \qquad \max(a_1, a_2) < Re(v) < \min(b_1, b_2),$$

where $F(v)$ and $G(v)$ are the Mellin transforms of f and g, respectively. The inverse Mellin transform related to (1) is

$$x(\tau) = \mathcal{M}^{-1}[X(v)] = \frac{1}{2\pi i} \int_\gamma X(v)\tau^v dv, \quad \tau \in \mathbb{R}^+,$$

where γ is vertical straight line in the ROC of the transform.

2.2. Scale-Derivatives

Definition 2. *Let $\alpha \in \mathbb{R}$. We define the α-order scale derivative (SD) as the operator $\mathfrak{D}_s$ obeying the rule [16,23]*

$$\mathfrak{D}_s^\alpha \tau^v = v^\alpha \tau^v, \quad \tau \in \mathbb{R}^+, v \in \mathbb{C},$$

for $Re(v) > 0$ (expansion or stretching case) or $Re(v) < 0$ (shrinking case).

If a function $x(\tau)$ has Mellin transform $X(v)$, then it has *fractional scale-derivative* that is given by

$$\mathfrak{M}[\mathcal{D}_s^\alpha x(\tau)] = v^\alpha X(v), \tag{2}$$

for a suitable ROC. The way how we express v^α imposes a form for the derivative. To start, we notice that we can consider two situations corresponding to the sign of $Re(v)$. If it is positive, we obtain stretching derivatives, while if it is negative, we obtain the shrinking one. For both, we can express the inverse Mellin transform of $v^\alpha X(v)$ in two different forms: summation or integral.

2.2.1. Stretching Derivatives: $Re(v) > 0$ [16]

Let $\varepsilon(\tau)$ be Heaviside step function. We have two ways of expressing v^α:

$$v^\alpha = \begin{cases} \lim_{q \to 1^+} \left[\dfrac{(1-q^{-v})}{\ln q} \right]^\alpha = \sum\limits_{n=0}^{\infty} \dfrac{(-\alpha)_n}{n!} q^{-nv} \\ \mathcal{M}\left[\dfrac{\ln^{-\alpha-1}(\tau)}{\Gamma(-\alpha)} \varepsilon(\tau-1) \right] \end{cases} \tag{3}$$

These expressions lead to the following scale derivative [16]:

$$\mathfrak{D}_{s+}^\alpha x(\tau) = \begin{cases} \lim\limits_{q \to 1^+} \ln^{-\alpha}(q) \sum\limits_{n=0}^{\infty} \frac{(-\alpha)_n}{n!} x(\tau q^{-n}) \\ \dfrac{1}{\Gamma(-\alpha)} \int\limits_0^\tau \left[x(u) - \sum\limits_{n=0}^{N-1} (-1)^n \dfrac{\mathfrak{D}_{s+}^N x(\tau)}{n!} \ln^n(\tau/u) \right] \ln^{-\alpha-1}(\tau/u) \dfrac{du}{u} \end{cases} \tag{4}$$

(the last expression is valid for any real order, provided that we assume the summation to be null for $N \leq 0$). These relations can alternatively be expressed by the Hadamard derivatives:

1. Hadamard right derivative [17,24]

$$\mathfrak{D}_{s+}^\alpha x(\tau) = \frac{1}{\Gamma(N-\alpha)} \mathfrak{D}_{s+}^N \int\limits_1^\infty x(\tau/\eta) \ln^{N-\alpha-1}(\eta) \frac{d\eta}{\eta}. \tag{5}$$

2. Hadamard–Liouville right derivative [16]

$$\mathfrak{D}_{s+}^\alpha x(\tau) = \frac{1}{\Gamma(N-\alpha)} \int\limits_1^\infty \left[\mathfrak{D}_{s+}^N x(\tau) \right] \ln^{N-\alpha-1}(\tau/u) \frac{du}{u}.$$

These derivatives are equivalent from the Mellin transform point of view, although not from numerical aspects.

2.2.2. Shrinking Derivatives: $Re(v) < 0$ [16]

We have again two ways of expressing v^α:

$$v^\alpha = \begin{cases} \lim_{q\to 1^+}(-1)^\alpha \left[\frac{(1-q^v)}{\ln q}\right]^\alpha = \sum_{n=0}^{\infty} \frac{(-\alpha)_n}{n!} q^{nv} \\ \mathcal{M}\left[\frac{\ln^{-\alpha-1}(1/\tau)}{\Gamma(-\alpha)}\varepsilon(1-\tau)\right] \end{cases}$$

These expressions lead to the following scale derivative [16]:

$$\mathfrak{D}^\alpha_{s-}x(\tau) = \begin{cases} \lim_{q\to 1^+} (-1)^\alpha \ln^{-\alpha}(q) \sum_{n=0}^{\infty} \frac{(-\alpha)_n}{n!} x(\tau q^n) \\ \frac{1}{\Gamma(-\alpha)} \int_\tau^\infty \left[x(u) - \sum_{n=0}^{N-1} \frac{\mathfrak{D}^N_{s-}x(\tau)}{n!} \ln^n(u/\tau)\right] \ln^{-\alpha-1}(u/\tau)\frac{du}{u} \end{cases} \tag{6}$$

that can alternatively be expressed by the Hadamard derivatives

1. Hadamard left derivative [17,24]

$$\mathfrak{D}^\alpha_{s-}x(\tau) = \frac{1}{\Gamma(N-\alpha)}\mathfrak{D}^N_{s-} \int_0^1 x(\tau/\eta) \ln^{N-\alpha-1}(1/\eta)\frac{d\eta}{\eta}.$$

2. Hadamard–Liouville left derivative [16]

$$\mathfrak{D}^\alpha_{s-}x(\tau) = \frac{1}{\Gamma(N-\alpha)} \int_0^1 \left[\mathfrak{D}^N_{s-}x(\tau)\right] \ln^{N-\alpha-1}(u/\tau)\frac{du}{u}.$$

2.3. ARMA Type Systems

Definition 3. *We define the dilation (scale)-invariant fractional autoregressive-moving average (DI-FARMA) system through*

$$\sum_{k=0}^{N_0} a_k \mathfrak{D}^{\alpha_k}_{s\pm} y(\tau) = \sum_{k=0}^{M_0} b_k \mathfrak{D}^{\beta_k}_{s\pm} x(\tau), \qquad \tau \in \mathbb{R}^+, \tag{7}$$

where $\mathfrak{D}^{\alpha_k,(\beta_k)}_{s\pm}$, $k = 0,1,2,\cdots$, *mean the fractional* $\alpha_k(\beta_k)$*-order scale-derivatives and* N_0, M_0 *are the system orders. The parameters* a_k, b_k, $k = 0,1,\cdots$, *are considered real numbers. Without losing generality, we set* $a_{N_0} = 1$.

The results in [25] can be easily adapted. As the power τ^v is the eigenfunction of (7), we obtain easily the transfer function

$$G(v) = \frac{\sum_{k=0}^{M_0} b_k v^{\beta_k}}{\sum_{k=0}^{N_0} a_k v^{\alpha_k}},$$

which is a bit difficult to manipulate [26]. In the following, we shall be considering the so-called "commensurate" systems described by differential equations with the format

$$\sum_{k=0}^{N_0} a_k \mathfrak{D}^{k\alpha}_{s\pm} y(\tau) = \sum_{k=0}^{M_0} b_k \mathfrak{D}^{k\alpha}_{s\pm} x(\tau), \qquad \tau \in \mathbb{R}^+.$$

The corresponding transfer function is

$$G(v) = \frac{\sum_{k=0}^{M_0} b_k v^{k\alpha}}{\sum_{k=0}^{N_0} a_k v^{k\alpha}},$$

where we assume that $M_0 < N_0$, for simplicity. The objective of our work is to find the impulse and step responses of systems. As expected, we have two cases in agreement with the assumed ROC.

3. The Algebraic Framework for Solving DI-FARMA Systems

3.1. Sequence of Basic Functions for Fractional Scale Derivatives

Definition 4. *Let $\mathcal{S}$ be an operator and $\{u_k(\tau)\}_{k\in\mathbb{Z}}$ a sequence of functions, verifying*

$$\mathcal{S}u_k(\tau) = u_{k-1}(\tau), \qquad k \in \mathbb{Z}. \tag{8}$$

We say that $\mathcal{S}$ is decremental index operator of the sequence of functions $\{u_k(\tau)\}_{k\in\mathbb{Z}}$.

Remark 1. *A well known example involves the generalized shift-invariant derivatives, D, and the power functions, stating*

$$D\frac{t^n}{n!}\varepsilon(t) = \frac{t^{n-1}}{(n-1)!}\varepsilon(t), \qquad n \in \mathbb{Z}$$

It has been extended and studied by several researchers [27–29].

The main goal in this section is to find sequence of functions $\{u_k(\tau)\}_{k\in\mathbb{Z}}$ verifying (8) for the scale derivatives, mainly the Hadamard's.

Hadamard Right (Left) Derivative

In the following we shall be addressing the stretching derivative case ($Re(v) > 0$); the case of the shrinking derivative ($Re(v) < 0$) is analogous. We remember the result shown in Section 2.2.1

$$\mathcal{M}^{-1}\left[v^{-\alpha}\right](\tau) = \frac{\ln^{\alpha-1}(\tau)}{\Gamma(\alpha)}\varepsilon(\tau-1), \quad Re(v) > 0, \tag{9}$$

which will be used in this subsection.

Theorem 1. *Let $u_k(\tau)$ be given by*

$$u_k(\tau) = \frac{\ln^{k\alpha-1}(\tau)}{\Gamma(k\alpha)}\varepsilon(\tau-1), \quad k \in \mathbb{N}. \tag{10}$$

Then,

$$\mathfrak{D}^{\alpha}_{s+}u_k(\tau) = u_{k-1}(\tau), \qquad k \in \mathbb{N}. \tag{11}$$

Proof. Let $\alpha > 0, 1 \leq \tau$ and $k \in \mathbb{N}$. Using (9) with order $k\alpha$,

$$\mathcal{M}\left[\frac{\ln^{k\alpha-1}(\tau)}{\Gamma(k\alpha)}\varepsilon(\tau-1)\right] = v^{-k\alpha}, \qquad \alpha > 0, \quad k \geq 1. \tag{12}$$

Following (2), the derivative $\mathfrak{D}^{\alpha}_{s+}\left(\frac{\ln^{k\alpha-1}(\tau)}{\Gamma(k\alpha)}\varepsilon(\tau-1)\right)$ is given by

$$\begin{aligned}\mathfrak{D}^{\alpha}_{s+}\left(\frac{\ln^{k\alpha-1}(\tau)}{\Gamma(k\alpha)}\varepsilon(\tau-1)\right) &= \mathcal{M}^{-1}\left[v^{\alpha}\mathcal{M}\left[\frac{\ln^{k\alpha-1}(\tau)}{\Gamma(k\alpha)}\varepsilon(\tau-1)\right]\right](\tau)\\ &= \mathcal{M}^{-1}\left[v^{-(k-1)\alpha}\right](\tau)\end{aligned}$$

Finally, from (12) we obtain that

$$\mathfrak{D}^{\alpha}_{s+}\frac{\ln^{k\alpha-1}(\tau)}{\Gamma(k\alpha)}\varepsilon(\tau-1) = \frac{\ln^{(k-1)\alpha-1}(\tau)}{\Gamma((k-1)\alpha)}\varepsilon(\tau-1).$$

for $\alpha > 0$ and $k \geq 1$. □

Remark 2. *For the next result, we need to observe that [30]*

$$u_0(\tau) = \frac{\ln^{-1}(\tau)}{\Gamma(0)}\varepsilon(\tau-1) = \delta(\ln(\tau))\varepsilon(\tau-1) = \delta(\tau-1).$$

Lemma 1. *Let $\alpha > 0$ and $1 \leq \tau$. For $u_0(\tau) = \frac{\ln^{-1}(\tau)}{\Gamma(0)}\varepsilon(\tau-1)$,*

$$\mathfrak{D}^{\alpha}_{s+}u_0(\tau) = \frac{\ln^{-\alpha-1}(\tau)}{\Gamma(-\alpha)}\varepsilon(\tau-1).$$

Proof. From Remark 2 and (5) we obtain

$$\mathfrak{D}^{\alpha}_{s+}u_0(\tau) = \frac{1}{\Gamma(N-\alpha)}\mathfrak{D}^{N}_{s+}\int_1^{\infty}\delta\left(\frac{\tau}{\eta}-1\right)\ln^{N-\alpha-1}(\eta)\frac{d\eta}{\eta}$$

Performing the variable change $\omega = \frac{\tau}{\eta}$ we have that

$$\int_1^{\infty}\delta\left(\frac{\tau}{\eta}-1\right)\ln^{N-\alpha-1}(\eta)\frac{d\eta}{\eta} = \int_0^{\tau}\delta(\omega-1)\ln^{N-\alpha-1}\left(\frac{\tau}{\omega}\right)\frac{d\omega}{\omega}.$$

It follows that

$$\frac{1}{\Gamma(N-\alpha)}\mathfrak{D}^{N}_{s+}\int_0^{\tau}\delta(\omega-1)\ln^{N-\alpha-1}\left(\frac{\tau}{\omega}\right)\frac{d\omega}{\omega} = 0, \qquad \tau < 1$$

and

$$\frac{1}{\Gamma(N-\alpha)}\mathfrak{D}^{N}_{s+}\int_0^{\tau}\delta(\omega-1)\ln^{N-\alpha-1}\left(\frac{\tau}{\omega}\right)\frac{d\omega}{\omega} = \frac{\ln^{-\alpha-1}(\tau)}{\Gamma(-\alpha)}, \qquad \tau \geq 1.$$

Therefore

$$\mathfrak{D}^{\alpha}_{s+}u_0(\tau) = \frac{\ln^{-\alpha-1}(\tau)}{\Gamma(-\alpha)}\varepsilon(\tau-1).$$

□

The previous Lemma tells us that $\mathfrak{D}^{\alpha}_{s+}u_0(\tau) = u_{-1}(\tau)$. So, we wonder what about $\mathfrak{D}^{\alpha}_{s+}u_{-1}(\tau)$. For this, from the additivity of operator $\mathfrak{D}^{\alpha}_{s+}$ we have that

$$\begin{aligned} \mathfrak{D}^{\alpha}_{s+}u_{-1}(\tau) &= \mathfrak{D}^{\alpha}_{s+}(\mathfrak{D}^{\alpha}_{s+}u_0(\tau)) \\ &= \mathfrak{D}^{2\alpha}_{s+}u_0(\tau) \\ &= \frac{\ln^{-2\alpha-1}(\tau)}{\Gamma(-2\alpha)}\varepsilon(\tau-1) \\ &= u_{-2}(\tau) \end{aligned} \tag{13}$$

The penultimate equality follows from Lemma 1 with the order of the derivative equal to 2α. Following this reasoning we obtain that $\mathfrak{D}^{\alpha}_{s+}u_{-k}(\tau) = \mathfrak{D}^{\alpha}_{s+}u_{-k-1}(\tau), k \in \mathbb{N}$. Finally, we conclude that

Corollary 1.

$$\mathfrak{D}^{\alpha}_{s+}u_k(\tau) = \mathfrak{D}^{\alpha}_{s+}u_{k-1}(\tau), \text{ for any } k \in \mathbb{Z}. \tag{14}$$

Therefore Hadamard right (left) derivative is a decremental index operator on the sequence of functions (10).

Remark 3. *The condition $Re(v) < 0$ leads to the $0 < \tau \leq 1$ case. The construction of the $u_k(\tau)$'s is similar to case $1 \leq \tau$. Here we get that*

$$u_k(\tau) = \frac{\ln^{k\alpha-1}\left(\frac{1}{\tau}\right)}{\Gamma(k\alpha)}\varepsilon(1-\tau).$$

It is not difficult to verify that

$$\mathfrak{D}^{\alpha}_{s+}u_k(\tau) = u_{k-1}(\tau), \text{ for any } k \in \mathbb{Z}.$$

Remark 4. *As we previously mentioned the Hadamard right (left) derivative and scale derivative of type Grünwald-Letnikov are equivalent. Despite this, in Appendix A we verify that the scale derivative of type Grünwald-Letnikov is a decremental index operators on the same sequence of functions* (10).

In some situations, it is more convenient to use the step response instead of the impulse response because this one has a singularity at $\tau = 1$. Therefore, another definition of $u_k(\tau)$ for which both Hadamard right (left) derivative and fractional scale derivative of type Grünwald-Letnikov are decremental index operators is possible and desired. For $1 \leq \tau$

$$u_k(\tau) = \frac{\ln^{k\alpha}(\tau)}{\Gamma(k\alpha+1)}\varepsilon(\tau-1), \qquad k \in \mathbb{Z},$$

and when $0 < \tau \leq 1$

$$u_k(\tau) = \frac{\ln^{k\alpha}\left(\frac{1}{\tau}\right)}{\Gamma(k\alpha+1)}\varepsilon(1-\tau), \qquad k \in \mathbb{Z}.$$

The justification can be seen in Appendix B.

3.2. The Framework

Let $u_k(\tau), k \in \mathbb{Z}$, having Mellin transform $U_k(v)$. Then, for any $k, m \in \mathbb{N}$

$$\mathcal{M}[u_k(\tau) \star u_m(\tau)](v) = U_k(v)U_m(v).$$

As $U_k(v) = v^{k\alpha}$ and $U_m(v) = v^{m\alpha}$, hence

$$U_k(v)U_m(v) = v^{(k+m)\alpha}, \qquad Re(v) > 0,$$

and

$$u_k(\tau) \star u_m(\tau) = \mathcal{M}^{-1}\Big[v^{(k+m)\alpha}\Big] = u_{k+m}(\tau).$$

Therefore, we extend this product to any $k, m \in \mathbb{Z}$ as follows

$$u_k(\tau) \star u_m(\tau) = u_{k+m}(\tau). \tag{15}$$

Remark 5. *Observe that*

$$\mathfrak{D}^{n\alpha}_{s+} u_k(\tau) = u_{-n}(\tau) \star u_k(\tau) = u_{k-n}(\tau), \qquad k \in \mathbb{Z}, \quad n \in \mathbb{N}.$$

Consider $\{u_k(\tau)\}_{k\in\mathbb{Z}}$ as a sequence of basic functions. Let $\mathcal{F}$ be the set of all the formal Laurent series

$$\mathcal{F} = \left\{ \sum_{k=-n}^{\infty} c_k u_k(\tau) : n \in \mathbb{N}_0, c_k \in \mathbb{C} \right\}.$$

Several properties of $\mathcal{F}$ and the product (15) can be founded in [20,31]. Observe that

- $u_0(\tau)$ is the neutral element of the Mellin convolution, $u_0(\tau) \star u_k(\tau) = u_k(\tau)$;
- the inverse element of $u_k(\tau)$ is $u_{-k}(\tau)$, $u_k(\tau) \star u_{-k}(\tau) = u_0(\tau)$.

By means of Cauchy series product, we can extend the Mellin product, $\star$, to any elements of $\mathcal{F}$ as follows. Let a_j, b_j, two sequences of real numbers and define

$$a = \sum_{j=-k_a}^{\infty} a_j u_j(\tau),$$

and

$$b = \sum_{j=-k_b}^{\infty} b_j u_j(\tau),$$

as elements of $\mathcal{F}$. Then

$$a \star b = f = \sum_{n=-k_a-k_b}^{\infty} f_n u_n(\tau),$$

where

$$f_n = \sum_{-k_a \le k \le n+k_b} a_k b_{n-k}.$$

This product is associative and commutative. Under this multiplication $\mathcal{F}$ is a field.

Definition 5. *Let us define the function*

$$\mathcal{E}_{\gamma,n}(\tau) = \sum_{k=n+1}^{\infty} \binom{k-1}{n} \gamma^{k-n-1} u_k(\tau), \quad \gamma \in \mathbb{C}, n \in \mathbb{N}_0.$$

that we will call α–log-exponential function.

We could define an analogue to the Mittag-Leffler function [16], but this one is more useful.

Let us introduce also the sequential convolution

$$(u_{-1}(\tau) - \gamma u_0(\tau))^{m+1}_{\star} = \underbrace{(u_{-1}(\tau) - \gamma u_0(\tau)) \star \cdots \star (u_{-1}(\tau) - \gamma u_0(\tau))}_{m+1-times}.$$

It is not difficult to verify that

$$(u_{-1}(\tau) - \gamma u_0(\tau)) \star \mathcal{E}_{\gamma,0}(\tau) = u_0(\tau),$$

and in general,

$$(u_{-1}(\tau) - \gamma u_0(\tau))_\star^{n+1} \star \mathcal{E}_{\gamma,n}(\tau) = u_0(\tau).$$

The α–log-exponential function has some useful properties [31]:

1. Derivative on a parameter

$$\frac{D_\gamma^n}{n!} \mathcal{E}_{\gamma,0}(\tau) = \mathcal{E}_{\gamma,n}(\tau),$$

where D_γ means usual derivative with respect to γ.

2. Convolution of two different α–log-exponential functions, but with the same parameter γ

$$\mathcal{E}_{\gamma,m}(\tau) \star \mathcal{E}_{\gamma,n}(\tau) = \mathcal{E}_{\gamma,m+n+1}(\tau).$$

3. Convolution of two different γ parameters α–log-exponential functions

For $\gamma_1 \neq \gamma_2$,

$$\mathcal{E}_{\gamma_1,0}(\tau) \star \mathcal{E}_{\gamma_2,0}(\tau) = \frac{\mathcal{E}_{\gamma_1,0}(\tau) - \mathcal{E}_{\gamma_2,0}(\tau)}{\gamma_1 - \gamma_2},$$

$$\mathcal{E}_{\gamma_1,m}(\tau) \star \mathcal{E}_{\gamma_2,n}(\tau) = \sum_{l=0}^{m} \frac{\binom{n+l}{l}(-1)^l}{(\gamma_1 - \gamma_2)^{1+n+l}} \mathcal{E}_{\gamma_1,m-l}(\tau) + \sum_{k=0}^{n} \frac{\binom{m+k}{k}(-1)^k}{(\gamma_2 - \gamma_1)^{1+m+k}} \mathcal{E}_{\gamma_2,n-k}(\tau).$$

Next, we will introduce and prove some other properties which will allow us to deduce that functions $\mathcal{E}_{\gamma,m}(\tau)$ are the generating elements of solution space of fractional scale-invariant systems.

Theorem 2. *Let $n \geq 1$. Then*

$$u_{-1}(\tau) \star \mathcal{E}_{\gamma,n}(\tau) = \mathcal{E}_{\gamma,n-1}(\tau) + \gamma \mathcal{E}_{\gamma,n}(\tau).$$

Proof. Observe that

$$\begin{aligned} u_{-1}(\tau) \star \mathcal{E}_{\gamma,n}(\tau) &= u_{-1}(\tau) \star \sum_{k=n+1}^{\infty} \binom{k-1}{n} \gamma^{k-n-1} u_k(\tau) \\ &= \sum_{k=n+1}^{\infty} \binom{k-1}{n} \gamma^{k-n-1} u_{k-1}(\tau). \end{aligned}$$

Using the basic recurrence $\binom{k-1}{n} = \binom{k-2}{n-1} + \binom{k-2}{n}$, we obtain

$$\begin{aligned} u_{-1}(\tau) \star \mathcal{E}_{\gamma,n}(\tau) &= \sum_{k=n+1}^{\infty} \left[\binom{k-2}{n-1} + \binom{k-2}{n} \right] \gamma^{k-n-1} u_{k-1}(\tau) \\ &= \sum_{k=n+1}^{\infty} \binom{k-2}{n-1} \gamma^{k-n-1} u_{k-1}(\tau) + \sum_{k=n+2}^{\infty} \binom{k-2}{n} \gamma^{k-n-1} u_{k-1}(\tau) \\ &= \sum_{k=n}^{\infty} \binom{k-1}{n-1} \gamma^{k-n} u_k(\tau) + \gamma \sum_{k=n+1}^{\infty} \binom{k-1}{n} \gamma^{k-n-1} u_k(\tau) \\ &= \mathcal{E}_{\gamma,n-1}(\tau) + \gamma \mathcal{E}_{\gamma,n}(\tau). \end{aligned}$$

□

Remark 6. *Observe that letting $n = 0$ in Theorem 2 we get*

$$u_{-1}(\tau) \star \mathcal{E}_{\gamma,0}(\tau) = u_0(\tau) + \gamma \mathcal{E}_{\gamma,0}(\tau) \tag{16}$$

Theorem 3. *Let N and n be positive integers such that $N \leq n$. Then we have*

$$u_{-N}(\tau) \star \mathcal{E}_{\gamma,n}(\tau) = \sum_{k=0}^{N} \binom{N}{k} \gamma^{N-k} \mathcal{E}_{\gamma,n-k}(\tau).$$

Proof. The proof is done by induction with $N \leq n$. For the base step of the induction ($N = 1$), we appeal to Lemma 2. For $N = 2$, due to $u_{-2}(\tau) = u_{-1}(\tau) \star u_{-1}(\tau)$ we have that

$$\begin{aligned} u_{-2}(\tau) \star \mathcal{E}_{\gamma,n}(\tau) &= u_{-1}(\tau) \star (u_{-1}(\tau) \star \mathcal{E}_{\gamma,n}(\tau)) \\ &= u_{-1}(\tau) \star (\mathcal{E}_{\gamma,n-1}(\tau) + \gamma \mathcal{E}_{\gamma,n}(\tau)) \\ &= \gamma^2 \mathcal{E}_{\gamma,n}(\tau) + 2\gamma \mathcal{E}_{\gamma,n-1}(\tau) + \mathcal{E}_{\gamma,n-2}(\tau). \end{aligned}$$

Suppose that theorem is valid for $N - 1$. This is

$$u_{-N+1}(\tau) \star \mathcal{E}_{\gamma,n}(\tau) = \sum_{k=0}^{N-1} \binom{N-1}{k} \gamma^{N-k-1} \mathcal{E}_{\gamma,n-k}(\tau). \tag{17}$$

Now, we will prove that theorem is valid for N. Observe that

$$\begin{aligned} u_{-N}(\tau) \star \mathcal{E}_{\gamma,n}(\tau) &= u_{-1}(\tau) \star (u_{-N+1}(\tau) \star \mathcal{E}_{\gamma,n}(\tau)) \\ &= \sum_{k=0}^{N-1} \binom{N-1}{k} \gamma^{N-k-1} (u_{-1}(\tau) \star \mathcal{E}_{\gamma,n-k}(\tau)) \\ &= \sum_{k=0}^{N-1} \binom{N-1}{k} \gamma^{N-k-1} (\mathcal{E}_{\gamma,n-k-1}(\tau) + \gamma \mathcal{E}_{\gamma,n-k}(\tau)) \\ &= \sum_{k=0}^{N} \binom{N}{k} \gamma^{N-k} \mathcal{E}_{\gamma,n-k}(\tau). \end{aligned} \tag{18}$$

□

Theorem 4. *Let $l \in \mathbb{N}$. Then*

$$u_{-n-l}(\tau) \star \mathcal{E}_{\gamma,n}(\tau) = \sum_{k=n+1}^{n+l} \binom{k-1}{n} \gamma^{k-n-1} u_{k-n-l}(\tau) + \sum_{k=0}^{n} \binom{n+l}{n-k} \gamma^{k+l} \mathcal{E}_{\gamma,k}(\tau). \tag{19}$$

Proof. The proof is by induction on $l \in \mathbb{N}$. For the base step of the induction ($l = 1$) we have that

$$\begin{aligned} u_{-n-1}(\tau) \star \mathcal{E}_{\gamma,n}(\tau) &= u_{-1}(\tau) \star (u_{-n}(\tau) \star \mathcal{E}_{\gamma,n}(\tau)) \\ &= u_{-1}(\tau) \star \left(\sum_{k=0}^{n} \binom{n}{k} \gamma^k \mathcal{E}_{\gamma,k}(t) \right) \\ &= u_0(\tau) + \gamma \mathcal{E}_{\gamma,0}(\tau) + \sum_{k=1}^{n} \binom{n}{k} \gamma^k (\mathcal{E}_{\gamma,k-1}(\tau) + \gamma \mathcal{E}_{\gamma,k}(\tau)) \\ &= u_0(\tau) + \sum_{k=0}^{n} \binom{n+1}{k+1} \gamma^{k+1} \mathcal{E}_{\gamma,k}(\tau). \end{aligned}$$

In the penultimate equality we apply the Remark 6 to the first term of the sum. Suppose that the theorem is valid for $l-1$, this is

$$u_{-n-l+1}(\tau)\star\mathcal{E}_{\gamma,n}(\tau)=\sum_{k=n+1}^{n+l-1}\binom{k-1}{n}\gamma^{k-n-1}u_{k-n-l+1}(\tau)+\sum_{k=0}^{n}\binom{n+l-1}{n-k}\gamma^{k+l-1}\mathcal{E}_{\gamma,k}(\tau). \tag{20}$$

Now, we will prove that theorem is valid for l. Observe that

$$\begin{aligned} u_{-n-l}(\tau)\star\mathcal{E}_{\gamma,n}(\tau) &= u_{-1}(\tau)\star(u_{-n-l+1}(\tau)\star\mathcal{E}_{\gamma,n}(\tau)) \\ &= \sum_{k=n+1}^{n+l-1}\binom{k-1}{n}\gamma^{k-n-1}u_{k-n-l}(\tau)+\sum_{k=0}^{n}\binom{n+l-1}{n-k}\gamma^{k+l-1}(u_{-1}(\tau)\star\mathcal{E}_{\gamma,k}(\tau)) \\ &= \sum_{k=n+1}^{n+l}\binom{k-1}{n}\gamma^{k-n-1}u_{k-n-l}(\tau)+\sum_{k=0}^{n}\binom{n+l}{n-k}\gamma^{k+l}\mathcal{E}_{\gamma,k}(\tau). \end{aligned} \tag{21}$$

Again, Remark 6 is applied in the last equality. □

Theorem 4 suggests that impulse (step) response to a fractional scale-invariant system is a linear combination of functions $\mathcal{E}_{\gamma,n}(t)$.

4. Impulse and Step Responses

4.1. The AR Case

Consider an AR system. Its impulse response is given by the solution of the equation

$$p(\mathfrak{D}_{s+}^{\alpha})y(\tau)=\delta(\tau-1), \tag{22}$$

where $p(x)=a_m x^m+a_{m-1}x^{m-1}+\cdots+a_1x+a_0$, $a_n\in\mathbb{C}$, $a_m=1$, and its roots $\gamma_1,\gamma_2,\ldots,\gamma_m$ have multiplicity 1. Consider that $y(\tau)\in\mathcal{F}$. In terms of the convolution $\star$, the Equation (22) can be rewritten as

$$(a_m u_{-m}(\tau)+a_{m-1}u_{-m+1}(\tau)+\cdots+a_1u_{-1}(\tau)+a_0u_0(\tau))\star y(\tau)=u_0(\tau).$$

Assume that impulse response is given by a linear combination of α–log-exponential functions

$$r_\delta(\tau)=c_1\mathcal{E}_{\gamma_1,0}(\tau)+\cdots+c_m\mathcal{E}_{\gamma_m,0}(\tau).$$

From (19), it is not difficult to deduce that

$$u_{-m}(\tau)\star\mathcal{E}_{\gamma_i,0}(\tau)=\sum_{k=1}^{m}\gamma_1^{k-1}u_{-m+k}(\tau)+\gamma_i^m\mathcal{E}_{\gamma_i,0}(t),\qquad \text{for any } m\in\mathbb{N}.$$

A simple computation leads to

$$(a_m u_{-m}(\tau)+a_{m-1}u_{-m+1}(\tau)+\cdots+a_0u_0(\tau))\star r_\delta(\tau)=\sum_{k=1}^{m}c_k\sum_{j=0}^{m-1}\sum_{i=0}^{m-j-1}a_{i+1}\gamma_k^i u_{-j}(\tau). \tag{23}$$

Now, in order to find the impulse response we obtain a linear system with m equations which can be reduced recursively to

$$\begin{aligned} c_1+c_2+c_3+\cdots+c_m &= 0 \\ \gamma_1c_1+\gamma_2c_2+\gamma_3c_3+\cdots+\gamma_mc_m &= 0 \\ \vdots\quad &= \vdots \\ \gamma_1^{m-1}c_1+\gamma_2^{m-1}c_2+\gamma_3^{m-1}c_3+\cdots+\gamma_m^{m-1}c_m &= 1. \end{aligned}$$

The coefficient matrix is invertible, since it has Vandermonde format and the roots γ_j are distinct. Therefore, the system has a unique solution. Finally, using the c_i's, we obtain $r_\delta(\tau)$, the solution to fractional system (22).

For the case of roots with multiplicity greater than one, we must propose an alternative solution. Consider that a given root, γ_k, has multiplicity $m_k > 1$. To obtain the solution, we need to add another linear combination of α–log-exponentials to the previous solution

$$c_{k,0}\mathcal{E}_{\gamma_k,0}(\tau) + c_{k,1}\mathcal{E}_{\gamma_k,1}(\tau) + \cdots + c_{k,m_k}\mathcal{E}_{\gamma_1,m_k}(\tau)$$

With the obtained guess of the solution we are led to a linear system with m equations. The coefficient matrix is of generalized Vandermonde-type [32] having non null determinant. To fix ideas, consider the system (22) but with $\gamma_4, \gamma_5, \ldots, \gamma_m$ simple roots of $p(x)$ and γ_1 a root with multiplicity 3 ($\gamma_1 = \gamma_2 = \gamma_3$). The proposed solution assumes the form

$$r_\delta(\tau) = c_1\mathcal{E}_{\gamma_1,0}(\tau) + c_2\mathcal{E}_{\gamma_2,1}(\tau) + c_3\mathcal{E}_{\gamma_3,2}(\tau) + c_4\mathcal{E}_{\gamma_4,0}(\tau) + \cdots + c_m\mathcal{E}_{\gamma_m,0}(\tau)$$

As in the previous case, from

$$(a_m u_{-m}(\tau) + a_{m-1}u_{-m+1}(\tau) + \cdots + a_1 u_{-1}(\tau) + a_0 u_0(\tau)) \star r_\delta(\tau) = u_0(\tau)$$

we obtain a system of m linear equations that can be recursively reduced to the following system

$$\begin{aligned}
c_1 + c_4 + \cdots + c_m &= 0 \\
\gamma_1 c_1 + c_2 + \gamma_4 c_4 + \cdots + \gamma_m c_m &= 0 \\
\gamma_1^2 c_1 + 2\gamma_2 c_2 + \gamma_3 c_3 + \gamma_4^2 c_4 + \cdots + \gamma_m^2 c_m &= 0 \\
\vdots \qquad &= \vdots \\
\gamma_1^{m-1} c_1 + (m-1)\gamma_2^{m-2} c_2 + \frac{(m-1)(m-2)}{2!}\gamma_3^{m-1} c_3 + \gamma_4^{m-1} c_4 + \cdots + \gamma_m^{m-1} c_m &= 1.
\end{aligned}$$

This system has a coefficient matrix of generalized Vandermonde-type whose determinant is equal to

$$\prod_{3<i<j\leq m} (\gamma_i - \gamma_j)^{m_i m_j},$$

where m_i, m_j are the multiplicities of the roots γ_i, γ_j, respectively. It follows that the system has a unique solution.

We have proven that the solution to system (22) is an element of vector space generated by the set

$$\{\mathcal{E}_{\gamma,n}(\tau) : \gamma \in \mathbb{C}, n \in \mathbb{N}_0\}. \tag{24}$$

Furthermore, in (p. 338, [31]) it is proved that the set (24) is linearly independent.

4.2. The ARMA Case

By means of the method above described, we can solve the more general problem

$$p(\mathfrak{D}^\alpha_{s+})y(\tau) = q(\mathfrak{D}^\alpha_{s+})\delta(\tau - 1),$$

where $p(x) = a_m x^m + a_{m-1}x^{m-1} + \cdots + a_1 x + a_0$ and $q(x) = b_r x^r + b_{r-1}x^{r-1} + \cdots + b_1 x + b_0$ are polynomials of degree m and r, respectively, with constant coefficients in $\mathbb{C}$. We procedure as follows. Firstly, we compute the impulsive response $r_\delta(\tau)$. In different words, we solve the fractional system

$$p(\mathfrak{D}^\alpha_{s+})y(\tau) = \delta(\tau - 1).$$

Later, the solution is given by the convolution

$$y(\tau) = (b_r u_{-r}(\tau) + b_{r-1}u_{-r+1}(\tau) + \cdots + b_1 u_{-1}(\tau) + b_0 u_0(\tau)) \star r_\delta(\tau).$$

This is known as cascade connection of two systems

$$\begin{array}{ll} \text{System } S_1: & p(\mathfrak{D}^{\alpha}_{s+})r_\delta(\tau) = \delta(\tau-1) \\ \text{System } S_2: & y(\tau) = q(\mathfrak{D}^{\alpha}_{s+})r_\delta(\tau) \end{array} \tag{25}$$

5. Examples

In all the following examples, we will compute both impulse and step response, by means of operational method. In order to compare ours with the classic transform method, we include the computation of impulse response in Example 1 using the Mellin transform.

Example 1. *Consider the fractional scale-invariant linear system*

$$p(\mathfrak{D}^{\alpha}_{s+})y(\tau) = \delta(\tau-1). \tag{26}$$

with $p(x) = x^2 + 2$. *The roots of* $p(x)$ *are* $\sqrt{2}i$ *and* $-\sqrt{2}i$ *of multiplicity 1.*

- *Operational method:*
  By means of our operational method, the system can be rewritten as

$$(u_{-2}(\tau) + 2u_0(\tau)) \star y(\tau) = u_0(\tau).$$

We propose the solution

$$y(\tau) = c_1\mathcal{E}_{\sqrt{2}i,0}(\tau) + c_2\mathcal{E}_{-\sqrt{2}i,0}(\tau).$$

Following the presented in Section 3.2 we obtain the system of equations

$$\begin{array}{ccccc} c_1 & + & c_2 & = & 0 \\ \sqrt{2}ic_1 & - & \sqrt{2}ic_2 & = & 1 \end{array}.$$

The solution to system of equations is $c_1 = \frac{1}{2\sqrt{2}i}$ *and* $c_2 = -\frac{1}{2\sqrt{2}i}$. *Therefore, for* $\tau \geq 1$ *the impulse response is*

$$\begin{aligned} r_\delta(\tau) &= \frac{1}{2\sqrt{2}i}\left(\sum_{k=1}^{\infty}\left((\sqrt{2}i)^{k-1} - (-\sqrt{2}i)^{k-1}\right)\frac{\ln^{k\alpha-1}(\tau)}{\Gamma(k\alpha)}\varepsilon(\tau-1)\right) \\ &= \sum_{k=1}^{\infty}(-2)^{k-1}\frac{\ln^{2k\alpha-1}(\tau)}{\Gamma(2k\alpha)}\varepsilon(\tau-1), \end{aligned}$$

and step response

$$r_u(\tau) = \sum_{k=1}^{\infty}(-2)^{k-1}\frac{\ln^{2k\alpha}(\tau)}{\Gamma(2k\alpha+1)}\varepsilon(\tau-1).$$

Remark 7. *When* $\alpha = 1$, $r_\delta(\tau) = \dfrac{1}{\sqrt{2}}\sin(\sqrt{2}\ln(\tau))$ *and* $r_u(\tau) = \dfrac{1-\cos(\sqrt{2}\ln(\tau))}{2}$.

The Figures 1 and 2 show the graphical representation of the solutions with $\tau \geq 1$ *and several values of* α.

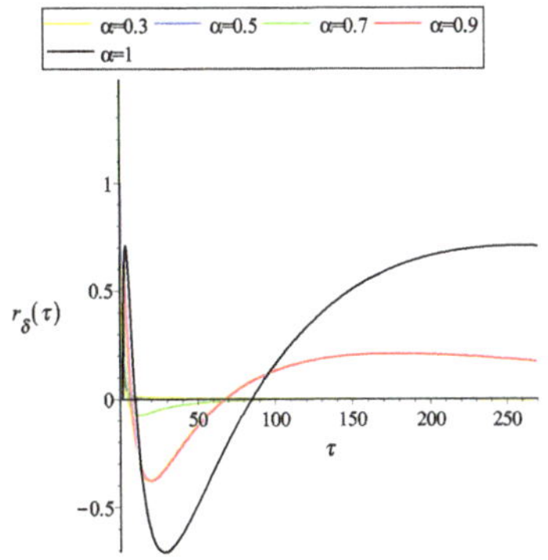

Figure 1. Impulse response of Example 1 with $1 \leq \tau$ and several values of α.

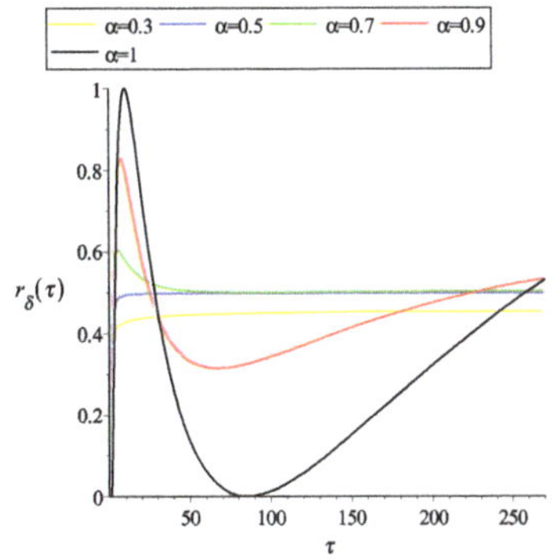

Figure 2. Step response of Example 1 with $1 \leq \tau$ and several values of α.

For $0 < \tau \leq 1$, the impulse response is

$$r_\delta(\tau) = \sum_{k=1}^{\infty} (-2)^{k-1} \frac{\ln^{2k\alpha-1}\left(\frac{1}{\tau}\right)}{\Gamma(2k\alpha)} \varepsilon(1-\tau),$$

and step response

$$r_u(\tau) = \sum_{k=1}^{\infty} (-2)^{k-1} \frac{\ln^{2k\alpha}\left(\frac{1}{\tau}\right)}{\Gamma(2k\alpha+1)} \varepsilon(1-\tau).$$

Remark 8. *When $\alpha = 1$,*

$$r_\delta(\tau) = \frac{1}{\sqrt{2}} \sin(\sqrt{2}\ln\left(\frac{1}{\tau}\right))\varepsilon(1-\tau),$$

and

$$r_u(\tau) = \frac{1-\cos(\sqrt{2}\ln\left(\frac{1}{\tau}\right))}{2} \varepsilon(1-\tau).$$

The Figures 3 and 4 show the graphical representation of the solutions with $0 < \tau \leq 1$ and several values of α.

- *Mellin transform:*
  We only consider the case $\tau \geq 1$, *the case* $0 < \tau \leq 1$ *is analog. By means of Mellin transform, the system* (26) *can be transformed to equation*

$$\begin{aligned} Y(v) &= \frac{1}{v^{2\alpha}+2} \\ &= \frac{i}{2\sqrt{2}}\frac{1}{v^{\alpha}+\sqrt{2}i} - \frac{i}{2\sqrt{2}}\frac{1}{v^{\alpha}-\sqrt{2}i} \\ &= v^{-\alpha}\frac{\frac{i}{2\sqrt{2}}}{1+\frac{\sqrt{2}i}{v^{\alpha}}} - v^{-\alpha}\frac{\frac{i}{2\sqrt{2}}}{1-\frac{\sqrt{2}i}{v^{\alpha}}} \end{aligned}$$

Using the geometric series, with $\sqrt{2} < v^{\alpha}$, *we obtain that*

$$\begin{aligned} Y(v) &= \frac{i}{4}v^{-\alpha}\sum_{k=0}^{\infty}(-1)^k\left(\frac{2i}{v^{\alpha}}\right)^k - \frac{i}{4}v^{-\alpha}\sum_{k=0}^{\infty}\left(\frac{2i}{v^{\alpha}}\right)^k \\ &= \sum_{k=1}^{\infty}(-2)^{k-1}v^{-2k\alpha}. \end{aligned}$$

Computing the inverse Mellin transform we obtain the impulsive response

$$\begin{aligned} r_{\delta}(\tau) &= \mathcal{M}^{-1}\left[\sum_{k=1}^{\infty}(-2)^{k-1}v^{-2k\alpha}\right] \\ &= \sum_{k=1}^{\infty}(-2)^{k-1}\frac{\ln^{2k\alpha-1}(\tau)}{\Gamma(2k\alpha)}\varepsilon(\tau-1). \end{aligned}$$

For the step response we apply (A1) *and obtain*

$$r_u(\tau) = \sum_{k=1}^{\infty}(-2)^{k-1}\frac{\ln^{2k\alpha}(\tau)}{\Gamma(2k\alpha+1)}\varepsilon(\tau-1).$$

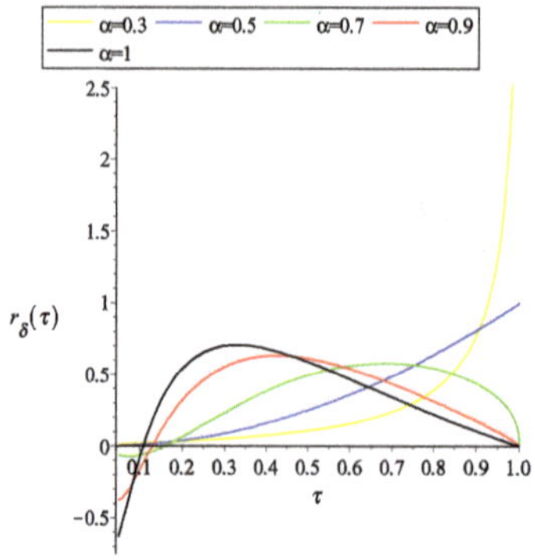

Figure 3. Impulse response of Example 1 with $0 < \tau \leq 1$ and several values of α.

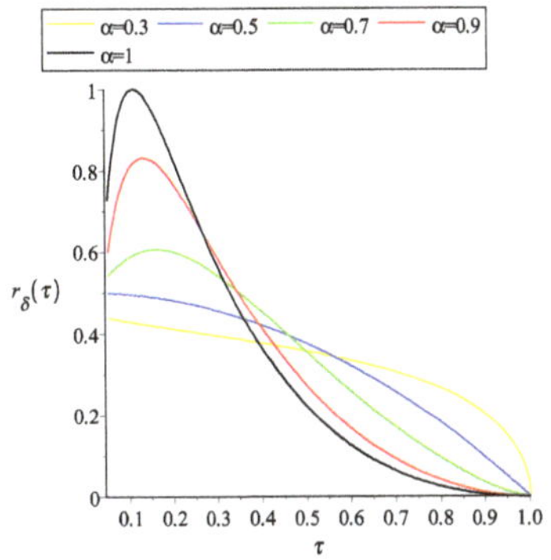

Figure 4. Step response of Example 1 with $0 < \tau \leq 1$ and several values of α.

Example 2. *Consider the fractional scale-invariant linear system*

$$p(\mathfrak{D}^{\alpha}_{s+})y(\tau) = q(\mathfrak{D}^{\alpha}_{s+})\delta(\tau - 1),$$

with $p(x) = x^2 + 2$ *and* $q(x) = x - \sqrt{2}$*. Observe that system is related with the Example 1. Following* (25) *we only need to compute the convolution*

$$y(\tau) = \left(u_{-1}(\tau) - \sqrt{2}u_0(\tau)\right) \star \left(\frac{1}{2\sqrt{2}i}\mathcal{E}_{\sqrt{2}i,0}(\tau) - \frac{1}{2\sqrt{2}i}\mathcal{E}_{-\sqrt{2}i,0}(\tau)\right).$$

Simplifying we obtain that

$$\begin{aligned} y(\tau) &= \left(u_{-1}(\tau) - \sqrt{2}u_0(\tau)\right) \star \left(\sum_{k=1}^{\infty}(-2)^{k-1}u_{2k}(\tau)\right) \\ &= \sum_{k=1}^{\infty}(-2)^{k-1}u_{2k-1}(\tau) - \sqrt{2}\sum_{k=1}^{\infty}(-2)^{k-1}u_{2k}(\tau). \end{aligned}$$

For $\tau \geq 1$*, the impulse response is*

$$r_\delta(\tau) = \sum_{k=1}^{\infty}(-2)^{k-1}\frac{\ln^{(2k-1)\alpha-1}(\tau)}{\Gamma((2k-1)\alpha)}\varepsilon(\tau-1) - \sqrt{2}\sum_{k=1}^{\infty}(-2)^{k-1}\frac{\ln^{2k\alpha-1}(\tau)}{\Gamma(2k\alpha)}\varepsilon(\tau-1),$$

and step response

$$r_u(\tau) = \sum_{k=1}^{\infty}(-2)^{k-1}\frac{\ln^{(2k-1)\alpha}(\tau)}{\Gamma((2k-1)\alpha+1)}\varepsilon(\tau-1) - \sqrt{2}\sum_{k=1}^{\infty}(-2)^{k-1}\frac{\ln^{2k\alpha}(\tau)}{\Gamma(2k\alpha+1)}\varepsilon(\tau-1).$$

The Figures 5 and 6 show the graphical representation of the solutions with $\tau \geq 1$ *and several values of* α*.*

For $0 < \tau \leq 1$*, the impulse response is*

$$r_\delta(\tau) = \sum_{k=1}^{\infty}(-2)^{k-1}\frac{\ln^{(2k-1)\alpha-1}\left(\frac{1}{\tau}\right)}{\Gamma((2k-1)\alpha)}\varepsilon(1-\tau) - \sqrt{2}\sum_{k=1}^{\infty}(-2)^{k-1}\frac{\ln^{2k\alpha-1}\left(\frac{1}{\tau}\right)}{\Gamma(2k\alpha)}\varepsilon(1-\tau),$$

and step response

$$r_u(\tau)) = \sum_{k=1}^{\infty}(-2)^{k-1}\frac{\ln^{(2k-1)\alpha}\left(\frac{1}{\tau}\right)}{\Gamma((2k-1)\alpha+1)}\varepsilon(1-\tau) - \sqrt{2}\sum_{k=1}^{\infty}(-2)^{k-1}\frac{\ln^{2k\alpha}\left(\frac{1}{\tau}\right)}{\Gamma(2k\alpha+1)}\varepsilon(1-\tau).$$

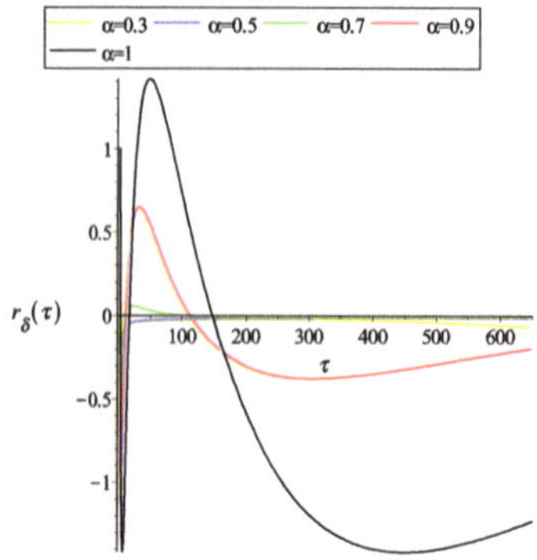

Figure 5. Impulse response of Example 2 with $1 \le \tau$ and several values of α.

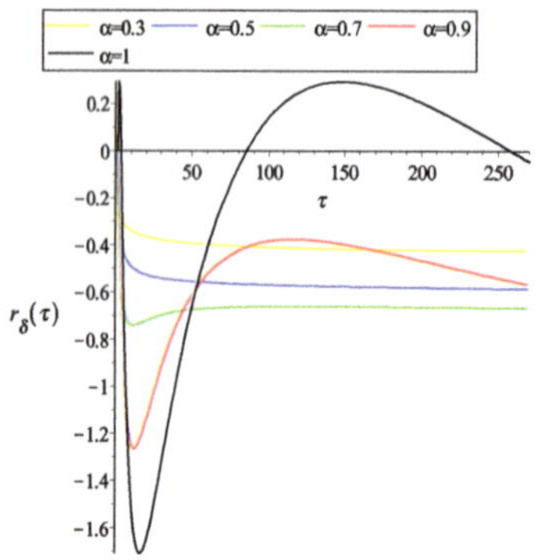

Figure 6. Step response of Example 2 with $1 \le \tau$ and several values of α.

The Figures 7 and 8 show the graphical representation of the solutions with $0 < \tau \le 1$ *and several values of* α.

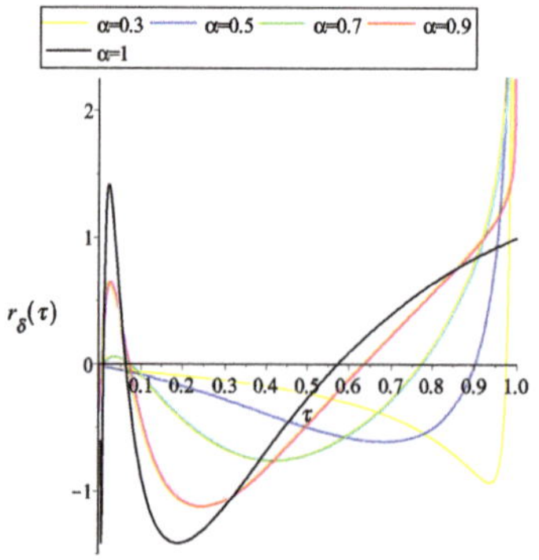

Figure 7. Impulse response of Example 2 with $0 < \tau \le 1$ and several values of α.

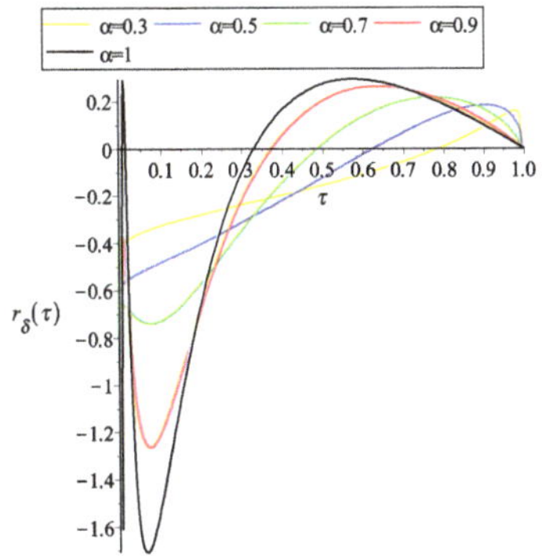

Figure 8. Step response of Example 2 with $0 < \tau \leq 1$ and several values of α.

6. Conclusions

We have proved that both Hadamard right (left) derivative and fractional scale derivative of type Grünwald-Letnikov are decremental index operators on the same sequence of functions $\{u_k\}_{k\in\mathbb{Z}}$. The Mellin convolution suggested to us how to define an algebraic product, which allowed us to construct a simple mathematical method to resolve fractional scale-invariant systems. The method relies on the roots of characteristic polynomial and the resolution of a linear system of equations. As expected, in our simulations, there is no convergence issue.

Author Contributions: Conceptualization, G.B. and M.O.; Methodology, G.B. and M.O.; Formal analysis, G.B. and M.O.; Writing—original draft, G.B. and M.O. All authors have read and agreed to the published version of the manuscript.

Funding: The second author was partially funded by National Funds through the Foundation for Science and Technology of Portugal, under the projects UIDB/00066/2020.

Conflicts of Interest: The authors declare no conflict of interest.

Appendix A

The fractional scale derivatives of type Grünwald-Letnikov were defined in (4) and (6).

Definition A1. *Let $q > 1$. The following expressions,*

$$\mathfrak{D}^{\alpha}_{s+}x(\tau) = \lim_{q\to1^+} \ln^{-\alpha}(q) \sum_{n=0}^{\infty} \frac{(-\alpha)_n}{n!} x(\tau q^{-n}),$$

and

$$\mathfrak{D}^{\alpha}_{s-}x(\tau) = \lim_{q\to1^+} (-1)^{\alpha} \ln^{-\alpha}(q) \sum_{n=0}^{\infty} \frac{(-\alpha)_n}{n!} x(\tau q^{n}),$$

represent scale-derivatives that we can call stretching and shrinking Grünwald-Letnikov type derivatives, respectively.

Suppose that $\tau > 1$ and $k \geq 1$. Hence

$$\mathfrak{D}^{\alpha}_{s+} \frac{\ln^{k\alpha-1}(\tau)}{\Gamma(k\alpha)} \varepsilon(\tau-1) = \lim_{q\to1^+} \ln^{-\alpha}(q) \sum_{n=0}^{\infty} \frac{(-\alpha)_n}{n!} \frac{\ln^{k\alpha-1}(\tau q^n)}{\Gamma(k\alpha)}.$$

Using the Mellin transform and its inverse the previous relation can be rewritten as

$$\mathfrak{D}^{\alpha}_{s+}\frac{\ln^{k\alpha-1}(\tau)}{\Gamma(k\alpha)}\varepsilon(\tau-1) = \lim_{q\to 1^+}\ln^{-\alpha}(q)\sum_{n=0}^{\infty}\frac{(-\alpha)_n}{n!}\frac{1}{2\pi i}\int_{\gamma}\mathcal{M}\left[\frac{\ln^{k\alpha-1}(\tau q^{-n})}{\Gamma(k\alpha)}\right]\tau^{v}dv$$
$$= \frac{1}{2\pi i}\int_{\gamma}\lim_{q\to 1^+}\frac{\sum_{n=0}^{\infty}\frac{(-\alpha)_n}{n!}q^{-nv}}{\ln^{\alpha}(q)}\mathcal{M}\left[\frac{\ln^{k\alpha-1}(\tau)}{\Gamma(k\alpha)}\right]\tau^{v}dv.$$

By binomial theorem and properties of limits it is not difficult to verify that

$$v^{\alpha} = \left[\frac{(1-q^{-v})}{\ln(q)}\right]^{\alpha} = \lim_{q\to 1^+}\frac{\sum_{n=0}^{\infty}\frac{(-\alpha)_n}{n!}q^{-nv}}{\ln^{\alpha}(q)}, \qquad Re(v) > 0.$$

It follows that

$$\mathfrak{D}^{\alpha}_{s+}\frac{\ln^{k\alpha-1}(\tau)}{\Gamma(k\alpha)}\varepsilon(\tau-1) = \frac{1}{2\pi i}\int_{\gamma}v^{\alpha}\mathcal{M}\left[\frac{\ln^{k\alpha-1}(\tau)}{\Gamma(k\alpha)}\right]\tau^{v}dv$$
$$= \frac{1}{2\pi i}\int_{\gamma}v^{-(k-1)\alpha}\tau^{v}dv$$
$$= \frac{\ln^{(k-1)\alpha-1}(\tau)}{\Gamma((k-1)\alpha)}\varepsilon(\tau-1).$$

The last equal follows from (3).

Theorem A1. *Let $\alpha < 0$ and $\tau > 1$. Then*

$$\mathfrak{D}^{\alpha}_{s+}\frac{\ln^{-1}(\tau)}{\Gamma(0)}\varepsilon(\tau-1) = \frac{\ln^{-\alpha-1}(\tau)}{\Gamma(-\alpha)}\varepsilon(\tau-1).$$

Proof. Observe that

$$\frac{\ln^{-1}(\tau)}{\Gamma(0)}\varepsilon(\tau-1) = \delta(\tau-1).$$

Hence

$$\mathfrak{D}^{\alpha}_{s+}\frac{\ln^{-1}(\tau)}{\Gamma(0)}\varepsilon(\tau-1) = \mathfrak{D}^{\alpha}_{s+}\delta(\tau-1)$$
$$= \lim_{q\to 1^+}\ln^{-\alpha}(q)\sum_{n=0}^{\infty}\frac{(-\alpha)_n}{n!}\delta(\tau q^{-n}-1).$$

By properties of delta function, $\delta(\tau q^{-n}-1) = q^n\delta(\tau-q^n)$. It follows that

$$\mathfrak{D}^{\alpha}_{s+}\frac{\ln^{-1}(\tau)}{\Gamma(0)}\varepsilon(\tau-1) = \lim_{q\to 1^+}\ln^{-\alpha}(q)\sum_{n=0}^{\infty}\frac{(-\alpha)_n}{n!}q^n\delta(\tau-q^n).$$

By Mellin transform we get that $\delta(\tau-q^n) = \frac{1}{2\pi i}\int_{\gamma}q^{n(v-1)}\tau^{v}dv$. So

$$\mathfrak{D}^{\alpha}_{s+}\frac{\ln^{-1}(\tau)}{\Gamma(0)}\varepsilon(\tau-1) = \lim_{q\to 1^+}\ln^{-\alpha}(q)\sum_{n=0}^{\infty}\frac{(-\alpha)_n}{n!}q^n\frac{1}{2\pi i}\int_{\gamma}q^{n(v-1)}\tau^{v}dv$$
$$= \frac{1}{2\pi i}\int_{\gamma}\lim_{q\to 1^+}\sum_{n=0}^{\infty}\frac{(-\alpha)_n}{n!}\ln^{-\alpha}(q)q^{nv}\tau^{v}dv.$$

By binomial Theorem and properties of limits we have that

$$\lim_{q\to1^+}\sum_{n=0}^{\infty}\frac{(-\alpha)_n}{n!}\ln^{-\alpha}(q)q^{nv}=\lim_{q\to1^+}\left(\frac{q^v-1}{\ln q}\right)^{\alpha}=v^{\alpha}.$$

Therefore

$$\begin{aligned}\mathfrak{D}^{\alpha}_{s+}\frac{\ln^{-1}(\tau)}{\Gamma(0)}\varepsilon(\tau-1)&=\frac{1}{2\pi i}\int_{\gamma}v^{\alpha}\tau^{v}dv\\&=\frac{\ln^{-\alpha-1}(\tau)}{\Gamma(-\alpha)}\varepsilon(\tau-1).\end{aligned}$$

□

Finally, by means of reasoning similar to (14) we obtain that

$$\mathfrak{D}^{\alpha}_{s+}u_k(\tau)=\mathfrak{D}^{\alpha}_{s+}u_{k-1}(\tau),\text{ for any }k\in\mathbb{Z}.$$

Remark A1. *The case* $0<\tau\le1$ *is similar to case* $1\le\tau$.

Appendix B

Observe that (3) is valid for all $\alpha>0$. If $\alpha>0$, then $\alpha+1>0$. So

$$\mathcal{M}^{-1}\left[v^{-(\alpha+1)}\right](\tau)=\frac{\ln^{\alpha}(\tau)}{\Gamma(\alpha+1)}\varepsilon(\tau-1),\qquad Re(v)>0. \tag{A1}$$

The case $Re(v)<0$ is analogous. With this inverse Mellin transform we can prove that

$$\mathfrak{D}^{\alpha}_{s+}\frac{\ln^{k\alpha}(\tau)}{\Gamma(k\alpha+1)}\varepsilon(\tau-1)=\frac{\ln^{(k-1)\alpha}(\tau)}{\Gamma((k-1)\alpha+1)}\varepsilon(\tau-1),\qquad k\in\mathbb{N}.$$

In the case when $k=0$, it is true that

$$\mathfrak{D}^{\alpha}_{s+}\varepsilon(\tau-1)=\frac{\ln^{-\alpha}(\tau)}{\Gamma(-\alpha+1)}\varepsilon(\tau-1).$$

The proof runs as Lemma 1. The same argument as in (13) applies to show

$$\mathfrak{D}^{\alpha}_{s+}\frac{\ln^{-k\alpha}(\tau)}{\Gamma(-k\alpha+1)}\varepsilon(\tau-1)=\frac{\ln^{(-k-1)\alpha}(\tau)}{\Gamma((-k-1)\alpha+1)}\varepsilon(\tau-1),\qquad k\in\mathbb{N}.$$

Therefore the new definition is given by

$$u_k(\tau)=\frac{\ln^{k\alpha}(\tau)}{\Gamma(k\alpha+1)}\varepsilon(\tau-1).$$

References

1. Roberts, M.J. *Signals and Systems: Analysis Using Transform Methods and Matlab*; McGraw-Hill: New York, NY, USA, 2003.
2. Shmaliy, Y. *Continuous-Time Systems*; Springer Science & Business Media: Berlin/Heidelberg, Germany, 2007.
3. Braccini, C.; Gambardella, G. Form-invariant linear filtering: Theory and applications. *IEEE Trans. Acoust. Speech Signal Process.* **1986**, *34*, 1612–1628. [CrossRef]
4. Yazici, B.; Kashyap, R. A class of second-order stationary self-similar processes for 1/f phenomena. *IEEE Trans. Signal Process.* **1997**, *45*, 396–410. [CrossRef]
5. Ortigueira, M.D. On the fractional linear scale invariant systems. *IEEE Trans. Signal Process.* **2010**, *58*, 6406–6410. [CrossRef]
6. Nottale, L. The theory of scale relativity. *Int. J. Mod. Phys. A* **1992**, *7*, 4899–4936. [CrossRef]
7. Narasimha, R.; Rao, R. Modeling variable-bit-rate video traffic using linear scale-invariant systems. In *Wavelet and Independent Component Analysis Applications IX*; SPIE: Bellingham, WA, USA, 2002; Volume 4738, pp. 79–89.

8. Cresson, J. Scale relativity theory for one-dimensional non-differentiable manifolds. *Chaos Solitons Fractals* **2002**, *14*, 553–562. [CrossRef]
9. Cresson, J. Scale calculus and the Schrödinger equation. *J. Math. Phys.* **2003**, *44*, 4907–4938. [CrossRef]
10. Khaluf, Y.; Ferrante, E.; Simoens, P.; Huepe, C. Scale invariance in natural and artificial collective systems: A review. *J. R. Soc. Interface* **2017**, *14*, 20170662. [CrossRef] [PubMed]
11. Rao, R.; Zhao, W. Image modeling with linear scale-invariant systems. In *Wavelet Applications VI*; SPIE: Bellingham, WA, USA, 1999; Volume 3723, pp. 407–418.
12. Gorenflo, R.; Luchko, Y.; Mainardi, F. Wright functions as scale-invariant solutions of the diffusion-wave equation. *J. Comput. Appl. Math.* **2000**, *118*, 175–191. [CrossRef]
13. Herrmann, R. *Fractional Calculus: An Introduction for Physicists*; World Scientific: Singapore, 2014.
14. Hirschman, I.I.; Widder, D.V. *The Convolution Transform*; Courier Corporation: Honolulu, HI, USA, 2012.
15. Poularikas, A. *The Transforms and Applications Handbook*; CRC Press LLC: Boca Raton, FL, USA, 2000.
16. Ortigueira, M.; Bohannan, G. Fractional Scale Calculus: Hadamard vs. Liouville. *Fractal Fract.* **2023**, *7*, 296. [CrossRef]
17. Samko, S.; Kilbas, A.; Marichev, O. *Fractional Integrals and Derivatives*; Gordon and Breach: New York, NY, USA, 1993.
18. Ortigueira, M.; Valério, D. *Fractional Signals and Systems*; De Gruyter: Berlin, Germany, 2020.
19. Ortigueira, M.D.; Machado, J.T. The 21st century systems: An updated vision of continuous-time fractional models. *IEEE Circuits Syst. Mag.* **2022**, *22*, 36–56. [CrossRef]
20. Bengochea, G.; Ortigueira, M. An operational approach to solve fractional continuous–time linear systems. *Int. J. Dyn. Control* **2017**, *5*, 61–71. [CrossRef]
21. Butzer, P.; Jansche, S. A direct approach to the Mellin transform. *J. Fourier Anal. Appl.* **1997**, *3*, 325–376. [CrossRef]
22. Luchko, Y.; Kiryakova, V. The Mellin integral transform in fractional calculus. *Fract. Calc. Appl. Anal.* **2013**, *16*, 405–430. [CrossRef]
23. Hadamard, J. Essai sur l'étude des fonctions données par leur développement de Taylor. *J. Math. Pures Appl.* **1892**, *8*, 101–186.
24. Kilbas, A.; Srivastava, H.; Trujillo, J. *Theory and Applications of Fractional Differential Equations*; North-Holland Mathematics Studies; Elsevier: Amsterdam, The Netherlands, 2006; Volume 204.
25. Ortigueira, M.; Bengochea, G.; Machado, J. Substantial, tempered, and shifted fractional derivatives: Three faces of a tetrahedron. *Math. Methods Appl. Sci.* **2021**, *44*, 9191–9209. [CrossRef]
26. Ortigueira, M.; Bengochea, G. Non-commensurate fractional linear systems: New results. *J. Adv. Res.* **2020**, *25*, 11–17. [CrossRef] [PubMed]
27. Appell, P. Sur une classe de polynômes. *Ann. Sci. de l'École Norm. Supérieure.* **1880**, *9*, 119–144. [CrossRef]
28. Rota, G.; Taylor, B. The classical umbral calculus. *SIAM J. Math. Anal.* **1994**, *25*, 694–711. [CrossRef]
29. Roman, S. *The Umbral Calculus*; Springer: Berlin/Heidelberg, Germany, 2005.
30. Gel'fand, I.; Shilov, G. *Generalized Functions*; Academic Press: Cambridge, MA, USA, 1964.
31. Bengochea, G.; Verde-Star, L. Linear algebraic foundations of the operational calculi. *Adv. Appl. Math.* **2011**, *47*, 330–351. [CrossRef]
32. Verde-Star, L. Inverses of generalized Vandermonde matrices. *J. Math. Anal. Appl.* **1988**, *131*, 341–353. [CrossRef]

fractal and fractional

Article

Quantum Creation of a Friedmann-Robertson-Walker Universe: Riesz Fractional Derivative Applied

Daniel L. Canedo [1,*], Paulo Moniz [2] and Gil Oliveira-Neto [1]

1 Departamento de Física, Instituto de Ciências Exatas, Universidade Federal de Juiz de Fora, Juiz de Fora 36036-330, MG, Brazil; gilnetojf@ufjf.br
2 Departamento de Física, Centro de Matemática e Aplicações (CMA-UBI), Universidade da Beira Interior, Rua Marquês d'Ávila e Bolama, 6200 Covilhã, Portugal; pmoniz@ubi.pt
* Correspondence: daniel.canedo@estudante.ufjf.br

Abstract: In this work, we apply fractional calculus to study quantum cosmology. Specifically, our Wheeler-DeWitt (WDW) equation includes a Friedman-Robertson-Walker (FRW) geometry, a radiation fluid, a positive cosmological constant (Λ), and an *ad-hoc* potential. We employ the Riesz fractional derivative, which introduces a parameter α, where $1 < \alpha \leq 2$, in the WDW equation. We investigate numerically the tunneling probability for the Universe to emerge using a suitable WKB approximation. Our findings are as follows. When we decrease the value of α, the tunneling probability also decreases, suggesting that if fractional features could be considered to ascertain among different early universe scenarios, then the value $\alpha = 2$ (meaning strict locality and standard cosmology) would be the most likely. Finally, our results also allow for an interesting discussion between selecting values for Λ (in a non-fractional conventional set-up) versus balancing, e.g., both Λ and α in the fractional framework.

Keywords: fractional calculus; quantum cosmology; tunneling probabilities; dark energy

1. Introduction

Since the introduction of the Wheeler-DeWitt equation [1,2], intending to describe the Universe as a quantum mechanical system, quantum cosmology (QC) [3–7] has steadily developed and achieved significant results concerning the quest to understand the origin of the Universe. For seminal contributions and recent reviews, cf. references [8,9].

The framework of QC includes audacious scenarios, namely the spontaneous creation from nothing [10–14]: our time and space emerge through a potential barrier. The universe (we will find ourselves in and observe) tunneling through the potential barrier and appearing to the right of it with a finite size and free from the initial singularity. This concept was broadly embraced, leading to the study of tunneling probabilities (TP) for the birth of the Universe for different cosmological models [15]. Because the regime is of high energy and the time is of the order of Planck time, quantum cosmology has no observable data. For more information on observables in quantum cosmology, their contributions of the theory and future predictions, we suggest reading reference [16].

Given the discussion in the above paragraph it is immensely tempting to explore QC further, trying new tools to better understand the Universe's origin. One such tool that recently gathered interest is fractional calculus [17], an extension of traditional calculus that allows for the modelling of complex systems and thus may be applied to describe phenomena in classical and quantum cosmology. See, e.g., [18,19] for a broad sample of recently published contributions.

Originating from the works of G. l'Hopital and G. W. Leibniz, and subsequently developed by mathematicians such as Abel, Liouville, and Riemann, an innovative mathematical tool was introduced, allowing derivatives and integrals to assume non-integer orders. This tool enabled the development of fractional calculus and is currently applied in various branches of physics, including field theory, particle physics, and atomic and molecular physics [17]. In addition, fractional calculus has also been used in engineering, biophysics and biomedicine, with encouraging results. For more information see [20–22], e.g., and the many references therein.

Depending on the phenomenon to be described, the system of fractional differential equations can be linear [23–26] or nonlinear [27–29]. Especially, there are many important phenomena in nature that can be described by the nonlinear fractional differential equations [27–29] or by the nonlinear integer differential equations [30–32]. In the present work we will focus on the study of cosmological systems described by linear fractional differential equations.

The application of Fractional calculus to quantum mechanics has allowed a generalization of path integrals and the Schrödinger equation, giving rise to fractional quantum mechanics (FQM) [33]. This new research area has gathered interest, and quite a few publications have appeared in the literature, pointing to potential benefits and new tests of traditional quantum mechanics. There still exist significant open problems to address in FQM. Please, see references [23,24,34,35] for more information. In particular, one of such open problems concerns the tunneling effect. Let us be more concrete. In [36,37], the authors studied quantum tunneling through delta potential barriers and through a rectangular barrier, respectively, using a space fractional Schrödinger equation. Tunneling with fractional time derivatives (Caputo derivative) can be found in [38]. In the first paper, the authors found an analytical expression for the TP as a function of the fractional parameter (α): the TP increased as α decreased. In the latter paper, the authors obtained a numerical solution where the TP decreased as α decreased. The scenarios were not so qualitatively different, nevertheless, fractional calculus generated discrepant results regarding the behavior of TP, in terms of α.

The application of fractional calculus in classical and quantum cosmology has also been of recent interest. The application of fractional calculus in quantum cosmology is usually designated as fractional quantum cosmology (FQC). Let us point out the following references [25,26,39,40]. Notably, FQC usually means taking (spatial) fractional derivatives. An application of interest is the Riesz derivative which affects the kinetic term of the Hamiltonian. Overall, for derivatives with a non-integer (e.g., fractional) order, we can suitably modify the Wheeler-DeWitt equation, which governs the quantum state of the Universe, and discuss fractional dimensions and, most importantly, non-local effects [25,36–38]. In fact, the Riesz fractional derivative operates as a non-local operator unless $\alpha = 2$. We can also anticipate scale-dependent geometries, which can emerge subtly as mimicked quantum gravity effects.

To be more precise, the Riesz fractional derivative has been considered non-local because its definition involves a convolution between a function and a kernel that considers the function's values over a certain domain, not just at a single point [17]. In the classical calculus, derivatives measure a function's local rate of the change at a given point [41]. In contrast, the fractional derivatives, particularly the Riesz fractional derivative, produces a non-local interaction with the function, where the behavior at a point depends on the values of the function at other (even distant) points [17]. Mathematically, the Riesz fractional derivative is often defined as [17],

$$D^{\alpha} f(x) = \frac{1}{2\pi} \int_{-\infty}^{\infty} \hat{f}(k)\, |k|^{\alpha} e^{ikx}\, dk.$$

In this definition, there is a Fourier transformation and a power-law factor that introduces the fractional differentiation order (α). Its non-local nature arises because the Fourier transform representation incorporates the global information of the function (i.e., the entire function in the frequency domain) rather than just the local information around a point. Consequently, the Riesz derivative responds to changes in the function's behavior over a wide region, constituting a non-local derivative. This contrasts with the classical derivative, which is strictly local and focuses only on the function's behavior near the point of interest. If we apply those ideas to a fractional Wheeler-DeWitt equation, we conclude that the behavior of the wave function in a specific region is influenced by the conditions in that region and in other regions, possibly in the entire domain. Thus, a broader influence of quantum mechanical features on semiclassical domains can be substantial. Namely, within a WKB tunneling discussion.

Based in the above discussion, our present work bears a twofold purpose. Firstly, we want contributing to the solution of the problem of seemingly distinct results in references [36,37], regarding tunneling in FQM. In particular, in reference [37] the authors employ a realistic (albeit simplified) approximation for the potential barrier, being rectangular and having a finite width and height, allowing one to estimate TP's and other effects. As a result of their calculations, they concluded that fractional parameters seem to alter the tunneling dynamics. However, the authors in [37] suggest that more realistic and elaborate potentials should be probed in order to solve the issue: how the TP's would change when one varies the fractional parameter α? That is exactly what we are going to do here. We will investigate a cosmological model endowed with a more realistic and elaborate potential.

Secondly, we are widening the scope of references [15,42] using the fractional Riesz derivative. It is tempting to check if a variation of α can mimic any other alteration we could make in Λ, or another parameter in references [15,42], and within which range this may be possible. Moreover, by investigating the fractional Riesz derivative in FQC, we will be studying the TP for the birth of a FRW Universe. As mentioned, above, our cosmological model is endowed with a more realistic and elaborate potential and the TP will be a function of the fractional parameter α. Our potential barrier was first introduced in references [15,42] and bears the curvature constant of the Universe (k), the cosmological constant (Λ), that plays the role of dark energy, and a parameter associated with the magnitude of the *ad-hoc* potential (σ). Thus, we are interested in comparing our results with the ones obtained in references [15,37,42], contributing to a still scarce study area.

Our paper is structured as follows. In Section 2, we introduce the Wheeler-DeWitt equation and then construct the fractional Schrödinger equation for our model. We solve the WDW equation using the WKB approximation and determine the WKB tunneling probability (TP_{WKB}). In Section 3, we present the numerical results of TP_{WKB}, for different selected parameters (namely, $\alpha, \Lambda, k, \sigma$). We, also, compare the TP_{WKB} obtained here, with the ones obtained in references [15,42]. Finally, Section 4 presents our conclusions and discussions about our work. This paper brings new results for the application of fractional calculus in quantum cosmology, thus contributing to the development and comprehension of the area.

2. Fractional WKB Tunneling Probabilites

We want to study how fractional calculus modifies the quantum tunneling studied in references [15,42], where the authors studied the classical and quantum dynamics of the universe with radiation, cosmological constant and an ad hoc potential, for different curvatures.

Starting from the FRW metric, using the ADM formalism [43] and the Schutz variational formalism [44,45], the total Hamiltonian of the Universe (H) is written as [15,42],

$$NH = -\frac{p_a^2}{12} + p_T - 3ka^2 + \Lambda a^4 + V_{ah}, \tag{1}$$

where p_a and p_T are the canonically conjugated momenta to a and T, respectively. Here we are using the natural unit system where $\hbar = c = k_B = 8\pi G = 1$. The Schutz variational formalism is used to recover the covariance that is lost when using the ADM formalism by rewriting the fluid in terms of potentials, one of which is entropy. In this way, the variable T, associated with the radiation fluid, plays the role of time in this model. For more information see the "Appendix: Hamiltonian for the radiation fluid" in reference [42]. The parameter Λ is the cosmological constant and V_{ah} is the ad hoc potential, first introduced in reference [15]. It is written as,

$$V_{ah} = -\frac{\sigma^2 a^4}{(a^3+1)^2} \tag{2}$$

where σ is a dimensionless parameter associated to the magnitude of that potential.

We study the creation of this universe within a quantized model. Specifically, the total Hamiltonian (1) is transformed into an operator using the usual commutation relations. Afterward, we introduce a wave function Ψ that depends on the canonical variables. Imposing that the total Hamiltonian operator annihilates the wave function, we obtain the Wheeler-DeWitt equation,

$$\begin{gathered}\hat{H}\Psi(a,T) = 0, \\ \left(\frac{1}{12}\frac{\partial^2}{\partial a^2} - i\frac{\partial}{\partial T} - 3ka^2 + \Lambda a^4 - \frac{\sigma^2 a^4}{(a^3+1)^2}\right)\Psi(a,T) = 0.\end{gathered} \tag{3}$$

Equation (3) can be re-cast in the form of a time-dependent Schrödinger equation, with the aid of a new variable $\tau = -T$,

$$\left(\frac{1}{12}\frac{\partial^2}{\partial a^2} - 3ka^2 + \Lambda a^4 - \frac{\sigma^2 a^4}{(a^3+1)^2}\right)\Psi(a,\tau) = -i\frac{\partial}{\partial \tau}\Psi(a,\tau). \tag{4}$$

The application of fractional calculus, using the Riesz derivative in the kinetic term of the Hamiltonian operator is given by [25,46],

$$\hat{H}_\alpha(p,r) = D_\alpha |p|^\alpha + V(r), \tag{5}$$

where D_α is a coefficient. For the standard textbook Schrödinger equation we have $i\hbar\frac{\partial \Psi}{\partial t} = -\frac{\hbar^2}{2m}\Delta\Psi + V\Psi$, whereas the fractional QM imports that $\frac{\hbar^2}{2m} \to D_\alpha(-\hbar^2\Delta)^{\frac{\alpha}{2}}$ and with $1 < \alpha \leq 2$ [23]. The fractional Hamiltonian operator (5) is Hermitian [24,47], that is, it has real eigenvalues that can be related to physical observables. When the eigenvalues associated with the Hamiltonian are not real, one may have complex dimensions. For more information on complex dimension, see reference [48].

Therefore, applying the Riesz derivative in the kinetic term of the Hamiltonian operator (4), we find the equation,

$$\left(D_\alpha\left[\frac{\partial^2}{\partial a^2}\right]^{\frac{\alpha}{2}} - 3ka^2 + \Lambda a^4 - \frac{\sigma^2 a^4}{(a^3+1)^2}\right)\Psi(a,\tau) = -i\frac{\partial}{\partial \tau}\Psi(a,\tau), \tag{6}$$

where we take $\frac{1}{12} = D_\alpha$, when $\alpha = 2$. The Riesz fractional derivative is a spatial, symmetric, nonlocal, linear fractional derivative [17,23,24].

The parameter α is known as the Lévy index and has its domain defined as $\alpha \in (0, 2]$ [23,24,33,34]. This parameter allowed the generalization of Brownian motion to Lévy motion, so that Brownian motion became a particular case of Lévy motion when $\alpha = 2$. Thus, the path integral over Lévy trajectories allowed the generalization of the Schrödinger equation of quantum mechanics, leading to the fractional Schrödinger equation. However, due to the fractional dimension [33], the parameter α has its domain limited to $(1, 2]$ in the application of fractional calculus to quantum mechanics.

E. Capelas de Oliveira and Jayme Vaz Jr, in reference [36], solved the fractional Schrödinger equation for the delta and double delta potential, taking into account that the fractional derivative is a nonlocal operator. M. Hasan and B.P. Mandal, in chapter 4 of referenece [37], studied the tunneling time in space fractional quantum mechanics for a time-independent fractional Schrödinger equation, whose potential barrier was rectangular. Differently from what was proposed by these authors, in their studies, we will obtain the tunneling probability by solving the Wheeler-DeWitt equation, in the form of a time-dependent Schrödinger equation, for a more realistic and elaborate potential barrier. For this, we will use the WKB approximation.

So let us propose a solution for Equation (6) in the following form [42],

$$\Psi(a, \tau) := \psi(a) e^{-iE\tau} \tag{7}$$

where we choose $\psi(a) = A(a) e^{i\phi(a)}$, with $A(a)$ being the amplitude, $\phi(a)$ the phase, and E is the energy associated to the radiation fluid of the Universe [42].

Substituting Equation (7) into Equation (6), we obtain the following expression,

$$\left(D_\alpha \left[\frac{\partial^2}{\partial a^2} \right]^{\frac{\alpha}{2}} - 3ka^2 + \Lambda a^4 - \frac{\sigma^2 a^4}{(a^3+1)^2} \right) \psi(a) e^{-iE\tau} = -i \frac{\partial}{\partial \tau} \psi(a) e^{-iE\tau}, \tag{8}$$

and therefore,

$$\frac{\partial^\alpha \psi(a)}{\partial a^\alpha} + \frac{1}{D_\alpha} (E - V_{eff}(a)) \psi(a) = 0. \tag{9}$$

This last equation can be rewritten as,

$$\frac{\partial^\alpha \psi(a)}{\partial a^\alpha} + \hat{\mathcal{K}}(a)^\alpha \psi(a) = 0, \tag{10}$$

where $\hat{\mathcal{K}}(a) \equiv \left(\frac{1}{D_\alpha} (E - V_{eff}) \right)^{\frac{1}{\alpha}}$ and $V_{eff}(a)$ is the effective potential,

$$V_{eff}(a) \equiv 3ka^2 - \Lambda a^4 + \frac{\sigma^2 a^4}{(a^3+1)^2}. \tag{11}$$

The general solution to Equation (10) is given by,

$$\begin{aligned} \Psi(a) &= \frac{C_1}{\hat{\mathcal{K}}(a)^{\frac{1}{\alpha}}} e^{\pm i \int \hat{\mathcal{K}}(a) da}, \qquad E > V_{eff}, \\ \Psi(a) &= \frac{C_2}{\leq(a)^{\frac{1}{\alpha}}} e^{\pm \int \kappa(a) da}, \qquad E < V_{eff}, \end{aligned} \tag{12}$$

where C_1 and C_2 are constants and $\kappa(a) \equiv \left(\frac{1}{D_\alpha} (V_{eff} - E) \right)^{\frac{1}{\alpha}}$. When $\alpha = 2$, the standard solution in reference [49] is recovered.

The WKB tunneling probability is given by [49],

$$TP_{WKB} \equiv \frac{4}{(2\theta + \frac{1}{2\theta})^2}, \tag{13}$$

where θ measures the height and thickness of the barrier for a given energy [49]. For our model, we have,

$$\theta = e^{\int_{a_L}^{a_R} \kappa(a)da}. \tag{14}$$

Here, a_L and a_R are the turning points where the energy line crosses the potential barrier on the left and right sides, respectively. Substituting (14) into (13), we obtain the tunneling probability for a wave function to pass through a high and wide barrier ($\theta \gg 1$),

$$TP_{WKB} \equiv \frac{4}{\left(2e^{\int_{a_L}^{a_R} \kappa(a)da} + \frac{1}{2e^{\int_{a_L}^{a_R} \kappa(a)da}}\right)^2}, \tag{15}$$

where $\kappa(a) = \left(\frac{1}{D_\alpha}\left(3ka^2 - \Lambda a^4 + \frac{\sigma^2 a^4}{(a^3+1)^2} - E\right)\right)^{\frac{1}{\alpha}}$.

3. Results

With the Fractional WKB Tunneling Probability, Equation (15), we are now able to compute the tunneling probabilities for the creation of the universe: an application of a simplified version of fractional calculus, in other words, the Riesz derivative in QC. In order to help us computing the TP_{WKB} Equation (15), we will use the Maple 18 Symbolic Software.

Equation (15) has 5 (five) parameters: (1) the curvature k, (2) the radiation energy E, (3) the cosmological constant Λ, (4) the ad hoc potential parameter σ and (5) the FC α. D_α is a constant. We will investigate how the TP_{WKB} depends on each of these five parameters. In order to do that, we will fix the value of four parameters and compute the TP_{WKB} for several different the values of the remaining one. In this way, we will determine how the TP_{WKB} depends on this fixed parameter. Then, we will repeat the same procedure for the other four parameters. For a better visualization of our results, we will show several graphs of the TP_{WKB}. Let us be more concrete. To compare our results with the ones obtained in reference [42], we will use the same values for the four parameters k, E, Λ and σ, which the authors used in reference [42]. All our results for the cases where $\alpha \neq 2$ will be exhibited in Section 3.2. Before that, in Section 3.1, we will comment on the constant D_α.

3.1. Tunneling Probability When $\alpha = 2$

Here, we call attention to the constant D_α present in the TP_{WKB} Equation (15). This constant is dependent on the parameter α and its definition involves some arbitrariness. An important condition that quantity must satisfy is that, when $\alpha = 2$ the result must be the constant of the standard model, without the fractional calculus. For fractional quantum mechanics, the constant $D_\alpha = \frac{1}{2m}$ is recovered when $\alpha = 2$ [33,34].

In the present paper, we will choose one of the simplest possible values for D_α, such that it has the correct limit when $\alpha = 2$. In this way, we define $D_\alpha = (\frac{1}{12})^{\frac{\alpha}{2}}$. When we substitute $\alpha = 2$ in Equation (15), we obtain the same equation and results for the TP_{WKB} as in the model in reference [42]. In a future work, we want to explore in details this arbitrariness, which may lead to some quantitatively different results. In order to give some idea about these quantitatively different results, we show in Appendix A some results for TP_{WKB} obtained with a different choice for D_α.

3.2. Tunneling Probability When $\alpha \neq 2$

We now investigate quantitatively how the fractional calculus features, namely the presence of the Riesz derivative, modify the quantum tunneling probabilities. To do that, we will study how the TP_{WKB} Equation (15) depends on the parameters: k, E, Λ, σ and α. We will employ the same values used for these parameters in reference [42], in order to compare our results with theirs.

3.2.1. TP_{WKB} as a Function of E

Concerning the variation of the energy E, we will fix $\Lambda = 1.5$ and $\sigma = -50$ like in [42]. All values for the energy E are below $V_{eff} = 691.51$, which is the maximum value of the barrier. We computed numerically Equation (15) for different values of E, α ($1 < \alpha < 2$) and k. We found that when E and α increase, the tunneling probabilities increase too. When we vary only the geometry (k) keeping the other parameters fixed, we obtain that TP_{WKB} is larger for the hyperbolic spatial sections ($k = -1$). An example of these results can be found in Figure 1.

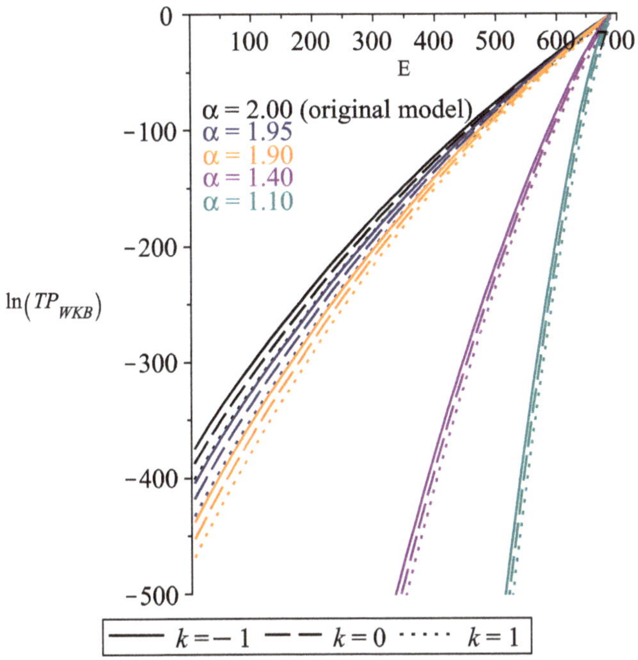

Figure 1. TP_{WKB}, in logarithmic scale, for the variation of the parameter E and for different values of the parameters α and k, with $\Lambda = 1.5$ and $\sigma = -50$. All parameters, with the exception of α, have the same value as in model [42].

3.2.2. TP_{WKB} as a Function of Λ

The following study is for the cosmological constant Λ, which plays the role of dark energy in this model. We compute numerically Equation (15), for different values of Λ, α ($1 < \alpha < 2$) and $k = 0, \pm 1$, but with $\sigma = -50$ and $E = 690$. We can see in Figure 2, as an example of our general result, that TP_{WKB} increases when α and Λ increase and is larger for $k = -1$.

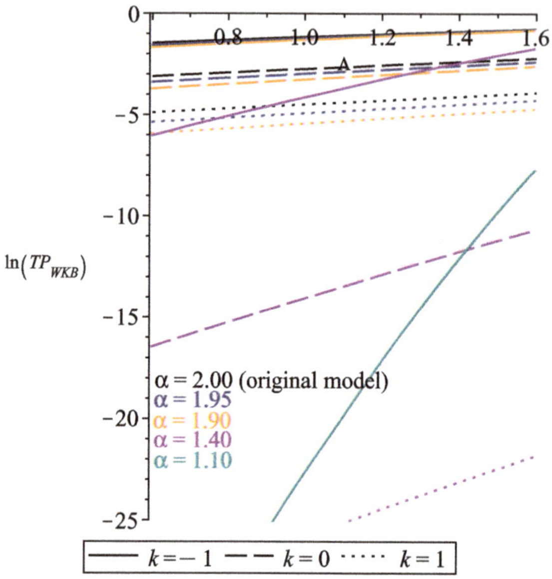

Figure 2. TP_{WKB}, in logarithmic scale, for the variation of the parameter Λ and for different values of the parameters α and k, with $\sigma = -50$ and $E = 690$. All parameters, with the exception of α, have the same value as in model [42]. In this figure, for $\alpha = 1.10$ we can only see the $k = -1$ curve.

3.2.3. TP_{WKB} as a Function of σ

Let us now vary the parameter σ, where σ is a dimensionless parameter associated with the magnitude of the ad hoc potential [15]. Following the same procedure, fixing the parameters $E = 680$ and $\Lambda = 1.5$, we vary and take several values of α and σ, for different curvatures of the space-like sections (k). As an example of our results, we can see in Figure 3, that TP_{WKB} increases when σ and α increase. The biggest value of TP_{WKB} is for $k = -1$ geometry, if compared to $k = 0, 1$ geometries.

3.3. Analysis and Implication of the Riesz Derivative in the Calculation of the Tunneling Probability

The Riesz derivative is an operator often used in fractional calculus and acts only on the kinetic term of the Hamiltonian operator (6). Thus, the effective potential (11) is identical to the effective potential of the model in reference [42]. In Section 3.2.1, we noticed that the TP_{WKB} decreases when we decrease the value of the parameter α, even when the energy E remains the same as the value used in reference [42]. In the non-fractional model, in order to decrease the TP, while keeping the energy fixed, we need to modify the potential barrier to become e.g., wider and higher. On the other hand, in the model with the Riesz derivative, this can go quite different. Let us be more specific.

In Figures 4–6, we draw the potential barriers for three different cases: (i) the fractional case with $\alpha = 1.9397961$ (blue line), (ii) the non-fractional case with $\Lambda = 0.7$ (red line), and (iii) the non-fractional case with the same values of Λ, σ, k as in case (i) (gold dot line). This last case (iii), is the one studied in reference [42]. In each Figure, the three cases are models with the same values of k. The horizontal black line, representing the constant energy $E = 200$, illustrates how the energy line intersects the barriers. We can see that the potential barriers in cases (i) and (iii) coincide. However, they generate different TP_{WKB}'s for the same energy, as per informed from Figures 1–3. It means that, the introduction of the Riesz derivative modifies in a significant way the TP_{WKB}'s associated with a given QC model.

On the other hand, we find that the results of TP_{WKB} for the non-fractional model with $\Lambda = 0.7$ closely mimic the results found for the fractional model with $\Lambda = 1.5$ and $\alpha = 1.9397961$, as we can see from the Figures 7–9. In each Figure, the two cases are models with the same values of k. The potential barriers of the two models can be seen in Figures 4–6.

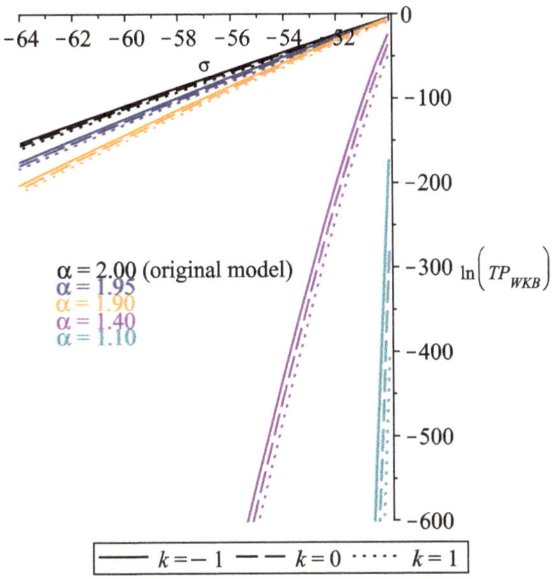

Figure 3. TP_{WKB}, in logarithmic scale, for the variation of the parameter σ and for different values of the parameters α and k, with $\Lambda = 1.5$ and $E = 680$. All parameters, with the exception of α, have the same value as in model [42].

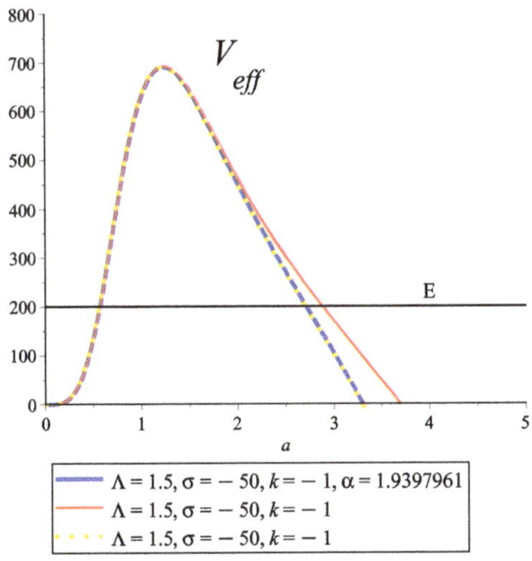

Figure 4. Effective potential for: fractional case (blue line), non-fractional case with $\Lambda = 0.7$ (red line) and non-fractional case studied in reference [42] (gold dot line). All of them with $k = -1$.

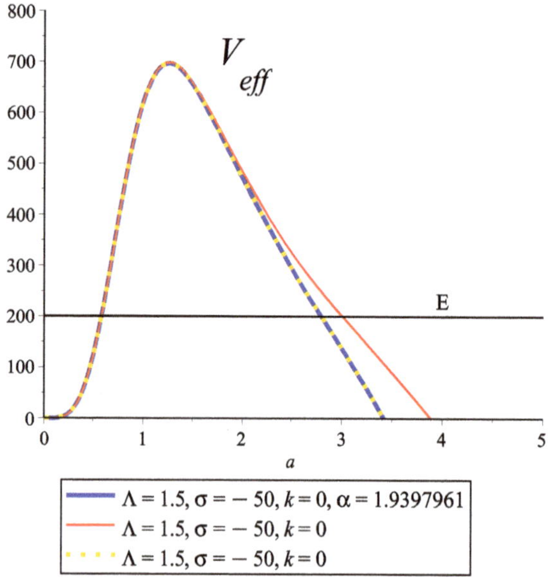

Figure 5. Effective potential for: fractional case (blue line), non-fractional case with $\Lambda = 0.7$ (red line) and non-fractional case studied in reference [42] (gold dot line). All of them with $k = 0$.

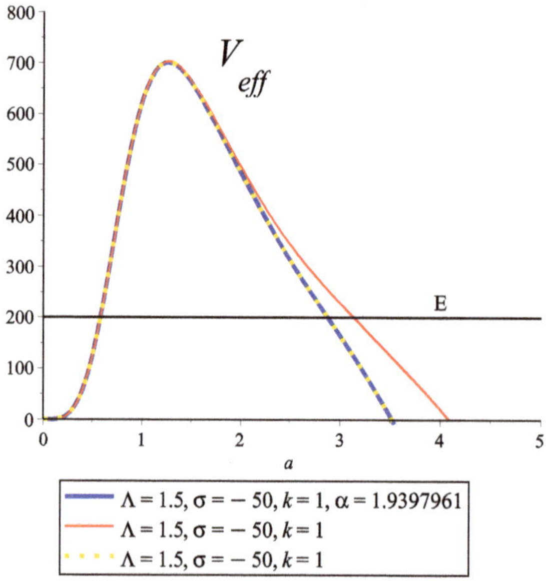

Figure 6. Effective potential for: fractional case (blue line), non-fractional case with $\Lambda = 0.7$ (red line) and non-fractional case studied in reference [42] (gold dot line). All of them with $k = 1$.

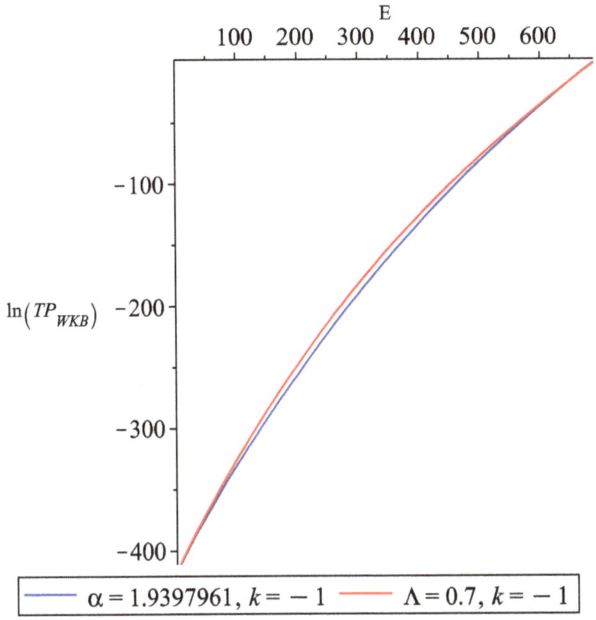

Figure 7. Comparison of TP_{WKB}, in logarithmic scale, for different energies E in the fractional (blue line) and non-fractional ($\Lambda = 0.7$), red line, models for $k = -1$.

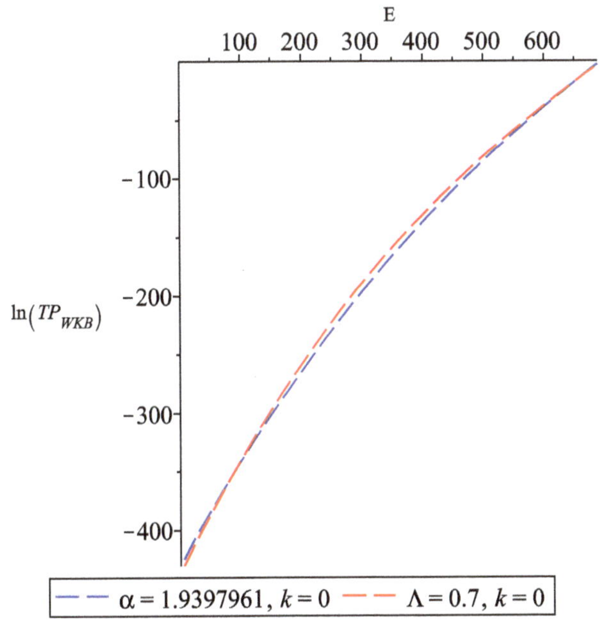

Figure 8. Comparison of TP_{WKB}, in logarithmic scale, for different energies E in the fractional (blue slash line) and non-fractional ($\Lambda = 0.7$), red slash line, models for $k = 0$.

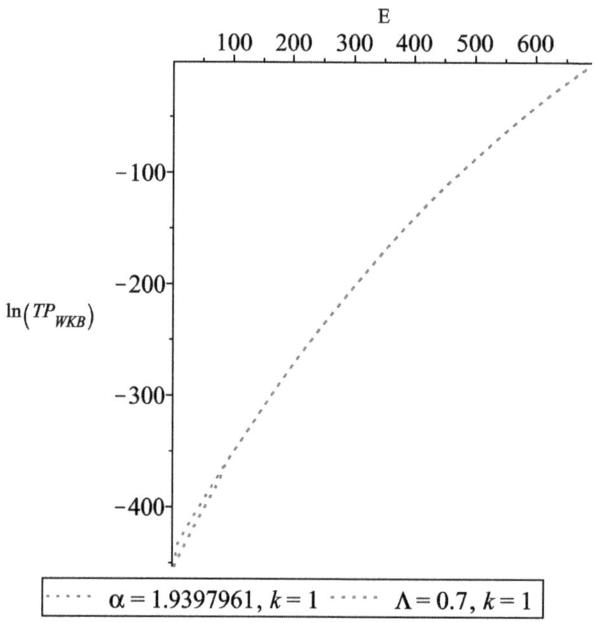

Figure 9. Comparison of TP_{WKB}, in logarithmic scale, for different energies E in the fractional (blue dot line) and non-fractional ($\Lambda = 0.7$), red dot line, models for $k = 1$.

This new and interesting result suggests that modifying the parameter α in the fractional model may be comparable to modifying the potential barrier in the non-fractional model, i.e., its height and width. In Tables 1–6, we show some results for θ Equation (14) and TP_{WKB} Equation (15) for different values of E, regarding the fractional model with $\Lambda = 1.5$ and $\alpha = 1.9397961$, and the non-fractional model with $\Lambda = 0.7$.

- For hyperbolic space-like sections

Table 1. Comparative table of θ for different energies in the fractional and non-fractional models for $k = -1$.

k	E	$\theta_{non-fractional}$ $(\Lambda = 0.7)$	$\theta_{fractional}$ $(\Lambda = 1.5)$ and $\alpha = 1.9397961$
	10	$1.002778169 \times 10^{88}$	$1.303841382 \times 10^{88}$
	170	$3.873356742 \times 10^{58}$	$1.577277123 \times 10^{60}$
-1	340	$3.066824521 \times 10^{34}$	$1.353799484 \times 10^{36}$
	500	$7.888358713 \times 10^{16}$	$5.091334256 \times 10^{17}$
	660	463.1719831	400.5848243

Table 2. Comparative table of tunneling probabilities for different energies in the fractional and non-fractional models for $k = -1$.

k	E	$TP_{WKB_{non-fractional}}$ $(\Lambda = 0.7)$	$TP_{WKB_{fractional}}$ $(\Lambda = 1.5)$ and $\alpha = 1.9397961$
	10	$9.944667312 \times 10^{-177}$	$5.882344812 \times 10^{-177}$
	170	$6.665381380 \times 10^{-118}$	$4.019610680 \times 10^{-121}$
-1	340	$1.063217573 \times 10^{-69}$	$5.456212944 \times 10^{-73}$
	500	$1.607040038 \times 10^{-34}$	$3.857773981 \times 10^{-36}$
	660	0.000004661379104	0.000006231744824

- For flat space-like sections

Table 3. Comparative table of the parameter θ for different energies in the fractional and non-fractional models for $k = 0$.

k	E	$\theta_{non-fractional}$ $(\Lambda = 0.7)$	$\theta_{fractional}$ $(\Lambda = 1.5)$ and $\alpha = 1.9397961$
	10	$1.793016944 \times 10^{92}$	$1.146483507 \times 10^{91}$
	170	$1.379498224 \times 10^{61}$	$1.674829609 \times 10^{62}$
0	340	$5.585366235 \times 10^{35}$	$2.076589094 \times 10^{37}$
	500	$3.790604212 \times 10^{17}$	$2.537403708 \times 10^{18}$
	660	1191.527234	1069.113378

Table 4. Comparative table of tunneling probabilities for different energies in the fractional and non-fractional models for $k = 0$.

k	E	$TP_{WKB_{non-fractional}}$ $(\Lambda = 0.7)$	$TP_{WKB_{fractional}}$ $(\Lambda = 1.5)$ and $\alpha = 1.9397961$
	10	$3.110507212 \times 10^{-185}$	$7.607892668 \times 10^{-183}$
	170	$5.254818360 \times 10^{-123}$	$3.564993479 \times 10^{-125}$
0	340	$3.205506704 \times 10^{-72}$	$2.318989928 \times 10^{-75}$
	500	$6.959581392 \times 10^{-36}$	$1.553176674 \times 10^{-37}$
	660	$6.959581392 \times 10^{-7}$	$8.748876416 \times 10^{-7}$

- For spherical space-like sections

Table 5. Comparative table of the parameter θ for different energies in the fractional and non-fractional models for $k = 1$.

k	E	$\theta_{non-fractional}$ $(\Lambda = 0.7)$	$\theta_{fractional}$ $(\Lambda = 1.5)$ and $\alpha = 1.9397961$
	10	$1.577640978 \times 10^{97}$	$1.907005973 \times 10^{94}$
	170	$1.313683533 \times 10^{64}$	$2.830562481 \times 10^{64}$
1	340	$1.380589165 \times 10^{37}$	$3.946000113 \times 10^{38}$
	500	$1.992360778 \times 10^{18}$	$1.370930167 \times 10^{19}$
	660	3160.340886	2945.792223

Table 6. Comparative table of tunneling probabilities for different energies in the fractional and non-fractional models for $k = 1$.

k	E	$TP_{WKB_{non-fractional}}$ $(\Lambda = 0.7)$	$TP_{WKB_{fractional}}$ $(\Lambda = 1.5)$ and $\alpha = 1.9397961$
	10	$4.017756788 \times 10^{-195}$	$2.749766985 \times 10^{-189}$
	170	$5.794533632 \times 10^{-129}$	$1.248114729 \times 10^{-129}$
1	340	$5.246516932 \times 10^{-75}$	$6.422229384 \times 10^{-78}$
	500	$2.519208036 \times 10^{-37}$	$5.320706876 \times 10^{-39}$
	660	$1.001226000 \times 10^{-7}$	$1.152380106 \times 10^{-7}$

Thus, analyzing the results qualitatively through the Figures 4–9 and quantitatively through the Tables 1–6, we see that the shapes of the barriers and the results for θ and TP_{WKB}, of the fractional model with $\Lambda = 1.5$ and $\alpha = 1.9397961$ and the non-fractional model with $\Lambda = 0.7$, are close. This convergence between the fractional and non-fractional models is lost for small Λ, on the order of 10^{-2}, since the behavior of the effective potential for $k = 1$ is modified.

4. Conclusions and Discussions

In this work, we investigated whether a concrete tool of fractional calculus may influence the tunneling probability computed using the WKB approximation. For this purpose, a FRW model was employed, containing a radiation fluid, a positive cosmological constant, and an *ad-hoc* potential. Moreover, we used the Riesz fractional derivative in the

Hamiltonian operator, which was applied to the kinetic term. In this manner, we made it possible to investigate the behavior of the tunneling probability as a function of the new fractional parameter α.

Our results show that when $\alpha = 2$, we obtain the same results found in the study carried out in reference [42]. When we allow α to vary, we observe that when α decreases, within its domain $1 < \alpha \leq 2$, the tunneling probability decreases. Thus, the Universe is more likely to be created for higher values of α, namely $\alpha = 2$.

These results allowed us to conclude that although our potential barrier is the same as that established in reference [42], applying fractional calculus in the kinetic term of the Hamiltonian operator modifies the tunneling probabilities. Upon investigating this feature in more detail, we noticed that the decrease of the parameter α seems to produce an effect similar to a modification on the potential barrier of the non-fractional model in reference [42]. More precisely, in order to achieve that we have to make the potential barrier broader and higher by modifying its parameters Λ, σ, k. To substantiate this observation, we presented an example with a fractional model where $\Lambda = 1.5$ and $\alpha = 1.9397961$ and a non-fractional model with $\Lambda = 0.7$. We showed that the tunneling probabilities computed for both models are very close. This was checked for other ranges, as presented in the previous section. Please compare Tables 1–6 and Figures 4–9.

In addition to the qualitative analysis of the potential barriers in the fractional and non-fractional models, through the Figures 4–9, we performed a quantitative analysis through θ, which informs about the height and length of the barriers. The results, found in Tables 1–3, confirm the similarity of the barriers and the values of the tunneling probabilities between the models.

Finally, our results also allow for an interesting discussion between selecting values for Λ (in a non-fractional conventional set-up) versus balancing, e.g., both Λ and α in the fractional framework. Concretely, as pointed out above, the TP_{WKB} in the non-fractional model if, e.g., $\Lambda = 0.7$, is very close to the TP_{WKB} computed if in the fractional model we choose, e.g., $\Lambda = 1.5, \alpha = 1.9397961$. This suggests that if fractional derivatives were present in a model with a certain Λ, the universe described by this model could be born with almost the same probability of another universe with a smaller value of Λ, provided that in the second model there were only usual derivatives.

These new results also contribute and shed additional light on the use of fractional calculus in quantum cosmology. More precisely, on the calculation of tunneling probabilities by using a more realistic and elaborate potential than those studied in references [37] and [36]. Lastly, the application of fractional calculus in quantum cosmology, specially in the calculation of tunneling probabilities, is relatively new and requires further investigation.

Author Contributions: Conceptualization, P. M.; methodology, P.M.; software, D.L.C.; formal analysis, D.L.C. and P. M.; investigation, D.L.C.; writing—original draft preparation, D.L.C., P. M. and G.O.-N.; writing—review and editing, D.L.C., P. M. and G.O.-N.; supervision, P. M. and G.O.-N. All authors have read and agreed to the published version of the manuscript.

Funding: D. L. Canedo thanks Coordenação de Aperfeiçoamento de Pessoal de Nível Superior (CAPES) and Universidade Federal de Juiz de Fora (UFJF) for his scholarships and the Universidade da Beira Interior (UBI) for academic support in the PDSE-CAPES program. PM acknowledges the FCT grant UID-B-MAT/00212/2020 at CMA-UBI plus the COST Actions CA23130 (Bridging high and low energies in search of quantum gravity (BridgeQG)) and CA23115 (Relativistic Quantum Information (RQI)). G. Oliveira-Neto thanks FAPEMIG (APQ-06640-24) for partial financial support.

Data Availability Statement: Data is contained within the article.

Conflicts of Interest: The funders had no role in the design of the study; in the collection, analyses, or interpretation of data; in the writing of the manuscript, or in the decision to publish the results.

Appendix A. D_α Analysis

In Section 3.1, we reported some arbitrariness in choosing the constant D_α. This constant is a function of the Riesz parameter α, which also appears explicitly in the tunneling probability expression (15). Let us write again this equation here,

$$TP_{WKB} \equiv \frac{4}{\left(2e^{\int_{a_L}^{a_R}\kappa(a)da} + \frac{1}{2e^{\int_{a_L}^{a_R}\kappa(a)da}}\right)^2}$$

where $\kappa(a) = \left(\frac{1}{D_\alpha}\left(3ka^2 - \Lambda a^4 + \frac{\sigma^2 a^4}{(a^3+1)^2} - E\right)\right)^{\frac{1}{\alpha}}$.

By analyzing this equation in detail, we can see that the fractional exponent α present in the term $\kappa(a)$ acts faster than the constant D_α, a multiplicative factor. Thus, the definition of D_α only changes the result quantitatively, not qualitatively.

We will show here a brief study as a concrete example to determine the influence of the constant D_α on the tunneling probability. We present below an analysis for two choices of this constant: $D_\alpha = (\frac{1}{12})^{\frac{\alpha}{2}}$ and $D_\alpha = (\frac{1}{12})^{\frac{2}{\alpha}}$. Note that there are other possible choices for D_α that satisfy the condition that $D_\alpha = \frac{1}{12}$, when $\alpha = 2$. However, for simplicity, we will only analyze these two examples here, leaving a broader analysis of the possible choices for D_α for a future paper.

In Figures A1 and A2, we can see, as an example, the TP_{WKB}'s, in logarithmic scale, for different energies E, different curvatures k and two values of the fractional parameter α. We have the parameters $\Lambda = 1.5$ and $\sigma = -50$ fixed in both figures.

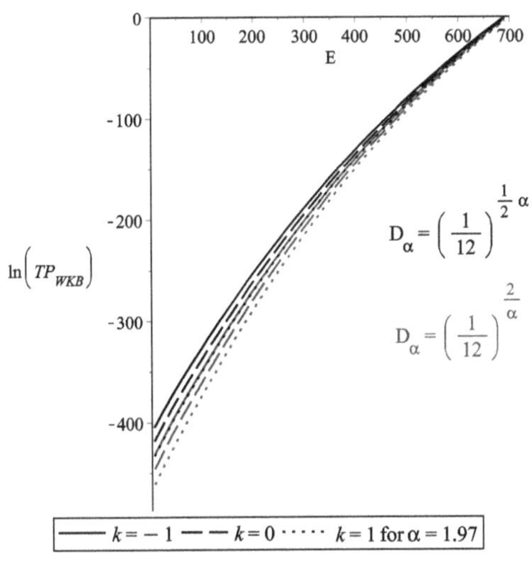

Figure A1. TP_{WKB}, in logarithmic scale, as a function of energy E and curvature k, when $\alpha = 1.97$, $\Lambda = 1.5$ and $\sigma = -50$, for $D_\alpha = (\frac{1}{12})^{\frac{\alpha}{2}}$ (black color) and $D_\alpha = (\frac{1}{12})^{\frac{2}{\alpha}}$ (purple color).

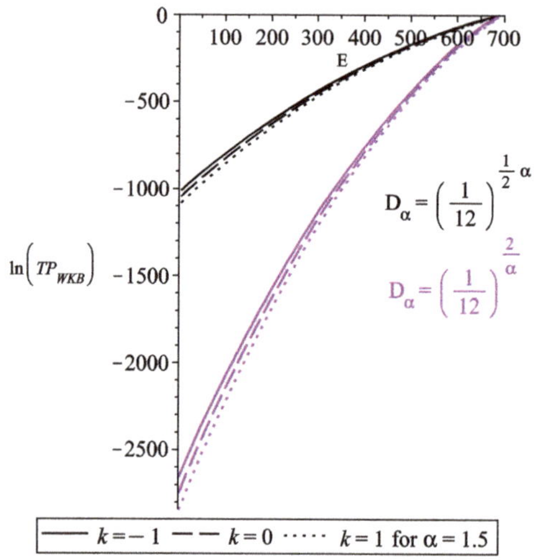

Figure A2. TP_{WKB}, in logarithmic scale, as a function of energy E and curvature k, when $\alpha = 1.5$, $\Lambda = 1.5$ and $\sigma = -50$, for $D_\alpha = (\frac{1}{12})^{\frac{\alpha}{2}}$ (black color) and $D_\alpha = (\frac{1}{12})^{\frac{2}{\alpha}}$ (purple color).

Thus, it can be observed that the constant D_α can be more influential in the result of the tunneling probability when $\alpha \to 1$, where $\alpha \in (1, 2]$. However, as discussed at the beginning of the Appendix A, the behavior of the tunneling probability as a function of the model parameters remains unchanged, that is, we will not have qualitative differences in the results, only quantitative ones.

References

1. DeWitt, B.S. Quantum Theory of Gravity. I. The Canonical Theory. *Phys. Rev. D* **1967**, *160*, 1113. [CrossRef]
2. Wheeler, J.A. *Battelles Rencontres*; DeWitt, C., Wheeler, J.A., Eds.; Benjamin: New York, NY, USA, 1968.
3. Grishchuk, L.P.; Zeldovich, Y.B. *Quantum Structure of Space and Time*; Duff, M., Isham, C., Eds.; Cambridge University Press: Cambridge, UK, 1982.
4. Hawking, S.W. Quantum Cosmology. In *Relativity, Groups and Topology II: Proceedings of the 1983 Les Houches Summer School, Session XL*; DeWitt, B.S., Stora, R., Eds.; North-Holland: Amsterdam, The Netherlands, 1984; pp. 333–379.
5. Halliwell, J.; Hawking, S. Quantum Cosmology—Beyond Minisuperspace. In *Proceedings of the Fourth Marcel Grossmann Meeting on General Relativity, Rome, Italy, 1985*; Ruffini, R., Ed.; North-Holland: Amsterdam, The Netherlands, 1986; Part A, pp. 65–83.
6. Bojowald, M. *Quantum Cosmology: A Fundamental Description of the Universe*; Lecture Notes in Physics; Springer: New York, NY, USA, 2011; Volume 835.
7. Bojowald, M. Quantum cosmology: A review. *Rep. Prog. Phys.* **2015**, *78*, 023901. [CrossRef] [PubMed]
8. Pinto-Neto, N.; Fabris, J.C. Quantum cosmology from the de Broglie–Bohm perspective. *Class. Quantum Grav.* **2013**, *30*, 143001. [CrossRef]
9. Jalalzadeh, S.; Moniz, P.V. *Challenging Routes in Quantum Cosmology*; World Scientific Publishing Co. Pte. Ltd.: Singapore, 2023.
10. Vilenkin, A. Creation of universes from nothing. *Phys. Lett. B* **1982**, *117*, 25. [CrossRef]
11. Vilenkin, A. Quantum creation of universes. *Phys. Rev. D* **1984**, *30*, 509. [CrossRef]
12. Vilenkin, A. Boundary conditions in quantum cosmology. *Phys. Rev. D* **1986**, *33*, 3560. [CrossRef]
13. Linde, A.D. Quantum creation of the inflationary universe. *Lett. Nuovo Cim.* **1984**, *39*, 401. [CrossRef]
14. Rubakov, V.A. Quantum mechanics in the tunneling universe. *Phys. Lett. B* **1984**, *148*, 280. [CrossRef]
15. Monerat, G.A.; Alvarenga, F.G.; Gonçalves, S.V.B.; Oliveira-Neto, G.; Santos, C.G.M.; Silva, E.V.C. The effects of dark energy on the early Universe with radiation and an ad hoc potential. *Eur. Phys. J. Plus* **2022**, *137*, 117. [CrossRef]
16. Chataignier, L.; Kiefer, C.; Moniz, P. Observations in quantum cosmology. *Class. Quantum Grav.* **2023**, *40*, 223001. [CrossRef]
17. Herrman, R. *Fractional Calculus: An Introduction for Physicists*, 2nd ed.; World Scientific: Singapore, 2014.
18. Rasouli, S.M.M.; Costa, E.W.d.; Moniz, P.; Jalalzadeh, S. Inflation and Fractional Quantum Cosmology. *Fractal Fract.* **2022**, *6*, 655. [CrossRef]

19. González, E.; Leon, G.; Fernandez-Anaya, G. Exact Solutions and Cosmological Constraints in Fractional Cosmology. *Fractal Fract.* **2023**, *7*, 368. [CrossRef]
20. Hilfer, R. *Applications of Fractional Calculus in Physics*; World Scientific: Singapore, 2000.
21. Ross, B. A brief history and exposition of the fundamental theory of fractional calculus. In *Fractional Calculus and Its Applications*; Lecture Notes in Mathematics; Ross, B., Ed.; Springer: Berlin/Heidelberg, Germany, 1975; Volume 457.
22. Ortigueira, D.M. *Fractional Calculus for Scientists and Engineers*; Springer: Dordrecht, The Netherlands; Berlin/Heidelberg, Germany; London, UK; New York, NY, USA, 2011.
23. Laskin, N. Fractional Schrödinger equation. *Phys. Rev. E* **2002**, *66*, 056108. [CrossRef] [PubMed]
24. Laskin, N. Principles of Fractional Quantum Mechanics. *arXiv* **2010**, arXiv:1009.5533.
25. Jalalzadeh, S.; Costa, E.W.O.; Moniz, P.V. de Sitter fractional quantum cosmology. *Phys. Rev. D* **2022**, *105*, L121901. [CrossRef]
26. Rasouli, S.M.M.; Cheraghchi, S.; Moniz, P. Fractional Scalar Field Cosmology. *Fractal Fract.* **2024**, *8*, 281. [CrossRef]
27. Jarad, F.; Abdeljawad, T.; Hammouch, Z. On a class of ordinary differential equations in the frame of Atangana–Baleanu fractional derivative. *Chaos Solitons Fractals* **2018**, *117*, 16–20. [CrossRef]
28. Syam, M.I.; Al-Refai, M. Fractional differential equations with Atangana–Baleanu fractional derivative: Analysis and applications. *Chaos Solitons Fractals X* **2019**, *2*, 100013. [CrossRef]
29. Kucche, K.D.; Sutar, S.T. Analysis of nolinear fractional differential equations involving Atangana-Baleanu-Caputo derivative. *Chaos Solitons Fractals* **2021**, *143*, 110556. [CrossRef]
30. Gao, X.Y. Hetero-Bäcklund transformation, bilinear forms and multi-solitons for a (2+1)-dimensional generalized modified dispersive water-wave system for the shallow water. *Chin. J. Phys.* **2024**, *92*, 1233–1239. [CrossRef]
31. Gao, X.Y. Open-Ocean Shallow-Water Dynamics via a (2+1)-Dimensional Generalized Variable-Coefficient Hirota-Satsuma-Ito System: Oceanic Auto-Bäcklund Transformation and Oceanic Solitons. *China Ocean Eng.* **2025**, *in press*. [CrossRef]
32. Gao, X.Y. In an Ocean or a River: Bilinear Auto-Bäcklund Transformations and Similarity Reductions on an Extended Time-Dependent (3+1)-Dimensional Shallow Water Wave Equation. *China Ocean Eng.* **2025**, *39*, 160–165. [CrossRef]
33. Laskin, N. Fractional quantum mechanics. *Phys. Rev. E* **2000**, *62*, 3135–3145. [CrossRef] [PubMed]
34. Laskin, N. Fractional quantum mechanics and Lévy path integrals. *Phys. Lett. A* **2000**, *268*, 298. [CrossRef]
35. Rabei, E.M.; Altarazi, I.M.A.; Muslih, S.I; Baleanu, D. Fractional WKB approximation. *Nonlinear Dyn.* **2009**, 57, 171–175. [CrossRef]
36. de Oliveira, E.C.; Vaz, J., Jr. Tunneling in fractional quantum mechanics. *J. Phys. A Math. Theor.* **2011**, *44*, 185303. [CrossRef]
37. Hasan, M.; Mandal, B.P. Tunneling time in space fractional quantum mechanics. *Phys. Lett. A* **2018**, *382*, 248–252. [CrossRef]
38. Duan, X.; Ma, C.; Huang, H.; Deng, K. Uniform Operator: Aligning Fractional Time Quantum Mechanics with Basic Physical Principles. *SSRN* **2024**, *preprint*. [CrossRef]
39. Costa, E.W.d.O.; Jalalzadeh, R.; Junior, P.F.d.; Rasouli, S.M.M.; Jalalzadeh, S. Estimated Age of the Universe in Fractional Cosmology. *Fractal Fract.* **2023**, *7*, 854. [CrossRef]
40. Tare, J.D.; Esguerra, J.P.H. Transmission through locally periodic potentials in space-fractional quantum mechanics. *Physical A* **2014**, *407*, 43–53. [CrossRef]
41. Piskunov, N. *Differential and Integral Calculus*; CBS Publishers and Distributors: New Delhi, India, 1996; Volume I, Chapter 3.
42. Oliveira-Neto, G.; Canedo, D.L.; Monerat, G.A. Tunneling probabilities for the birth of universes with radiation, cosmological constant and an ad hoc potential. *Eur. Phys. J. Plus* **2023**, *138*, 400. [CrossRef]
43. Misner, C.W.; Thorne, K.S.; Wheeler, J.A. *Gravitation*; W. H. Freeman: San Francisco, CA, USA, 1973.
44. Schutz, B.F. Perfect Fluids in General Relativity: Velocity Potentials and a Variational Principle. *Phys. Rev. D* **1970**, *2*, 2762. [CrossRef]
45. Schutz, B.F. Hamiltonian Theory of a Relativistic Perfect Fluid. *Phys. Rev. D* **1971**, *4*, 3559. [CrossRef]
46. Moniz, P.V.; Jalalzadeh, S. From Fractional Quantum Mechanics to Quantum Cosmology: An Overture. *Mathematics* **2020**, *8*, 313. [CrossRef]
47. Calcagni, G. Multifractional theories: An unconventional review. *J. High Energ. Phys.* **2017**, *2017*, 138. [CrossRef]
48. Calcagni, G. Complex dimensions and their observability. *Phys. Rev. D* **2017**, *96*, 046001. [CrossRef]
49. Merzbacher, E. *Quantum Mechanics*, 3rd ed.; John Wiley and Sons, Inc.: New York, NY, USA, 1998; Chapter 7.

fractal and fractional

MDPI

Article

Advanced Stability Analysis for Fractional-Order Chaotic DC Motors Subject to Saturation and Rate Limitations

Esmat Sadat Alaviyan Shahri [1,†], Yangquan Chen [2,*,†] and Naser Pariz [3,†]

1 Electrical and Computer Engineering Department, University of Gonabad, Gonabad 9691880002, Iran; alaviyan@gonabad.ac.ir
2 Mechatronics, Embedded Systems and Automation Lab, University of California, Merced, CA 95343, USA
3 Department of Electrical Engineering, Ferdowsi University of Mashhad, Mashhad 9177948974, Iran; n-pariz@um.ac.ir
* Correspondence: ychen53@ucmerced.edu
† These authors contributed equally to this work.

Abstract: Chaotic behavior and memory-dependent dynamics in fractional-order brushless DC motors (FOBLDCMs) pose significant challenges for robust and stable control design, particularly when physical constraints such as actuator saturation and rate limitations are present. Existing control frameworks often neglect these nonlinear limitations, resulting in performance degradation and potential instability in practical applications. Motivated by these challenges, this paper presents a comprehensive Lyapunov-based stability and control synthesis framework for FOBLDCMs within the fractional-order (FO) range $0 < v < 1$. The proposed methodology employs indirect, direct, and composite Lyapunov functions to derive sufficient stability conditions under four scenarios: unconstrained input, saturation-only, rate-limited-only, and combined constraints. For each case, a family of stabilizing controllers is designed to explicitly handle the respective limitations. To the best of our knowledge, this is the first study to rigorously address both saturation and rate limitations in the control design of FO chaotic systems. Numerical simulations confirm that the proposed controllers significantly improve performance over existing methods. Specifically, the unconstrained controller achieves a notable reduction in control energy (from 2.72×10^5 to 1.83×10^5), a 26.3% decrease in maximum control effort, and enhanced or comparable tracking accuracy, as indicated by lower ISE and RMSE values. These results highlight the robustness and practical applicability of the proposed control framework for real-world FO electromechanical systems.

Keywords: chaotic system; saturation; rate limitation; stability; indirect Lyapunov method

1. Introduction

Fractional calculus (FC), an extension of classical integer-order calculus, offers a powerful framework for capturing memory and hereditary properties in complex dynamical systems. By introducing non-local operators, FC enables more accurate descriptions of processes where current states depend not only on present conditions but also on historical trajectories. This capability makes it highly relevant for modeling and analysis in control engineering, signal processing, viscoelasticity, and beyond. Recent works have increasingly leveraged FC to study physical and engineering systems where conventional integer-order models fall short [1–4]. Particularly, the mathematical richness of fractional-order (FO) derivatives has facilitated nuanced modeling of nonlinear, chaotic, and high-dimensional systems.

1.1. Motivation and Background

FO modeling techniques have gained substantial attention across various engineering disciplines due to their superior ability to capture complex dynamics with fewer parameters and enhanced accuracy compared to their classical integer-order counterparts [5–7]. These methods have proven particularly useful in analyzing chaotic systems, where nonlinearities and sensitivity to initial conditions demand more refined modeling tools. Prominent examples include the FO Lorenz, Chen, and Lü systems, as well as FO models of brushless DC motors (BLDCMs) [8–11]. The pioneering work by Hemati [12] introduced chaotic dynamics in BLDCMs, while subsequent studies such as [13] utilized both analytical and computational tools to characterize chaotic regimes and design stabilizing strategies. Researchers in [11] further extended the analysis by deriving bifurcation properties of FO BLDCMs (FOBLDCMs), and detailed investigations in [14–16] explored their bifurcation structures and qualitative behaviors. These studies confirmed that while chaos poses risks to the performance and reliability of actuators, it can be rigorously studied and mitigated through advanced modeling approaches.

In terms of control strategies for FO chaotic systems, numerous methods have been proposed within the FO domain ($0 < v < 1$). For instance, Ref. [17] proposed a Lyapunov-based stabilization approach leveraging a single state variable. In a related work, the authors of [18] analyzed the stabilization of a nonlinear FOBLDCM using Caputo derivatives, supported by mathematical tools such as the Laplace transform, the Mittag–Leffler function, Jordan decomposition, and Grönwall's inequality. Moreover, Ref. [19] introduced a novel adaptive control strategy based on the Immersion and Invariance (I&I) theorem and fuzzy systems to synchronize chaotic BLDCM dynamics with desired trajectories, especially for electric vehicle applications. Alternative formulations such as FO operators—including the Caputo, Caputo–Fabrizio, and Atangana–Baleanu definitions—have also been employed in modeling and control, as seen in [20]. Sensorless control approaches have also been developed for high-speed BLDCMs, using digital signal processors (DSPs) to enhance commutation accuracy, as discussed in [21]. Bifurcation-based anti-control techniques were proposed in [22], where various external periodic and constant signals were shown to influence complex bifurcation structures, including Hopf, Bogdanov–Takens, and period-doubling types. Additionally, works such as [23] explored single-input stabilization, [24] analyzed quasi-Mittag–Leffler stability for distributed-order systems, and the authors' contributions in [25] addressed delay-induced instability in FO power systems using Lyapunov functionals. However, many of these studies still assume idealized conditions and often neglect key practical constraints such as actuator saturation and input rate limitations—challenges that are critical in real-world applications.

1.2. Modeling with Input Constraints

The integration of actuator saturation into FO system modeling yields a block-oriented structure, notably resembling Hammerstein models, where a static nonlinearity (saturation) precedes a linear or nonlinear FO dynamic system. This opens a promising avenue for system identification and control. Recent contributions in FO Hammerstein modeling include the development of smoothed functional algorithms with norm-limited update vectors for the identification of continuous-time FO Hammerstein systems [26]. Similarly, iterative parameter estimation methods were applied in [27] to FO Hammerstein systems under colored noise. However, these approaches primarily focus on identification, not stabilization or constrained control design. The current work seeks to bridge this gap by formulating a control-oriented FO Hammerstein framework for systems with both amplitude and rate limitations, a direction previously unexplored.

Furthermore, in recent years, significant advancements have been made in the control of BLDCMs, particularly through the application of FO control theory. Classical control strategies have been extended with robust, adaptive, and intelligent features to handle system nonlinearities, parameter uncertainties, and external disturbances more effectively. For instance, the authors of [28] proposed a finite-time super-twisting algorithm based on recurrent neural networks for FO systems, demonstrating improved transient and steady-state performance. In another direction, Ref. [29] tackled the challenges of rate-limited control in FO systems by introducing flat phase constraints derived from Bode integrals. Furthermore, Ref. [30] presented a novel integration of active disturbance rejection control (ADRC) with compensation for actuator rate limitations, validating its effectiveness through experimental results on benchmark systems. Despite these promising developments, most control approaches for FO chaotic systems—including BLDCMs—do not simultaneously consider both actuator saturation and rate limitations, which are frequently encountered in practice. Instead, these limitations are typically addressed separately, with many designs assuming ideal actuator behavior.

A contribution addressing input constraints can be found in the work of Alavian Shahri et al. [31–35], who analyzed saturation effects on control inputs in both linear and nonlinear systems, including cases with and without time delays. These studies offered valuable insights into the impact of input bounds in FO systems. However, they primarily focused on saturation constraints, leaving rate limitations either unaddressed or only marginally considered. Moreover, their scope did not encompass chaotic dynamics or FOBLDCMs specifically, where the interaction of saturation and rate constraints plays a critical role in achieving safe and stable operation.

Beyond constraint handling, another common limitation in current control designs lies in the underlying assumptions regarding system observability and feedback availability. Many approaches rely heavily on direct Lyapunov methods and presume access to full state measurements or multiple sensors—conditions often impractical in embedded or resource-limited systems. Additionally, few controllers incorporate physical actuator characteristics such as limited bandwidth or maximum permissible control effort during the synthesis process. Neglecting these constraints can result in suboptimal tracking performance, delayed response, or even destabilization of the closed-loop system under real-world operating conditions.

1.3. Gap and Contribution Overview

To the best of our knowledge, no prior work has systematically addressed the stabilization of FO chaotic BLDCMs under both amplitude saturation and rate-limited control inputs. Motivated by this practical need, this paper proposes a unified framework for stability analysis and controller synthesis using novel Lyapunov candidates for various constrained scenarios. The proposed approach accommodates single, dual, and triple input cases, reducing sensor dependency while ensuring robust performance under physical limitations. By extending FO system modeling to include block-oriented nonlinearities, this research also lays a theoretical foundation for FO Hammerstein-type control architectures.

1.4. Main Contributions

The primary contributions of this work are summarized as follows:

- Unified stability framework: A comprehensive Lyapunov-based stability framework is developed for FO chaotic BLDCMs under input constraints including saturation, rate limits, and their combination. To our knowledge, this is the first study that considers both rate and amplitude limitations simultaneously in FO chaotic control design.

- Novel Lyapunov candidates: Tailored Lyapunov functions are constructed for each control scenario—unconstrained, saturated, rate-limited, and jointly constrained—based on a combination of direct and indirect Lyapunov methods.
- Input-constrained controller design: Multiple controller configurations are derived from stability conditions, enabling implementations with reduced sensor requirements (single-, double-, and triple-input variants).
- Benchmark validation: The effectiveness of the proposed framework is demonstrated through extensive simulations on FOBLDCMs with varying degrees of input constraints and nonlinear behavior.

1.5. Organization

The organization of this paper is as follows: Section 2 delineates the requisite definitions and preliminaries imperative for comprehending the concepts and methods employed in subsequent sections. Section 3 details the stability analysis and controller design methodologies, underscoring the introduced indirect Lyapunov method without and with limitations. Section 4 presents comprehensive simulation results, corroborating the efficacy of the proposed methods in stabilizing FOBLDCMs. Finally, Section 5 encapsulates the study, summarizing salient findings and suggesting potential trajectories for future exploration.

2. Preliminaries

In this section, the preliminary mathematical concepts are presented.

Definition 1 ([2]). *The Caputo derivative of a smooth function, denoted by $g(t) : \mathbb{R}^+ \longrightarrow \mathbb{R}$, with an FO v, can be expressed as follows:*

$$ {}_{t_0}^{C}D_t^{v} g(t) = \frac{1}{\Gamma(n-v)} \int_{t_0}^{t} \frac{g^{(n)}(\tau)}{(t-\tau)^{v-n+1}} d\tau, \tag{1} $$

where $n \in \mathbb{N}$, $n-1 < v < n$, is the nth derivative of the function $g(t)$.

The Laplace transform of $g(t)$ can be expressed as follows:

$$ \ell\left\{ {}_{t_0}^{C}D_t^{v} g(t) \right\} = s^{v} G(s) - \sum_{k=0}^{n-1} s^{v-k-1} g^{(k)}(0). \tag{2} $$

Theorem 1 ([36,37]). *The following equation satisfies the condition for any $s \in \mathbb{C}$ and $0 < v < 1$:*

$$ \int_{0}^{\infty} \frac{\mu_v(\omega)}{s+\omega} d\omega = \frac{1}{s^{v}}, \tag{3} $$

where $\mu_v(\omega) = \frac{\sin(v\pi)}{\pi\omega^{v}}$.

By applying the Laplace transform to Equation (3), we obtain

$$ \int_{0}^{\infty} \mu_v(\omega) e^{-\omega t} d\omega = \frac{t^{v-1}}{\Gamma(v)}. \tag{4} $$

Theorem 2 ([37]). *The FO nonlinear differential equation* ${}_{t_0}^{C}D_t^{v}y(t) = g(t)$ *can be interpreted using the continuous-frequency-distributed model of the fractional integrator as follows:*

$$\frac{\partial z(\omega,t)}{\partial t} = -\omega z(\omega,t) + g(t), \tag{5}$$

In this context, the variable $z(\omega,t) \in \mathbb{R}$ *represents the frequency-distributed state, and the output* $y(t)$ *corresponds to the weighted integral of* $z(\omega,t)$.

$$y(t) = \int_0^\infty \mu_v(\omega) z(\omega,t) d\omega, \tag{6}$$

with $y(t) = 0$ *and* $0 < v < 1$.

Lemma 1 ([38]). *For any real matrices M and N of appropriate dimensions, the following inequality is satisfied for any scalar k:*

$$MN + M^T N^T < kMM^T + k^{-1} NN^T \tag{7}$$

3. Main Results

Consider the FO brushless DC motor (FOBLDCM) described by the following equation [39]:

$$\begin{cases} {}^{C}D_t^{v} i_d = Sat(u_d) - \delta i_d + i_q w, & \| \dot{u_d} \| \leqslant c_d \\ {}^{C}D_t^{v} i_q = Sat(u_q) - i_q - i_d w + \gamma w, & \| \dot{u_q} \| \leqslant c_q \ ,0 < v < 1 \\ {}^{C}D_t^{v} w = \sigma(i_q - w) - Sat(T_l), & \| \dot{T_l} \| \leqslant c_T \end{cases} \tag{8}$$

where w, i_q, and i_d represent the angular speed, quadrature-axis current, and direct-axis current of the motor, respectively. The system also includes positive parameters δ, γ, and σ, which determine the specific dynamical behavior of the motor. Additionally, the controls u_d, u_q, and T play a role in governing the system dynamics. Furthermore, c_d, c_q, and c_T are positive numbers that show rate limitation in specific inputs. Figure 1 shows the control system block diagram of the FOBLDCM. The function $Sat(\cdot)$ represents the saturation function, defined as $Sat(r) = sign(r)Min(r,$ a), that has the saturation level **a**. This function is shown in Figure 2.

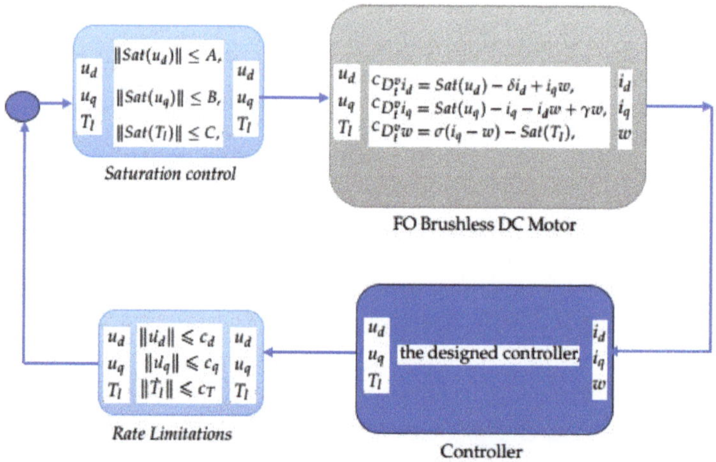

Figure 1. Block diagram of the FOBLDCM.

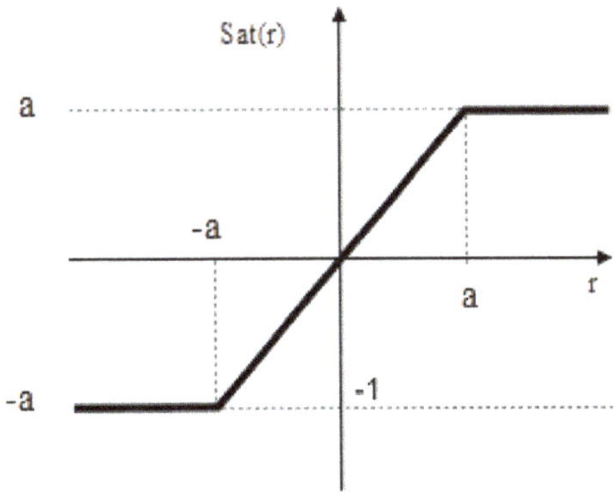

Figure 2. Saturation function.

As a first step, we have to make some assumptions about the control input, as follows:

$$\| Sat(u_d) \| \leq A, A \in R^+ \tag{9}$$

$$\| Sat(u_q) \| \leq B, B \in R^+ \tag{10}$$

$$\| Sat(T_l) \| \leq C, C \in R^+ \tag{11}$$

The open-loop behavior of the FOBLDCM is illustrated in Figures 3 and 4 for different values of the fractional derivative. Specifically, when $\sigma = 4$, $\gamma = 55$, and $\delta = 0.875$, and with initial condition $\begin{bmatrix} 10 & 3 & -12 \end{bmatrix}^T$, the system exhibits aperiodic, sudden, random, or morbid oscillations, indicating chaotic behavior. These chaotic oscillations can have detrimental effects on system stability. Therefore, it is of utmost importance to address the challenges posed by the chaotic FOBLDCM and develop effective control methods to stabilize the system.

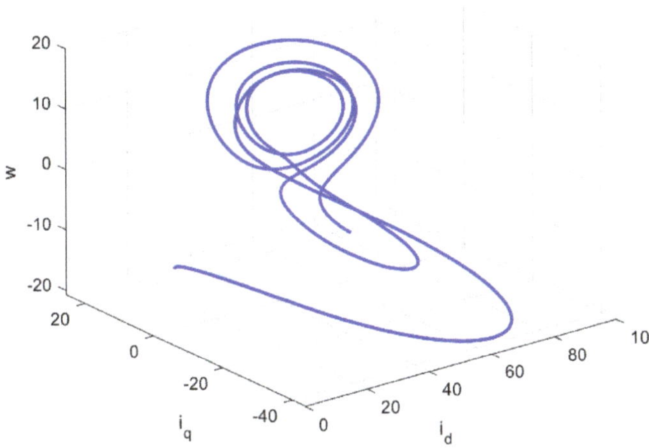

Figure 3. Space representation $[i_d \; i_q \; w]$ of the chaotic attractor with $v = 0.968$ for the open-loop FOBLDCM.

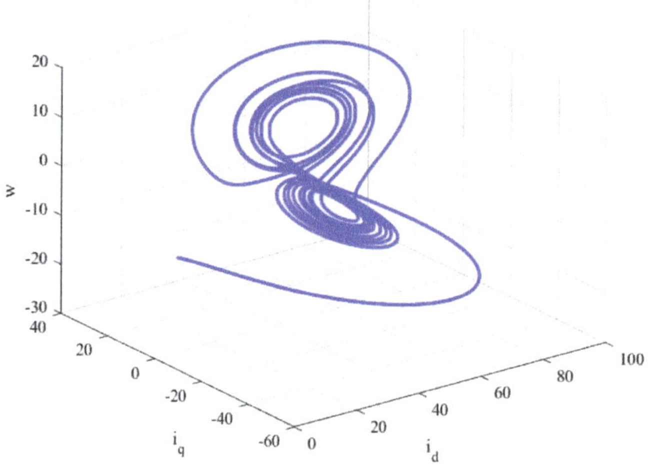

Figure 4. Space representation $[i_d \ i_q \ w]$ of the chaotic attractor with $v = 0.99$ for the open-loop FOBLDCM.

3.1. No Limitation Control

We consider the present analysis step by step. In the first step, study Equation (8) without any limitation, as described by the following equation [39]:

$$\begin{cases} {}^{C}D_t^{v} i_d = u_d - \delta i_d + i_q w \\ {}^{C}D_t^{v} i_q = u_q - i_q - i_d w + \gamma w \quad , 0 < v < 1 \\ {}^{C}D_t^{v} w = \sigma\left(i_q - w\right) - T_l \end{cases} \tag{12}$$

Theorem 3. *The system described in Equation (12) can achieve global stability at the equilibrium point by implementing the following controller:*

$$i_d u_d + i_q u_q + (\sigma + \gamma) w i_q - w T_l \leq 0. \tag{13}$$

where u_d, u_q, and T_l are the control inputs. By substituting this controller into Equation (12) and satisfying the inequality constraint given by Equation (13), then the closed loop system is asymptotically stable.

Note 1. *Theorem 3 is satisfied with the necessary condition that none of the eigenstates, i_d or i_q or w, are included in the denominator of the designed controller.*

Proof. Based on Theorem 2, we can alternatively express the system described by Equation (12) as

$$\begin{cases} \frac{\partial z_1(\omega,t)}{\partial t} = -\omega z_1(\omega,t) + u_d - \delta i_d + i_q w \\ i_d = \int\limits_0^\infty \mu_v(\omega) z_1(\omega,t) d\omega, \\ \mu_v(\omega) = \frac{\sin(v\pi)}{\pi \omega^{v}} \end{cases} \tag{14}$$

$$\begin{cases} \frac{\partial z_2(\omega,t)}{\partial t} = -\omega z_2(\omega,t) + u_q - i_q - i_d w + \gamma w \\ i_q = \int\limits_0^\infty \mu_v(\omega) z_2(\omega,t) d\omega, \\ \mu_v(\omega) = \frac{\sin(v\pi)}{\pi \omega^{v}} \end{cases} \tag{15}$$

$$\begin{cases} \frac{\partial z_3(\omega,t)}{\partial t} = -\omega z_3(\omega,t) + \sigma(i_q - w) - T_l \\ w = \int\limits_0^\infty \mu_v(\omega) z_3(\omega,t) d\omega, \\ \mu_v(\omega) = \frac{\sin(v\pi)}{\pi\omega^v} \end{cases} \tag{16}$$

Consider two Lyapunov functions for the system, denoted as $V_1(\omega,t) = z_1^2 + z_2^2 + z_3^2$, which represents the monochromatic Lyapunov function based on the elementary frequency, and $V(t)$, which is defined as the sum of all the monochromatic functions $V_1(t)$ weighted by the function $\mu_v(\omega)$; see Equation (17). The monochromatic Lyapunov function $V_1(\omega,t)$ captures the energy associated with each individual frequency component of the system. It quantifies the stability of the system with respect to the elementary frequency components, considering their magnitudes in the squared sum.

$$V = \frac{1}{2}\sum_{i=1}^{3}\int\limits_0^\infty \mu_v(\omega) z_i(\omega,t)^2 d\omega. \tag{17}$$

It can easily be derived from Equation (17) that

$$\frac{dV}{dt} = \sum_{i=1}^{3}\int\limits_0^\infty \mu_v(\omega) z_i(\omega,t)\frac{\partial z_i(\omega,t)}{\partial t} d\omega \tag{18}$$

Simplifying Equation (18),

$$\begin{aligned} \tfrac{dV}{dt} &= \int\limits_0^\infty \mu_v(\omega) z_1(\omega,t)\tfrac{\partial z_1(\omega,t)}{\partial t} d\omega \\ &+ \int\limits_0^\infty \mu_v(\omega) z_2(\omega,t)\tfrac{\partial z_2(\omega,t)}{\partial t} d\omega + \int\limits_0^\infty \mu_v(\omega) z_3(\omega,t)\tfrac{\partial z_3(\omega,t)}{\partial t} d\omega \end{aligned} \tag{19}$$

Substituting Equations (14)–(16) into Equation (19), we have

$$\begin{aligned} \tfrac{dV}{dt} &= \int\limits_0^\infty \mu_v(\omega) z_1(\omega,t)\big(-\omega z_1(\omega,t) + u_d - \delta i_d + i_q w\big) d\omega \\ &+ \int\limits_0^\infty \mu_v(\omega) z_2(\omega,t)\big(-\omega z_2(\omega,t) + u_q - i_q - i_d w + \gamma w\big) d\omega \\ &+ \int\limits_0^\infty \mu_v(\omega) z_3(\omega,t)\big(-\omega z_3(\omega,t) + \sigma(i_q - w) - T_l\big) d\omega \end{aligned} \tag{20}$$

This can be rewritten as

$$\begin{aligned} \tfrac{dV}{dt} &= \int\limits_0^\infty -\omega\mu_v(\omega)\big\{z_1^2(\omega,t) + z_2^2(\omega,t) + z_3^2(\omega,t)\big\} d\omega \\ &+ \int\limits_0^\infty \mu_v(\omega) z_1(\omega,t) d\omega\big(u_d - \delta i_d + i_q w\big) \\ &+ \int\limits_0^\infty \mu_v(\omega) z_2(\omega,t) d\omega\big(u_q - i_q - i_d w + \gamma w\big) \\ &+ \int\limits_0^\infty \mu_v(\omega) z_3(\omega,t) d\omega\big(\sigma(i_q - w) - T_l\big) \end{aligned} \tag{21}$$

Simplifying Equation (21), we have

$$\begin{aligned} \tfrac{dV}{dt} &= \int\limits_0^\infty -\omega\mu_v(\omega)\big\{z_1^2(\omega,t) + z_2^2(\omega,t) + z_3^2(\omega,t)\big\} d\omega \\ &+ i_d\big(u_d - \delta i_d + i_q w\big) + i_q\big(u_q - i_q - i_d w + \gamma w\big) \\ &+ w\big(\sigma(i_q - w) - T_l\big) \end{aligned} \tag{22}$$

Classifying Equation (22), it can be presented as

$$\begin{aligned} &\tfrac{dV}{dt} = \int_0^\infty -\omega\mu_v(\omega)\left\{z_1^2(\omega,t) + z_2^2(\omega,t) + z_3^2(\omega,t)\right\}d\omega \\ &-\left\{\delta i_d^2 + i_q^2 + \sigma w^2\right\} \\ &+\left(i_d u_d + i_d i_q w + i_q u_q - i_q i_d w + \gamma w i_q + w\sigma i_q - wT_l\right) \end{aligned} \tag{23}$$

The first and second terms of (23) are negative definite due to $\omega \geq 0$, $\mu_{v_i} > 0$, and $\varepsilon_i > 0$. The third term is negative semi-definite to satisfy the stability condition $\frac{dV}{dt} < -\omega V$. Therefore, the true states will tend to zero and the FOBLDCM will be asymptotically stable. Thus, the proof is complete. □

3.2. Saturation Control

In this section, we assume there is just the limitation of saturation on the controller, then (8) can be expressed as follows:

$$\begin{cases} {}^C D_t^v i_d = Sat(u_d) - \delta i_d + i_q w \\ {}^C D_t^v i_q = Sat(u_q/) - i_q - i_d w + \gamma w \quad ,0 < v < 1 \\ {}^C D_t^v w = \sigma(i_q - w) - Sat(T_l) \end{cases} \tag{24}$$

In the presence of saturation control, stability analysis and design controller must be different. If we can introduce a group of controllers, it has a special condition. This section considers the system shown in Equation (24) and studies this special condition.

Theorem 4. *Consider system (24) under assumptions (9)–(11). If there exist three positive numbers, k_1, k_2, and k_3, such that Equations (25) and (26) are satisfied, then the closed-loop system is globally exponentially stable at the zero equilibrium point:*

$$p_1 i_d u_d + (p_1 - p_2) i_d i_q w + p_2 i_q u_q + (p_2\gamma + p_3\sigma) w i_q - p_3 w T_l \leq 0 \tag{25}$$

$$\begin{aligned} &p_1 i_d\left(k_1 + k_1^{-1}A^2\right) + (p_1 - p_2) i_d i_q w + p_2 i_q\left(k_2 + k_2^{-1}B^2\right) + (p_2\gamma + p_3\sigma) w i_q \\ &-p_3 w\left(k_3 + k_3^{-1}C^2\right) \leq 0 \end{aligned} \tag{26}$$

where k_i and p_i, $i = 1,2,3$ are positive scalars and A, B, and C satisfy assumptions (9)–(11).

Proof. Based on Theorem 2, the system specified by Equation (24) can alternatively be expressed in another form as

$$\begin{cases} \frac{\partial z_1(\omega,t)}{\partial t} = -\omega z_1(\omega,t) + Sat(u_d) - \delta i_d + i_q w \\ i_d = \int_0^\infty \mu_v(\omega) z_1(\omega,t) d\omega, \\ \mu_v(\omega) = \frac{\sin(v\pi)}{\pi\omega^v} \end{cases} \tag{27}$$

$$\begin{cases} \frac{\partial z_2(\omega,t)}{\partial t} = -\omega z_2(\omega,t) + Sat(u_q) - i_q - i_d w + \gamma w \\ i_q = \int_0^\infty \mu_v(\omega) z_2(\omega,t) d\omega, \\ \mu_v(\omega) = \frac{\sin(v\pi)}{\pi\omega^v} \end{cases} \tag{28}$$

$$\begin{cases} \frac{\partial z_3(\omega,t)}{\partial t} = -\omega z_3(\omega,t) + \sigma(i_q - w) - Sat(T_l) \\ w = \int_0^\infty \mu_v(\omega) z_3(\omega,t) d\omega, \\ \mu_v(\omega) = \frac{\sin(v\pi)}{\pi\omega^v} \end{cases} \tag{29}$$

□

Consider two Lyapunov functions. $V_1(\omega,t) = p_1 z_1^2 + p_2 z_2^2 + p_3 z_3^2$ is the monochromic Lyapunov function based on the elementary frequency, and the other Lyapunov function $V(t)$ is the sum of all the monochromatic $V_1(t)$s with the weight function $\mu_v(\omega)$:

$$V = \frac{1}{2}\sum_{i=1}^{3}\int_0^\infty \mu_v(\omega)p_i z_i(\omega,t)^2 d\omega. \tag{30}$$

It can easily be derived from Equation (30) that

$$\frac{dV}{dt} = \sum_{i=1}^{3}\int_0^\infty \mu_v(\omega)p_i z_i(\omega,t)\frac{\partial z_i(\omega,t)}{\partial t}d\omega \tag{31}$$

Simplifying Equation (30),

$$\begin{aligned}
&\tfrac{dV}{dt} = \int_0^\infty \mu_v(\omega)p_1 z_1(\omega,t)\tfrac{\partial z_1(\omega,t)}{\partial t}d\omega \\
&+\int_0^\infty \mu_v(\omega)p_2 z_2(\omega,t)\tfrac{\partial z_2(\omega,t)}{\partial t}d\omega + \int_0^\infty \mu_v(\omega)p_3 z_3(\omega,t)\tfrac{\partial z_3(\omega,t)}{\partial t}d\omega
\end{aligned} \tag{32}$$

Substituting Equations (27)–(29) into Equation (32), we have

$$\begin{aligned}
&\tfrac{dV}{dt} = \int_0^\infty \mu_v(\omega)p_1 z_1(\omega,t)\big(-\omega z_1(\omega,t) + Sat(u_d) - \delta i_d + i_q w\big)d\omega \\
&+\int_0^\infty \mu_v(\omega)p_2 z_2(\omega,t)\big(-\omega z_2(\omega,t) + Sat(u_q) - i_q - i_d w + \gamma w\big)d\omega \\
&+\int_0^\infty \mu_v(\omega)p_3 z_3(\omega,t)\big(-\omega z_3(\omega,t) + \sigma(i_q - w) - Sat(T_l)\big)d\omega
\end{aligned} \tag{33}$$

This can be rewritten as

$$\begin{aligned}
&\tfrac{dV}{dt} = \int_0^\infty -\omega\mu_v(\omega)\{p_1 z_1^2(\omega,t) + p_2 z_2^2(\omega,t) + p_3 z_3^2(\omega,t)\}d\omega \\
&+\int_0^\infty \mu_v(\omega)p_1 z_1(\omega,t)d\omega\big(Sat(u_d) - \delta i_d + i_q w\big) \\
&+\int_0^\infty \mu_v(\omega)p_2 z_2(\omega,t)d\omega\big(Sat(u_q) - i_q - i_d w + \gamma w\big) \\
&+\int_0^\infty \mu_v(\omega)p_3 z_3(\omega,t)d\omega\big(\sigma(i_q - w) - Sat(T_l)\big)
\end{aligned} \tag{34}$$

Simplifying Equation (34), we have

$$\begin{aligned}
&\tfrac{dV}{dt} = \int_0^\infty -\omega\mu_v(\omega)\{p_1 z_1^2(\omega,t) + p_2 z_2^2(\omega,t) + p_3 z_3^2(\omega,t)\}d\omega \\
&+p_1 i_d\big(Sat(u_d) - \delta i_d + i_q w\big) + p_2 i_q\big(Sat(u_q) - i_q - i_d w + \gamma w\big) \\
&+p_3 w\big(\sigma(i_q - w) - Sat(T_l)\big)
\end{aligned} \tag{35}$$

Classifying Equation (35), it can be presented as

$$\begin{aligned}
&\tfrac{dV}{dt} = \int_0^\infty -\omega\mu_v(\omega)\{p_1 z_1^2(\omega,t) + p_2 z_2^2(\omega,t) + p_3 z_3^2(\omega,t)\}d\omega \\
&-\left\{p_1\delta i_d^2 + p_2 i_q^2 + p_3\sigma w^2\right\} \\
&+\big(p_1 i_d Sat(u_d) + p_1 i_d i_q w + p_2 i_q Sat(u_q) - p_2 i_q i_d w + p_2\gamma w i_q + p_3 w\sigma i_q - p_3 w Sat(T_l)\big)
\end{aligned} \tag{36}$$

The first and the second items of Equation (36) are negative definite since $\omega > 0$, $\mu_{vi} > 0$, and for the third term, we must consider two cases. The first case is when the saturation element is in the linear domain, $Sat(r) = r$, this means that there is no limitation on control; then the third term of Equation (36) can be rewritten as follows:

$$p_1 i_d u_d + (p_1 - p_2) i_d i_q w + p_2 i_q u_q + (p_2 \gamma + p_3 \sigma) w i_q - p_3 w T_l \leq 0 \tag{37}$$

If Equation (37) is negative, then the stability condition is satisfied in the linear case.

If there exists the limitation of saturation, then the third term of Equation (36) is as follows:

$$p_1 i_d Sat(u_d) + (p_1 - p_2) i_d i_q w + p_2 i_q Sat(u_q) + (p_2 \gamma + p_3 \sigma) w i_q - p_3 w Sat(T_l) \tag{38}$$

Based on Lemma 1, we have

$$\begin{aligned} & p_1 i_d (k_1 + k_1^{-1} Sat^2(u_d)) + (p_1 - p_2) i_d i_q w + p_2 i_q \left(k_2 + k_2^{-1} Sat^2(u_q)\right) \\ & + (p_2 \gamma + p_3 \sigma) w i_q - p_3 w (k_3 + k_3^{-1} Sat^2(T_l)) \end{aligned} \tag{39}$$

Considering the three assumptions in Equations (9)–(11),

$$\begin{aligned} & p_1 i_d \left(k_1 + k_1^{-1} A^2\right) + (p_1 - p_2) i_d i_q w + p_2 i_q \left(k_2 + k_2^{-1} B^2\right) \\ & + (p_2 \gamma + p_3 \sigma) w i_q - p_3 w \left(k_3 + k_3^{-1} C^2\right) \leq 0 \end{aligned} \tag{40}$$

Equation (40) is negative until the stability condition holds. Thus, the proof is complete.

3.3. Rate Limitations

Rate limitation is a crucial aspect of control engineering, involving constraints on how quickly a system can change states or execute commands. Addressing rate limitations is essential for designing controllers that ensure stable and precise system responses. Research in this area is vital for improving control strategies and advancing control theory, leading to more adaptable systems in various real-world scenarios. Therefore, the study focuses on systems with up to two rate limitations as follows:

$$\begin{cases} {}^{C}D_t^{v} i_d = u_d - \delta i_d + i_q w, & \| \dot{u_d} \| \leqslant c_d \\ {}^{C}D_t^{v} i_q = u_q - i_q - i_d w + \gamma w, & \| \dot{u_q} \| \leqslant c_q \ ,0 < v < 1 \\ {}^{C}D_t^{v} w = \sigma(i_q - w) - T_l, & \| \dot{T_l} \| \leqslant c_T \end{cases} \tag{41}$$

where c_d, c_q, and c_T are positive numbers that show rate limitation in specific inputs.

In the following, we present some theorems that consider the FOBLDCM system subject to rate limitations.

Theorem 5. *The system described in Equation (41) can achieve global stability at the equilibrium point if the desired controller satisfies the following inequality:*

$$(i_d + c_d sgn(\dot{u}_d)) u_d + (i_q + c_q sgn(\dot{u}_q)) u_q + (\gamma + \sigma) w i_q - \left(w - c_T sgn\left(\dot{T}_l\right)\right) T_l \leq 0. \tag{42}$$

where u_d, u_q, and T_l are the control inputs and c_d, c_q, and c_T are, respectively, their rate limitations.

By substituting this controller into Equation (41) and satisfying the inequality constraint given by Equation (42), we can ensure the desired stability property.

Note 2. *Note 1 is satisfied for Theorem 5.*

Proof. We can alternatively consider a new Lyapunov candidate $V(t)$, which is defined as the sum of all the monochromatic functions $V_1(t)$ weighted by the function $\mu_v(\omega)$ and another functions as follows:

$$V = \frac{1}{2}\sum_{i=1}^{3}\int_0^\infty \mu_v(\omega)z_i(\omega,t)^2 d\omega + \frac{1}{2}\left(u_q^2 + u_d^2 + T_l^2\right) \tag{43}$$

It can easily be derived from Equation (43) that

$$\frac{dV}{dt} = \sum_{i=1}^{3}\int_0^\infty \mu_v(\omega)z_i(\omega,t)\frac{\partial z_i(\omega,t)}{\partial t}d\omega + \left(\dot{u_q}u_q + \dot{u_d}u_d + \dot{T_l}T_l\right) \tag{44}$$

Simplifying Equation (44),

$$\begin{aligned}
&\tfrac{dV}{dt} = \int_0^\infty \mu_v(\omega)z_1(\omega,t)\tfrac{\partial z_1(\omega,t)}{\partial t}d\omega \\
&+ \int_0^\infty \mu_v(\omega)z_2(\omega,t)\tfrac{\partial z_2(\omega,t)}{\partial t}d\omega + \int_0^\infty \mu_v(\omega)z_3(\omega,t)\tfrac{\partial z_3(\omega,t)}{\partial t}d\omega \\
&+\dot{u}_q u_q + \dot{u}_d u_d + \dot{T}_l T_l
\end{aligned} \tag{45}$$

Substituting Equations (14)–(16) into Equation (45), we have

$$\begin{aligned}
&\tfrac{dV}{dt} = \int_0^\infty \mu_v(\omega)z_1(\omega,t)(-\omega z_1(\omega,t) + u_d - \delta i_d + i_q w)d\omega \\
&+ \int_0^\infty \mu_v(\omega)z_2(\omega,t)(-\omega z_2(\omega,t) + u_q - i_q - i_d w + \gamma w)d\omega \\
&+ \int_0^\infty \mu_v(\omega)z_3(\omega,t)(-\omega z_3(\omega,t) + \sigma(i_q - w) - T_l)d\omega \\
&+\dot{u_q}u_q + \dot{u_d}u_d + \dot{T_l}T_l
\end{aligned} \tag{46}$$

Applying the rate limitation, we have

$$\begin{aligned}
&\tfrac{dV}{dt} \leqslant \int_0^\infty -\omega\mu_v(\omega)\{z_1^2(\omega,t) + z_2^2(\omega,t) + z_3^2(\omega,t)\}d\omega \\
&+ \int_0^\infty \mu_v(\omega)z_1(\omega,t)d\omega(u_d - \delta i_d + i_q w) \\
&+ \int_0^\infty \mu_v(\omega)z_2(\omega,t)d\omega(u_q - i_q - i_d w + \gamma w) \\
&+ \int_0^\infty \mu_v(\omega)z_3(\omega,t)d\omega(\sigma(i_q - w) - T_l) \\
&c_q sgn(\dot{u}_q)u_q + c_d sgn(\dot{u}_d)u_d + c_T sgn\left(\dot{T}_l\right)T_l
\end{aligned} \tag{47}$$

Simplifying Equation (47), we have

$$\begin{aligned}
&\tfrac{dV}{dt} \leqslant \int_0^\infty -\omega\mu_v(\omega)\{z_1^2(\omega,t) + z_2^2(\omega,t) + z_3^2(\omega,t)\}d\omega \\
&+i_d(u_d - \delta i_d + i_q w) + i_q(u_q - i_q - i_d w + \gamma w) \\
&+w(\sigma(i_q - w) - T_l) \\
&c_q sgn(\dot{u}_q)u_q + c_d sgn(\dot{u}_d)u_d + c_T sgn\left(\dot{T}_l\right)T_l
\end{aligned} \tag{48}$$

Classifying Equation (48), it can be presented as

$$\begin{aligned}&\tfrac{dV}{dt} \leqslant \int_0^\infty -\omega\mu_v(\omega)\{z_1^2(\omega,t)+z_2^2(\omega,t)+z_3^2(\omega,t)\}d\omega\\&-\left\{\delta i_d^2+i_q^2+\sigma w^2\right\}+\{((i_d+c_d sgn(\dot{u}_d))u_d+\\&(i_q+c_q sgn(\dot{u}_q))u_q+(\gamma+\sigma)wi_q-\left(w-c_T sgn\left(\dot{T}_l\right)\right)T_l)\}\end{aligned} \tag{49}$$

The first and second terms of (49) are negative definite due to $\omega \geq 0$, $\mu_{v_i} > 0$, and $\varepsilon_i > 0$. The third term must be negative semi-definite to satisfy the stability condition $\frac{dV}{dt} < -\omega V$. Therefore, the true states will tend to zero and the FOBLDCM will be asymptotically stable. Thus, the proof is complete. □

Corollary 1. *The system described in Equation (41) can achieve global stability at the equilibrium point if there are three positive numbers, k_1, k_2, and k_3, and the following inequality is satisfied:*

$$\left(i_d+\left(k_1c_d^2+k_1^{-1}\right)\right)u_d+\left(i_q+\left(k_2c_q^2+k_2^{-1}\right)\right)u_q+(\gamma+\sigma)wi_q-(w-(k_3c_T^2+k_3^2))T_l \leq 0 \tag{50}$$

where u_d, u_q, and T_l are the control inputs and c_d, c_q, and c_T are, respectively, their rate limitations.

Proof. The proof is similar to Theorem 5; the third term of Equation (49) based on Lemma 1 can be rewritten as

$$\begin{aligned}&(i_d+c_d sgn(\dot{u}_d))u_d+(i_q+c_q sgn(\dot{u}_q))u_q+(\gamma+\sigma)wi_q-\left(w-c_T sgn\left(\dot{T}_l\right)\right)T_l)=\\&\left(i_d+\left(k_1c_d^2+k_1^{-1}\right)\right)u_d+\left(i_q+\left(k_2c_q^2+k_2^{-1}\right)\right)u_q+(\gamma+\sigma)wi_q-(w-(k_3c_T^2+k_3^2))T_l \leq 0\end{aligned} \tag{51}$$

The proof is completed. □

3.4. Saturation and Rate Limitation Simultaneously

In this section, we consider saturation and rate limitations in the input control simultaneously. We conduct a stability analysis and derive the stability conditions under these limitations.

Theorem 6. *Consider system (8) under assumptions (9)–(11). If there exist six positive numbers, $k_1, \ldots k_6$, such that Equations (52) and (53) are satisfied simultaneously, then the closed-loop system is globally exponentially stable at the zero equilibrium point:*

$$\begin{aligned}&(p_1i_d+c_d sgn(\dot{u}_d))u_d+(p_1-p_2)i_di_qw+(p_2i_q+c_q sgn(\dot{u}_q))u_q+(p_2\gamma+p_3\sigma)wi_q\\&+\left(c_T sgn\left(\dot{T}_l\right)-p_3w\right)T_l \leq 0\end{aligned} \tag{52}$$

$$\begin{aligned}&p_1i_d\left(k_1+k_1^{-1}A^2\right)+(p_1-p_2)i_di_qw+p_2i_q\left(k_2+k_2^{-1}B^2\right)+(p_2\gamma+p_3\sigma)wi_q\\&-p_3w\left(k_3+k_3^{-1}C^2\right)+c_q\left(k_4+k_4^{-1}B^2\right)+c_d\left(k_5+k_5^{-1}A^2\right)+c_T\left(k_5+k_6^{-1}C^2\right) \leq 0\end{aligned} \tag{53}$$

where k_i and p_i, $i = 1,2,3$ are positive scalars and A, B, and C satisfy assumptions (9)–(11).

Note 3. *Note 1 is satisfied for this theorem.*

Proof. Consider a Lyapunov function as follows:

$$V=\frac{1}{2}\sum_{i=1}^{3}\int_0^\infty \mu_v(\omega)p_iz_i(\omega,t)^2d\omega.+\frac{1}{2}\left(u_q^2+u_d^2+T_l^2\right) \tag{54}$$

It can easily be derived from Equation (54) that

$$\frac{dV}{dt} = \sum_{i=1}^{3} \int_0^\infty \mu_v(\omega) p_i z_i(\omega,t) \frac{\partial z_i(\omega,t)}{\partial t} d\omega + \left(\dot{u_q} u_q + \dot{u_d} u_d + \dot{T_l} T_l\right) \tag{55}$$

Simplifying Equation (55),

$$\begin{aligned} &\tfrac{dV}{dt} = \int_0^\infty \mu_v(\omega) p_1 z_1(\omega,t) \tfrac{\partial z_1(\omega,t)}{\partial t} d\omega + \int_0^\infty \mu_v(\omega) p_2 z_2(\omega,t) \tfrac{\partial z_2(\omega,t)}{\partial t} d\omega + \\ &\int_0^\infty \mu_v(\omega) p_3 z_3(\omega,t) \tfrac{\partial z_3(\omega,t)}{\partial t} d\omega + \left(\dot{u_q} u_q + \dot{u_d} u_d + \dot{T_l} T_l\right) \end{aligned} \tag{56}$$

Substituting Equations (27)–(29) into Equation (56), we have

$$\begin{aligned} &\tfrac{dV}{dt} = \int_0^\infty \mu_v(\omega) p_1 z_1(\omega,t) \left(-\omega z_1(\omega,t) + Sat(u_d) - \delta i_d + i_q w\right) d\omega \\ &+ \int_0^\infty \mu_v(\omega) p_2 z_2(\omega,t) \left(-\omega z_2(\omega,t) + Sat(u_q) - i_q - i_d w + \gamma w\right) d\omega \\ &+ \int_0^\infty \mu_v(\omega) p_3 z_3(\omega,t) \left(-\omega z_3(\omega,t) + \sigma(i_q - w) - Sat(T_l)\right) d\omega + \left(\dot{u_q} u_q + \dot{u_d} u_d + \dot{T_l} T_l\right) \end{aligned} \tag{57}$$

This can be rewritten as

$$\begin{aligned} &\tfrac{dV}{dt} = \int_0^\infty -\omega \mu_v(\omega) \left\{ p_1 z_1^2(\omega,t) + p_2 z_2^2(\omega,t) + p_3 z_3^2(\omega,t) \right\} d\omega \\ &+ \int_0^\infty \mu_v(\omega) p_1 z_1(\omega,t) d\omega \left(Sat(u_d) - \delta i_d + i_q w\right) \\ &+ \int_0^\infty \mu_v(\omega) p_2 z_2(\omega,t) d\omega \left(Sat(u_q) - i_q - i_d w + \gamma w\right) \\ &+ \int_0^\infty \mu_v(\omega) p_3 z_3(\omega,t) d\omega \left(\sigma(i_q - w) - Sat(T_l)\right) + \left(\dot{u_q} u_q + \dot{u_d} u_d + \dot{T_l} T_l\right) \end{aligned} \tag{58}$$

Simplifying Equation (58), we have

$$\begin{aligned} &\tfrac{dV}{dt} = \int_0^\infty -\omega \mu_v(\omega) \left\{ p_1 z_1^2(\omega,t) + p_2 z_2^2(\omega,t) + p_3 z_3^2(\omega,t) \right\} d\omega \\ &+ p_1 i_d \left(Sat(u_d) - \delta i_d + i_q w\right) + p_2 i_q \left(Sat(u_q) - i_q - i_d w + \gamma w\right) \\ &+ p_3 w \left(\sigma(i_q - w) - Sat(T_l)\right) + \left(\dot{u_q} u_q + \dot{u_d} u_d + \dot{T_l} T_l\right) \end{aligned} \tag{59}$$

Classifying Equation (59) and applying the rate limitation, we have

$$\begin{aligned} &\tfrac{dV}{dt} = \int_0^\infty -\omega \mu_v(\omega) \left\{ p_1 z_1^2(\omega,t) + p_2 z_2^2(\omega,t) + p_3 z_3^2(\omega,t) \right\} d\omega - \left\{ p_1 \delta i_d^2 + p_2 i_q^2 + p_3 \sigma w^2 \right\} \\ &+ \left(p_1 i_d Sat(u_d) + p_1 i_d i_q w + p_2 i_q Sat(u_q) - p_2 i_q i_d w + p_2 \gamma w i_q + p_3 w \sigma i_q - p_3 w Sat(T_l)\right) + \\ &c_q sgn(\dot{u}_q) u_q + c_d sgn(\dot{u}_d) u_d + c_T sgn\left(\dot{T_l}\right) T_l \end{aligned} \tag{60}$$

Based on Lemma 1, we have three positive scalars, k_1, k_2, and k_3, that satisfy the following equation:

$$\begin{aligned} &\tfrac{dV}{dt} = \int_0^\infty -\omega \mu_v(\omega) \left\{ p_1 z_1^2(\omega,t) + p_2 z_2^2(\omega,t) + p_3 z_3^2(\omega,t) \right\} d\omega - \left\{ p_1 \delta i_d^2 + p_2 i_q^2 + p_3 \sigma w^2 \right\} \\ &+ \left(p_1 i_d Sat(u_d) + p_1 i_d i_q w + p_2 i_q Sat(u_q) - p_2 i_q i_d w + p_2 \gamma w i_q + p_3 w \sigma i_q - p_3 w Sat(T_l)\right) \\ &\left(c_q sgn(\dot{u}_q) u_q + c_d sgn(\dot{u}_d) u_d + c_T sgn\left(\dot{T_l}\right) T_l\right) \leq 0 \end{aligned} \tag{61}$$

The first and the second items of Equation (61) are negative definite since $\omega > 0$, $\mu_{vi} > 0$, and for the third term, we must consider two cases. The first case is when the saturation element is in the linear domain, $Sat(r) = r$, this means that there is no limitation on control; then the third term of Equation (61) can be rewritten as follows:

$$\begin{aligned}&(p_1 i_d + c_d sgn(\dot{u}_d))u_d + (p_1 - p_2)i_d i_q w + (p_2 i_q + c_q sgn(\dot{u}_q))u_q + (p_2\gamma + p_3\sigma)wi_q + \\ &\left(c_T sgn\left(\dot{T}_l\right) - p_3 w\right)T_l \le 0\end{aligned} \tag{62}$$

If Equation (62) is negative, then the stability condition is satisfied in the linear case.

If there exists the limitation of saturation, then the third and fourth terms of Equation (61) are as follows:

$$\begin{aligned}&p_1 i_d Sat(u_d) + (p_1 - p_2)i_d i_q w + p_2 i_q Sat(u_q) + (p_2\gamma + p_3\sigma)wi_q - p_3 w Sat(T_l) + \\ &\left(c_q sgn(\dot{u}_q)u_q + c_d sgn(\dot{u}_d)u_d + c_T sgn\left(\dot{T}_l\right)T_l\right) \le 0\end{aligned} \tag{63}$$

In the worst case, when saturation control occurs, e.g., u_d could not violate $Sat(u_d)$, then the above equation must be rewritten as

$$\begin{aligned}&p_1 i_d Sat(u_d) + (p_1 - p_2)i_d i_q w + p_2 i_q Sat(u_q) + (p_2\gamma + p_3\sigma)wi_q - p_3 w Sat(T_l) + \\ &\left(c_q sgn(\dot{u}_q)Sat(u_q) + c_d sgn(\dot{u}_d)Sat(u_d) + c_T sgn\left(\dot{T}_l\right)Sat(T_l) \le 0\right.\end{aligned} \tag{64}$$

Based on Lemma 1, we have

$$\begin{aligned}&p_1 i_d\left(k_1 + k_1^{-1}Sat^2(u_d)\right) + (p_1 - p_2)i_d i_q w + p_2 i_q\left(k_2 + k_2^{-1}Sat^2(u_q)\right) \\ &+(p_2\gamma + p_3\sigma)wi_q - p_3 w\left(k_3 + k_3^{-1}Sat^2(T_l)\right) + \\ &c_q\left(k_4 + k_4^{-1}Sat^2(u_q)\right) + c_d\left(k_5 + k_5^{-1}Sat^2(u_d)\right) + c_T\left(k_5 + k_6^{-1}Sat^2(T_l)\right) \le 0\end{aligned} \tag{65}$$

Considering the three assumptions of Equations (9)–(11),

$$\begin{aligned}&p_1 i_d\left(k_1 + k_1^{-1}A^2\right) + (p_1 - p_2)i_d i_q w + p_2 i_q\left(k_2 + k_2^{-1}B^2\right) + (p_2\gamma + p_3\sigma)wi_q \\ &-p_3 w\left(k_3 + k_3^{-1}C^2\right) + c_q\left(k_4 + k_4^{-1}B^2\right) + c_d\left(k_5 + k_5^{-1}A^2\right) + c_T\left(k_5 + k_6^{-1}C^2\right) \le 0\end{aligned} \tag{66}$$

Equation (66) is negative until the stability condition holds. Thus, the proof is complete. □

Corollary 2. *Consider system (8) under assumptions (9)–(11). If there exist nine positive numbers, $k_1, \ldots k_9$, such that Equations (67) and (68) are satisfied simultaneously, then the closed-loop system is globally exponentially stable at the zero equilibrium point:*

$$\begin{aligned}&\left(p_1 i_d + \left(k_7 c_d^2 + k_7^{-1}\right)\right)u_d + (p_1 - p_2)i_d i_q w + \left(p_2 i_q + \left(k_8 c_q^2 + k_8^{-1}\right)\right)u_q + \\ &(p_2\gamma + p_3\sigma)wi_q + \left(\left(k_9 c_T^2 + k_9^{-1}\right) - p_3 w\right)T_l \le 0\end{aligned} \tag{67}$$

$$\begin{aligned}&p_1 i_d\left(k_1 + k_1^{-1}A^2\right) + (p_1 - p_2)i_d i_q w + p_2 i_q\left(k_2 + k_2^{-1}B^2\right) + (p_2\gamma + p_3\sigma)wi_q \\ &-p_3 w\left(k_3 + k_3^{-1}C^2\right) + c_q\left(k_4 + k_4^{-1}B^2\right) + c_d\left(k_5 + k_5^{-1}A^2\right) + c_T\left(k_5 + k_6^{-1}C^2\right) \le 0\end{aligned} \tag{68}$$

where k_i and p_i, $i = 1, 2, 3$ are positive scalars and A, B, and C satisfy assumptions (9)–(11).

Note 4. *Note 1 is satisfied for this theorem.*

Proof. The proof is similar to Theorem 6 based on Lemma 1. □

Note 5. *In certain applications, it is crucial to utilize a single input. This is particularly relevant when contemplating the obtained theorems by adjusting a single input. We suggest employing straightforward controllers that involve only one state variable. This implies the need for just one sensor instead of the usual requirement of two or more in practical applications.*

4. Numerical Simulations and Performance Evaluation

In this section, we first design a set of controllers that satisfy the stability conditions established by the theorems presented in this study, particularly those with single sufficient conditions, such as Theorems 3 and 5 in Sections 3.1 and 3.3. These controllers are then validated through comprehensive numerical simulations conducted on the FOBLDCM model.

To assess the performance of the proposed control strategies, we employ the following quantitative criteria:

- Integral of squared error (ISE): Measures the accumulated squared tracking error over the simulation time for each state variable, reflecting the long-term tracking performance of the system.
- Root mean square error (RMSE): Evaluates the average deviation between the system outputs and their reference trajectories, providing a normalized metric for comparison.
- Control energy: Represents the total energy consumed by the control inputs, calculated as the integral of the squared control signal, and is used to evaluate the energy efficiency of the controller.
- Maximum control effort ($u_{\max}$): Denotes the peak value of the control input, serving as an indicator of actuator feasibility and the extent of input constraints such as saturation.

These criteria enable a fair and systematic comparison between different control approaches, particularly in the presence of input constraints. The numerical results for each case are presented and discussed in the following subsections.

After evaluating controllers designed based on single-condition theorems, we also propose and implement controllers that satisfy multi-condition theorems, such as those involving composite Lyapunov approaches.

Overall, the simulations are carried out across three general control scenarios:

1. Scenario 1: Control without any actuator limitations;
2. Scenario 2: Control with rate limitation constraint only;
3. Scenario 3: Control under both saturation and rate limitation constraints simultaneously.

Scenario 1: Control Without Any Actuator Limitations

Table 1 presents a set of controllers based on Theorem 3. This set of controllers is designed without any constraints. We offer a range of controllers, including single-input, double-input, and triple-input controllers, tailored to meet different design requirements and conditions.

Table 1. Some desired controllers satisfying Theorem 3.

Input	Design Controller	
Single Input	$\begin{cases} u_d = 0 \\ u_q = 0 \\ T_l = (\sigma+\gamma)i_q \end{cases}$	$\begin{cases} u_d = 0 \\ u_q = -(\sigma+\gamma)w \\ T_l = 0 \end{cases}$
Double Input	$\begin{cases} u_d = 0 \\ u_q = -\sigma w \\ T_l = \gamma i_q \end{cases}$	$\begin{cases} u_d = 0 \\ u_q = -\gamma w \\ T_l = \sigma i_q \end{cases}$
Triple Input	$\begin{cases} u_d = -i_q \\ u_q = i_d \\ T_l = (\gamma+\sigma)i_q \end{cases}$	$\begin{cases} u_d = i_q \\ u_q = -i_d \\ T_l = (\gamma+\sigma)i_q \end{cases}$

Table 1. *Cont.*

Input	Design Controller	
Triple Input	$\begin{cases} u_d = i_q \\ u_q = -(i_d + (\sigma+\gamma-1)w) \\ T_l = i_q \end{cases}$	$\begin{cases} u_d = w \\ u_q = w \\ T_l = i_d + (\gamma+\sigma+1)i_q \end{cases}$

First Scenario: we consider the $\sigma = 4$, we choose $v = 0.97$ as the FO and an initial condition of $[10, 3, -12]^T$. Based on the stability conditions derived from Theorem 3, the controller needs to satisfy the inequality $i_d u_d + i_q u_q + \gamma w i_q + w\sigma i_q - wT_l \leq 0$ in the absence of limitations. One possible choice for the controller is $u_d = -i_q$, $u_q = i_d$, and $T_l = (\gamma+\sigma)i_q$. Figures 5 and 6 illustrate the behavior of the closed-loop system and the phase plot of the FOBLDCM for the chosen FO $v = 0.97$. It can be observed that after 4 s, the states of the FOBLDCM converge to the equilibrium point of the system. This demonstrates the effectiveness of the designed controller in achieving stability and graceful behavior of the FOBLDCM.

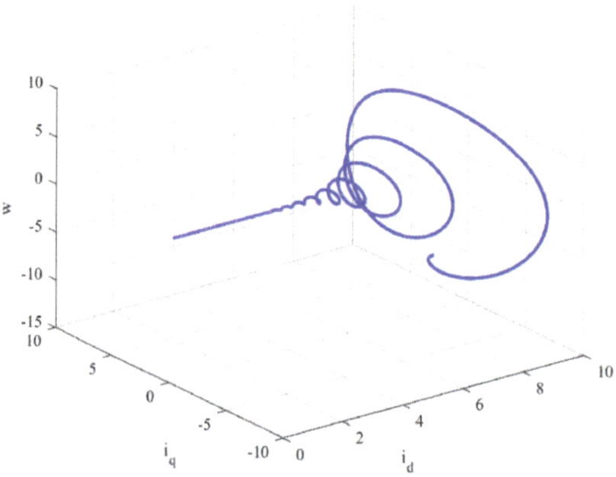

Figure 5. w, i_d, and i_q for the closed-loop FOBLDCM when $v = 0.97$.

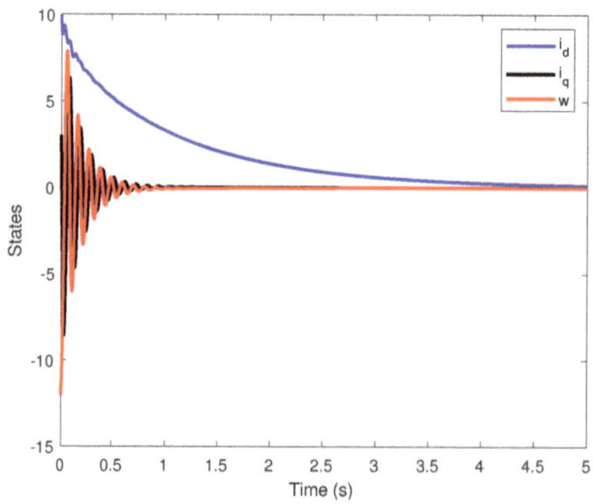

Figure 6. Phase plot of i_d, i_q, and w of the closed-loop FOBLDCM for $v = 0.97$.

To benchmark the effectiveness of the proposed control framework, we perform a comparative analysis against an existing FOBLDCM control method reported in the literature. Specifically, the study in [39] addresses the stabilization of an FOBLDCM without considering any actuator constraints. The control law proposed in that work is

$u_q = -80\omega$, which directly regulates the mechanical subsystem of the motor. Among the various controller configurations developed in the present work, the closest in structure to the method in [39] is given by $u_q = -(\sigma + \gamma)\omega = -59\omega$, highlighting a similar yet more energy-efficient approach.

To facilitate a fair and quantitative comparison, we evaluate several standard performance indices, including ISE, RMSE, control energy, and the maximum control input $u_{\max}$. The results are summarized in Table 2. As shown, our proposed controller demonstrates superior performance in terms of lower control energy and reduced maximum control effort, while maintaining comparable or improved tracking accuracy across all state variables. These results underscore the practicality and robustness of the proposed controller under both constrained and unconstrained input scenarios.

Table 2. Performance indices for comparison with Ref. [39].

Performance Indices	ISE	RMSE	Control Energy	$u_{\max}$
Controller from [39]	$\text{ISE}_{i_d} = 76.063$ $\text{ISE}_{i_q} = 318.447$ $\text{ISE}_w = 76.063$	$\text{RMSE}_{i_d} = 0.019$ $\text{RMSE}_{i_q} = 0.0064$ $\text{RMSE}_w = 0.0016$	2.7153×10^5	$u_{i_q} = 96$
Our proposed controller (close to [39])	$\text{ISE}_{i_d} = 81.945$ $\text{ISE}_{i_q} = 291.604$ $\text{ISE}_w = 78.002$	$\text{RMSE}_{i_d} = 0.0173$ $\text{RMSE}_{i_q} = 0.000229$ $\text{RMSE}_w = 0.0012$	1.8321×10^5	$u_{i_q} = 70.8$
Proposed controller Scenario 1	$\text{ISE}_{i_d} = 66.685$ $\text{ISE}_{i_q} = 70.044$ $\text{ISE}_w = 78.953$	$\text{RMSE}_{i_d} = 0.081$ $\text{RMSE}_{i_q} = 0.084$ $\text{RMSE}_w = 0.088$	2.4383×10^5	$u_{i_d} = 2.27$ $u_{i_q} = 1$ $u_w = 177$

Second scenario: In the second scenario, we consider the case where only rate limitations exist. Based on Theorem 5 and Note 2, we have $u_d = w$, $u_q = 0$, and $T_l = c_d \,\text{sgn}(\dot{w}) + i_d + (\gamma + \sigma)i_q$.

Implementing $c_T = 0$, $c_q = 10$, and $c_d = 10$ in the proposed controller for the FOBLDCM yields encouraging outcomes, as evidenced by the convergence of the closed-loop system behaviors illustrated in Figures 7 and 8 in the presence of rate limitations. The rapid stabilizing of the system, coupled with the manifestation of stability, underscores the efficacy and efficiency of the applied control strategy, aligning with the desired performance characteristics for practical applications.

Table 3 presents several desired controllers that satisfy Theorem 5 and Note 1. This table also offers various controllers based on the available sensors or specific applications. It includes a new column labeled "rate limitation" where $c_d \neq 0$. It is essential to note that when $c_d = 0$, Note 1 is not satisfied. This is because the polynomial $(\sigma + \gamma)i_q w$ lacks the presence of i_d. Consequently, for the designed controller, i_d must appear in the denominator to meet the requirements of Note 1. Therefore, Note 1 is not satisfied in this case.

Third scenario: We consider both saturation and rate limitations in the input control. Under the previous conditions, the closed-loop system is unstable when saturation and rate limitations are applied to the input control. We assume that $A = B = C = 10$ and the initial state is $(1, 3, -1.2)$. By applying Theorem 6 and considering Corollary 2, we utilize the Matlab function `Fmincon` to achieve stability. We apply the control input as follows: $u_d = 0$, $u_q = 0$, and $T_l = -(\sigma + \gamma)u_q w/(c_T^2 + 1 - w) + 1$. This control input makes the closed-loop system asymptotically stable, and the states converge to zero. Figure 9 shows the time evolution of the state variables of the closed-loop system, while Figure 10 illustrates the input control. We deduce that the system can achieve stability even with saturation and rate limitations.

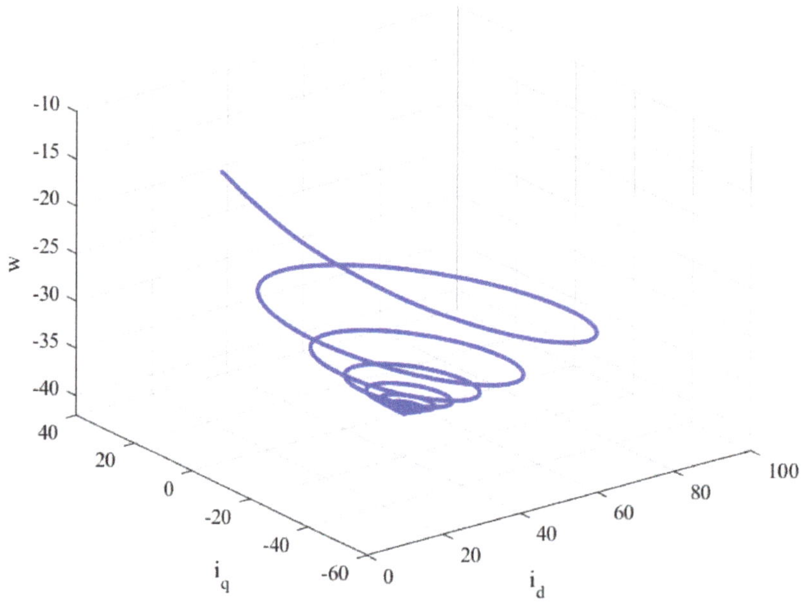

Figure 7. Phase plot of $i_d, i_q,$ and w of the closed-loop FOBLDCM for $v = 0.97$ in presence of rate limitations.

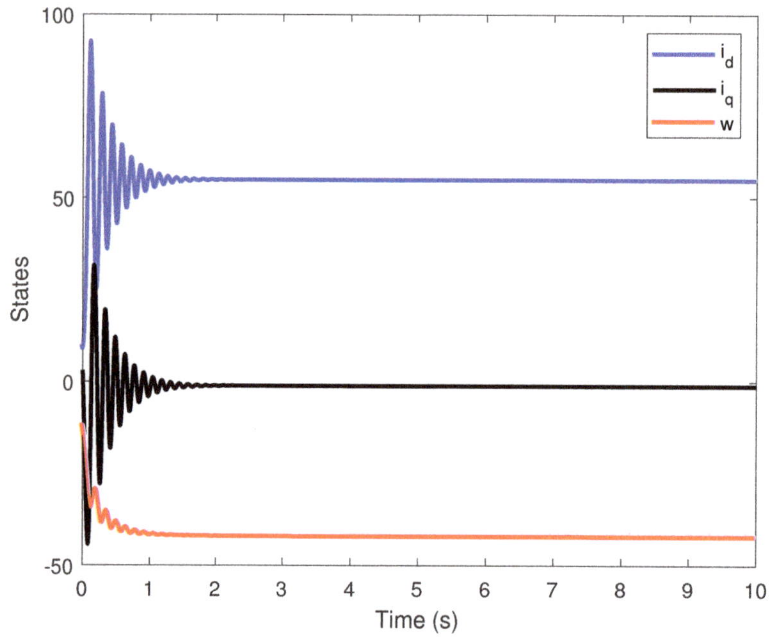

Figure 8. Time evolution of state variables $i_d, i_q,$ and w for the closed-loop FOBLDCM for $v = 0.97$ in presence of rate limitations.

Table 3. Some desired controllers satisfying Theorem 5.

Rate Limitation	Input	Design Controller
$c_T = 0$, $c_q \geqslant 0$, $c_d \geqslant 0$	Single Input	$\begin{cases} u_d = 0 \\ u_q = 0 \\ T_l = (\sigma + \gamma) i_q \end{cases}$
	Double Input	$\begin{cases} u_d = w \\ u_q = 0 \\ T_l = c_d sgn(\dot{w}) + i_d + (\gamma + \sigma) i_q \end{cases}$
	Triple Input	$\begin{cases} u_d = w \\ u_q = w \\ T_l = (\gamma + \sigma + 1) i_q + i_d + sgn(\dot{w})(c_q + c_d) \end{cases}$
$c_q = 0$, $c_d \geqslant 0$, $c_T \geqslant 0$	Single Input	$\begin{cases} u_d = 0 \\ T_l = 0 \\ u_q = -(\sigma + \gamma) w \end{cases}$
	Double Input	$\begin{cases} u_d = i_q \\ u_q = -\left(i_d + c_d sgn\left(\dot{i}_q\right)\right) - (\gamma + \sigma) w \\ T_l = 0 \end{cases}$
	Double Input	$\begin{cases} u_d = 0 \\ u_q = \left(w + c_T sgn\left(\dot{i}_q\right)\right) - (\gamma + \sigma) w \\ T_l = i_q \end{cases}$
	Triple Input	$\begin{cases} u_d = i_q \\ u_q = -i_d - (c_d + c_T) sgn\left(\dot{i}_q\right) - (\gamma + \sigma - 1) w \\ T_l = i_q \end{cases}$

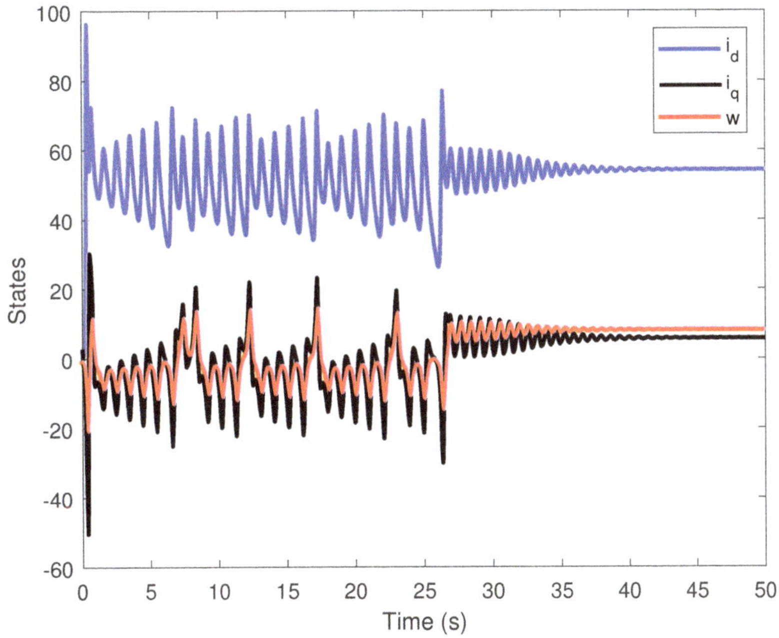

Figure 9. Time evolution of state variables i_d, i_q, and w for the closed-loop FOBLDCM for 0.99.

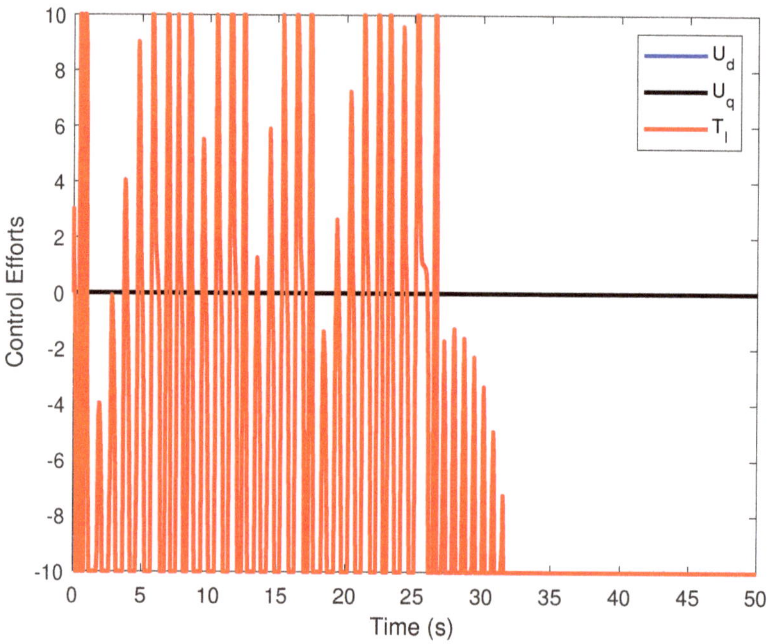

Figure 10. Input controls for the closed-loop FOBLDCM for 0.99.

These improved and extended simulation results provide strong evidence of the effectiveness of the proposed control approaches for the FOBLDCM.

Table 4 presents the performance indices for the third control scenario, where both input saturation and rate limitation are simultaneously imposed. The proposed controller demonstrates satisfactory tracking performance under these challenging constraints. Specifically, the ISE for the direct-axis current (i_d), quadrature-axis current (i_q), and angular speed (w) is kept within acceptable bounds, with $ISE_{i_d} = 2.65 \times 10^5$, $ISE_{i_q} = 1.075 \times 10^4$, and $ISE_w = 4.27 \times 10^4$, respectively. Furthermore, the RMSE indicates relatively smooth tracking with minimal steady-state deviation. The control energy remains moderate (6.63×10^5), highlighting the controller's efficiency in regulating the system without excessive actuation effort. Notably, the maximum control efforts ($u_{\max}$) remain within the saturated limits—$u_{i_d} = 0$, $u_{i_q} = 0$, and $u_w = 10$—demonstrating that the designed control law successfully respects both the amplitude and rate constraints while maintaining system stability and tracking accuracy.

Table 4. Performance indices for third scenario.

Performance Indices	ISE	RMSE	Control Energy	$u_{\max}$
Proposed controller Scenario 3	$\text{ISE}_{i_d} = 2.6524 \times 10^5$ $\text{ISE}_{i_q} = 1.075 \times 10^4$ $\text{ISE}_w = 4.2702 \times 10^4$	$\text{RMSE}_{i_d} = 50.2996$ $\text{RMSE}_{i_q} = 1.9848$ $\text{RMSE}_w = 1.0439$	6.63×10^5	$u_{i_d} = 0$ $u_{i_q} = 0$ $u_w = 10$

Although the overall performance is not as favorable as in scenario 1, this decline is directly attributed to the presence of two stringent nonlinear constraints—saturation and rate limitation—imposed concurrently. Nevertheless, the results still validate the effectiveness and robustness of the proposed Lyapunov-based approach under severe practical limitations, reinforcing its applicability in real-world systems where such constraints are unavoidable.

Comparison with the results obtained in [34] demonstrates several key distinctions, as highlighted below:

- Proposed set of controllers based on available sensors: This paper introduces a comprehensive set of controllers tailored to the available sensors. In contrast, Ref. [34] proposed only a feedback linear controller, which can be considered a subset of the more general controller set presented in this work.
- Simultaneous consideration of saturation and rate limitation on the controller: This study addresses the FOBLDCM under the simultaneous constraints of saturation and rate limitation on the controller. In comparison, Ref. [34] only considered saturation as a limitation without accounting for rate limitation. Furthermore, other valuable papers did not consider any constraints [17–19,23,24,39].
- Robust solution approach: The proposed results in this paper are derived using a presented novel Lyapunov candidate to establish novel stability conditions in the presence of rate limitations and saturated control inputs. On the other hand, Ref. [34] relied on estimations of the solutions to the given equations, which presents a less robust approach than the one presented in this paper.

Table 5 summarizes the above statements.

Table 5. Comparison of proposed work with related studies.

Feature	Proposed Work	[34]	[39]
Controller design based on sensor availability	Comprehensive set (single/double/triple input)	Only feedback linearization	Only feedback linearization
Constraints considered	Both saturation and rate limitation	Only saturation	No constraints
Stability analysis method	Lyapunov-based analytical approach	Estimation-based	Estimation-based
Robustness	High (based on derived sufficient conditions)	Moderate lack of rate-limit handling	Moderate lack of saturation and rate-limit handling

The achieved stability, convergence, and desired system behavior highlight the practical applicability and potential of the proposed methods in real-world applications. These findings contribute to the advancement of control techniques for FOBLDCMs, opening up new possibilities for their utilization in various domains.

5. Conclusions

This work addresses the stabilization problem of fractional-order chaotic brushless DC motors (FOBLDCMs) subject to input constraints, including saturation and rate limits, within the fractional domain $0 < v < 1$. The proposed approach overcomes the limitations of classical methods by developing a unified framework that explicitly incorporates actuator constraints into the control design process. The primary contributions of this research can be summarized as follows:

- Novel Lyapunov candidates: Dedicated Lyapunov functions are constructed for each control scenario—namely, unconstrained, saturated, rate-limited, and jointly constrained—by integrating both direct and indirect Lyapunov-based techniques tailored to fractional-order dynamics.
- **Input-constrained controller design:** Multiple controller configurations are derived based on the developed stability conditions, enabling practical implementation with reduced sensor dependencies through single-input, double-input, and triple-input

controller variants. To the best of our knowledge, this is the first study to simultaneously address both amplitude and rate constraints in the control design of FO chaotic systems.

- **Benchmark validation:** The effectiveness of the proposed framework is validated through extensive numerical simulations conducted on FO chaotic BLDCMs under varying degrees of nonlinear behavior and input limitations, providing a solid benchmark for future studies.

Practical significance: The proposed framework is particularly beneficial for precision motion control applications where BLDC motors are subjected to strict actuator limitations—common in electric vehicles, robotic manipulators, unmanned aerial vehicles (UAVs), and industrial automation. By explicitly considering actuator constraints, the designed controllers prevent performance degradation, avoid instability caused by saturation-induced limit cycles, and ensure safe motor operation, especially in embedded and energy-limited platforms.

Technological recommendations:

- *For manufacturers:* It is recommended to embed FO control logic and constraint-aware algorithms within motor control chips or firmware, enabling higher-fidelity performance in FO dynamic environments. Support for configurable constraint-aware control modules should be considered during motor drive design.
- *For system integrators and end users:* When selecting control algorithms for high-precision or safety-critical systems, priority should be given to those that explicitly handle rate and amplitude constraints. The use of adaptable multi-input controllers can provide significant performance benefits when sensor configurations are flexible.

In conclusion, this study offers a scalable, constraint-aware control strategy for a class of nonlinear FO systems, addressing both theoretical and practical challenges. Future work will focus on real implementation, robustness under parametric uncertainty, and experimental validation on physical motor platforms.

Author Contributions: Methodology, E.S.A.S.; software, E.S.A.S.; validation, E.S.A.S., N.P., and Y.C.; formal analysis, E.S.A.S.; investigation, N.P. and Y.C.; writing—original draft preparation, E.S.A.S.; writing—review and editing, N.P. and Y.C.; supervision, N.P. and Y.C.; project administration, N.P. and Y.C. All authors have read and agreed to the published version of the manuscript.

Funding: This research received no external funding.

Data Availability Statement: All data generated or analyzed during this study are included in this article.

Conflicts of Interest: The authors declare that they have no conflict of interest.

Abbreviations

The following abbreviations are used in this manuscript:

FOBLDCM	Fractional-order brushless DC motor
FC	Fractional calculus
FO	Fractional order
BLDCM	Brushless DC motor
PID	Proportional–integral–derivative
ADRC	Active disturbance rejection control
I&I	Immersion and Invariance
DSPs	Digital signal processors

ISE	Integral of squared error
RMSE	Root mean square error
UAVs	Unmanned aerial vehicles

References

1. Fu, H.; Wu, G.C.; Yang, G.; Huang, L.L. Fractional calculus with exponential memory. *Chaos Interdiscip. J. Nonlinear Sci.* **2021**, *31*, 031103. [CrossRef] [PubMed]
2. Wang, S.; Zhang, S. The global classical solution to compressible system with fractional viscous term. *Nonlinear Anal. Real World Appl.* **2024**, *75*, 103963. [CrossRef]
3. Jiang, K.; Liu, Z.; Zhou, L. Global existence and asymptotic dynamics in a 3D fractional chemotaxis system with singular sensitivity. *Nonlinear Anal. Real World Appl.* **2020**, *54*, 103103. [CrossRef]
4. Luo, H.; Tang, X. Ground state and multiple solutions for the fractional Schrödinger–Poisson system with critical Sobolev exponent. *Nonlinear Anal. Real World Appl.* **2018**, *42*, 24–52. [CrossRef]
5. Zhang, Y.; Li, J.; Zhu, S.; Zhao, H. Bifurcation and chaos detection of a fractional Duffingvan der Pol oscillator with two periodic excitations and distributed time delay. *Chaos Interdiscip. J. Nonlinear Sci.* **2023**, *33*, 083153. [CrossRef]
6. Tian, Q.; Yang, X.; Zhang, H.; Xu, D. An implicit robust numerical scheme with graded meshes for the modified Burgers model with nonlocal dynamic properties. *Comput. Appl. Math.* **2023**, *42*, 246. [CrossRef]
7. Alaviyan Shahri, E.S.; Alfi, A.; Tenreiro Machado, J.A. Robust stability and stabilization of uncertain fractional order systems subject to input saturation. *J. Vib. Control.* **2018**, *24*, 3676–3683. [CrossRef]
8. Chen, L.; Huang, C.; Liu, H.; Xia, Y. Anti-synchronization of a class of chaotic systems with application to Lorenz system: A unified analysis of the integer order and fractional order. *Mathematics* **2019**, *7*, 559. [CrossRef]
9. Li, C.; Chen, G. Chaos in the fractional order Chen system and its control. *Chaos Solitons Fractals* **2004**, *22*, 549–554. [CrossRef]
10. Lu, J.G. Chaotic dynamics of the fractional-order Lü system and its synchronization. *Phys. Lett. A* **2006**, *354*, 305–311. [CrossRef]
11. Rajagopal, K.; Vaidyanathan, S.; Karthikeyan, A.; Duraisamy, P. Dynamic analysis and chaos suppression in a fractional order brushless DC motor. *Electr. Eng.* **2017**, *99*, 721–733. [CrossRef]
12. Hemati, N. Strange attractors in brushless DC motors. *IEEE Trans. Circuits Syst. Fundam. Theory Appl.* **1994**, *41*, 40–45. [CrossRef]
13. Liu, D.; Zhou, G.; Liao, X. Global exponential stabilization for chaotic brushless DC motor with simpler controllers. *Trans. Inst. Meas. Control.* **2019**, *41*, 2678–2684. [CrossRef]
14. Faradja, P.; Qi, G. Analysis of multistability, hidden chaos and transient chaos in brushless DC motor. *Chaos Solitons Fractals* **2020**, *132*, 109606. [CrossRef]
15. Bi, H.; Qi, G.; Hu, J. Modeling and analysis of chaos and bifurcations for the attitude system of a quadrotor unmanned aerial vehicle. *Complexity* **2019**, *2019*, 6313925. [CrossRef]
16. Kingni, S.T.; Cheukem, A.; Tsafack, A.S.; Kengne, R.; Mboupda Pone, J.R.; Wei, Z. Spiking oscillations and multistability in nonsmoothairgap brushless direct current motor: Analysis, circuit validation and chaos control. *Int. Trans. Electr. Energy Syst.* **2021**, *31*, 12575.
17. Zhou, P.; Cai, H.; Yang, C. Stabilization of the unstable equilibrium points of the fractional-order BLDCM chaotic system in the sense of Lyapunov by a single-state variable. *Nonlinear Dyn.* **2016**, *84*, 2357–2361. [CrossRef]
18. Zafar, Z.U.A.; Ali, N.; Tunc, C. Mathematical modelling and analysis of fractional-order brushless DC motor. *Adv. Differ. Equations* **2021**, *2021*, 433. [CrossRef]
19. Mohammadzadeh, A.; Ahmadian, A.; Elkamel, A.; Alhameli, F. Chaos synchronization of brushes direct current motors for electric vehicle: Adaptive fuzzy immersion and invariance approach. *Trans. Inst. Meas. Control.* **2021**, *43*, 178–193. [CrossRef]
20. Abro, K.A.; Atangana, A.; Gómez-Aguilar, J.F. Chaos control and characterization of brushless DC motor via integral and differential fractal-fractional techniques. *Int. J. Model. Simul.* **2023**, *43*, 416–425. [CrossRef]
21. Zhang, H.; Wu, H.; Jin, H.; Li, H. High-dynamic and low-cost sensorless control method of high-speed brushless DC motor. *IEEE Trans. Ind. Inform.* **2022**, *19*, 5576–5584. [CrossRef]
22. Souhail, W.; Khammari, H. Sensorless anti-control and synchronization of chaos of brushless DC motor driver. *Sci. Rep.* **2025**, *15*, 13899. [CrossRef] [PubMed]
23. Zhou, P.; Bai, R.J.; Zheng, J.M. Stabilization of a fractional-order chaotic brushless DC motor via a single input. *Nonlinear Dyn.* **2015**, *82*, 519–525. [CrossRef]
24. Zhong, X.; Shahidehpour, M.; Zou, Y. Global quasi-Mittag-Leffler stability of distributed-order BLDCM system. *Nonlinear Dyn.* **2022**, *108*, 2405–2416. [CrossRef]
25. Yu, Z.; Sun, Y.; Dai, X. Stability and stabilization of the fractional-order power system with time delay. *IEEE Trans. Circuits Syst. II Express Briefs* **2021**, *68*, 3446–3450. [CrossRef]
26. Mok, R.; Ahmad, M.A. Smoothed functional algorithm with norm-limited update vector for identification of continuous-time fractional-order Hammerstein models. *IETE J. Res.* **2024**, *70*, 1814–1832. [CrossRef]

27. Wang, J.; Ji, Y.; Ding, F. Iterative parameter estimation for a class of fractional-order Hammerstein nonlinear systems disturbed by colored noise. *Proc. Inst. Mech. Eng. Part I J. Syst. Control. Eng.* **2025**. [CrossRef]
28. Alsaadi, F.E.; Jahanshahi, H.; Yao, Q.; Mou, J. Recurrent neural network-based technique for synchronization of fractional-order systems subject to control input limitations and faults. *Chaos Solitons Fractals* **2023**, *173*, 113717. [CrossRef]
29. Yuan, J.; Fei, S.; Chen, Y.; Ding, Y. Robust feedback compensation and PID Tuning under actuator rate limit effect based on Bode s integrals. *Control. Eng. Pract.* **2022**, *129*, 105347. [CrossRef]
30. Wu, Z.; Yuan, J.; Liu, Y.; Li, D.; Chen, Y. An active disturbance rejection control design with actuator rate limit compensation for the ALSTOM gasifier benchmark problem. *Energy* **2021**, *227*, 120447. [CrossRef]
31. Alaviyan Shahri, E.S.; Balochian, S. An analysis and design method for fractional order linear systems subject to actuator saturation and disturbance. *Optim. Control. Appl. Methods* **2016**, *37*, 305–322. [CrossRef]
32. Shahri, E.S.A.; Balochian, S. Stability region for fractional-order linear system with saturating control. *J. Control. Autom. Electr. Syst.* **2014**, *25*, 283–290. [CrossRef]
33. Alaviyan Shahri, E.S.; Balochian, S. A stability analysis on fractional order linear system with nonlinear saturated disturbance. *Natl. Acad. Sci. Lett.* **2015**, *38*, 409–413. [CrossRef]
34. Alaviyan Shahri, E.S.; Alfi, A.; Tenreiro Machado, J.A. Stability analysis of a class of nonlinear fractional order systems under control input saturation. *Int. J. Robust Nonlinear Control.* **2018**, *28*, 2887–2905. [CrossRef]
35. Alaviyan Shahri, E.S.; Pariz, N.; Chen, Y. Stabilization of a Class of Fractional-Order Nonlinear Systems Subject to Actuator Saturation and Time Delay. *Appl. Sci.* **2025**, *15*, 1851. [CrossRef]
36. Chen, Y.; Wei, Y.; Zhou, X.; Wang, Y. Stability for nonlinear fractional order systems: An indirect approach. *Nonlinear Dyn.* **2017**, *89*, 1011–1018. [CrossRef]
37. Wang, B.; Ding, J.; Wu, F.; Zhu, D. Robust finite-time control of fractional-order nonlinear systems via frequency distributed model. *Nonlinear Dyn.* **2016**, *85*, 2133–2142. [CrossRef]
38. Tan, Y.; Xiong, M.; Du, D.; Fei, S. Observer-based robust control for fractional-order nonlinear uncertain systems with input saturation and measurement quantization. *Nonlinear Anal. Hybrid Syst.* **2019**, *34*, 45–57. [CrossRef]
39. Huang, S.; Wang, B. Stabilization of a fractional-order nonlinear brushless direct current motor. *J. Comput. Nonlinear Dyn.* **2017**, *12*, 041005. [CrossRef]

MDPI

Article

Control Error Convergence Using Lyapunov Direct Method Approach for Mixed Fractional Order Model Reference Adaptive Control

Gustavo E. Ceballos Benavides [1,2,*], Manuel A. Duarte-Mermoud [1] and Lisbel Bárzaga Martell [3]

1 Facultad de Ingeniería y Arquitectura, Universidad Central de Chile, Av. Santa Isabel 1186, Santiago 8330601, Chile; manuel.duarte@ucentral.cl

2 Escuela de Negocios y Tecnología, Universidad Gabriela Mistral, Av. Andrés Bello 1337, Santiago 7500533, Chile

3 Departamento de Electricidad, Universidad Tecnológica Metropolitana (UTEM), Av. José Pedro Alessandri 1242, Santiago 7800002, Chile; lisbel.barzaga@utem.cl

* Correspondence: gustavo.ceballos@ucentral.cl

Abstract: This paper extends Lyapunov stability theory to mixed fractional order direct model reference adaptive control (FO-DMRAC), where the adaptive control parameter is of fractional order, and the control error model is of integer order. The proposed approach can also be applied to other types of model reference adaptive controllers (MRACs), provided the form of the control error dynamics and the fractional order adaptive control law are similar. This paper demonstrates that the control error will converge to zero, even if the derivative of the classical Lyapunov function $\dot{V}$ is positive during a transient period, as long as $\dot{V}(e,\phi)$ tends to zero as time approaches infinity. Finally, this paper provides application examples that illustrate both the convergence of the control error to zero and the behavior of $\dot{V}(e,\phi)$.

Keywords: Lyapunov function; fractional order control; fractional order direct model reference adaptive control (FO-DMRAC); convergence of the control error

1. Introduction

This paper extends the classical Lyapunov stability theory to mixed fractional order direct model reference adaptive control (FO-DMRAC), providing a theoretical foundation for analyzing the stability of fractional order dynamic systems. The principal aim of this paper is to demonstrate that, for such systems, the control error $e_1(t)$ approaches zero as time tends to infinity, leveraging the classical Lyapunov stability approach.

This work prioritizes establishing that the control error $e_1(t) = y_p(t) - y_m(t)$ converges to zero, even if the Lyapunov method ($\dot{V}(e,\phi) \leq 0$) conditions are not met for all t The analysis shows that this convergence holds as long as the difference between the plant output $y_p(t)$ and the reference model output $y_m(t)$ approaches zero as $t \to \infty$.

Numerous methods applied to fractional adaptive systems rely on fractional Lyapunov functions [1,2], resulting in analyses that primarily ensure the stability of the mean square of the control error [3–7]. For instance, the approach presented in [4] develops a specialized fractional Lyapunov function tailored for fractional order dynamic systems. Similarly, the works of [5] and [6] propose the use of fractional Lyapunov derivatives to address an adaptive class of fractional systems, but those methods do not use the classical or integer Lyapunov approach. Additionally, other noteworthy approaches include the utilization of fractional gradients for control applications [8–15] and adaptive laws based on the MIT

 https://doi.org/10.3390/fractalfract9020098

rule [8–10]. However, these approaches often lack rigorous stability analysis, and the proposed fractional Lyapunov functions tend to be quite complex.

For this reason, this work seeks to perform a stability analysis using a classical Lyapunov function but applied to a fractional controller, thus decreasing the analysis's complexity level. To conduct this analysis, we utilized the adaptive error model 3, which operates without access to the system's states. This approach adds complexity and generality to the analysis while simultaneously ensuring that the control error converges to zero [1,2]. It is worth mentioning that fractional calculus could be used in the case of Lyapunov exponent problems if we change the classical derivative to a fractional one [16].

This paper is structured as follows: Section 2 presents the classical integer order implementation of direct model reference adaptive control (IO-DMRAC). In Section 3, we explore fundamental concepts and key results from fractional calculus, which serve as the foundation for analyzing the stability of FO-DMRAC systems. Section 4 addresses the challenges associated with proving the convergence of the control error $e_1(t)$ to zero and introduces the proposed methodology for establishing this convergence. Section 5 showcases the simulation results across various examples that illustrate both the convergence of the control error to zero and the behavior of the function $\dot{V}(e, \phi)$ Lastly, Section 6 summarizes the conclusions.

2. Control Model System

Figure 1 shows a simplified block diagram for the classical integer order direct model reference adaptive control (DMRAC), in which control parameters k and θ are adjusted using their corresponding adaptive laws to keep the control error as small as possible.

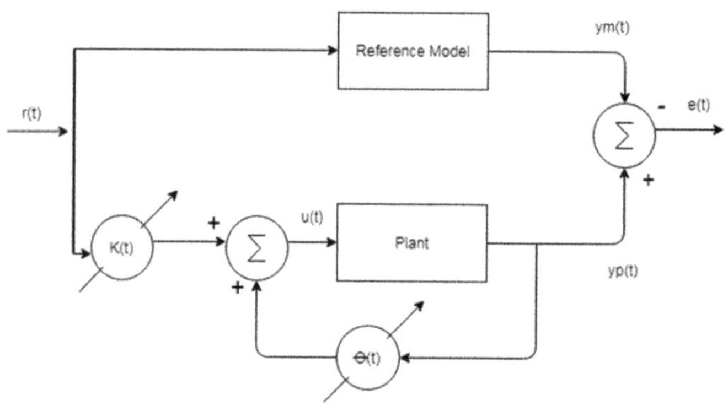

Figure 1. Classical DMRAC block diagram.

DMRAC Algorithm

The objective of the DMRAC is to minimize the control error $e_1(t)$ This approach simplifies implementation by eliminating the need for an identification block, as asymptotic convergence of the controller parameters to their ideal values is not required, making parameter adjustments less critical [17].

In Figure 2, a detail DMRAC adaptive control scheme of a linear (or linearized) nth order plant, with relative degree 1 ($n^* = 1$), is shown. In this scheme, only the control error $e_1(t)$ is accessible (error model 3), while the full state error vector $e(t)$ is not. This limitation simplifies the analysis of the stability conditions [17]. Next, we show the differences between error models 2 and 3, respectively.

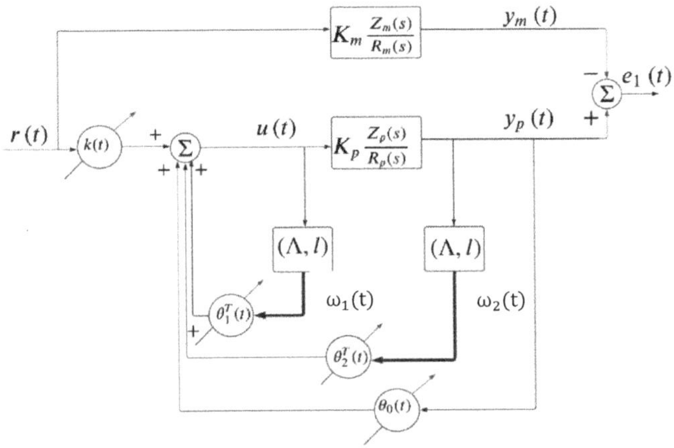

Figure 2. DMRAC block diagram for plant with relative degree 1 ($n^* = 1$).

Model error 2:

${}_{t_0}^{C}D_t^{\beta}e(t) = A_{mn}e(t) + b_{mn}\left[\phi^T(t)\omega(t)\right], e(t_0) = e_0$. In this case, the whole sate error vector $e(t)$ is accessible, including the output or control error $e_1(t)$, which is one element of the state vector.

Model error 3:

$${}_{t_0}^{C}D_t^{\beta}e(t) = A_{mn}e(t) + b_{mn}\left[\phi^T(t)\omega(t)\right], e(t_0) = e_0,$$

$e_1(t) = h_{mn}^T e(t),\ e_1(t_0) = e_{10}$. In this case, we only have access to the output of the system or control error $e_1(t)$.

The control law has the following form

$u(t) = \theta^T(t)\cdot\omega(t)$ where $\theta(t) = \left[k(t),\ \theta_1^T,\ \theta_0(t),\ \theta_2^T\right]^T \in \mathbb{R}^{2n}$ and

$\omega(t) = \left[r(t),\ \omega_1^T,\ y_p(t),\ \omega_2^T\right]^T \in \mathbb{R}^{2n}$ are the controller parameters and the auxiliary signals, respectively, and n is the order of the plant.

The parameters error vector controller is as follows:

$$\phi(t) = \begin{bmatrix} \psi(t) \\ \phi_1(t) \\ \phi_0(t) \\ \phi_2(t) \end{bmatrix} = \begin{bmatrix} k(t) - k^* \\ \theta_1(t) - \theta_1^* \\ \theta_0(t) - \theta_0^* \\ \theta_2(t) - \theta_2^* \end{bmatrix} \in \mathbb{R}^{2n} \text{ with}$$

$$\theta^* = \begin{bmatrix} k^* \\ \theta_1^* \\ \theta_0^* \\ \theta_2^* \end{bmatrix} \text{ the ideal controller parameters.}$$

The auxiliary signals are defined by the following:

$$\dot{\omega}_1(t) = \Lambda\omega_1 + lu(t),$$
$$\dot{\omega}_2(t) = \Lambda\omega_2 + ly(t),$$

with $k(t),\ \theta_0(t),\ r(t),\ y_p(t) \in \mathbb{R},\ \theta_1(t),\ \theta_2(t),\ \omega_1(t),\ \omega_2(t) \in \mathbb{R}^{n-1}$ and (Λ, l) is any arbitrary stable and controllable pair with $\Lambda \in \mathbb{R}^{n-1xn-1}$, a Hurwitz matrix.

For simplicity, we choose (Λ, l) in the controllable canonical form. Furthermore, when $n^* = 1$, the control parameters for the classical or integer order adaptive laws (IO-DMRAC) can be chosen as follows:

$$\begin{aligned}\dot{k}(t) &= -sgn(k_p)e_1(t)r(t),\\ \dot{\theta}_0(t) &= -sgn(k_p)e_1(t)y_p(t),\\ \dot{\theta}_1(t) &= -sgn(k_p)e_1(t)\omega_1(t),\\ \dot{\theta}_2(t) &= -sgn(k_p)e_1(t)\omega_2(t).\end{aligned}$$

and the output control error $e_1(t) = y_p(t) - y_m(t)\mathbb{R}$, can be expressed as $e_1(t) = \frac{k_p}{k_m}W_m(s)\phi^T(t)\omega(t)$, where $W_m(s)$ is a strictly positive real (SPR) transfer function.

On the other hand, for the fractional order adaptive laws (FO-DMRAC) case, these adaptive laws can be written as

$$ {}_{t_0}^{C}D_t^{\alpha}\theta(t) = {}_{t_0}^{C}D_t^{\alpha}\phi(t) = -sgn(k_p)e_1(t)\omega(t) \tag{1}$$

where $\alpha \in (0, 1]$ is a fractional derivative term.

3. Fractional Calculus Preliminaries

In this section, we present some definitions and the main advances in the stability of fractional order model reference adaptive control systems.

3.1. Basic Concepts of Fractional Calculus

The basic definitions of fractional derivative and integral most used in engineering are presented in [18,19], which will be useful for implementing the FO-DMRAC.

Definition 1 ([19]). *The Riemann–Liouville fractional integral of order $\alpha > 0$ of a function $f(t) \in \mathbb{R}$ is defined by*

$$I_{t_0}^{\alpha} f(t) = \frac{1}{\Gamma(\alpha)}\int_{t_0}^{t}\frac{f(\tau)}{(t-\tau)^{1-\alpha}}d\tau \ , \ t > t_0 \ and \alpha > 0, \tag{2}$$

where $\Gamma(\alpha)$ is the Gamma function defined as

$$\Gamma(\alpha) = \int_0^{\infty} t^{\alpha-1}e^{-t}dt. \tag{3}$$

Definition 2 ([19]). *Let $\alpha \geq 0$ and $n = [\alpha] + 1$. The Caputo fractional derivative of order α of a function $f(t) \in \mathbb{R}$ is defined as*

$${}_{t_0}^{C}D_t^{\alpha} f(t) = \frac{1}{\Gamma(n-\alpha)}\int_{t_0}^{t}\frac{f^{(n)}(\tau)}{(t-\tau)^{\alpha-n+1}}d\tau; \text{ as long as } f^{(n)} \in L_1[t_0, t]. \tag{4}$$

Some additional lemmas and a theorem are important for the stability analysis of fractional order adaptive control systems. In what follows, we will mention these and reference their proofs.

Lemma 1 (Principle of fractional comparison). *Let $e(t) \in \mathbb{R}^n$ be a vector of differentiable functions. Then,$\forall\, t \geq t_0$ the following inequality holds* [1,2].

$${}_{t_0}^{C}D_t^{\alpha}\left\{e^T(t)Pe(t)\right\} \leq 2e^T(t)P\,{}_{t_0}^{C}D_t^{\alpha}e(t),\ \forall\alpha \in (0,1],$$

where $P \in \mathbb{R}^{nxn}$ is a symmetric square matrix of constant coefficients and positive definite. Proof of this Lemma can be found in [2].

3.2. Principal Advances in Stability of Fractional Order Systems

Theorem 1. *Let the state error $e(t)$ and the control error $e_1(t)$ be represented by equations (model error 3)*

$$
\begin{aligned}
{}^{C}_{t_0}D^{\beta}_{t}e(t) &= A_{mn}e(t) + b_{mn}\left[\phi^T(t)\omega(t)\right], \qquad & e(t_0) = e_0, \\
e_1(t) &= h^T_{mn}e(t), & e_1(t_0) = e_{10},
\end{aligned}
\tag{5}
$$

where $A_{mn} \in \mathbb{R}^{nxn}$ is a Hurwitz matrix, such that there is a given matrix $Q = Q^T > 0 \in \mathbb{R}^{nxn}$. Then, there exists a matrix $P = P^T > 0 \in \mathbb{R}^{nxn}$, such that

$$
\begin{aligned}
A^T_{mn}P + PA_{mn} &= -Q, \\
Pb_{mn} &= h_{mn}
\end{aligned}
$$

whose adaptive adjustment laws to estimate the unknown controller parameters are given by

$$
{}^{C}_{t_0}D^{\alpha}_{t}\phi(t) = {}^{C}_{t_0}D^{\alpha}_{t}\theta(t) = -\gamma sgn(k_p)e_1(t)\omega(t), \qquad \phi(t_0) = \phi_0 \tag{6}
$$

where $k_p > 0$ is the gain of the plant, which is unknown, but the sign is known. Also, $\alpha < \beta$ and $\alpha \in (0,1]$. Then, if $e(t)$ and $\phi(t)$ are differentiable and uniformly continuous functions, it holds that

(a) The parametric error $\phi(t)$ the state error $e(t)$ and the control error $e_1(t)$ remain bounded for all time.
(b) Furthermore, if the auxiliary signal $\omega(t)$ is bounded, then ${}^{C}_{t_0}D^{\alpha}_{t}\phi(t)$ and ${}^{C}_{t_0}D^{\beta}_{t}e(t)$ also remain bounded.
(c) The mean value of the squared norm of the state error $\overline{\|e(t)\|^2}$ is $o(t^{\varepsilon-\alpha})$ $\forall\varepsilon > 0$, or equivalently

$$
\lim_{t\to\infty}\left[t^{\alpha-\varepsilon}\frac{\int_{t_0}^{t} e(\tau)^2 d\tau}{t}\right] = 0,\ \forall\varepsilon > 0 \tag{7}
$$

where $o(t^{\varepsilon-\alpha})$ means that the speed of converges to zero is higher than $t^{-\alpha}$ The proof of this theorem can be found in [3].

Remark 1. *This theorem applies to systems whose relative degree n^* is greater than one as long as the model transfer function $W_m(s)$ is strictly positive real. Otherwise, it is necessary to modify $W_m(s)$ to meet this condition.*

From Theorem 1, since $e_1(t) = h^T_{mn}e(t)$ with h^T_{mn} is a constant vector, then the control error $e_1(t)$ will also be $(t^{\varepsilon-\alpha})$ $\forall\varepsilon > 0$.

If (c) holds, it must also hold for the mean value of the square norm of $e_1(t)$ since $e_1(t) = h^T_{mn}e(t)$ with h^T_{mn} a vector whose components are constants.

There is a lemma that relaxes hypothesis (b) imposed from Theorem 1 when $\beta = 1$ (i.e., the error model equation is of integer order); therefore, all the internal signals $\omega(t)$ are bounded, and there is no need to impose the boundedness condition over $\omega(t)$. The proof of this lemma can be found in [20].

Furthermore, as the auxiliary signal $\omega(t)$ is bounded and Theorem 1 guarantees (c), the squared norm of the control error $|e_1(t)|^2$ also tends to 0 as t tends to infinity. That is

$$\lim_{t\to\infty}\left[t^{\alpha-\varepsilon}\frac{\int_{t_0}^{t}e_1(\tau)^2d\tau}{t}\right]=0,\ \forall\varepsilon>0 \tag{8}$$

Therefore, the stability of the proposed FO-DMRAC is guaranteed.

Nevertheless, it is impossible to conclude the convergence of the errors ($e(t)$ and $e_1(t)$) to 0 as t tends to ∞. Also, it is still a pending issue to prove the analytical differentiability of $\phi(t)$.

The high-frequency gain of the plant b_p is supposed to be unknown, but its sign is assumed to be known $(sgn(b_p) > 0)$.

4. Some Issues That Difficult to Prove Convergence of Errors to 0 in Adaptive Fractional Order Systems

In the well-known classical (or integer order) DMRAC, the proof of the convergence of the state error and the control error ($e(t)$ and $e_1(t)$, respectively) to 0 rests on the Barbalat Lemma. That is, the derivative of the Lyapunov function

$$\dot{V}(e,\phi) = -e^T(t)Qe(t) \le 0.$$

Then, using the Barbalat Lemma, we can conclude that the state error tends to 0 $(\lim_{t\to\infty} e(t) = 0)$; therefore, the control error $e_1(t) = h_{mn}^T e(t)$ also tends to 0 $(\lim_{t\to\infty} e_1(t) = 0)$ [17].

Nevertheless, even though it is not explicitly mentioned in the literature, because of the above, it must also be satisfied that $\lim_{t\to\infty} \dot{V}(e,\phi) = 0$.

In the mixed fractional order direct model reference adaptive control (FO-MRAC), there is no equivalent Barbalat Lemma like in the integer order case. Therefore, it is not possible to conclude the convergence of the state error $e(t)$ and the control error $e_1(t)$ to 0.

If we write the Lyapunov function for the mixed adaptive system, we have (considering, from Figure 3, $k_p = 1$ for simplicity)

$$V(e,\phi) = e^T(t)Pe(t) + \phi^T(t)\phi(t) \tag{9}$$

therefore,

$$\dot{V}(e,\phi) = -e^TQe + 2\phi^T(t)\left\{e_1(t)\omega(t) - D^{1-\alpha}(e_1(t)\omega(t))\right\} \tag{10}$$

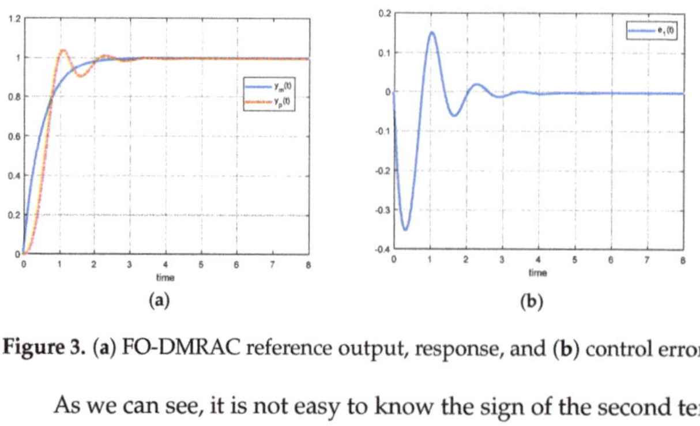

(a) (b)

Figure 3. (**a**) FO-DMRAC reference output, response, and (**b**) control error when $r(t) = 1$.

As we can see, it is not easy to know the sign of the second term

$2\phi^T(t)\{e_1(t)\omega(t) - D^{1-\alpha}(e_1(t)\omega(t))\}$ or the term

$$\phi^T(t)\left\{e_1(t)\omega(t) - D^{1-\alpha}(e_1(t)\omega(t))\right\} \tag{11}$$

with $\alpha \in (0,1)$. To make the notation easier, we can make the variable change $\gamma = 1-\alpha$; therefore, $\gamma \in (0,1)$. Then, (11) could be rewritten as

$$\phi^T(t)\{e_1(t)\omega(t) - D^{\gamma}(e_1(t)\omega(t))\} \tag{12}$$

By Lemma 2 [20], we know that $\omega(t)$ is boundness. By part (a) of Theorem 1, $e_1(t)$ is boundness; therefore, $D^{\gamma}(e_1(t)\omega(t)) = 0$ (when t tends to infinity) by Caputo derivative properties. Moreover, as $\phi(t)$ is boundness by the same theorem, (12) is a boundedness term.

Still, we cannot prove that the term

$$\dot{V}(e,\phi) = -e^TQe + 2\phi^T(t)\{e_1(t)\omega(t) - D^{\gamma}(e_1(t)\omega(t))\} \leq 0$$

Remark 2. *If the signals are of the PE type (Persisting Excitation type) class of an adequate order,* $\lim\limits_{t\to\infty}\phi(t)$ *could converge to 0, but this is more related to the case of identification problems* [17,21]. *In the direct model reference adaptive control (DMRAC) case, it is not necessarily* $\lim\limits_{t\to\infty}\phi(t) = 0$.

Even in this case, we can only show that $\lim\limits_{t\to\infty}\dot{V}(e,\phi) = \lim\limits_{t\to\infty} -e^TQe$, but it is not enough to conclude that $\lim\limits_{t\to\infty}\dot{V}(e,\phi) = 0$ or $\lim\limits_{t\to\infty} -e^TQe = 0$, and thus that $\lim\limits_{t\to\infty} e = 0$ with Q as a constant and symmetric matrix.

Therefore, we must explore what happens with the term inside the parenthesis. That is, the term $\{e_1(t)\omega(t) - D^{\gamma}(e_1(t)\omega(t))\}$.

First, we know that all the signals inside the parenthesis are bounded; then, $\lim\limits_{t\to\infty}\{e_1(t)\omega(t) - D^{\gamma}(e_1(t)\omega(t))\} = \lim\limits_{t\to\infty} e_1(t)\omega(t)$ because as we showed before, by Caputo derivative properties [18,19], $D^{\gamma}(e_1(t)\omega(t)) = 0$, as t tends to ∞, because the term $e_1(t)\omega(t)$ will be at least constant. Then, as $\omega(t)$ is a bounded signal, if $\lim\limits_{t\to\infty} e_1(t) = 0$, then $\lim\limits_{t\to\infty}\dot{V}(e,\phi) = 0$ and $\lim\limits_{t\to\infty} -e^TQe = 0$; therefore, $\lim\limits_{t\to\infty} e = 0$ will prove the convergence to 0 of all errors (state error $e(t)$ and control error $e_1(t)$). But we assume that $\lim\limits_{t\to\infty} e_1(t) = 0$, which is not possible to establish a priori.

It is important to mention that several fractional adaptive systems present this behavior. That is, $\lim\limits_{t\to\infty}\dot{V}(e,\phi) = 0$ and $\lim\limits_{t\to\infty} e_1(t) = 0$. In the Simulation Results Section (Section 5), we will show some examples that show this behavior for both stable and unstable systems.

Now, from (7), as ε is arbitrary, as long as $\varepsilon > 0$, we can choose $\varepsilon = \alpha$; therefore, (7) can be rewritten as

$\lim\limits_{t\to\infty}\left[\frac{\int_{t_0}^{t} e(\tau)^2 d\tau}{t}\right] = 0$ which gives a term that is divided by ∞ Even more, as part (a) of Theorem 1, $e(t)$ is bounded, and by part (b) of the same theorem, $\dot{e}(t)$ is bounded and $e(t)$ is part of (5); all the other terms ($\phi(t)$ and $\omega(t)$) are bounded. Therefore, the numerator of (5) $\left(\lim\limits_{t\to\infty}\int_{t_0}^{t} e(\tau)^2 d\tau\right)$ can be infinite or constant (if $e(t)$ is square integrable), and then we can use the L'Hôpital rule, that is, if $e(t)^2$ and 1 are continuous and differentiable functions, then

If $\lim\limits_{t\to\infty}\left[\frac{e(t)^2}{1}\right] = \lim\limits_{t\to\infty} e(t)^2 \Rightarrow \lim\limits_{t\to\infty} e(t) = 0$ then $\lim\limits_{t\to\infty}\left[\frac{\int_{t_0}^{t} e(\tau)^2 d\tau}{t}\right] = 0$ which has been proved in [3].

That is to say, as the L'Hôpital's rule states, if $\lim_{t\to\infty}\frac{f'(t)}{g'(t)} = \lim_{t\to\infty}\left[\frac{e(t)^2}{1}\right] = 0 \Rightarrow \lim_{t\to\infty}\frac{f(t)}{g(t)} = \lim_{t\to\infty}\left[\frac{\int_{t_0}^{t} e(\tau)^2 d\tau}{t}\right] = 0$.

Therefore, as $\lim_{t\to\infty} e(t) = 0 \Rightarrow \lim_{t\to\infty} e_1(t) = 0$ because $e_1(t) = h_{mn}^T e(t)$ with h_{mn}^T a vector of constants elements, this means that the control error $e_1(t)$ tends to 0 conform t tends to ∞ Therefore, we have proven the convergence of the state and control error to 0, which is a new result for fractional order direct model reference adaptive control systems (FO-DMRAC). Also, this result means that $\lim_{t\to\infty} \dot{V}(e,\phi) = 0$, as in the integer order case.

5. Simulation Results

In this section, we will show some examples (of different relative degree plants) that support what has been developed and concluded in Section 4. The simulations were performed using Matlab–Simulink [22–24]. For all examples, zero initial conditions were considered.

For simplicity of the analysis but without loss of generality, $k_p = 1$ is considered. Then, as was said before (9), a typical Lyapunov function can be chosen, such as $V(e,\phi) = e^T(t)Pe(t) + \phi^T(t)\phi(t)$. Therefore,

$\dot{V}(e,\phi) = -e^T Qe + 2\phi^T(t)\{e_1(t)\omega(t) - D^{1-\alpha}(e_1(t)\omega(t))\}$ If $\gamma = 1-\alpha$ then the above term can be rewritten as

$$\dot{V}(e,\phi) = -e(t)^T Qe(t) + 2\phi^T(t)\{e_1(t)\omega(t) - D^{\gamma}(e_1(t)\omega(t))\} \tag{13}$$

Unlike the classic case, in (13), a term with a fractional derivative appears. For doing the simulation analysis, the designer can choose any $\alpha, \gamma \in (0,1]$, such as $\gamma = 1-\alpha$. In this case, we will choose $\alpha = 0.8 \Rightarrow \gamma = 0.2$, but any combination of values of α and γ could be chosen as long as $\alpha + \gamma = 1$.

In the mixed FO-DMRAC case, where the error model dynamic is of integer order and the adaptive laws are fractional (see Equation (1)), the dynamic of the state error $e(t)$ considering the plant together with the controller (error model 3) [17], is

$$\begin{aligned} \dot{e}(t) &= A_{mn}e(t) + b_{mn}\left[\phi^T(t)\omega(t)\right] \\ e_1(t) &= h_{mn}^T e(t) \end{aligned} \tag{14}$$

where

$$A_{mn} = \begin{bmatrix} A_p + b_p\theta_0^* h_p^T & b_p\theta_1^{*T} & b_p\theta_2^{*T} \\ l\theta_0^* h_p^T & \Lambda + l\theta_1^{*T} & l\theta_2^{*T} \\ lh_p^T & 0 & \Lambda \end{bmatrix} \quad b_{mn} = \begin{bmatrix} b_p \\ l \\ 0 \end{bmatrix}$$

and

$h_{mn} = \begin{bmatrix} h_p^T & 0 & 0 \end{bmatrix}^T$, $x(t) = \begin{bmatrix} x_p^T(t) & \omega_1^T(t) & \omega_2^T(t) \end{bmatrix}^T$ and

$x_{mn}(t) = \begin{bmatrix} x_p^{*T}(t) & \omega_1^{*T}(t) & \omega_2^{*T}(t) \end{bmatrix}^T$, where $e(t) = x(t) - x_{mn}(t)$.

Although, from a theoretical point of view, it is not necessary to calculate the value of P from Q since it is enough that the conditions of the Meyer–Kalman–Yakubovich (MKY) lemma are met, it is important for the purposes of carrying out the calculation of $\dot{V}(e,\phi)$.

Next, we present some examples to show the behavior of the control error $e_1(t)$ and the derivative of the Lyapunov function $\dot{V}(e,\phi)$ that confirm the convergence to zero of $e_1(t)$, which is the main result of this paper, and this was proven in the previous section.

5.1. Scalar Stable Plant

Example 1. *($n = 1$ and $n^* = 1$).*

Remark 3. *In the scalar case, $\theta_0^* = \theta^* = \frac{a_m - a_p}{b_p}$ and $k^* = \frac{b_m}{b_p}$, where θ^* and k^* are the ideal control parameters and $u(t) = k(t)r(t) + \theta(t)x_p(t)$ is the control law.*

Then, using the MKY lemma, that is, for any $Q = Q^T > 0$ a $P = P^T > 0$ exists, such that

$$A_{mn}^T P + PA_{mn} = -Q.$$
$$Pb_{mn} = h_{mn}.$$

we may calculate A_{mn}, P, and Q for the system of Example 1 and thus be able to calculate $\dot{V}(e, \phi)$.

In this example, $A_{mn} = -2$, $P = 1$, $Q = 2$, $k^* = \frac{b_m}{b_p} = 2$, and $\theta^* = \frac{a_m - a_p}{b_p} = -1$. In Table 1 the differential equations and values of Example 1 are shown.

Table 1. FO-DMRAC implementation for a stable plant.

Plant Model	Reference Model
$\dot{x}_p(t) = -x_p(t) + u(t)$. $y_p(t) = x_p(t)$. $W_p(s) = \frac{1}{s+1}$. $a_p = -1,\ b_p = 1,\ h_p = h_p^T = 1$.	$\dot{x}_m(t) = -2(t) + 2r(t)$. $r(t) = 1$. $y_m(t) = x_m(t)$. $W_m(s) = \frac{2}{s+2}$. $a_m = -2,\ b_m = 2,\ h_m = h_m^T = 1$.
$\Lambda = 0,\ l = 0,\ A_{mn} = -2,\ b_{mn} = -1,\ e(t) = e_1(t) = x_p - x_m$	

The fractional adaptive laws were implemented using the Ninteger Toolbox [23]. Specifically, the NID block was used based on the Oustaloup method [24].

Figure 3 shows the plant response $y_p(t)$, reference output $y_m(t)$, and control error $e_1(t)$, respectively. From Figure 4, we can see the evolution of $\dot{V}(e, \phi)$, respectively.

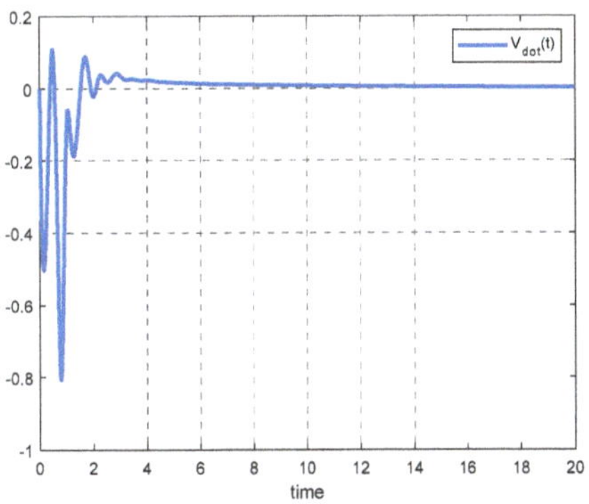

Figure 4. FO-DMRAC graph of $\dot{V}(e, \phi) vs\ t$ when $r(t) = 1$.

Additionally, as shown in Figures 3 and 4, the control error $e_1(t)$ converges to zero, and while $\dot{V}(e, \phi)$ may be greater than zero in certain time intervals, it ultimately converges to zero as $t \to \infty$, like the classical case.

If we change $r(t)$ by a sinusoidal signal such as $r(t) = 2\sin(t)$, the response, control error, and the graph of $\dot{V}(e, \phi)$ are shown in Figures 5 and 6, respectively.

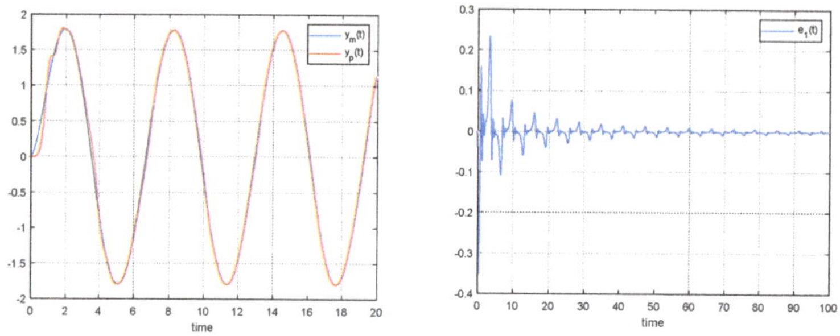

(**a**) (**b**)

Figure 5. (**a**) FO-DMRAC reference output, response, and (**b**) control error when $r(t) = 2\sin(t)$.

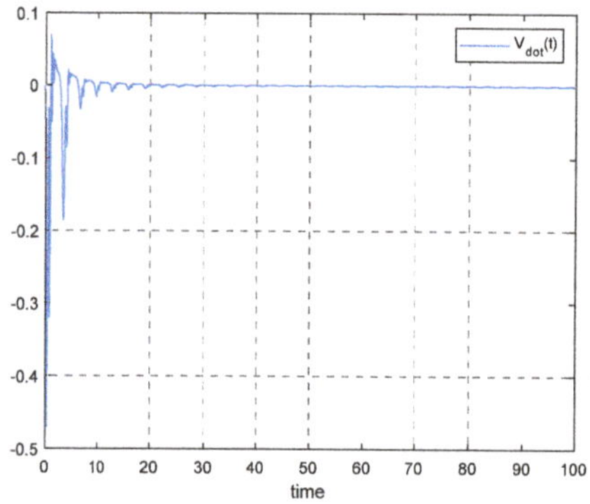

Figure 6. FO-DMRAC graph of $\dot{V}(e, \phi)$ when $r(t) = 2\sin(t)$.

From Figure 5, the control error $e_1(t)$ convergence takes more time than the stable case, but the convergence is assured anyway. A similar convergence behavior can be seen from Figure 6.

5.2. Scalar Unstable Plant

Example 2. *($n = 1$ and $n^* = 1$).*

$A_{mn} = -2$, $P = 1$, $Q = 2$, $k^* = \frac{b_m}{b_p} = 2$ and $\theta^* = \frac{a_m - a_p}{b_p} = -3$. Table 2 shows the differential equations and values of Example 2.

Table 2. FO-DMRAC implementation for an unstable plant.

Plant Model	Reference Model
$\dot{x}_p(t) = 1(t) + 1u(t)$. $y_p(t) = x_p(t)$. $W_p(s) = \frac{1}{s-1}$. $a_p = 1,\ b_p = 1,\ h_p = h_p^T = 1$.	$\dot{x}_m(t) = -2(t) + 2r(t)$. $r(t) = 1$. $y_m(t) = x_m(t)$. $W_m(s) = \frac{2}{s+2}$. $a_m = -2,\ b_m = 2,\ h_m = h_m^T = 1$.
$\Lambda = 0,\ l = 0,\ A_{mn} = -2,\ b_{mn} = -1,\ e(t) = e_1(t) = x_p - x_m$	

The next figures (Figures 7 and 8) show similar convergence behavior as the graphics of Example 1 for the unstable plant.

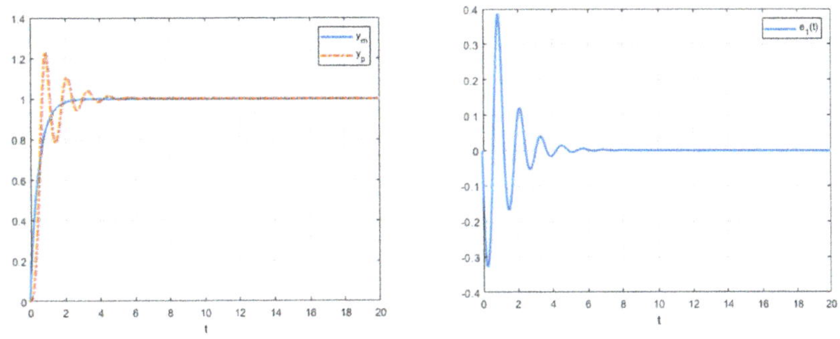

(**a**) (**b**)

Figure 7. (**a**) FO-DMRAC reference output, response, and (**b**) control error when $r(t) = 1$.

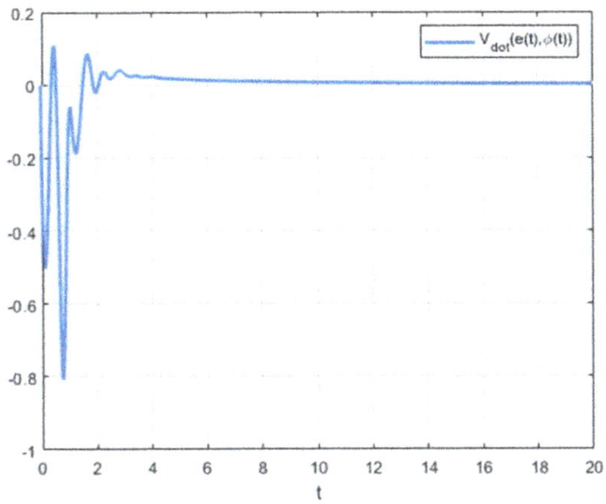

Figure 8. FO-DMRAC graph of $\dot{V}(e,\phi) vs\ t$ when $r(t) = 1$.

Now, if we change the reference to $r(t) = 2\sin(t)$, the figures are as follows (Figures 9 and 10).

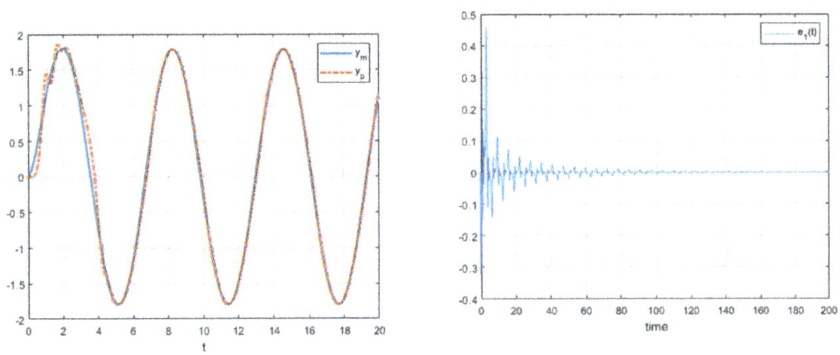

(**a**) (**b**)

Figure 9. (**a**) FO-DMRAC reference output, response, and (**b**) control error when $r(t) = 2\sin(t)$.

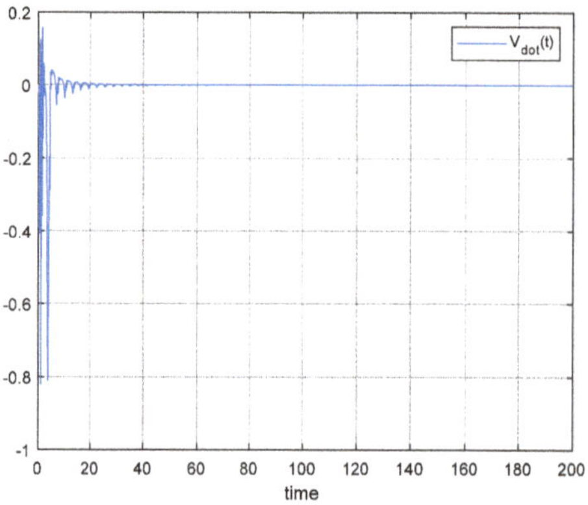

Figure 10. FO-DMRAC graph of $\dot{V}(e,\phi)$ when $r(t) = 2\sin(t)$.

As we can see, from Figures 10 and 11, both the control error $e_1(t)$ and $\dot{V}(e,\phi)$ converge to 0, even if $\dot{V}(e,\phi)$ can take positive values in some time intervals.

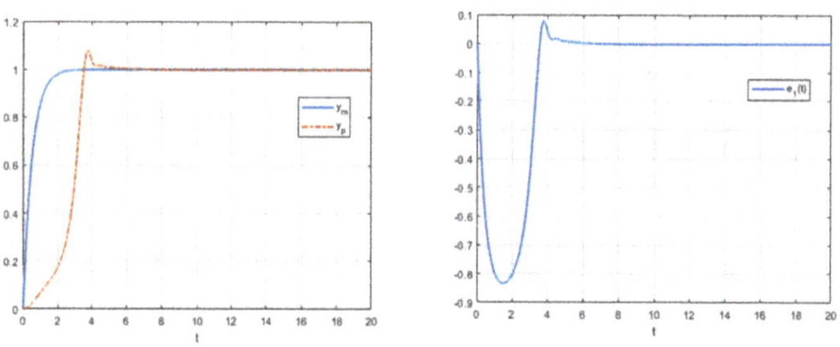

(a) (b)

Figure 11. (**a**) FO-DMRAC reference output, response, and (**b**) control error when $r(t) = 1$.

5.3. Vectorial Case (Stable Plant)

Example 3. *($n = 2$ and $n^* = 1$).*

Table 3 shows the differential equations and values of Example 3.

Table 3. FO-DMRAC implementation.

Plant Model	Reference Model
$\dot{x}_p(t) = A_p(t)x_p(t) + b_p u(t)$. $y_p(t) = h_p^T x_p(t)$. $W_p(s) = \frac{s+1}{s^2+7s+12}$	$\dot{x}_m(t) = -2(t) + 2r(t)$. $y_m(t) = x_m(t)$. $r(t) = 1$. $W_m(s) = \frac{2}{s+2}\frac{(s+1)}{(s+1)}$
Controllable canonical form: $A_p = \begin{bmatrix} 0 & 1 \\ -12 & -7 \end{bmatrix}$, $b_p = \begin{bmatrix} 0 \\ 1 \end{bmatrix}$, $h_p^T = [1\,1]$	Controllable canonical form: $A_p = \begin{bmatrix} 0 & 1 \\ -2 & -3 \end{bmatrix}$, $b_p = \begin{bmatrix} 0 \\ 1 \end{bmatrix}$, $h_m^T = [1\,1]$
$\Lambda = -1,\ l = 1,\ b_{mn} = [0\,1\,1\,0]^T,\ h_{mn}^T = [1\,1\,0\,0]$ $e(t) = x(t) - x_{mn}(t)\ e_1(t) = h_{mn}^T e(t)$	

Remark 4. *The reference model transfer function* $W_m(s)$ *has been changed (order 2) just to match the conditions for finding the control ideal parameters* θ^**, but the behavior is the same as the original transfer function* $W_m(s) = \frac{2}{s+2}$.

Control Laws:

$$\theta(t) = \begin{bmatrix} k(t) & \theta_1^T(t)\,\theta_0(t) & \theta_2^T(t) \end{bmatrix}^T \in \mathbb{R}^4$$
$$\omega(t) = \begin{bmatrix} r(t) & \omega_1^T(t)\,y_p(t) & \omega_2^T(t) \end{bmatrix}^T \in \mathbb{R}^4$$
$$u(t) = \theta^T(t)\omega(t)$$

Note: $\theta_1^T(t)$ and $\theta_2^T(t) \in \mathbb{R}$
Internal auxiliary signals:

$$\dot{\omega}_1(t) = \Lambda\omega_1(t) + lu(t)$$
$$\dot{\omega}_2(t) = \Lambda\omega_2(t) + ly_p(t)$$
$$\Lambda = -1$$
$$l = 1$$

Fractional order adaptive laws:

$${}_{t_0}^{C}D_t^{\alpha_i}\theta(t) = -\Gamma_i e_1(t)\omega(t)$$

Remark 5. Γ_i *is a diagonal matrix where* $i = 1, \ldots, 4$*. For practical implementation simplicity, we choose* $\Gamma_i = I$ *(identity matrix of appropriated dimension).*

$\phi(t) = \begin{bmatrix} \psi(t) \\ \phi_1(t) \\ \phi_0(t) \\ \phi_2(t) \end{bmatrix} = \begin{bmatrix} k(t) - k^* \\ \theta_1(t) - \theta_1^* \\ \theta_0(t) - \theta_0^* \\ \theta_2(t) - \theta_2^* \end{bmatrix} \in \mathbb{R}^4$ are the parameters error vector controllers and

$\theta^* = \begin{bmatrix} k^* \\ \theta_1^* \\ \theta_0^* \\ \theta_2^* \end{bmatrix} = \begin{bmatrix} 2 \\ 0 \\ 4 \\ 6 \end{bmatrix}$ are the ideal controller parameters.

Finally, $A_{mn} = \begin{bmatrix} 0 & 1 & 0 & 0 \\ -8 & -3 & 0 & 6 \\ 4 & 4 & -1 & 6 \\ 1 & 1 & 0 & -1 \end{bmatrix}$
whose eigenvalues are −1, −2, −1, and −1; therefore, A_{mn} is Hurwitz. Also, if

$Q = \begin{bmatrix} 2 & 26.5 & -23.5 & -6 \\ 26.5 & 33 & -16.5 & -8 \\ -23.5 & -16.5 & 4 & 0 \\ -6 & -8 & 0 & 2 \end{bmatrix}$, which is a symmetrical and positive defined matrix,

then

$P = \begin{bmatrix} 4 & 0.5 & 0.5 & 1 \\ 0.5 & 3 & -2 & 0 \\ 0.5 & -2 & 2 & 0 \\ 1 & 0 & 0 & 1 \end{bmatrix}$, which is also a symmetrical and positive defined matrix that

satisfies the MKY Lemma. That is

$$A_{mn}^T P + P A_{mn} = -Q,$$
$$P b_{mn} = h_{mn}.$$

As before, Figures 11 and 12 show the response, control error $e_1(t)$ and $\dot{V}(e, \phi)$ behavior, respectively.

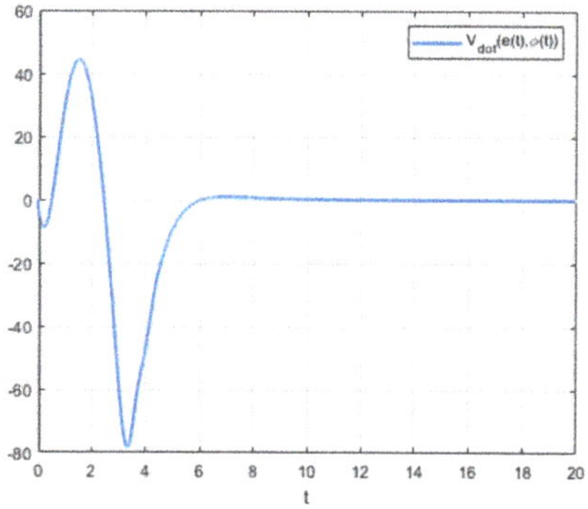

Figure 12. FO-DMRAC graph of $\dot{V}(e, \phi)$ when $r(t) = 1$.

Figure 11 shows similar behavior as Examples 1 and 2; that is, the plant output $y_p(t)$ converges to the model reference output $y_m(t)$, which is equivalent to saying that the control error tends to 0 as $t \to \infty$. Also, from Figure 12, we confirm that $\lim_{t\to\infty} \dot{V}(e, \phi) = 0$, even if in some time intervals (mainly in the transient period), $\dot{V}(e, \phi)$ can be positive.

Now, by changing the reference signal to a sinusoidal one as in the previous example, that is, $r(t) = 2\sin(t)$, we obtain the following dynamic behavior, which is shown in the next figures (Figures 13 and 14 respectively).

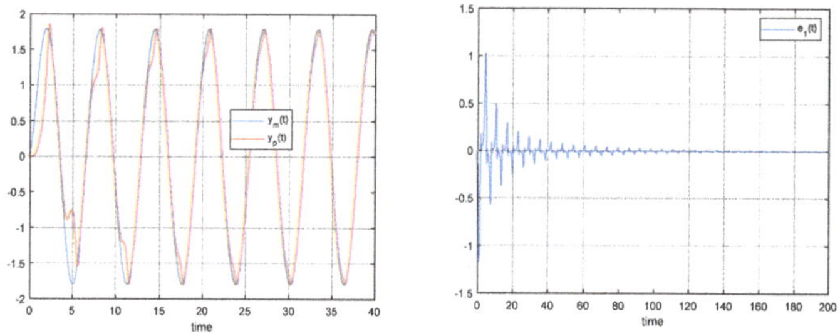

(**a**) (**b**)

Figure 13. (**a**) FO-DMRAC reference output, response, and (**b**) control error when $r(t) = 2\sin(t)$.

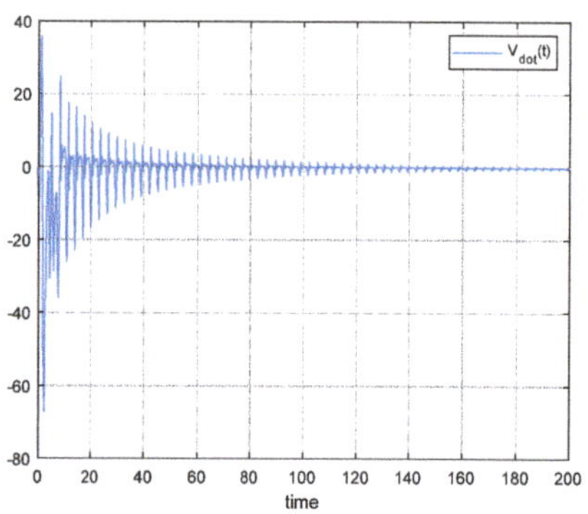

Figure 14. FO-DMRAC graph of $\dot{V}(e, \phi)$ when $r(t) = 2\sin(t)$.

Remark 6. *These simulations are made to show that* $\lim_{t \to \infty} e_1(t) = 0$ *(the control error converges to 0) in the case of fractional order model reference adaptive control implementation (FO-DMRAC) and not to show the performance of the controllers. Better performance can be achieved by using an optimization algorithm such as PSO* [25] *or another one in such a way as to choose the fractional parameters* α_i *and adaptive gains* Γ_i *more conveniently.*

Finally, new conditions of the Lyapunov method can be established and applied to FO-DMRAC. That is, let $V(e, \phi)$ be a continuous and derivable function, then

1. $V(e, \phi) > 0$.
2. $\dot{V}(0, 0) = 0$.
3. If $\lim_{t \to \infty} \dot{V}(e, \phi) = 0$, then, $\lim_{t \to \infty} e(t) = 0$, which implies that the control error $e_1(t)$ also converges to 0.

6. Conclusions

In this article, we have proven that in the FO-DMRAC case, the control error $e_1(t) = y_p(t) - y_m(t)$ converges to 0 even if the derivative of the Lyapunov function $V(e, \phi)$ is greater than 0 in some time intervals (mainly in the transient periods). Some examples have been presented to show the convergence of the control error $e_1(t)$ and the behavior of the function $\dot{V}(e, \phi)$ as t approaches infinity.

One of the main difficulties in carrying out the synthesis of $\dot{V}(e, \phi)$, for simulation purposes, is that we need to compute the ideal control parameters θ^* analytically and the matrix Q explicitly, which is not an easy task when the order of the plant to control grows in order. One practical approach to determine the ideal controller parameters θ^* is to implement the controller system using a Persistent Excitation (PE) reference input signal and wait for convergence. Sometimes, it could take a long time, depending on the system order, because the higher the order, the more parameters we must compute.

In conclusion, the convergence of the state error $e(t)$ and the control error $e_1(t)$ to zero has been demonstrated for a class of fractional adaptive control systems (FO-DMRAC) using the classical Lyapunov approach, avoiding additional complexities in the analysis. Previously, it had only been established that the mean square errors converge to zero as time approaches infinity; however, the convergence of errors themselves had not been explicitly demonstrated until now.

Author Contributions: G.E.C.B.: Conceptualization, methodology, investigation, writing—original draft, and validation; M.A.D.-M.: writing—original draft and validation, L.B.M.: writing—review and editing. All authors have read and agreed to the published version of the manuscript.

Funding: The authors are grateful for the support obtained from the Universidad Central de Chile.

Data Availability Statement: The data are contained within the article.

Acknowledgments: The research presented in this paper has been supported by the Faculty of Engineering and Architecture (FINARQ) of the Universidad Central de Chile.

Conflicts of Interest: The authors declare no conflicts of interest.

References

1. Duarte-Mermoud, M.A.; Aguila-Camacho, N.; Gallegos, J.A.; Castro-Linares, R. Using General Quadratic Lyapunov Functions to Prove Lyapunov Uniform Stability for Fractional Order Systems. *Commun. Nonlinear Sci. Numer. Simul.* **2015**, *22*, 650–659. [CrossRef]
2. Aguila-Camacho, N.; Gallegos, J.; Duarte-Mermoud, M.A. Analysis of fractional order error models in adaptive systems: Mixed order cases. *Fract. Calc. Appl. Anal.* **2019**, *22*, 1113–1132. [CrossRef]

3. Aguila-Camacho, N.; Duarte-Mermoud, M.A.; Gallegos, J.A. Lyapunov Functions for Fractional Order Systems. *Commun. Nonlinear Sci. Numer. Simul.* **2014**, *19*, 2951–2957. [CrossRef]
4. Hu, J.-B.; Lu, G.-P.; Zhang, S.-B.; Zhao, L.-D. Lyapunov Stability Theorem about Fractional System Without and with Delay. *Commun. Nonlinear Sci. Numer. Simul.* **2015**, *2*, 905–913. [CrossRef]
5. Balaska, H.; Ladaci, S.; Djouambi, A.; Schulte, H.; Bourouba, B. Fractional Order Tube Model Reference Adaptive Control for a Class of Fractional Order Linear Systems. *Int. J. Appl. Math. Comput. Sci.* **2020**, *30*, 501–515. [CrossRef]
6. Hu, C.; Qi, Z.; Ma, Q.; Zhou, X. Factional Order Model Reference Adaptive Control based on Lyapunov Stability Theory. In Proceedings of the 35th Chinese Control Conference, Chengdu, China, 27–29 July 2016.
7. Zhang, R.; Liu, Y. A new Barbalat's Lemma and Lyapunov stability theorem for Fractional order Systems. In Proceedings of the 2017 29th Chinese Control and Decision Conference (CCDC), Chongqing, China, 28–30 May 2017.
8. Ladaci, S.; Charef, A. On fractional adaptive control. *Nonlinear Dyn.* **2006**, *43*, 365–378. [CrossRef]
9. Petrás, I. An Adaptive Fractional-Order Controller. In Proceedings of the 2013 14th International Carpathian Control Conference (ICCC), Rytro, Poland, 26–29 May 2013; pp. 297–301.
10. Vinagre, B.M.; Petrás, I.; Podlubny, I.; Chen, Y. Using fractional order adjustment rules and fractional order reference models in model-reference adaptive control. *Nonlinear Dyn.* **2002**, *29*, 269–279. [CrossRef]
11. Chen, Y.; Gao, Q.; Wei, Y.; Wang, Y. Study on fractional order gradient methods. *Appl. Math. Comput.* **2017**, *314*, 310–321. [CrossRef]
12. Sheng, D.; Wei, Y.; Chen, Y.; Wang, Y. Convolutional neural networks with fractional order gradient method. *Neurocomputing* **2020**, *408*, 42–50. [CrossRef]
13. Liu, J.; Chen, S.; Cai, S.; Xu, C. The Novel Adaptive Fractional Order Gradient Decent Algorithms Design via Robust Control. *arXiv* **2023**, arXiv:2303.04328.
14. Liu, J.; Zhai, R.; Liu, Y.; Li, W.; Wang, B.; Huang, L. A quasi fractional order gradient descent method with adaptive stepsize and its application in system identification. *Appl. Math. Comput.* **2021**, *393*, 125797. [CrossRef]
15. Hai, P.V.; Rosenfeld, J.A. The gradient descent method from the perspective of fractional calculus. *Math. Methods Appl. Sci.* **2021**, *44*, 5520–5547. [CrossRef]
16. Haghighinia, A.; Tabatabaei, S.M.; Movahedirad, S. A novel geometrically-hybrid microchannel for performance enhancement in mass transfer: Description of Lyapunov exponent and Poincaré map. *Int. J. Heat Mass Transf.* **2021**, *165*, 120700. [CrossRef]
17. Narendra, K.S.; Annaswamy, A.M. *Stable Adaptive Systems*; Dover Publications Inc.: Mineola, NY, USA, 2005.
18. Kilbas, A.; Srivastava, H.; Trujillo, J. *Theory and Applications of Fractional Differential Equations*; Elsevier: Amsterdam, The Netherlands, 2006.
19. Diethelem, K. *The Analysis of Fractional Differential Equations*; Springer: Berlin/Heidelberg, Germany, 2010.
20. Benavides, G.E.C.; Duarte-Mermoud, M.A.; Orchard, M.E.; Travieso-Torres, J.C. Pitch Angle Control of an Airplane Using Fractional Order Direct Model Reference Adaptive Controllers. *Fractal Fract.* **2023**, *7*, 342. [CrossRef]
21. Narendra, K.S.; Annaswamy, A.M. Persistent excitation in adaptive systems. *Int. J. Control* **1987**, *45*, 127–160. [CrossRef]
22. The Math Works Inc. Control System Toolbox User's Guide. 1998. Available online: https://www.mathworks.com (accessed on 4 December 2024).
23. Valerio, D.; da Costa, J.S. Ninteger: A non-integer control toolbox for matlab. In *Fractional Derivatives and Applications*; OIFAC: Bordeaux, France, 2004.
24. Sabatier, J.; Aoun, M.; Oustaloup, A.; Gregoire, G.; Ragot, F.; Roy, P. Fractional system identification for lead acid battery state of charge estimation. *Signal Process.* **2006**, *86*, 2645–2657. [CrossRef]
25. Clerc, M. *Particle Swarm Optimization*; ISTE Ltd.: London, UK, 2006.

fractal and fractional

MDPI

Article

Fractional Gradient-Based Model Reference Adaptive Control Applied on an Inverted Pendulum-Cart System

Maibeth Sánchez-Rivero [1], Manuel A. Duarte-Mermoud [2], Lisbel Bárzaga-Martell [3,*], Marcos E. Orchard [1] and Gustavo Ceballos-Benavides [2,4]

1 Departamento de Ingeniería Eléctrica, Facultad de Ciencias Físicas y Matemáticas, Universidad de Chile, Av. Tupper 2007, Santiago 8370451, Región Metropolitana, Chile; maibeth.sanchez@ug.uchile.cl (M.S.-R.); morchard@ing.uchile.cl (M.E.O.)
2 Facultad de Ingeniería y Arquitectura, Universidad Central de Chile, Av. Santa Isabel 1186, Santiago 8330601, Región Metropolitana, Chile; manuel.duarte@ucentral.cl (M.A.D.-M.); gustavo.ceballos@ucentral.cl (G.C.-B.)
3 Departamento de Electricidad, Universidad Tecnológica Metropolitana, Av. José Pedro Alessandri 1242, Ñuñoa 7800002, Región Metropolitana, Chile
4 Escuela de Negocios y Tecnología, Universidad Gabriela Mistral, Av. Andrés Bello 1337, Santiago 7500533, Región Metropolitana, Chile
* Correspondence: lisbel.barzaga@utem.cl

Abstract

This study introduces a novel model reference adaptive control (MRAC) framework that incorporates fractional-order gradients (FGs) to regulate the displacement of an inverted pendulum-cart system. Fractional-order gradients have been shown to significantly improve convergence rates in domains such as machine learning and neural network optimization. Nevertheless, their integration with fractional-order error models within adaptive control paradigms remains unexplored and represents a promising avenue for research. The proposed control scheme extends the classical MRAC architecture by embedding Caputo fractional derivatives into the adaptive law governing parameter updates, thereby improving both convergence dynamics and control flexibility. To ensure optimal performance across multiple criteria, the controller parameters are systematically tuned using a multi-objective Particle Swarm Optimization (PSO) algorithm. Two fractional-order error models (FOEMs) incorporating fractional gradients (FOEM2-FG, FOEM3-FG) are investigated, with their stability formally analyzed via Lyapunov-based methods under conditions of sufficient excitation. Validation is conducted through both simulation and real-time experimentation on a physical pendulum-cart setup. The results demonstrate that the proposed fractional-order MRAC (FOMRAC) outperforms conventional MRAC, proportional-integral-derivative (PID), and fractional-order PID (FOPID) controllers. Specifically, FOMRAC-FG achieved superior tracking performance, attaining the lowest Integral of Squared Error (ISE) of 2.32×10^{-5} and the lowest Integral of Squared Input (ISI) of 6.40 in simulation studies. In real-time experiments, FOMRAC-FG maintained the lowest ISE (5.11×10^{-6}). Under real-time experiments with disturbances, it still achieved the lowest ISE (1.06×10^{-5}), highlighting its practical effectiveness.

Keywords: fractional-order model reference adaptive control (FOMRAC); fractional-order gradient (FG); Lyapunov stability; inverted pendulum-cart system

1. Introduction

The inverted pendulum-cart system remains a paradigmatic benchmark in nonlinear control theory due to its underactuated nature, structural instability, and rich dynamic behavior. This system serves as a standard platform for evaluating advanced control strategies and finds practical applications in robotics (e.g., bipedal locomotion), aerospace (e.g., satellite orientation), and civil engineering (e.g., structural vibration mitigation) [1–3].

The fundamental control objective is to stabilize the pendulum around its unstable upright equilibrium by applying horizontal forces to the cart. In recent decades, a wide range of control strategies have been proposed to address this challenge, including proportional-integral-derivative (PID) control, linear quadratic regulators (LQRs) [4], sliding mode control (SMC) [5,6], fuzzy logic [7], and model reference adaptive control (MRAC) [8], as well as hybrid and intelligent approaches that integrate multiple control paradigms. These control schemes can be broadly categorized into classical, robust, and intelligent control strategies.

Classical controllers, such as PID, are frequently employed due to their simplicity and ease of implementation. However, they exhibit limited robustness and adaptability. As reported in [7], while PID controllers achieve faster settling times, they underperform in adaptability compared to fuzzy logic, particularly under varying conditions such as inclined surfaces.

Robust controllers, including LQRs and SMC, provide improved stability and disturbance rejection. LQRs offer guaranteed stability under quadratic cost functions, although their effectiveness depends heavily on the appropriate selection of weight matrices [4]. SMC, on the other hand, exhibits strong robustness to model uncertainties and external disturbances, and is often combined with observers for state and disturbance estimation [5,9].

Intelligent control techniques, such as fuzzy logic, neural networks, and reinforcement learning, have gained traction in recent years for handling system nonlinearities and adaptability challenges. Fuzzy controllers enhance adaptability compared to PID [7]. Hybrid approaches that combine energy-based swing-up control with LQRs or SMC have been proposed for complex configurations such as rotary or double inverted pendulum systems [6,10]. Reinforcement learning methods, including Q-learning adapted to continuous control domains, have shown promise in simulation environments [11], although they remain sensitive to modeling inaccuracies and hardware constraints.

Robust and intelligent controllers continue to evolve. For instance, adaptive fuzzy terminal sliding mode control (AFFTSMC) [9] demonstrates experimental fault tolerance and reduced chattering. In [12], a second-order sliding mode controller is used to stabilize a pendulum mounted on an omnidirectional mobile robot, achieving semi-global asymptotic stability. Neural-based PID (PIDNN) architectures, optimized using Ant Colony Optimization [13], exhibit improved tracking and robustness compared to PSO-tuned PID/FOPID schemes, although they introduce increased model complexity and typically lack hardware validation. Experimental comparisons in [14], using an Arduino-based platform, demonstrate that both indirect adaptive control (IAC) and neuro-fuzzy control (NFC) outperform PID in terms of robustness and transient response.

While several advanced nonlinear control strategies have been proposed in recent years—such as BELBIC [15], fuzzy brain emotional learning controllers (FBELC) [16], neural PID structures [13], and deep reinforcement learning (DRL) approaches [17]—they still present major limitations. These include reliance on trial-and-error tuning [15], increased structural and computational complexity [16], and strong sensitivity to hyperparameter selection and model architecture [17]. Moreover, many of these methods are data-driven and lack analytical guarantees for convergence and stability, which limits their applicability in safety-critical real-time systems.

In contrast, **fractional-order control** has emerged as a novel and promising approach that offers a sound mathematical foundation with greater flexibility for tuning and improved robustness. By generalizing classical calculus to non-integer orders, fractional-order controllers introduce additional degrees of freedom in controller design [18,19]. Among them, the fractional-order PID (FOPID) controller extends the classical PID by incorporating fractional-order integrals and derivatives, enabling improved performance in the presence of model uncertainties and disturbances. Experimental studies, such as [20], validate its effectiveness in various real-world settings without requiring changes to model order. Recent works have applied metaheuristic optimization techniques—such as Particle Swarm Optimization (PSO), genetic algorithms, and differential evolution—to fine-tune FOPID parameters for multi-objective performance indices, including ITSE, settling time, and rise time [21,22]. These results confirm that fractional-order strategies can outperform conventional PID and many existing nonlinear controllers in both performance and adaptability.

Despite these advances, an important research gap persists: the integration of **fractional-order gradients (FGs)** into adaptive control frameworks like model reference adaptive control (MRAC). While FG methods have demonstrated improved convergence rates in optimization and machine learning applications [23], their incorporation into real-time adaptive control—particularly for nonlinear systems—remains largely unexplored. Recent work [24] has introduced a first-order fractional error model with fractional gradients (FOEM1–FG), showing encouraging results in simulations and initial experimental validations. The present paper aims to build upon this foundation, offering a systematic development and analysis of a novel fractional gradient-based MRAC scheme with theoretical guarantees and practical relevance.

In this paper, we address this gap by proposing a novel fractional-order error model (FOEM) framework that systematically embeds Caputo fractional gradients into the parameter adaptation law. Two new formulations, **FOEM2–FG and FOEM3–FG**, are presented and analyzed using Lyapunov stability theory. The proposed controller is tuned using a multi-objective PSO algorithm and validated using simulations and real-time experiments on an inverted pendulum-cart system.

The main contributions of this work are as follows:

1. The formulation of two original architectures, FOEM2–FG and FOEM3–FG, that incorporate fractional gradients into the adaptive law via Caputo derivatives. This contribution systematically extends classical adaptive control theory to fractional-order systems.
2. A rigorous Lyapunov-based stability and convergence analysis demonstrating boundedness of the tracking error and asymptotic convergence under persistent excitation.
3. Extensive validation using simulations and real-time experiments, showing that the proposed FOEMRAC strategy outperforms conventional MRAC, PID, and FOPID controllers in tracking accuracy and convergence speed.

The paper is organized as follows: Section 2 introduces the fundamentals of fractional calculus and fractional gradient methods. Section 3 formally defines the fractional-order error models (FOEM1–3) using Caputo derivatives and the Lyapunov-based stability and convergence analysis. Section 4 presents the case study and experimental validation, discussing the results and implications of fractional-order MRAC in underactuated nonlinear systems. Conclusions are presented in Section 5.

2. Preliminaries

Fractional calculus generalizes conventional calculus by allowing for differentiation and integration to be defined for orders that are not necessarily integers [25].

Several definitions of fractional derivatives exist in the literature, including the *Riemann–Liouville* and *Grünwald–Letnikov* definitions. This research employs the *Caputo* fractional derivative [26], which is preferred in engineering due to its straightforward treatment of initial conditions, clear physical interpretation, and availability of effective numerical tools. These features make it a robust method for modeling and analyzing systems that exhibit fractional behavior in practical applications.

Definition 1 (Caputo fractional derivative). *The Caputo fractional derivative of order $\alpha \in \mathbb{R}$ of function $f(\cdot)$, defined in a finite interval $[t_0, t]$ in $\mathbb{R}^+$, is defined as*

$$
\begin{aligned}
{}_{t_0}^{C}D_t^{\alpha} f(t) &= {}_{t_0}I_t^{n-\alpha}[D^n f(t)] \\
&= \frac{1}{\Gamma(n-\alpha)} \int_{t_0}^{t} \frac{f^{(n)}(\tau)}{(t-\tau)^{\alpha-n+1}} d\tau, \qquad t > t_0
\end{aligned}
\tag{1}
$$

with $n = min\{k \in \mathbb{N}/k > \alpha\}$. Also, it can be defined in a series form as

$$
{}_{t_0}^{C}D_t^{\alpha} f(t) = \sum_{i=n}^{\infty} \frac{f^{i}(t_0)}{\Gamma(i+1-\alpha)} (t-t_0)^{i-\alpha}. \tag{2}
$$

2.1. Fractional Gradient Using Caputo Derivative

The main concept behind fractional gradient (FG) methods is to use fractional-order derivatives instead of first-order ones while ensuring that the algorithm still converges properly:

$$
t_{k+1} = t_k - \gamma {}_{t_0}^{C}D_{t_k}^{\beta} f(t). \tag{3}
$$

where t_k is the current position, t_{k+1} is the next position, and $\gamma > 0$ is the learning rate.

In [23], the authors address the challenge that the fractional-order optimal point does not always align with the true optimum of the objective function [23,27,28]. To overcome this limitation, they propose three algorithms leveraging the Caputo fractional derivative. The first approach, called the fixed memory step method, takes advantage of the fractional derivative's long-memory property and then truncates it to a finite window. The second strategy simplifies the infinite series expansion of the fractional derivative by only retaining its leading term. The third technique dynamically adjusts the fractional order at each iteration based on the current loss function.

Moreover, these strategies are not mutually exclusive and can be combined in various ways. Together, they guarantee that a convergent algorithm will indeed approach the true extremum of the objective function. This makes the fractional-order gradient approach highly practical, versatile, and effective [23].

This paper builds upon the initial application of FG introduced in the authors' earlier research [24]. The FG equation is equal to

$$
t_{k+1} = t_k - \gamma \frac{f^{(1)}(t_k)}{\Gamma(2-\beta)} (|t_k - t_{k-1}| + \delta)^{1-\beta}, \tag{4}
$$

where γ is the adaptation gain, $\Gamma(\cdot)$ denotes the Gamma function, and $\delta > 0$ is a small constant to prevent numerical singularities.

Usually, γ is selected as a very small value to ensure the convergence of the FG so that $|t_k - t_{k-1}|$ decreases quickly below 1. The convergence speed of FG (4) for $0 < \beta < 1$ could be worse than in the conventional case because $\frac{\gamma}{\Gamma(2-\beta)}(|t_k - t_{k-1}| + \delta)^{1-\beta}$ can be viewed as the algorithm's step size. In contrast, the FG for $1 < \beta < 2$ will exhibit a convergence speed significantly faster than the conventional case.

2.2. Definitions

To analyze the convergence properties of fractional-order adaptive laws, we recall some fundamental concepts and results that establish the conditions under which the error dynamics are guaranteed to converge. The following definitions and properties summarize key notions of persistent and sufficient excitation for fractional-order systems, as well as their relationships:

Property 1 (Theorem 2, [29]). *For the FOEM-1, if $\omega \in PE(n,1)$ and $\alpha = 1$, then (ϕ, e) converges uniformly to zero. If $\omega \in SE(n,\alpha)$ and $0 < \alpha \leq 1$, then (ϕ, e) converges asymptotically to zero.*

Definition 2. *Let I_n be the $n \times n$ identity matrix and $\mathbb{R}^+$ the set of all real numbers greater than or equal to zero. Let us define the subset $SE(n,\alpha)$ in the space of bounded, continuously differentiable functions as the set of sufficiently exciting functions as follows:*

$$
\begin{aligned}
SE(n,\alpha) &:= \{\omega : [0,\infty) \to \mathbb{R}^n | (\exists f_\omega : [0,\infty) \to [0,\infty)), \\
s.t. \quad & \lim_{t\to\infty} I^\alpha f_\omega(t) = \infty \wedge (\forall t > 0)\omega(t)\omega^T(t) \leq f_\omega(t) I_n\}.
\end{aligned} \tag{5}
$$

Property 2 (Lemma 3, [29]). *Let $\omega \in \mathbb{R}^n$ be a uniformly continuous function. If $\omega \in PE(n,1)$, then $\omega \in SE(n,\alpha)$ for every $0 < \alpha < 1$.*

3. Fractional-Order Error Models with Fractional Gradient-Adaptive Laws

3.1. Fractional-Order Error Model 1 with Fractional Gradient-Adaptive Laws

In the work of [24], the fractional-order error model 1 with a fractional gradient (FOEM1-FG) is introduced. This model extends previous contributions [23,28] by incorporating both fixed-memory steps and truncated higher-order terms.

$$
\begin{aligned}
e_y(t) &= \phi^T(t)\omega(t), \\
D_{t_0}^\alpha \phi(t) &= \frac{-\gamma}{\Gamma(2-\beta)} e_y(t)\omega(t)(|\psi_t - \psi_{t-1}| + \delta)^{1-\beta}.
\end{aligned} \tag{6}
$$

$e_y(t)$ denotes the output error, and $D_{t_0}^\alpha \phi(t)$ represents the fractional update law. The signal $\omega(t) : \mathbb{R}^+ \to \mathbb{R}^n$ corresponds to the input or information vector (also referred to as the auxiliary signal). The term $\phi(t)$ captures the parameter error, while $\gamma \in \mathbb{R}^+$ is a constant adaptive gain, although it could be generalized to a time-varying gain with its own adaptation law. When $\beta = 1$, Equation (6) simplifies to fractional-order error model 1 (FOEM1), and when $\alpha = 1$, it transforms into the standard error model 1 (EM1) [30].

The simulation results reported in [24] confirm that the output error remains bounded and converges to zero for a wide range of signals, especially when the gradient order $\beta > 1$, which accelerates convergence. Theoretical analysis based on Lyapunov stability, fractional derivatives, and sufficient excitation ($SE(n,\alpha)$) confirms the boundedness and stability of the parameter error $\phi(t)$. While classical Barbalat-type results cannot be directly applied due to the properties of fractional integrals, parametric convergence is still guaranteed under specific conditions, particularly when the input signal belongs to $SE(n,\alpha)$. These results establish FOEM1-FG as a robust and flexible adaptive scheme suited for systems with limited plant information and fractional dynamics.

The analysis conducted for FOEM1-FG serves as the foundation for the subsequent subsections, in which FOEM2-FG and FOEM3-FG errors are presented.

3.2. *Fractional-Order Error Model 2 with Fractional Gradient-Adaptive Laws (FOEM2-FG)*

In the case of the fractional-order error model 2 (FOEM2), the error corresponds to the output of a dynamic system in which all state variables are accessible, as illustrated in Figure 1.

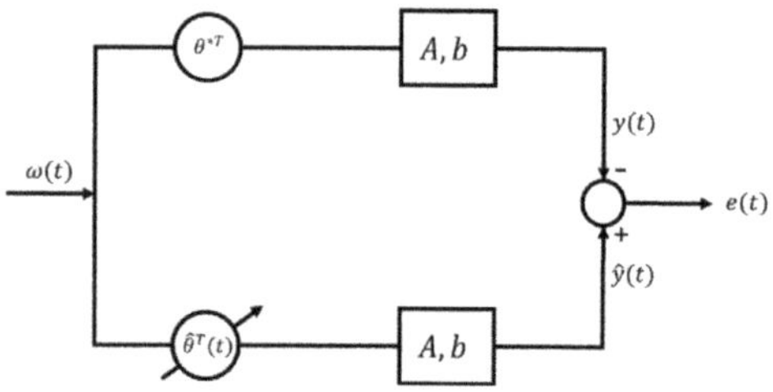

Figure 1. Fractional-order error model 2 scheme.

Since the full state vector is available, the error $e(t) : \mathbb{R}^+ \rightarrow \mathbb{R}^n$ can be defined using a fractional derivative of order η:

$$D_{t_0}^{\eta} e(t) = Ae(t) + b\phi^T(t)\omega(t), \tag{7}$$

where $D_{t_0}^{\eta}$ represents the fractional derivative of order η, which relies on the characteristics of the plant to be controlled. $y(t) = x(t)$ and $\hat{y}(t) = \hat{x}(t)$, where $x(t)$ represents the actual state and $\hat{x}(t)$ denotes the estimated state. $A \in \mathbb{R}^{n\times n}$ is an asymptotically stable matrix, $b \in \mathbb{R}^n$ is a known vector, and the pair (A, b) is controllable. The ideal parameter $\theta^* \in \mathbb{R}^m$ is assumed to be unknown, and $\theta(t) : \mathbb{R}^+ \rightarrow \mathbb{R}^m$ is the adjustable parameter that estimates the ideal parameter θ^*. The parametric error is defined as $\phi(t) = \theta(t) - \theta^*$.

If the loss function is defined as

$$L(\phi(t)) = \frac{d}{dt}\left\{\tfrac{e^T(t)Pe(t)}{2}\right\} + \frac{e^T(t)Qe(t)}{2}, \tag{8}$$

and the following fractional adjustment law is used,

$$\begin{aligned} D_{t_0}^{\alpha}\phi(t) &= -\gamma L^{(1)}(\phi(t)) \\ D_{t_0}^{\alpha}\phi(t) &= -\gamma e(t)^T Pb\omega(t), \end{aligned} \tag{9}$$

where $L^1(\phi(t))$ is the standard (integer-order) derivative of $L(\phi(t))$ and $P \in \mathbb{R}^{n\times n}$ is a symmetric positive definite matrix satisfying the equation $A^T P + PA = -Q < 0$ (where $Q \in \mathbb{R}^{n\times n}$ is an arbitrary symmetric positive definite matrix that penalizes the error). $\gamma \in \mathbb{R}^+$ is the adaptive gain, which is considered constant in this case.

The fractional adjustment law for the FOEM2 in (9), with the fractional gradient applied [23,28], is redefined as

$$D_{t_0}^{\alpha}\phi(t) = -\gamma \nabla_{\theta}^{\beta} L(\phi(t)) \tag{10}$$

where the term $\nabla_{\theta}^{\beta} L(\phi(t))$ is the gradient of the loss function $L(\phi(t))$ associated with the adaptive parameter θ.

$$\nabla_{\theta}^{\beta} L(\phi(t)) = \frac{L^{(1)}(\phi(t))}{\Gamma(2-\beta)}(|\theta_t - \theta_{t-1}| + \delta)^{1-\beta}, \tag{11}$$

$$\nabla_{\theta}^{\beta} L(\phi(t)) = \frac{e(t)^T Pb\omega(t)}{\Gamma(2-\beta)}(|\theta_t - \theta_{t-1}| + \delta)^{1-\beta}. \tag{12}$$

From Equation (12), retaining the value of the parameter θ from the previous moment (recorded data) is crucial. Consequently, the proposed adaptive law is

$$D_{t_0}^{\alpha}\phi(t) = -\gamma\frac{e(t)^T P b\omega(t)}{\Gamma(2-\beta)}(|\theta_t - \theta_{t-1}| + \delta)^{1-\beta}. \tag{13}$$

Equation (13) represents the fractional-order error model 2 with fractional gradient (FOEM2-FG) for the fractional error defined in Equation (7). Simulation studies of the FOEM2-FG for different values of α, and varying β, show that values of $\beta > 1$ significantly enhance the performance indices, regardless of the value of α. In the case of $\beta = 1$, (13) becomes the FOEM2 defined in [31].

We can state the following general conclusions regarding the two-dimensional vector case for the FOEM2-FG:

- The output error is bounded and converges to zero for all analyzed signals, regardless of the value of β for $0 < \beta < 2$.
- Values of $\beta > 1$ enhance the convergence speed of the output error, regardless of the value of α.
- The parametric error remains bounded, and its convergence to zero depends on the characteristics of the input signal $\omega(t)$ used.

Stability and Convergence Analysis for FOEM2-FG

For the stability analysis, it is assumed that $\eta = \alpha$. Although the case $\eta \neq \alpha$ has not yet been fully developed, it has been observed that the error model remains Lyapunov-stable within the FOEM2-FG framework (see Equation (13)).

ζ_t s defined as a positive definite adaptation gain matrix given by

$$\zeta_t = \frac{\gamma(|\theta_t - \theta_{t-1}| + \delta)^{1-\beta}}{\Gamma(2-\beta)}, \tag{14}$$

the behavior of ζ_t depends on β values (see Figure 2). For $\beta > 1$, if $|\theta_t - \theta_{t-1}| = 0$, then ζ_t is upper-bounded and remains finite. Conversely, if $\beta < 1$, simulations indicate that this does not improve the convergence speed of the algorithm, and, therefore, this range of β values is not recommended for FOEM2-FG.

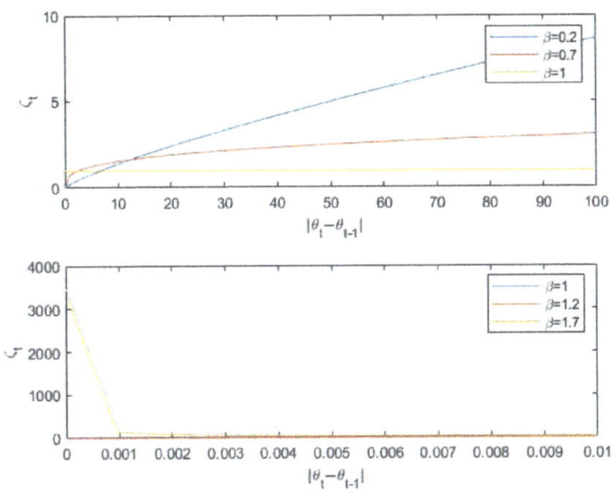

Figure 2. ζ_t performance as a function of $|\theta_t - \theta_{t-1}|$.

Additionally, if $|\theta_t - \theta_{t-1}| \to \infty$, then $\zeta_t \to \infty$. However, in practice, the objective of the optimization algorithm is to ensure that θ_t converges to θ_{t-1} through successive iterations. Consequently, abrupt parameter changes are unlikely, thereby guaranteeing that ζ_t remains bounded.

We now present the stability and convergence properties of the FOEM2-FG scheme; the results are summarized in the following theorem.

Theorem 1 (Lyapunov Stability of FOEM2-FG). *Consider the fractional-order error model FOEM2-FG with adaptation law given by*

$$D^{\alpha}\phi(t) = -e^{T}(t)\,P\,b\,\omega(t)\,\zeta_t, \tag{15}$$

and error dynamics defined by

$$D^{\alpha}e(t) = Ae(t) + b\,\phi^{T}(t)\omega(t), \tag{16}$$

where $A \in \mathbb{R}^{n\times n}$ is Hurwitz and $P = P^{T} > 0$. Then, under these conditions and assuming $\omega(t)$ is bounded, the closed-loop system is Lyapunov-stable, i.e.,

$$\|y(t)\| \le \|y(t_0)\|, \quad \forall t \ge t_0, \tag{17}$$

where $y(t) = \begin{bmatrix} Be(t) \\ \phi(t) \end{bmatrix}$ *and* $P = B^{T}B$.

Proof. Define the Lyapunov candidate function:

$$V(t) = e^{T}(t)Pe(t) + \phi^{T}(t)\,\zeta_t^{-1}\,\phi(t). \tag{18}$$

Taking the Caputo fractional derivative of order α and applying known bounds for FO derivatives of quadratic functions [32–34], we obtain

$$\begin{aligned} D^{\alpha}V(t) &\le 2\,e^{T}P\,D^{\alpha}e + 2\,K_{\zeta}^{-1}\,\phi^{T}D^{\alpha}\phi \\ &= 2\,e^{T}P\,(Ae + b\,\phi^{T}\omega) - 2\,\phi^{T}\,e^{T}Pb\,\omega \\ &= 2\,e^{T}PAe + 2\,e^{T}Pb\,\phi^{T}\omega - 2\,\phi^{T}e^{T}Pb\,\omega \\ &= 2\,e^{T}PAe. \end{aligned} \tag{19}$$

Using the property $A^{T}P + PA = -Q$ with $Q = Q^{T} > 0$, we have

$$e^{T}PAe = \frac{1}{2}e^{T}(A^{T}P + PA)e = -\frac{1}{2}e^{T}Qe. \tag{20}$$

Therefore,

$$D^{\alpha}V(t) \le -e^{T}Qe. \tag{21}$$

Since $Q > 0$, $V(t)$ is non-increasing. Integrating both sides yields

$$V(t) - V(t_0) \le -I_{t_0}^{\alpha}\left[e^{T}Qe\right] \le 0. \tag{22}$$

Recalling that $P = B^{T}B$, define

$$y(t) = \begin{bmatrix} Be(t) \\ \phi(t) \end{bmatrix}, \tag{23}$$

so that

$$\|y(t)\|^{2} = e^{T}Pe + \phi^{T}\phi = V(t). \tag{24}$$

Hence,

$$\|y(t)\|^2 - \|y(t_0)\|^2 \le 0, \tag{25}$$

implying:

$$\|y(t)\| \le \|y(t_0)\|, \quad \forall t \ge t_0. \tag{26}$$

This proves Lyapunov stability. □

Theorem 2 (Asymptotic Convergence under Sufficient Excitation). *Assume the conditions of Theorem 1. Furthermore, suppose that $\omega(t) \in SE(n,\alpha)$. Then, the tracking error $e(t)$ and the parameter estimation error $\phi(t)$ converge asymptotically to zero:*

$$\lim_{t\to\infty} e(t) = 0, \quad \lim_{t\to\infty} \phi(t) = 0. \tag{27}$$

Proof. Define the auxiliary error signal:

$$\epsilon(t) := D^\alpha e(t) - Ae(t) = b\,\phi^T(t)\,\omega(t). \tag{28}$$

Under the adaptive law,

$$D^\alpha \phi(t) = -\zeta_t\, e^T(t)\, P\, b\, \omega(t), \tag{29}$$

the coupled fractional-order system $(\phi(t), \epsilon(t))$ satisfies the hypotheses of Property 1. Therefore, if $\omega \in SE(n,\alpha)$, then $\epsilon(t) \to 0$ and $\phi(t) \to 0$ as $t \to \infty$. Since $\epsilon(t) \to 0$, consider

$$D^\alpha e(t) = Ae(t) + \epsilon(t). \tag{30}$$

Applying Theorem 5 in [35], it follows that $e(t) \to 0$ as $t \to \infty$. □

3.3. Fractional-Order Error Model 3 with Fractional Gradient-Adaptive Laws (FOEM3-FG)

The fractional-order error model 3 (referred to as FOEM3) has the same structure as FOEM2, with one key difference: access is restricted to an algebraic combination of its components, specifically $e_1(t) \in \mathbb{R}$. In contrast, FOEM2 allows for access to the entire error vector $e(t) \in \mathbb{R}^n$, which reflects the state access available in real plants. Generally, this error model arises when only the output of the plant being controlled or identified is accessible, making FOEM3 applicable to a broader range of problems compared to FOEM2. Figure 3 presents the diagram for FOEM3.

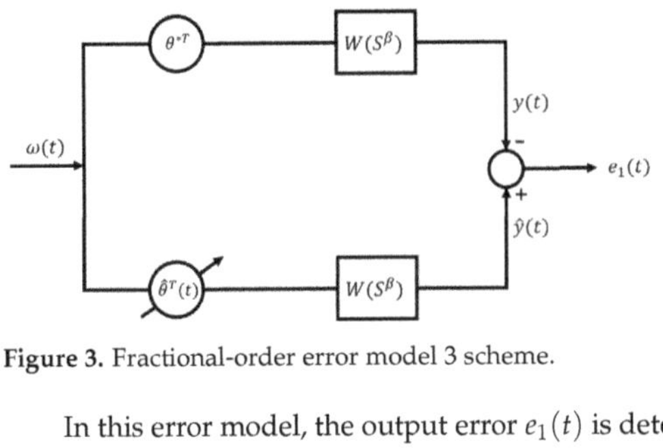

Figure 3. Fractional-order error model 3 scheme.

In this error model, the output error $e_1(t)$ is determined by

$$e_1(t) = h^T e(t), \tag{31}$$

where h^T is the output weighting vector and $e(t)$ is the state estimation error. Considering a dynamic system, the fractional error dynamics equation is similar to (7), where now the pair (h^T, A) must be observable. The fractional adjustment law for FOEM3 takes the following form:

$$D^{\alpha}_{t_0}\phi(t) = -\gamma \frac{e_1(t)\omega(t)}{\Gamma(2-\beta)}(|\theta_t - \theta_{t-1}| + \delta)^{1-\beta}, \tag{32}$$

where $\theta^* \in \mathbb{R}$ is the ideal parameter assumed to be unknown, $\theta(t) : \mathbb{R}^+ \to \mathbb{R}^m$ is the adjustable parameter that estimates θ^*, and $\phi(t) = \theta(t) - \theta^* : \mathbb{R}^* \to \mathbb{R}^m$ is the parametric error. $e(t) : \mathbb{R}^+ \to \mathbb{R}^n$ is the state error, $\omega(t) : \mathbb{R}^+ \to \mathbb{R}^m$ is the input signal, also known as the information signal, and $e_1(t) : \mathbb{R}^+ \to \mathbb{R}$ is the output error, which is assumed to be accessible.

As stated earlier, the fact that only $e_1(t)$ is available instead of the complete state vector makes this error model more commonly used than FOEM2. However, as anticipated, more restrictive conditions are placed on the transfer function $W(s^\beta)$ between $\phi^T(t)\omega(t)$ and $e_1(t)$, so that the tuning laws could be synthesized. Specifically, the triplet (h^T, A, b) must ensure that the transfer function $h^T(sI - A)^{-1}b$ is strictly positive real (SPR) [30].

The tuning law for this error model is expressed as $\gamma > 0$, which is related to the adaptive gain. This adaptive gain may be a constant or a time-varying scalar $\gamma \in \mathbb{R}$, or it might take the form of a constant or time-varying matrix $\Gamma \in \mathbb{R}^{m \times n}$ [30].

Stability and Convergence Analysis for FOEM3-FG

We now present the stability and convergence properties of the proposed FOEM3-FG scheme for the case $\eta = \alpha$. The results are summarized in the following theorem.

Theorem 3 (Lyapunov Stability of FOEM3-FG). *Consider the fractional-order error model FOEM3-FG with adaptation law governed by:*

$$D^{\alpha}_{t_0}\phi(t) = -e_1^T\omega(t)\,\zeta_t, \tag{33}$$

and error dynamics defined by:

$$D^{\alpha}e(t) = Ae(t) + b\,\phi^T(t)\omega(t), \tag{34}$$

where $A \in \mathbb{R}^{n\times n}$ is Hurwitz and the transfer function $h^T(sI - A)^{-1}b$ is strictly positive real (SPR). Then, under these conditions and assuming $\omega(t)$ is bounded, the closed-loop system is Lyapunov stable in the sense that:

$$\|y(t)\| \leq \|y(t_0)\|, \quad \forall t \geq t_0, \tag{35}$$

where $y(t) = \begin{bmatrix} Be(t) \\ \phi(t) \end{bmatrix}$ *with* $P = B^T B$ *a positive definite matrix.*

Proof. Let us define the Lyapunov candidate function:

$$V(t) = e^T(t)Pe(t) + K_\zeta^{-1}\phi^T(t)\phi(t), \tag{36}$$

where $P = P^T > 0$ is the solution of the Lyapunov equation:

$$A^TP + PA = -Q, \quad Q = Q^T > 0, \quad Pb = h. \tag{37}$$

Taking the Caputo fractional derivative of $V(t)$ of order α, we obtain

$$D^{\alpha}V(t) = D^{\alpha}\left[e^T Pe\right] + K_{\zeta}^{-1}D^{\alpha}\left[\phi^T\phi\right]$$
$$\leq e^T(A^T P + PA)e + 2e^T Pb\phi^T\omega - 2\phi^T e_1\omega$$
$$= -e^T Qe + 2e_1\phi^T\omega - 2\phi^T e_1\omega$$
$$= -e^T Qe. \tag{38}$$

Since $Q > 0$, this implies $D^{\alpha}V(t) \leq 0$, which shows that $V(t)$ is non-increasing. Integrating both sides yields

$$V(t) - V(t_0) \leq -\int_{t_0}^{t} \frac{1}{\Gamma(\alpha)}(t-\tau)^{\alpha-1}e^T(\tau)Qe(\tau)d\tau. \tag{39}$$

Rewriting $V(t)$ using $P = B^T B$, we define $y(t) = \begin{bmatrix} Be(t) \\ \phi(t) \end{bmatrix}$, so that

$$\|y(t)\|^2 = e^T Pe + \phi^T\phi = V(t). \tag{40}$$

Then the inequality becomes

$$\|y(t)\|^2 - \|y(t_0)\|^2 \leq -I_{t_0}^{\alpha}\left[e^T Qe\right] \leq 0, \tag{41}$$

which implies

$$\|y(t)\| \leq \|y(t_0)\|, \quad \forall t \geq t_0. \tag{42}$$

Thus, the system is Lyapunov-stable. □

Theorem 4 (Asymptotic Convergence under Persistent Excitation). *Assume the conditions of Theorem 3 hold. Furthermore, suppose that the regressor $\omega(t) \in SE(n,\alpha)$, i.e., it is α-persistently exciting. Then, the tracking error $e(t)$ and the parameter estimation error $\phi(t)$ converge asymptotically to zero:*

$$\lim_{t\to\infty} e(t) = 0, \qquad \lim_{t\to\infty} \phi(t) = 0. \tag{43}$$

Proof. Define the auxiliary signal:

$$\epsilon(t) := D^{\alpha}e(t) - Ae(t) = b\,\phi^T(t)\omega(t). \tag{44}$$

Under the adaptive law,

$$D^{\alpha}\phi(t) = -\zeta_t\epsilon(t)P\omega(t), \tag{45}$$

the pair $(\phi(t), \epsilon(t))$ forms a coupled fractional-order dynamic system. According to Property 1, if $\omega(t) \in \mathrm{SE}(n,\alpha)$, then both $\phi(t) \to 0$ and $\epsilon(t) \to 0$ as $t \to \infty$. Since $\omega(t)$ is bounded, this implies $\phi^T(t)\omega(t) \to 0$. Now consider the fractional-order linear system:

$$D^{\alpha}e(t) = Ae(t) + \epsilon(t), \tag{46}$$

with $\epsilon(t) \to 0$. Applying Theorem 5 in [35], it follows that $e(t) \to 0$ as $t \to \infty$. □

4. Results and Simulations

4.1. Case Study: The Inverted Pendulum

The advantages of the FOEM3-FG are examined in an experimental case of study: the inverted pendulum (InvP). The InvP is a servomechanism consisting of a pivot, which can swing freely about its axis and is mounted on a carriage (Figure 4). The carriage moves along a horizontal axis within a finite range, generating thus an oscillation in the pendulum. The objective is to keep the pendulum vertical and maintain it at equilibrium by implementing a control system [36]. Fractional-order PID (FOPID) controllers have already been experimentally validated in this plant [37].

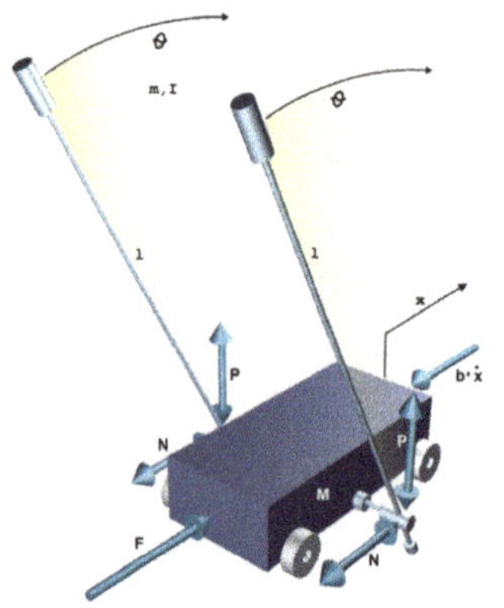

Figure 4. Inverted pendulum-cart system [36].

The carriage's movement is generated by the traction of a chain coupled to the shaft of a direct current (DC) motor located at the end of the rail. Applying voltage to the motor allows for the carriage's movement to be controlled in both directions. The two variables measured in the system using optical encoders are the carriage's position and the pendulum's inclination angle. Table 1 shows the parameters of the pendulum-cart system used in this study.

The control signal is limited in the range $[-2.5\,\text{V}\ldots+2.5\,\text{V}]$ and the magnitude of the generated force varies in the interval $[-20.0\,\text{N}\ldots+20.0\,\text{N}]$. The length of the rail physically limits the position of the carriage and is equal to $[-0.5\,\text{m}\ldots+0.5\,\text{m}]$.

The phenomenological model of the inverted pendulum is presented in Equation (47). By adding the forces acting on the pendulum and cart system, as well as the moments, the following nonlinear equations of motion are derived:

$$\begin{aligned} (m+M)\ddot{x} + b\dot{x} + ml\ddot{\theta}cos\theta - ml\dot{\theta}^2 sin\theta &= F, \\ (I+ml^2)\ddot{\theta} - mglsin\theta + ml\ddot{x}cos\theta + d\dot{\theta} &= 0, \end{aligned} \tag{47}$$

where x [m] is the cart position corresponding to the center of the rail, θ [rad] is the pendulum angular position concerning the vertical axis, g is the gravitational acceleration, l is the pendulum length, M is the mass of the cart, m is the mass of the pendulum, I is the moment of inertia, b is the friction coefficient of the cart, d is the viscous friction coefficient of the pendulum, and F is the force applied to the cart by the motor and corresponds to the input to the system. The parameter values are listed in Table 1. For the simplicity of presenting our theoretical results, the control input $u(t)$ used in the inverted pendulum state model is the force exerted on the cart, $u(t) = F$.

Next, we will analyze the equilibrium states of the pendulum and their effects on the phenomenological model. The pendulum has two equilibrium points: one occurs when $\theta = 0$ (inverted pendulum, unstable system), and the other occurs when $\theta = \pi$ (freely suspended, stable system). To demonstrate the applicability of the proposed adaptive controller, we will focus on the linearized model for the operating point $\theta = pi$. The position of the cart, denoted as x, will be controlled by letting the angle hang freely.

Table 1. Pendulum parameters.

Parameter	Value
g—Gravity	$9.81\ m/s^2$
l—Rod length	0.36 m
M—Cart mass	2.4 kg
m—Pendulum mass	0.23 kg
I—Moment of inertia	$0.099\ kg \cdot m^2$
b—Friction coefficient	0.05 Ns/m
d—Damping coefficient (negligible)	0.005 Ns/m

4.2. Linearized Model for Equilibrium Point $\theta = \pi$

To linearize the system with respect to the equilibrium point $\theta = \pi$, the following substitutions are made:

$$\begin{aligned} sin\theta &\cong -\theta, \\ cos\theta &\cong -1, \\ \dot{\theta}^2 &= 0, \end{aligned} \tag{48}$$

resulting in

$$\begin{aligned} (m+M)\ddot{x} + b\dot{x} - ml\ddot{\theta} &= F, \\ (I+ml^2)\ddot{\theta} + mgl\theta - ml\ddot{x} + d\dot{\theta} &= 0. \end{aligned} \tag{49}$$

Building the matrices in the state variable, we obtain

$$\begin{aligned} \dot{x}(t) &= A(t)x(t) + B(t)u(t), \\ y(t) &= C(t)x(t), \end{aligned} \tag{50}$$

with the state vector $x(t)$ defined as

$$\dot{x}(t) = \begin{bmatrix} x_1 \\ x_2 \\ x_3 \\ x_4 \end{bmatrix} = \begin{bmatrix} \theta(t) \\ \dot{\theta}(t) \\ x(t) \\ \dot{x}(t) \end{bmatrix}. \tag{51}$$

The state matrices ($A \in \mathbb{R}^{4\times4}$, $B \in \mathbb{R}^{4\times1}$) and output matrices ($C \in \mathbb{R}^{2\times4}$) become

$$A = \begin{bmatrix} 0 & 1 & 0 & 0 \\ -\frac{mgl(M+m)}{z} & -\frac{D(M+m)}{z} & 0 & -\frac{mlb}{z} \\ 0 & 0 & 0 & 1 \\ -\frac{gm^2l^2}{z} & -\frac{mlD}{z} & 0 & -\frac{by}{z} \end{bmatrix}; B = \begin{bmatrix} 0 \\ \frac{ml}{z} \\ 0 \\ \frac{y}{z} \end{bmatrix}; C = \begin{bmatrix} 1 & 0 & 0 & 0 \\ 0 & 0 & 1 & 0 \end{bmatrix}, \tag{52}$$

where

$$\begin{aligned} z &= I(M+m) + Mml^2, \\ y &= I + ml^2. \end{aligned}$$

4.3. Parameters Tuning

The controller parameters are tuned using the Particle Swarm Optimization (PSO) algorithm [38]. PSO is a population-based metaheuristic method inspired by swarm intelligence. It mimics the social behavior of a biological population (such as insects, birds, or fish) in their search for food. According to its creators, each individual (particle) interacts with another, exchanging experiences, so that the group will gradually move into better regions of the search space [38].

In PSO, Figure 5, the solution search for each particle is defined by the update of its speed and position inside the swarm, which are established as follows:

$$\begin{aligned} &V^{(j,t)} = \omega V^{(j,t-1)} + C_1 r_1 (Pb^j - X^{(j,t-1)}) + C_2 r_2 (Gb - X^{(j,t-1)}), \\ &whith \quad j = 1,\ldots,N \quad t = 1,\ldots,T \\ &and \quad X^{(j,t)} = X^{(j,t-1)} + V^{(j,t)}, \end{aligned} \tag{53}$$

where N and T are the number of particles of the swarm and the number of iterations, respectively. V and X are the speed and the position of the particle (i.e., the candidate solution), C_1 and C_2 are the acceleration coefficients (individual or population), Pb^j is the best position found by the particle in previous iterations, Gb is the best position found by the population, r_1 and r_2 are uniformly distributed random numbers in the interval $[0,1]$ used to keep the population diversity, and ω is the inertial weight.

Input: Parameters: C_1 (acceleration individual coefficients), C_2 (acceleration social coefficients), ω (inertia weight), N (population size),
Initialize X^0 and velocities V^0 randomly.
Initialize personal bests Pb = X^0.
Initialize Pareto archive.
Repeat
    For j = 1 to N /* Each individual */
        Evaluate objective functions at X^j.
        Update personal best Pb^j if necessary (random non-dominated solution).
    End For
    Update Pareto Front Archive
    For j = 1 to N /* Each individual */
        Select leader Gb (random non-dominated solution).
        Update velocities:
        $V^{(j,t)} = \omega V^{(j,t-1)} + C_1 r_1 \left(Pb^j - X^{(j,t-1)}\right) + C_2 r_2 \left(Gb - X^{(j,t-1)}\right)$
        Move to the new position: $X^{(j,t)} = X^{(j,t-1)} + V^{(j,t)}$
        Apply velocity and position constraints.
    End For
Until Stopping criteria /* ex: a given number of generations */
Output: Pareto front archive (best solutions found)

Figure 5. Pseudocode of the Multiobjective PSO algorithm.

A high value of ω implies greater exploration of the search space and a longer convergence time. In contrast, a small value reduces convergence time, but increases the risk of getting trapped in a local optimum. The value of ω is typically set to decrease linearly, promoting greater exploration at the beginning of the algorithm and greater exploitation of the solutions found as the search progresses.

In this work, a multi-objective problem is defined. A first primary objective function is defined as the Integral of Squared Error (ISE):

$$J_1 = ISE = \int_0^T e(t)^2 dt, \tag{54}$$

where $e(t)$ represents the control error, computed as the difference between the reference signal $r(t)$ and the system output $y(t)$, i.e., $e(t) = r(t) - y(t)$. A lower ISE indicates better tracking performance and improved accuracy.

Then, a second objective function is defined as the Quantitative Total Variation (QTV). The QTV metric is used to evaluate the variability of the control signal $u(t)$, reflecting the aggressiveness of its variation over time. The QTV is defined as

$$J_2 = QTV = \sum_{t=1}^{N-1} (u_{t+1} - u_t)^2, \tag{55}$$

where $u(t)$ is the control signal by the instant t and N is the total number of samples, taken with a sampling time of 0.001 s. J_2 is focused on minimizing highly abrupt behavior.

Although it is possible to aggregate the two objectives (J_1 and J_2) into a single weighted cost function, this study employs a Pareto-based approach to preserve the trade-offs between competing objectives. To this end, a Multiobjective Particle Swarm Optimization (MOPSO) algorithm is applied, which extends the classical PSO framework to handle multiple objectives simultaneously. Key modifications include the following:

- Maintaining an archive of non-dominated (Pareto-optimal) solutions found throughout the optimization process.
- Selecting a random leader from the Pareto front to maintain solution diversity and prevent premature convergence.

In MOPSO, each particle represents a candidate controller configuration defined by parameters such as gains or fractional orders. The algorithm evaluates each configuration using simulations of the cart-pendulum system, computing ISE and QTV as objective metrics for tracking accuracy and trajectory smoothness. These values define the fitness function, allowing for the construction of a Pareto front with non-dominated solutions. Particle positions and velocities are iteratively updated until a stopping criterion is met, enabling the simultaneous optimization of both performance objectives.

Three key performance indices—Integral of Squared Error (ISE) (54), Quantitative Total Variation (QTV) (55), and Integral of Squared Input (ISI)—are used to quantitatively evaluate the control performance of the different controllers implemented on the inverted pendulum-cart system. These indices measure tracking accuracy, control signal smoothness, and control effort.

The Integral of Squared Input (ISI) measures the energy associated with the control signal and is defined as

$$\mathrm{ISI} = \int_0^T u^2(t)\,dt. \tag{56}$$

A lower ISI implies reduced control effort and energy consumption, which are critical in real-time embedded systems and power-sensitive applications.

These indices collectively allow for a comprehensive evaluation of control performance, balancing accuracy (ISE), smoothness (QTV), and effort (ISI).

4.4. Controllers Design

4.4.1. PID and FOPID Controllers

The manufacturer provides a PID controller for controlling the car's movement on the rail [36]. Since the manufacturer's PID effectively meets the control objective, the performance of this controller will serve as a reference for the other designed controllers. The PID equation is described as follows:

$$u_{PID}(t) = K_p\, e(t) + K_i \int_0^t e(\tau)d\tau + K_d \frac{de(t)}{dt}. \tag{57}$$

To construct the fractional order of the FOPID controller, as shown in Equation (58), we utilize the structure of the manufacturer's PID controller, but with fractional parameters. The fractional parameters, denoted as λ and μ, are optimized using Multiobjective Particle Swarm Optimization (MOPSO). The numerical values for the PID and FOPID controllers are defined in Table 2.

A value of $\mu = 0.02$ indicates that the FOPID controller essentially behaves as a FOPI controller, since the derivative action effectively becomes a proportional action. It is also interesting to note that $\lambda = 1.15$ is greater than one, corresponding to the integer-order integration.

$$u_{FOPID}(t) = K_p\, e(t) + K_i\, D_t^{-\lambda} e(t) + K_d\, D_t^{\mu} e(t). \tag{58}$$

4.4.2. MRAC and FOMRAC Controllers

With the aim of controlling the position of the car x_3, without concern for the angular position of the pendulum, we include integral tracking of reference error, thus resulting in an extended state plant model given by

$$A_{ext} = \begin{bmatrix} & A & & & 0 \\ 0 & 0 & 1 & 0 & 0 \end{bmatrix}; B_{ext} = \begin{bmatrix} B \\ 0 \end{bmatrix}; B_m = \begin{bmatrix} 0 \\ -1 \end{bmatrix}; C_m = \begin{bmatrix} 0 & 0 & 1 & 0 & 0 \end{bmatrix}, \tag{59}$$

the reference model for the design of the MRAC [39] is defined as follows:

$$\begin{aligned} \dot{\hat{x}}_m &= A_m \hat{x}_m + B_m r(t), \\ \hat{y}_m &= C_m \hat{x}_m, \end{aligned} \tag{60}$$

where $A_m = A_{ext} - B_{ext}K$ and where the gain K is defined by linear quadratic regulator (LQR) methods that keep the system stable.

The control signal is defined as

$$F = -\phi(t)^T \omega(t), \tag{61}$$

where it is a negative linear combination of the information vector $\omega = [x(t), r(t)]$, weighted by adaptive parameters.

The control error is defined as the difference between the plant output in Equation (50) and the reference model described in (60), and the error dynamic $\dot{e}(t)$ is defined in Equation (7), with the corresponding adjustment law:

$$D_{t_0}^{\alpha} \phi(t) = -\gamma \frac{e_1^T(t)\omega(t)}{\Gamma(2-\beta)} (|\theta_t - \theta_{t-1}| + \delta)^{1-\beta}, \tag{62}$$

with $e_1(t) = h^T e(t)$, where $h = [0 \quad 1]$ and $\delta = 0.01$. The model reference adaptive control described by Equations (7) and (62), illustrated in Figure 6, corresponds to the FOEM3-FG, as complete access to the system output state vector is not available.

For the design of the integer-order MRAC, the tuning of γ_{θ_1} and γ_{θ_1} is performed individually, as separating the output error gains from the parameter adaptation gains proves to be more beneficial. The control signal is given by

$$u_{MRAC}(t) = u_{FOMRAC}(t) = -\phi(t)^T \omega(t), \tag{63}$$

with the error model $\dot{e}(t)$ and adaptation law $\phi(t)$ defined in Equations (7) and (62), respectively, and the information vector equal to $\omega = [x(t), r(t)]$. When $\alpha = 1$ and $\beta = 1$, the formulation corresponds to the standard MRAC. In contrast, when α and β differ from 1, the method corresponds to the fractional-order variant, FOMRAC.

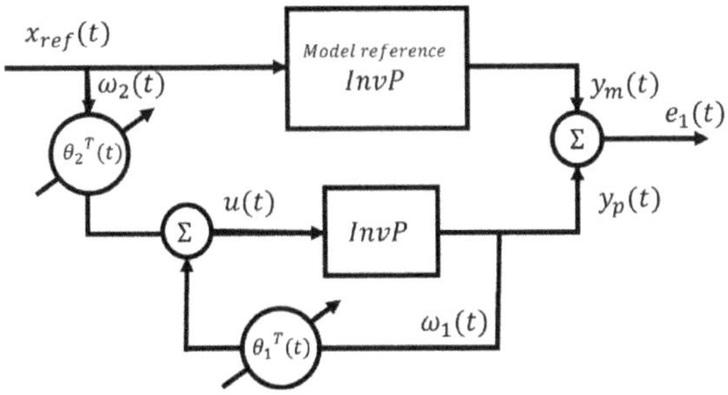

Figure 6. Block diagram of the inverted pendulum with the FOMRAC controller.

4.4.3. Simulations for the System of the Inverted Pendulum

Fractional operators were implemented using the Ninteger toolbox for MATLAB [40], specifically through the NID block, which approximates fractional-order transfer functions. Since the NID block does not handle initial conditions by default, the Caputo definition of the fractional derivative and relevant properties of fractional integrals were adopted in order to incorporate the system's initial states correctly.

The NID block operates based on the Oustaloup recursive approximation method. For this implementation, a configuration of ten poles and ten zeros was selected, with a frequency range of $[0.001, 1000]$ rad/s to ensure a reliable approximation across the operating bandwidth.

For all simulations, the initial conditions placed the cart at the center of the rail, while the pendulum started from the inverted position (180° from the vertical) and at rest. The simulation time was set to 60 s. The values of the linear quadratic regulator (LQR) matrices Q_{LQR} and R_{LQR}, as well as the gain matrix K, were defined using LQR methods to ensure closed-loop system stability.

$$Q_{LQR} = \begin{bmatrix} 0 & 0 & 0 & 0 & 0 \\ 0 & 0 & 0 & 0 & 0 \\ 0 & 0 & 0 & 0 & 0 \\ 0 & 0 & 0 & 0 & 0 \\ 0 & 0 & 0 & 0 & 1 \end{bmatrix}, \qquad R_{LQR} = 1, \tag{64}$$

where the gain K is equal to $K = [-0.0848; -0.1135; 2.7592; 3.7567; 1]$. The numerical values for the MRAC and FOMRAC controllers are defined in Table 2.

Table 2. Numerical values of the parameters for the PID, FOPID, MRAC, and FOMRAC controllers.

Controller	K_p	K_i	K_d	λ	μ	γ_{θ_1}	γ_{θ_2}	α	β
PID	27.3	50	3.9	1	1	–	–	–	–
FOPID	27.3	50	3.9	1.15	0.02	–	–	–	–
MRAC	–	–	–	–	–	594.44	632.85	1	1
FOMRAC	–	–	–	–	–	2.95	8.13	0.38	1.71

Figure 7 shows the pendulum position control simulation in response to a sinusoidal reference input, defined as $r(t) = 0.15sin(0.2073t)$, and the corresponding control signal $u(t)$ generated by the four designed controllers (PID, FOPID, MRAC, and FOMRAC). Table 3 presents a comparative analysis using the performance indices defined in Section 4.3.

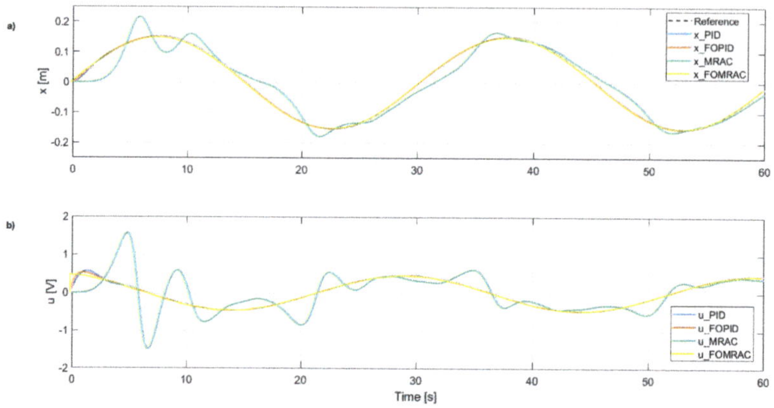

Figure 7. Simulation of control over the movement of the pendulum carriage on the rail. (**a**) Position x. (**b**) Control signal in volts v. PID (blue), FOPID (orange), MRAC (green), FOMRAC (yellow).

In Figure 7a, which shows the cart position x over time, the conventional MRAC controller exhibits significant overshoot and oscillatory behavior, indicating a less robust response to the system's nonlinear dynamics. The FOPID controller improves damping and reduces oscillatory behavior, but still displays a delayed and less accurate tracking of the reference. However, it achieves the best QTV score (Table 3). The proposed FOMRAC controller demonstrates the best tracking performance, following the desired reference with minimal error and the fastest convergence, as reflected by its superior ISE value (Table 3).

Figure 7b presents the control signal in volts. The MRAC controller generates the most aggressive control action, characterized by high peaks and rapid variations, which may lead to increased energy consumption and actuator wear. The FOPID controller provides a moderately smoother control effort, but exhibits noticeable transients. In contrast, the FOMRAC controller produces the softest and most efficient control signal among all methods, with minimal amplitude and variation, corresponding to the best ISI score (Table 3). This suggests a more energy-efficient use of control effort while maintaining high trajectory-tracking performance. Overall, the FOMRAC strategy outperforms the others in both reference tracking and control efficiency. Although the FOPID controller exhibits the best Quadratic Tracking Variation (QTV), the FOMRAC's performance remains comparable and well-balanced across all indices.

Including fractional-order gradients markedly enhances the adaptability and robustness of the control scheme, resulting in a notably smoother transient response. As shown in Table 2, the adaptive gain values γ_{k_c} and γ_{ϕ} required for the FOMRAC controller are significantly lower than those needed for the conventional MRAC approach. Despite these lower gains, FOMRAC not only outperforms the classical MRAC in terms of stability and tracking precision, but also delivers performance comparable to—and in some cases exceeding—that of the $FOPID$ controller. These results demonstrate that incorporating fractional calculus into adaptive control strategies introduces additional degrees of freedom that enhance flexibility, robustness, and overall control performance, particularly in scenarios where integer-order methods prove insufficient.

Table 3. Performance of controllers for simulation results.

Controller	ISE	QTV	ISI
PID	2.0248×10^{-4}	1.8299×10^{-3}	6.6207
FOPID	1.2303×10^{-4}	8.2456×10^{-4}	6.5697
MRAC	4.8070×10^{-2}	1.3485×10^{-2}	14.1294
FOMRAC	2.3248×10^{-5}	5.7534×10^{-3}	6.4062

4.4.4. Experimental Simulations for the System of Inverted Pendulum

The experimental results presented in Figure 8 were obtained experimentally in the research group's laboratory using the inverted pendulum model provided by Feedback Instruments [36].

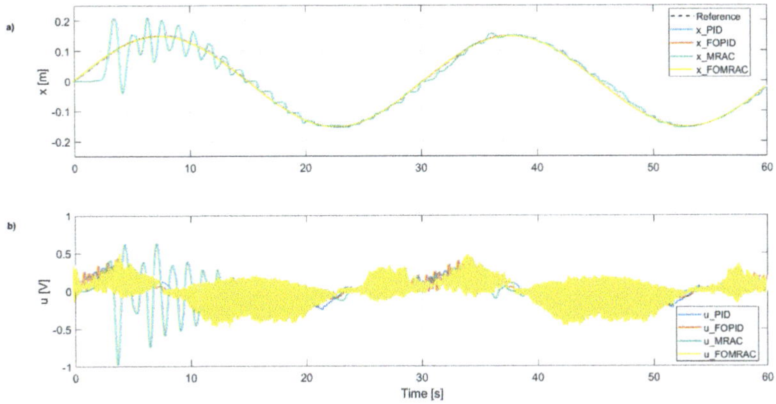

Figure 8. Experimental simulation of control over the movement of the pendulum carriage on the rail. (**a**) Position x. (**b**) Control signal in volts v. PID (blue), FOPID (orange), MRAC (green), FOMRAC (yellow).

In Figure 8a, the cart position x reveals a clear contrast between the control strategies. As observed in simulation, the MRAC controller (green) continues to display overshoot and oscillations, indicating limited robustness in handling real-world nonlinearities and noise. The FOPID controller (orange) improves greatly, reducing oscillatory behavior and showing a more stable trajectory than MRAC, obtaining the best QTV. The proposed FOMRAC controller (yellow) also accurately tracks the reference trajectory, achieving the best ISE. Despite the increased variability inherent in the physical setup, it minimizes the tracking error over the full time horizon and exhibits faster convergence than the other methods.

Figure 8b shows the control signals in volts. The control effort of the MRAC exhibits the highest amplitude signal, although it remains within the permissible range of the DC motor. The FOPID signal has a lower amplitude than the MRAC and achieves the best ISI (see Table 4), although it still displays visible transients. In contrast, the FOMRAC controller, in its practical implementation, produces control actions with more frequent abrupt changes than the other methods. Although the inverted pendulum setup applies constraints such as slew rate limiting, high-frequency filtering, and dead zone compensation to protect the motor from overvoltage, current spikes, and excessive wear, this behavior suggests a potential area for improvement in the FOMRAC design, since its control signal could impose considerable stress on the actuators in real-world applications. Overall, the FOMRAC strategy demonstrates superior experimental performance in precise reference tracking, even if this entails larger variations in the control signal, thereby validating the advantages of incorporating fractional-order gradients into adaptive control laws.

Table 4. Performance of controllers for experimental results.

Controller	ISE	QTV	ISI
PID	7.9273×10^{-5}	1.0607×10^{-1}	1.0670
FOPID	7.3898×10^{-5}	7.6233×10^{-2}	1.0172
MRAC	3.4059×10^{-2}	4.1561×10^{-2}	1.9829
FOMRAC	5.1070×10^{-6}	15.8057	1.6068

4.4.5. Experimental Simulations for the System of the Inverted Pendulum with Disturbances

To validate the robustness of the designed controllers against disturbances, simulations were carried out in which the pendulum was displaced from its stable equilibrium position at $\theta = \pi$ to $\theta = \frac{3}{2}\pi$. This scenario represents a significant alteration of the system dynamics and allows for assessments of how each control strategy maintains trajectory tracking performance under adverse conditions.

In the case of the PID controllers, both the classical integer-order and the fractional-order variants (see Figure 9a), it is observed that reference tracking is noticeably affected during the application of the disturbance. This performance degradation manifests as small oscillations superimposed on the reference trajectory, which tend to diminish progressively as the controllers increase the control action to compensate for the error. This behavior is numerically reflected in the performance indices presented in Table 5, where an increase in the ISE is evident. Likewise, Figure 9b shows that this compensation involves a considerable increase in the control signal amplitude and its transients, reflecting additional control effort that could compromise energy efficiency and actuator lifespan if sustained over time.

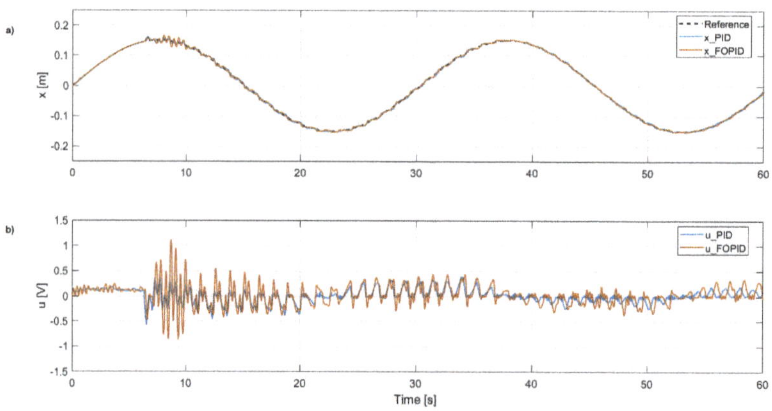

Figure 9. Experimental simulation of control over the movement of the pendulum carriage on the rail with disturbances. (**a**) Position x. (**b**) Control signal in volts v. PID (blue), FOPID (orange).

In the case of the conventional MRAC controller (Figure 10a), the system initially exhibits oscillations that gradually decrease until, after second 30, the disturbance is applied. The system then experiences a rise in oscillations around the reference, accompanied by a sustained increase in the control signal amplitude (Figure 10b). This increase highlights the limited capability of the conventional MRAC to dynamically adapt to abrupt changes in operating conditions, partially compromising tracking performance.

In contrast, the FOMRAC controller demonstrates more robust behavior against the disturbance. Although an increase in the magnitude of the control action is observed in the control signal (Figure 10b) when compensating for the perturbation, the reference tracking remains practically unaffected, without additional noticeable oscillations in the trajectory.

This result is quantitatively corroborated in Table 5, where the FOMRAC achieves the lowest ISE among all evaluated controllers, confirming its ability to maintain high-precision tracking despite sudden variations in the system dynamics. This superior performance is attributed to the combination of the adaptive law based on fractional gradients and the greater flexibility introduced by the non-integer order parameters, which enable a smoother and more efficient response to external disturbances.

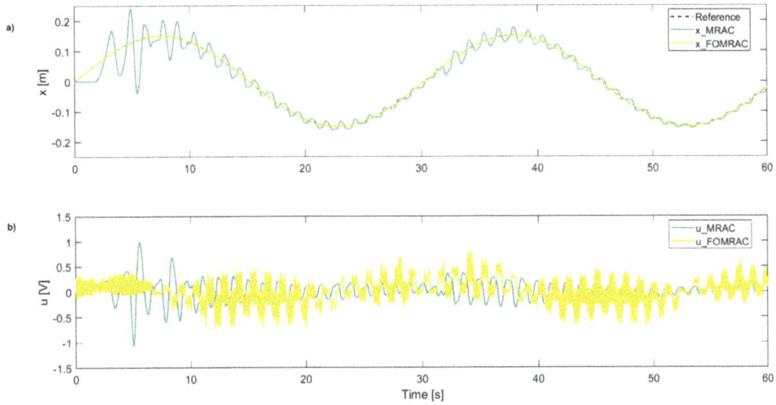

Figure 10. Experimental simulation of control over the movement of the pendulum carriage on the rail with disturbances. (**a**) Position x. (**b**) Control signal in volts v. MRAC (green), FOMRAC (yellow).

Table 5. Performance of controllers for experimental results with disturbances.

Controller	ISE	QTV	ISI
PID	6.0120×10^{-4}	3.1653×10^{-1}	1.2561
FOPID	8.0615×10^{-4}	3.7433×10^{-1}	3.1189
MRAC	3.7816×10^{-2}	6.7814×10^{-2}	2.2033
FOMRAC	1.0606×10^{-5}	15.6162	3.3372

In future work, the proposed fractional-order adaptive control strategies (FOEM2-FG and FOEM3-FG) could be extended beyond the inverted pendulum to a broader class of nonlinear and underactuated systems. For example, integrating fractional-order MRAC schemes with robust controllers, such as fractional-order sliding mode control (FOSMC), offers a promising research direction for differential-drive mobile robots subject to skidding, slipping, and unknown disturbances [41]. In this context, fractional gradient-adaptation laws can enable the online estimation of uncertain dynamic parameters without requiring prior knowledge of disturbance bounds, thereby enhancing adaptability and tracking performance under highly variable operating conditions. Such hybrid controllers may significantly improve convergence speed, disturbance rejection, and control smoothness in applications including payload stabilization in aerial drones, trajectory tracking in ground vehicles, and precise manipulation in robotic arms [42]. Further research will focus on developing composite Lyapunov-based stability proofs and experimentally validating the proposed methods on real-time embedded platforms.

5. Conclusions

This paper introduced two adaptive control strategies—fractional-order error models 2 and 3—incorporating a fractional gradient. Model 3 extends model 2 by relaxing the requirement of full plant knowledge, making it more suitable for practical implementations. Theoretical foundations for stability and convergence were established based on the Caputo fractional derivative, and the proposed methods were applied to the position control of an inverted pendulum system.

The experimental and simulation results demonstrate that, while the classical PID controller fulfilled the basic control objectives, it was outperformed by controllers utilizing fractional calculus. The FOPID controller, in particular, exhibited improved damping and smoother control signals compared to PID, highlighting the benefits of fractional-order dynamics for improving transient behavior.

Although the MRAC controller was developed based on a linearized model, its performance suffered from overshoot and aggressive control action both in the simulation and on the real system, suggesting limited robustness to nonlinearities and disturbances. In contrast, the proposed FOMRAC controller, which integrates the fractional gradient, achieved superior performance in both scenarios. It delivered more accurate trajectory tracking and enhanced disturbance rejection capabilities, validating the effectiveness of the fractional-order adaptive control framework in handling real-world nonlinear systems with greater precision, resilience, and efficiency.

Author Contributions: Conceptualization and methodology, M.S.-R., M.A.D.-M. and L.B.-M.; investigation, M.S.-R., M.A.D.-M., M.E.O. and L.B.-M.; validation, M.S.-R., M.A.D.-M., L.B.-M., M.E.O. and G.C.-B.; writing—original draft, M.S.-R. and L.B.-M.; writing—review and editing, M.S.-R., M.A.D.-M., M.E.O., L.B.-M. and G.C.-B. All authors have read and agreed to the published version of the manuscript.

Funding: The first author acknowledges CONICYT/ANID for its funding through the project National Doctoral Program 2020/21200215. ANID-FONDECYT partly supported this work under grant numbers 3240317 and 1250036. Marcos Orchard would like to thank the Advanced Center for Electrical and Electronic Engineering, ANID Basal, under Project AFB240002.

Data Availability Statement: Data are contained within the article.

Conflicts of Interest: The authors declare no conflicts of interest.

References

1. Hamza, M.F.; Yap, H.J.; Choudhury, I.A.; Isa, A.I.; Zimit, A.Y.; Kumbasar, T. Current development on using Rotary Inverted Pendulum as a benchmark for testing linear and nonlinear control algorithms. *Mech. Syst. Signal Process.* **2019**, *116*, 347–369. [CrossRef]
2. Kafetzis, I.; Moysis, L. Inverted Pendulum: A System with Innumerable Applications. In Proceedings of the 9th International Week Dedicated to Maths, Thessaloniki, Greece, 7–12 April 2017.
3. Boubaker, O. The inverted pendulum benchmark in nonlinear control theory: A survey. *Int. J. Adv. Robot. Syst.* **2013**, *10*, 233. [CrossRef]
4. Maity, S.; Luecke, G.R. Stabilization and optimization of design parameters for control of inverted pendulum. *J. Dyn. Syst. Meas. Control* **2019**, *141*, 081007. [CrossRef]
5. Jmel, I.; Dimassi, H.; Hadj-Said, S.; M'Sahli, F. An adaptive sliding mode observer for inverted pendulum under mass variation and disturbances with experimental validation. *ISA Trans.* **2020**, *102*, 264–279. [CrossRef] [PubMed]
6. Mathew, N.J.; Rao, K.K.; Sivakumaran, N. Swing up and stabilization control of a rotary inverted pendulum. *IFAC Proc. Vol.* **2013**, *46*, 654–659. [CrossRef]
7. Kharola, A.; Patil, P.; Raiwani, S.; Rajput, D. A comparison study for control and stabilisation of inverted pendulum on inclined surface (IPIS) using PID and fuzzy controllers. *Perspect. Sci.* **2016**, *8*, 187–190. [CrossRef]
8. Fan, X.; Wang, Z. A fuzzy Lyapunov function method to stability analysis of fractional-order T–S fuzzy systems. *IEEE Trans. Fuzzy Syst.* **2021**, *30*, 2769–2776. [CrossRef]
9. Zeghlache, S.; Ghellab, M.Z.; Djerioui, A.; Bouderah, B.; Benkhoris, M.F. Adaptive fuzzy fast terminal sliding mode control for inverted pendulum-cart system with actuator faults. *Math. Comput. Simul.* **2023**, *210*, 207–234. [CrossRef]
10. Singh, S.; Swarup, A. Control of Rotary Double Inverted Pendulum using Sliding Mode Controller. In Proceedings of the 2021 International Conference on Intelligent Technologies (CONIT), Hubli, India, 25–27 June 2021; IEEE: Piscataway, NJ, USA, 2021; pp. 1–6.

11. Safeea, M.; Neto, P. A Q-learning approach to the continuous control problem of robot inverted pendulum balancing. *Intell. Syst. Appl.* **2024**, *21*, 200313. [CrossRef]
12. Kao, S.T.; Ho, M.T. Balance control of a configurable inverted pendulum on an omni-directional wheeled mobile robot. *Appl. Sci.* **2022**, *12*, 10307. [CrossRef]
13. Mohsen, Z.S.; Mohamed, J. PID neural controller design for nonlinear inverted pendulum system. *Int. J. Intell. Eng. Syst.* **2023**, *16*, 783–798. [CrossRef]
14. de la Cruz-Alejo, J.; Beatriz-Cuellar, H.; Guillermo, I.C.A.; Ortega, A.M. A decision-making approach on control techniques for an inverted pendulum based on, neuro-fuzzy, indirect adaptive and PID controllers. *Discov. Appl. Sci.* **2024**, *6*, 251. [CrossRef]
15. Kim, J.W.; Oh, C.Y. Control of a rotary inverted pendulum system using brain emotional learning based intelligent controller. *J. Korean Soc. Manuf. Technol. Eng.* **2013**, *22*, 837–844. [CrossRef]
16. Lin, C.-M.; Chung, C.-C. Fuzzy brain emotional learning control system design for nonlinear systems. *Int. J. Fuzzy Syst.* **2015**, *17*, 117–128. [CrossRef]
17. Özalp, R.; Varol, N.K.; Taşci, B.; Uçar, A. A review of deep reinforcement learning algorithms and comparative results on inverted pendulum system. In *Machine Learning Paradigms: Advances in Deep Learning-Based Technological Applications*; Springer: Berlin/Heidelberg, Germany, 2020; pp. 237–256.
18. Mishra, S.K.; Chandra, D. Stabilization and tracking control of inverted pendulum using fractional order PID controllers. *J. Eng.* **2014**, *2014*, 752918. [CrossRef]
19. Patra, A.K.; Mishra, A.K.; Nanda, A.; Subudhi, D.K.; Agrawal, R.; Patra, A. Stabilizing and trajectory tracking of inverted pendulum based on fractional order PID control. In *Advances in Intelligent Computing and Communication: Proceedings of ICAC 2019*; Springer: Singapore, 2020; pp. 338–346.
20. Bettayeb, M.; Boussalem, C.; Mansouri, R.; Al-Saggaf, U.M. Stabilization of an inverted pendulum-cart system by fractional PI-state feedback. *ISA Trans.* **2014**, *53*, 508–516. [CrossRef] [PubMed]
21. Mondal, R.; Chakraborty, A.; Dey, J.; Halder, S. Optimal fractional order $PI\lambda D\mu$ controller for stabilization of cart-inverted pendulum system: Experimental results. *Asian J. Control* **2020**, *22*, 1345–1359. [CrossRef]
22. Mondal, R.; Dey, J. A novel design methodology on cascaded fractional order (FO) PI-PD control and its real time implementation to Cart-Inverted Pendulum System. *ISA Trans.* **2022**, *130*, 565–581. [CrossRef] [PubMed]
23. Wei, Y.; Kang, Y.; Yin, W.; Wang, Y. Generalization of the gradient method with fractional order gradient direction. *J. Frankl. Inst.* **2020**, *357*, 2514–2532. [CrossRef]
24. Sánchez-Rivero, M.; Duarte-Mermoud, M.A.; Travieso-Torres, J.C.; Orchard, M.E.; Ceballos-Benavides, G. Analysis of Fractional Order-Adaptive Systems Represented by Error Model 1 Using a Fractional-Order Gradient Approach. *Mathematics* **2024**, *12*, 3212. [CrossRef]
25. Vinagre, B.M.; Monje, C.A. Introducción al Control Fraccionario. *Rev. Iberoam. Autom. Inform. Ind.* **2006**, *3*, 5–23.
26. Kilbas, A.A.; Srivastava, H.M.; Trujillo, J.J. *Theory and Applications of Fractional Differential Equations*; North-Holland Mathematics Studies; Elsevier: Amsterdam, The Netherlands, 2006; Volume 204.
27. Pu, Y.F.; Zhou, J.L.; Zhang, Y.; Zhang, N.; Huang, G.; Siarry, P. Fractional Extreme Value Adaptive Training Method: Fractional Steepest Descent Approach. *IEEE Trans. Neural Netw. Learn. Syst.* **2015**, *26*, 653–662. [CrossRef] [PubMed]
28. Chen, Y.; Gao, Q.; Wei, Y.; Wang, Y. Study on fractional order gradient methods. *Appl. Math. Comput.* **2017**, *314*, 310–321. [CrossRef]
29. Gallegos, J.A.; Duarte-Mermoud, M.A. Convergence of fractional adaptive systems using gradient approach. *ISA Trans.* **2017**, *69*, 31–42. [CrossRef] [PubMed]
30. Narendra, K.S.; Annaswamy, A.M. *Stable Adaptive Systems*; Courier Corporation: Chelmsford, MA, USA 2012.
31. Aguila-Camacho, N. Análisis del Comportamiento de Sistemas Adaptables Fraccionarios Representados por Modelos de Error. Ph.D. Thesis, Universidad de Chile, Santiago, Chile, 2014.
32. Aguila-Camacho, N.; Duarte-Mermoud, M.A.; Gallegos, J.A. Lyapunov functions for fractional order systems. *Commun. Nonlinear Sci. Numer. Simul.* **2014**, *19*, 2951–2957. [CrossRef]
33. Tuan, H.T.; Trinh, H. Stability of fractional-order nonlinear systems by Lyapunov direct method. *IET Control Theory Appl.* **2018**, *12*, 2417–2422. [CrossRef]
34. Hai, P.V.; Rosenfeld, J.A. The gradient descent method from the perspective of fractional calculus. *Math. Methods Appl. Sci.* **2021**, *44*, 5520–5547. [CrossRef]
35. Gallegos, J.A.; Duarte-Mermoud, M.A. Boundedness and convergence on fractional order systems. *J. Comput. Appl. Math.* **2016**, *296*, 815–826. [CrossRef]
36. *Digital Pendulum Control Experiments, Manual: 33-936S*; Feedback Instruments Ltd.: Crowborough, UK, 2006.
37. Fernández-Jorquera, M.; Zepeda-Rabanal, M.; Aguila-Camacho, N.; Bárzaga-Martell, L. Design, Tuning, and Experimental Validation of Switched Fractional-Order PID Controllers for an Inverted Pendulum System. *Fractal Fract.* **2025**, *9*, 234. [CrossRef]

38. Kennedy, J.; Eberhart, R. Particle swarm optimization. In Proceedings of the ICNN'95-International Conference on Neural Networks, Perth, WA, Australia, 27 November–1 December 1995; IEEE: Piscataway, NJ, USA, 1995; Volume 4, pp. 1942–1948. [CrossRef]
39. Gaudio, J.E.; Annaswamy, A.M.; Lavretsky, E.; Bolender, M.A. Parameter estimation in adaptive control of time-varying systems under a range of excitation conditions. *IEEE Trans. Autom. Control* **2021**, *67*, 5440–5447. [CrossRef]
40. Oliveira Valerio, D. Ninteger v. 2.3, Fractional Control Toolbox for MatLab. 2005. Available online: https://web.ist.utl.pt/duarte.valerio/ninteger/ninteger.htm (accessed on 28 May 2025)
41. Aguilar-Pérez, J.I.; Duarte-Mermoud, M.A.; Velasco-Villa, M.; Castro-Linares, R. Fractional order tracking control of a disturbed differential mobile robot. *PLoS ONE* **2025**, *20*, e0321749. [CrossRef] [PubMed]
42. Govea-Vargas, A.; Castro-Linares, R.; Duarte-Mermoud, M.A.; Aguila-Camacho, N.; Ceballos-Benavides, G.E. Fractional order sliding mode control of a class of second order perturbed nonlinear systems: Application to the trajectory tracking of a quadrotor. *Algorithms* **2018**, *11*, 168. [CrossRef]

fractal and fractional

MDPI

Article

A Robust Fractional-Order Controller for Biomedical Applications

Nicoleta E. Badau, Teodora M. Popescu, Marcian D. Mihai, Isabela R. Birs and Cristina I. Muresan *

Automation Department, Technical University of Cluj-Napoca, Memorandumului Street No. 28, 400114 Cluj-Napoca, Romania; nicoleta.badau@aut.utcluj.ro (N.E.B.); teodora.popescu@aut.utcluj.ro (T.M.P.); marcian.mihai@aut.utcluj.ro (M.D.M.); isabela.birs@aut.utcluj.ro (I.R.B.)
* Correspondence: cristina.muresan@aut.utcluj.ro

Abstract

Automatic control in biomedicine has attracted the attention of clinicians to mitigate the side effects resulting from drug overdoses administered to patients. To provide the most optimal and accurate results, the computer-controlled systems in biomedical engineering require more advanced tuning procedures that tackle patient variability and ensure the robustness of the control system. This has been enhanced over the past two decades through the replacement of standard PID controllers with fractional-order controllers. However, most of the developed fractional-order control methods address only the robustness with respect to gain variations. In this study, a novel fractional-order control algorithm that is robust to time constant variations is developed. The control algorithm is designed for second-order plus dead time systems. A graphical solution is chosen to solve the nonlinear system of equations for the proposed approach. Three biomedical applications are employed as case studies. The first one consists in the control of the bispectral index in general anesthesia, the second one refers to the blood glucose level control for diabetic patients, and finally, the third one tackles computerized control in chemotherapy. The closed-loop simulation results validate the efficiency of the tuning method according to the accepted values of the performance specifications in the scientific literature.

Keywords: fractional order control; closed-loop control systems; biomedical applications; robustness; numerical simulations

1. Introduction

Fractional-order controllers are increasingly sought after in industrial applications alongside classical proportional integral derivative (PID) controllers, due to their robustness and efficiency [1]. Over the past twenty years, these controllers and their associated design methods have experienced significant growth [2]. The fractional-order PID (FO-PID) controller has two extra degrees of freedom, one for the fractional order of integration and the other one for differentiation. This is considered a generalization of the standard integer-order controller [3]. Due to these two degrees of freedom, the FO-PID design algorithm proves to be more robust and efficient than the traditional one [4].

The FO-PID controllers are generally designed in the frequency domain using performance specifications such as phase margin, gain margin, crossover frequency, and iso-damping property [5–8]. Noise attenuation and disturbance rejection are occasional performance criteria. The design of fractional-order PID controllers for various types of processes is discussed in several outstanding survey papers [3,7,8]. The robustness of the fractional-order controllers is also addressed in some of these review papers.

Compared to the classical PID controller, the FO-PID controller ensures greater robustness of the system. Robustness to gain variations is found in several studies for various system models, from simple first-order [9], to more complex higher-order processes [10] or those with time delay [11]. The tuning procedure of an FO-PID controller is proposed in [12] for robustness to gain variations by using the mentioned performance specifications, as well as the integral time absolute error (ITAE), which is a time domain specification. Another fractional-order controller is designed in [13] using the integral of absolute error (IAE). To ensure robustness, an additional constraint of maximum sensitivity is used. An FO-PID controller cascaded with a fractional-order filter is presented in [14]. The tuning method of this controller is based on Bode's ideal loop transfer function with dead time. For this control strategy, only robustness to gain variations is analyzed and tested. In [15] a tuning procedure of an FO-PID controller based on the same idea is proposed. In [16] a similar approach based on Bode's ideal loop transfer function is used to tune a fractional-order PI (FO-PI) controller for robustness to gain variations only. Bode's optimal loop transfer function is proposed also in [17] to design an FO-PI controller using the internal model control (IMC) approach. The previously presented fractional-order controllers are tuned to meet the performance specifications such as phase margin and gain crossover frequency. The method's robustness is tested and validated experimentally using a DC motor setup. The fractional-order PD (FO-PD) controllers are tuned in [18] using the iso-damping property and its associated robustness. The design method is again based on Bode's ideal loop transfer function.

By using both the gain and phase margin specifications, the robustness to gain and time constant variations are proposed in [19], although no method is provided by the authors on how to design the fractional-order controller to be robust to time constant variations. For diverse parameter uncertainties of the process, a tuning method based on probabilistic robustness is tackled in [20]. A similar idea is also presented in [21], but no design methods for the fractional-order controllers are provided. The robustness of the control structure for the cascaded fractional-order controllers tackled in [22] is tested on a hybrid electric vehicle considering parameter uncertainties. To optimize the primary and secondary controllers' gain, a multi-objective genetic algorithm is applied, considering settling time, maximum overshoot, and the minimization of IAE. In [23] a cascaded control strategy using two FO-PI controllers is designed. The robust control system is obtained through design based on optimizing the IAE. A tuning procedure for FO-PID controllers is developed in [6]. The proposed method ensures design specifications such as an imposed phase margin, gain crossover frequency, and iso-damping property. This procedure consists of tuning controllers for robustness to undamped natural frequency variations of a system. The oscillatory systems are represented by minimum phase rational transfer functions, whose dynamics must satisfy the interlacing property of pole-zero combinations on the imaginary axis. In [24] a novel approach is proposed to tune the fractional-order controllers using interval fractional-order pole placement. Compared to classical robust control, the proposed approach achieves improved transient response performance, as well as good control effort and robustness, and has been tested and experimentally validated in a thermal plant.

In [25] a robust stabilization criterion for fractional-order controllers, without tuning rules, is proposed for uncertainties in all process parameters. A toolbox for designing robust controllers based on the CRONE control system was developed in [26] for irrigation canals. A similar procedure based on a CRONE controller was recently designed and tested for robustness in wind energy systems [27]. Fractional-order robust controllers are developed using D-K iterations for interval plants in [28], but the tuning procedure is regarded as laborious. A robust stability area for FO-PID controller parameters is investigated in [29], using uncertain first-order plus dead time (FOPDT) systems. Most research papers that focus on the robustness of the control system to plant uncertainties provide an exact procedure for determining the actual value of the parameters, but in the case of the proposed method in this paper, such a tuning approach is not detailed.

Several papers introduce the concept of tuning fractional-order controllers for robustness, not only to gain variations but also to time constant variations. FO-PID controllers are designed and tested on an FOPDT system in [30], using a generalized iso-damping condition based on a min-max optimization problem. The obtained controllers validate the effectiveness of the approached method for 30% parameter variations. A tuning procedure based on the usual performance criteria, such as phase margin and gain crossover frequency, is tackled in [31] to design an FO-PD controller. Robustness to time constant variations is considered the third tuning constraint. To achieve the specified robustness for time constant variations, the basic idea consists in using the gradient of the phase margin and the cutoff frequency with respect to the time constant of the FOPDT process and to the actual frequency. Due to the nonlinear system equations, the optimization methods are used to compute the controller parameters. Hints about the parameter constraints and how to choose the gain crossover frequency are also provided. The efficiency of the tuning algorithm for robustness to time constant variations is proven through the closed-loop simulation results for $\pm 20\%$ time constant variations and through the experimental results using a servo system. A concept based on the same tuning method was subsequently introduced in [32]. The designed controller simultaneously satisfies the possible ranges for the gain crossover frequency and the phase margin, ensuring the robustness of the closed-loop system with respect to variations in the process time constant. Recently, a generalized tuning procedure of an FO-PID controller was introduced in [4]. The proposed design method is based on maintaining a constant phase margin to ensure that the tuned controller is robust to an uncertain parameter in the plant model. To determine the controller parameters using optimization routines, the partial derivatives of the phase margin and gain crossover frequency with respect to the process parameter are calculated and used alongside other specifications of the frequency domain.

Widely used methods that consider the trade-off between robustness and performance, using maximum sensitivity (MS) as a criterion to ensure a desired level of robustness, are introduced in [33,34]. Several methods that emphasize simple tuning rules for FO-PI controllers, as well as extensions of the kappa-tau methods to the fractional-order case, are presented in [35–38]. Modifications of the Ziegler–Nichols methods adapted to FO-PI controllers are also presented in [39–42].

The proposed control method in this article involves the tuning of the robust FO-PI controllers to time constant variations for a second-order plus dead time (SOPDT) process. To determine the controller parameters, the three performance criteria are also imposed, such as a certain phase margin (for the overshoot), a gain crossover frequency (for the settling time), and robustness to time constant variations. The key aspect of this approach is to ensure that a constant overshoot is obtained, despite variations in the time constant; the procedure is similar to that in [4,31,32]. The variation in the time constant will lead to changes in both the phase and magnitude of the open-loop system, causing modifications of the phase margin and gain crossover frequency. To preserve the imposed value of the phase margin, the partial derivatives of the magnitude and phase of the open-loop frequency response with respect to the variable time constant of the model and the frequency are used. For the tuning of the robust fractional-order controller, a complex system of analytical equations is developed. The system of nonlinear equations could be solved using optimization routines, but in this paper, a graphical method is chosen.

In this paper, case studies from biomedical engineering are considered to validate the proposed approach. The computer-controlled systems in biomedicine would be a safer option for the patients, being more robust to various disturbances that may occur, and with optimally computed drug doses. These features would reduce the side effects caused by drug overdose [43]. Some of the biomedical applications in which there is a growing preference to use automatic control are general anesthesia [44], diabetes [45], and cancer treatment [46]. Fractional-order controllers are potential candidates to provide the most accurate and optimal results in biomedical engineering. These would have to be robust to patient variability. As such, in this paper, three case studies are employed, where patient variability is directly addressed, in terms of time constant variations. The FO-PI controllers are designed based on a novel approach that follows in the remainder of the manuscript. The three case studies are bispectral index (BIS) control in anesthesia, blood glucose level control for diabetic patients, and automatic control of chemotherapy.

Patient variability represents the main challenge in developing a computer-controlled solution for managing the depth of hypnosis in general anesthesia [47,48], the blood glucose level of diabetic patients [45], and the drug concentration used in cancer treatment [49]. Undesirable side effects such as under- or overdosing of the required drugs may arise from modeling uncertainties that impact the closed-loop performance of the system, caused by inter- and intra-patient variability [50]. Thus, a controller that ensures the robustness to modeling uncertainties, such as time constant variations, is desirable.

The main objectives and the original elements of the current study consist of the following:

- The development of a fractional-order robust control algorithm for the process time constant variations.
- The design of an FO-PI controller that is robust to time constant variations for BIS level control in general anesthesia.
- The design of an FO-PI controller that is robust to time constant variations for blood glucose level control of diabetic patients.
- The design of an FO-PI controller that is robust to time constant variations for computer-controlled chemotherapy.

The manuscript consists of six sections. Following the Introduction, the algorithm for designing an FO-PI controller that is robust to time constant variations for a second-order model with dead time is described in Section 2. Three case studies of tuning robust fractional-order controllers for biomedical applications are included in Section 3. Comparative closed-loop results to demonstrate the efficiency of the proposed approach are included in Section 4. Some insights and limitations of the proposed method are indicated in Section 5. In Section 6 the concluding remarks and further research topics are given.

2. FO-PI Controller for Robustness to Time Constant Variations

The closed loop of the fractional-order control system is presented in Figure 1, $w(s)$ is the set-point signal, $C(s)$ is the FO-PI controller to be designed, $P(s)$ is the controlled process, and $y(s)$ is the output signal. The process P(s) is a SOPDT model defined by the following transfer function:

$$P(s) = \frac{K}{(T_1 s + 1)(T_2 s + 1)} e^{-\tau_d s} \quad (1)$$

where K is the process gain, T_1 and T_2 are the process time constants, and τ_d is the dead time. The SOPDT models discussed in this paper are characterized by a small (T_1) and a dominant time constant (T_2). Since the overall dynamics of the process is little influenced by the small time constant and its possible variations, only variations in the dominant time constant (T_2) are considered [51].

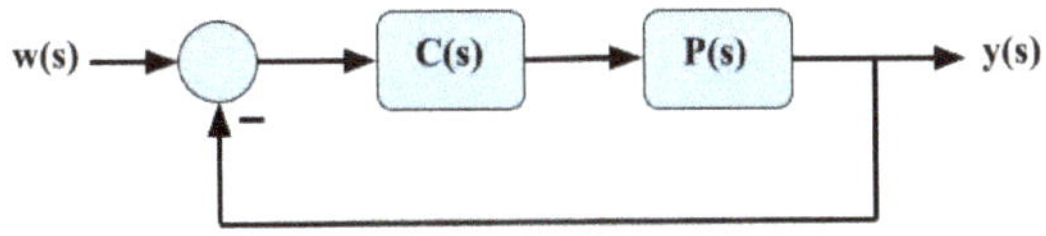

Figure 1. Block diagram of the fractional-order control system.

The transfer function of the FO-PI controller $C(s)$ is given as:

$$C(s) = \left(k_p + \frac{k_i}{s}\right)^{\lambda} \tag{2}$$

where k_p and k_i are the proportional and integral components, and $\lambda \in (0,1)$ is the fractional order. The FO-PI controller is equal to a standard PI controller, when $\lambda = 1$. The fractional order λ is used to increase the flexibility of the controller design and to ensure robustness to time constant T_2 variations.

Based on the block diagram from Figure 1, the open-loop system is given as follows:

$$H_{ol}(s) = P(s)C(s) \tag{3}$$

The frequency response of the open-loop transfer function $H_{ol}(s)$ can be written as:

$$H_{ol}(j\omega) = P(j\omega)C(j\omega) = \frac{k}{(j\omega T_1 + 1)(j\omega T_2 + 1)} e^{-j\tau_d\omega} \left(k_p + \frac{k_i}{j\omega}\right)^{\lambda} \tag{4}$$

The phase and magnitude of $H_{ol}(s)$ at any frequency ω can be calculated using (4):

$$|H_{ol}(j\omega)| = \frac{k}{\sqrt{(\omega T_1)^2 + 1}\sqrt{(\omega T_2)^2 + 1}} \left(k_p^2 + k_i^2\omega^{-2}\right)^{\frac{\lambda}{2}} \tag{5}$$

$$\angle H_{ol}(j\omega) = -\tan^{-1}(T_1\omega) - \tan^{-1}(T_2\omega) - \tau\omega + \lambda \tan^{-1}\left(\frac{k_p\omega}{k_i}\right) - \frac{\lambda\pi}{2} \tag{6}$$

To tune the FO-PI controller, three performance specifications are imposed. The first performance criterion consists in imposing a certain gain crossover frequency ω_c to ensure a specific settling time of the closed-loop system:

$$|H_{ol}(j\omega_c)| = \frac{k}{\sqrt{(\omega_c T_1)^2 + 1}\sqrt{(\omega_c T_2)^2 + 1}} \left(k_p^2 + k_i^2\omega_c^{-2}\right)^{\frac{\lambda}{2}} = 1 \tag{7}$$

The second performance criterion consists in imposing a certain phase margin φ_m to ensure a specific overshoot of the closed-loop system and stability:

$$\angle H_{ol}(j\omega_c) = -\pi + \varphi_m \tag{8}$$

and replacing (6) into (8) leads to:

$$-\tan^{-1}(T_1\omega_c) - \tan^{-1}(T_2\omega_c) - \tau\omega_c + \lambda \tan^{-1}\left(\frac{k_p\omega_c}{k_i}\right) - \frac{\lambda\pi}{2} = -\pi + \varphi_m \tag{9}$$

The third performance criterion refers to robustness to time constant T_2 variations, tackled by the extra design parameter of the FO-PI controller in (2). Any changes to the time constant T_2 in Equations (7) and (9) will cause variations in the two performance specifications, the phase margin φ_m, and the gain crossover frequency ω_c, respectively. The following two conditions must be satisfied for the system to be robust to time constant variations:

$$\left.\frac{\partial|H_{ol}(j\omega)|}{\partial\omega}\right|_{(\omega_c,T_2)}\Delta\omega+\left.\frac{\partial|H_{ol}(j\omega)|}{\partial T}\right|_{(\omega_c,T_2)}\Delta T=0 \tag{10}$$

$$\left.\frac{\partial\angle H_{ol}(j\omega)}{\partial\omega}\right|_{(\omega_c,T_2)}\Delta\omega+\left.\frac{\partial\angle H_{ol}(j\omega)}{\partial T}\right|_{(\omega_c,T_2)}\Delta T=0 \tag{11}$$

Rewriting (10) and (11) leads to:

$$\frac{\Delta T}{\Delta\omega}=-\frac{\left.\frac{\partial|H_{ol}(j\omega)|}{\partial\omega}\right|_{(\omega_c,T_2)}}{\left.\frac{\partial|H_{ol}(j\omega)|}{\partial T}\right|_{(\omega_c,T_2)}} \tag{12}$$

$$\frac{\Delta T}{\Delta\omega}=-\frac{\left.\frac{\partial\angle H_{ol}(j\omega)}{\partial\omega}\right|_{(\omega_c,T_2)}}{\left.\frac{\partial\angle H_{ol}(j\omega)}{\partial T}\right|_{(\omega_c,T_2)}} \tag{13}$$

From (12) and (13), the final equation is obtained for robustness to time constant variations:

$$\frac{\left.\frac{\partial|H_{ol}(j\omega)|}{\partial\omega}\right|_{(\omega_c,T_2)}}{\left.\frac{\partial|H_{ol}(j\omega)|}{\partial T}\right|_{(\omega_c,T_2)}}=\frac{\left.\frac{\partial\angle H_{ol}(j\omega)}{\partial\omega}\right|_{(\omega_c,T_2)}}{\left.\frac{\partial\angle H_{ol}(j\omega)}{\partial T}\right|_{(\omega_c,T_2)}} \tag{14}$$

Assumptions:

1. The notation $A=\frac{k_p\omega_c}{k_i}$, $A>0$ will be substituted into equations in what follows.
2. The fractional order $\lambda\in(0,1)$ is assumed to be known. A later procedure will show how to compute the actual value of λ.

Theorem 1. *Given a process described by second-order plus dead time dynamics, the parameter A of a fractional-order PI controller ensures robustness to time constant variations and can be determined by solving a quadratic equation, under the mentioned assumptions.*

Proof. The partial derivatives of the modulus with respect to ω and T are computed using (5):

$$\left.\frac{\partial|H_{ol}(j\omega)|}{\partial\omega}\right|_{(\omega_c,T_2)}=-\frac{{T_1}^2k\omega_c x^{\frac{\lambda}{2}}}{y^3\sqrt{z}}-\frac{T_2^2k\omega_c x^{\frac{\lambda}{2}-1}}{y\sqrt{z}^3}-\frac{\lambda k{k_i}^2x^{\frac{\lambda}{2}-1}}{{\omega_c}^3y\sqrt{z}^3} \tag{15}$$

$$\left.\frac{\partial|H_{ol}(j\omega)|}{\partial T}\right|_{(\omega_c,T_2)}=-\frac{T_2k{\omega_c}^2x^{\frac{\lambda}{2}}}{y\sqrt{z}^3} \tag{16}$$

where $x=\frac{k_i^2}{\omega_c^2}+k_p^2$, $y=\sqrt{{T_1}^2{\omega_c}^2+1}$, $z={T_2}^2{\omega_c}^2+1$.

In the same way, the partial derivatives of the phase are determined using (6):

$$\left.\frac{\partial\angle H_{ol}(j\omega)}{\partial\omega}\right|_{(\omega_c,T_2)}=\frac{\lambda k_p}{k_i\left(\frac{k_p^2{\omega_c}^2}{k_i^2}+1\right)}-\frac{T_1}{{T_1}^2{\omega_c}^2+1}-\frac{T_2}{{T_2}^2{\omega_c}^2+1}-\tau \tag{17}$$

$$\left.\frac{\partial\angle H_{ol}(j\omega)}{\partial T}\right|_{(\omega_c,T_2)}=-\frac{\omega_c}{\left({T_2}^2{\omega_c}^2+1\right)} \tag{18}$$

The following equation that assures robustness to time constant variations is obtained by replacing (15)–(18) in (14):

$$-\left({T_2}^2{\omega_c}^2+1\right)\frac{T(s)}{T_2{\omega_c}^3\left({k_i}^2+{k_p}^2{\omega_c}^2\right)\left({T_1}^2{\omega_c}^2+1\right)}=0 \quad (19)$$

where $T(s)$ has the following form:

$$\begin{aligned}T(s) = \lambda {k_i}^2 + \; & {T_1}^2{k_i}^2{\omega_c}^2 + {T_1}^2{k_p}^2{\omega_c}^4 + {T_1}^2\lambda{k_i}^2{\omega_c}^2 - T_1T_2{k_i}^2{\omega_c}^2 \\ & -T_1T_2{k_p}^2{\omega_c}^4 - T_2{k_i}^2\tau{\omega_c}^2 - T_2{k_p}^2\tau{\omega_c}^4 - {T_1}^2T_2{k_i}^2\tau{\omega_c}^4 \\ & -{T_1}^2T_2{k_p}^2\tau{\omega_c}^6 + T_2\lambda k_ik_p{\omega_c}^2 + {T_1}^2T_2\lambda k_ik_p{\omega_c}^4\end{aligned} \quad (20)$$

The quadratic equation is obtained by applying the notation $A=\frac{k_p\omega_c}{k_i}$, $A>0$ into (19):

$$z_1A^2+z_2A+z_3=0 \quad (21)$$

where

$$z_1=\omega_c^2(T_1^2-T_1T_2-T_2\tau-T_1^2T_2\omega_c^2\tau),$$
$$z_2=\omega_cT_2\lambda(1+T_2\omega_c^2),$$
$$z_3=\lambda+T_1^2{\omega_c}^2+T_1^2{\omega_c}^2\lambda-T_1T_2\omega_c^2-T_2\tau\omega_c^2-{T_1}^2T_2\tau{\omega_c}^4\tau$$

The A parameter is computed based on the fractional-order λ function, using assumption no. 2, as previously presented. Thus, the quadratic equation in (21) has two possible solutions:

$$A_{1,2}=\frac{-z_2\pm\sqrt{z_2^2-4z_1z_3}}{2z_1} \quad (22)$$

This completes the proof. □

Theorem 2. *The proportional and integral gains, k_p and k_i, of the fractional-order PI controller in (2) are determined as follows: $k_p=\frac{Ak_i}{\omega_c}$ and $k_i=\omega_c\sqrt{\frac{\left((\omega_cT_1)^2+1\right)\left((\omega_cT_2)^2+1\right)}{k^2(A^2+1)^\lambda}}^{\frac{1}{\lambda}}$.*

Proof. Considering the dominant time constant T_2 and applying the notation $A=\frac{k_p\omega_c}{k_i}$, the phase margin criterion in (9) has the following form:

$$-\tan^{-1}(T_1\omega_c)-\tan^{-1}(T_2\omega_c)-\tau\omega_c+\lambda\tan^{-1}(A)-\frac{\lambda\pi}{2}=-\pi+\varphi_m \quad (23)$$

The parameter A is determined as a function of the fractional order λ using (23):

$$A=\tan\left(\frac{\tan^{-1}(T_1\omega_c)+\tan^{-1}(T_2\omega_c)+\tau\omega_c+\frac{\lambda\pi}{2}-\pi+\varphi_m}{\lambda}\right) \quad (24)$$

Using Equations (22) and (24), the unknown parameters A and λ can be computed. Due to the tangent function in (24), the solution is not easily attainable. The graphical method is preferred instead of the analytical method to obtain a simplified solution. Therefore, the parameter A from (22) and (24) is computed for different values of the fractional order λ, taken in small increments of 0.01 within the interval [0, 1]. A smaller step size can be used to obtain an even more accurate solution. The determined A values are graphically represented with respect to λ, and the intersection point of the graphs yields the final solution. Using (7), the parameters k_p and k_i of the FO-PI controller are determined based on the results of the A and λ. Applying the notation $A = \frac{k_p\omega_c}{k_i}$ specified in Assumption no. 1, the proportional gain of the controller can be determined:

$$k_p = \frac{Ak_i}{\omega_c} \tag{25}$$

Substituting k_p into (7) yields:

$$\frac{k}{\sqrt{(\omega_c T_1)^2 + 1}\sqrt{(\omega_c T_2)^2 + 1}}\left(\frac{A^2k_i^2}{\omega_c^2} + k_i^2\omega_c^{-2}\right)^{\frac{\lambda}{2}} = 1 \tag{26}$$

which is used to compute the integral gain k_i:

$$k_i = \omega_c\left(\sqrt{\frac{\left[(\omega_c T_1)^2 + 1\right]\left[(\omega_c T_2)^2 + 1\right]}{k^2(A^2 + 1)^{\lambda}}}\right)^{\frac{1}{\lambda}} \tag{27}$$

□

The design of the fractional-order controller using the proposed approach ensures the robustness of the control system with respect to time constant variations. This means that the overshoot is expected to remain constant despite variations in the time constant. The tuning algorithm of the FO-PI controller that is robust to time constant variations for the BIS level control is given in the Appendix A.

3. Design of FO-PI Controllers for Biomedical Applications

3.1. BIS Level Control Using an FO-PI Controller for Robustness to Time Constant Variations

One of the biomedical applications where the design method of an FO-PI controller that is robust to time constant variations can be applied is the control of the BIS level in general anesthesia. The depth of hypnosis is measured by the BIS index using electroencephalography (EEG). To induce and maintain the hypnotic state, a short acting drug such as propofol is required [52]. A propofol bolus of 0.6 mg/kg/min is administered to the patient during the induction phase. The estimation method of a SOPDT model is tackled in [53] using the propofol infusion rate and the BIS signal. The transfer function that models a patient's bispectral index (BIS) response has the following form:

$$G(s) = \frac{42.34}{(7.325s + 1)(248.875s + 1)}e^{-19.7s} \tag{28}$$

where $k = 42.34$, $T_1 = 7.325$, and $T_2 = 248.875$.

To design an FO-PI controller for BIS level control, a gain crossover frequency $\omega_c = 0.0135$ rad/s and a phase margin $\varphi_m = 65°$ are imposed as performance criteria. Moreover, the robustness to time constant variations is additionally considered for the iso-damping property. As a function of fractional order λ, the values of the variable A are determined using (22) and (24). Figure 2 shows the resulting values, and the intersection point is given by $\lambda = 0.82$ and $A = 2.12$. Using (25) and (27), the proportional and integral gains of the controller are computed as $k_p = 0.0436$ and $k_i = 2.77 \cdot 10^{-4}$. The determined FO-PI controller has the following transfer function:

$$C_1(s) = \left(0.0436 + \frac{2.77 \cdot 10^{-4}}{s}\right)^{0.82} \tag{29}$$

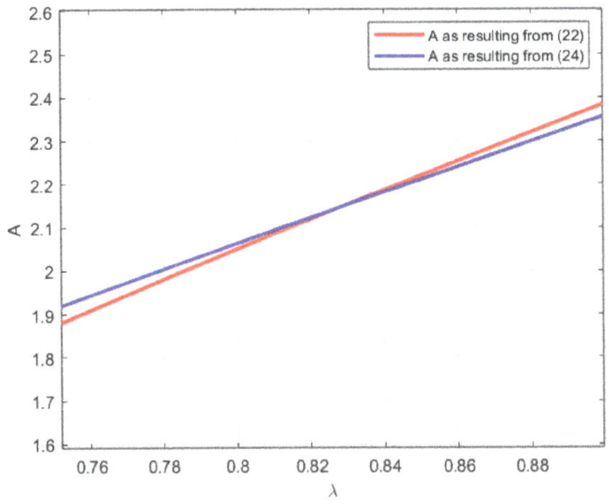

Figure 2. Graphical solution for A as a function of λ for BIS control.

To implement the controller, a direct discrete-time approximation method is used. The details are given in [54]. For this specific case study, a fourth-order approximation was considered, and the sampling period was chosen to be $T_s = 1$ s. The open-loop Bode diagram is included in Figure 3 and clearly shows that the performance specifications have been met.

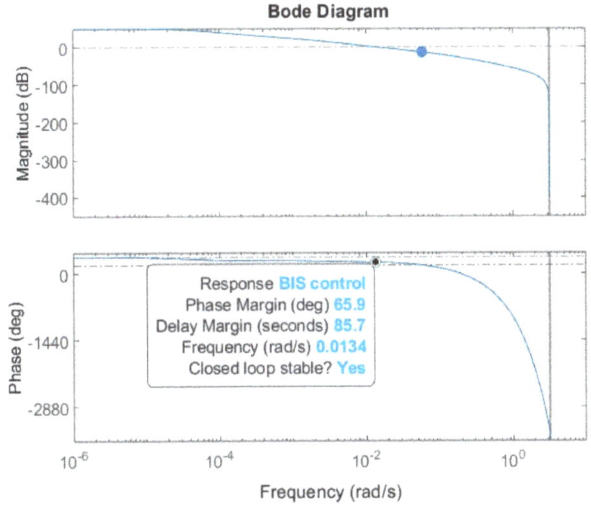

Figure 3. Bode diagram of the open-loop system for BIS control.

The closed-loop responses of the BIS signal are indicated in Figure 4, for a nominal value of the time constant T_2 as well as for the $\pm 20\%$ time constant variations. The T_2 variations are considered to test the robustness of the designed FO-PI controller. As can be seen in Figure 4, the maximum amplitude of the BIS signal ranges between 48 and 50 for the variations in the time constant T_2. In the nominal case, a maximum amplitude of 49 is obtained, whereas for time constant variations, no undershoot is indicated. For +20% variation in the time constant, the maximum BIS amplitude reaches 48, close to the nominal case. In this case, the computed undershoot yields 4%; thus only minor undershoot variations are present. The settling time for the level BIS control is considered as the time to target (TT), the time needed by the BIS signal to reach a band of 45–55 and remain within that range. In this case, TT varies between 99 and 142 s. According to the literature [55,56], accepted values for TT should not exceed 3 to 5 min (180–300 s). Consequently, the resulting TT represents a good performance, having a value smaller than 180 s.

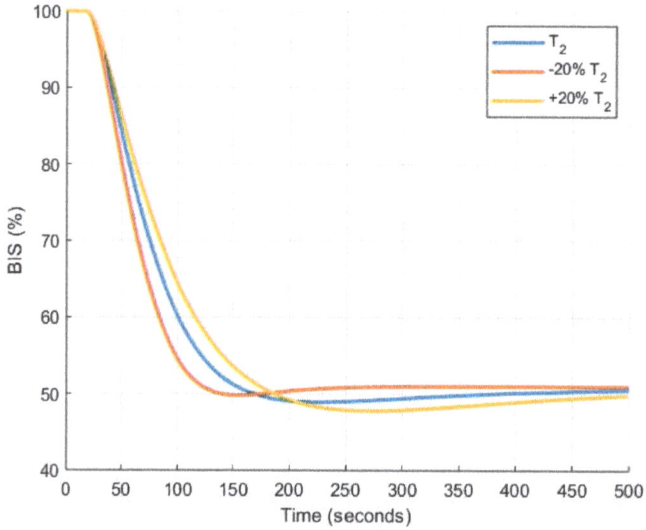

Figure 4. Closed-loop system responses of the BIS level, considering T_2 and ±20% variations.

The closed-loop control signals for the BIS level of ±20% time constant variations is depicted in Figure 5. Notice that the control signal reaches the steady state value at the required propofol infusion rate for the patient. These propofol boluses correspond to the accepted values in the literature [57–59]. Figure 6 shows the closed-loop responses of the BIS level for different variations in the variable time constant T_2. The undershoot is at approximately 0% for −5% variation, and this can increase up to 4% for +20% variation in T_2. Thus, it is clearly highlighted that the designed FO-PI controller ensures the robustness of the closed-loop system to the variations in T_2.

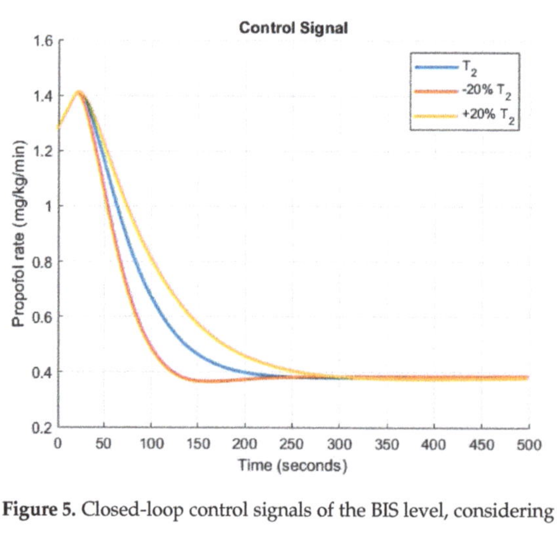

Figure 5. Closed-loop control signals of the BIS level, considering T_2 and ±20% variations.

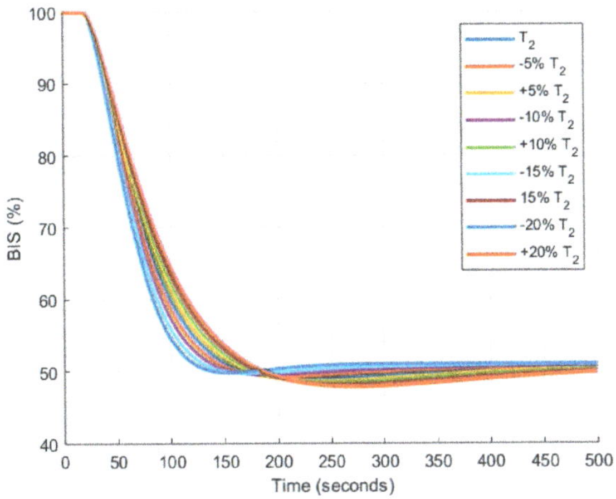

Figure 6. Closed-loop system responses for BIS control, considering T_2 and several variations in T_2.

When significantly larger variations of ±50% of the time constant T_2 are considered, larger differences in the BIS signals can be noticed, as illustrated in Figure 7. For −50% variation in T_2, the system shows a fairly large variation in BIS level between 45 and 55. The system becomes quite slow for +50% variation and the time to target (TT) is 168 s. This TT exceeds the obtained TT for a +20% variation, but remains below 180 s, which is regarded as a good performance in this case too. The undershoot in both +50% and −50% variation in T_2 reaches 10% (with a maximum amplitude of the BIS signal that decreases to 45, compared to the nominal case when the maximum amplitude was 49). This shows the efficiency of the designed controller that manages to maintain a low overshoot despite significant variations in the time constant. The control signals considering ±50% variations in T_2 are shown in Figure 8. For +50% variation in T_2, the administered propofol bolus to the patient stabilizes much more slowly at the required dose compared to +20% variation for the control signal depicted in Figure 5, but the system remains robust to such variations.

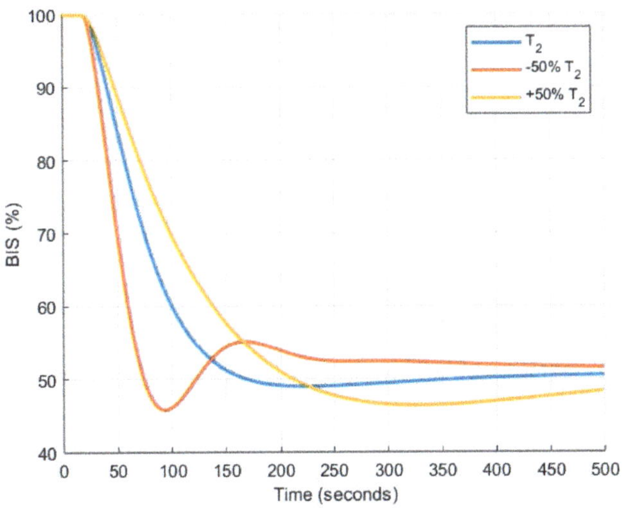

Figure 7. Closed-loop system responses of the BIS level, considering T_2 and ±50% variations.

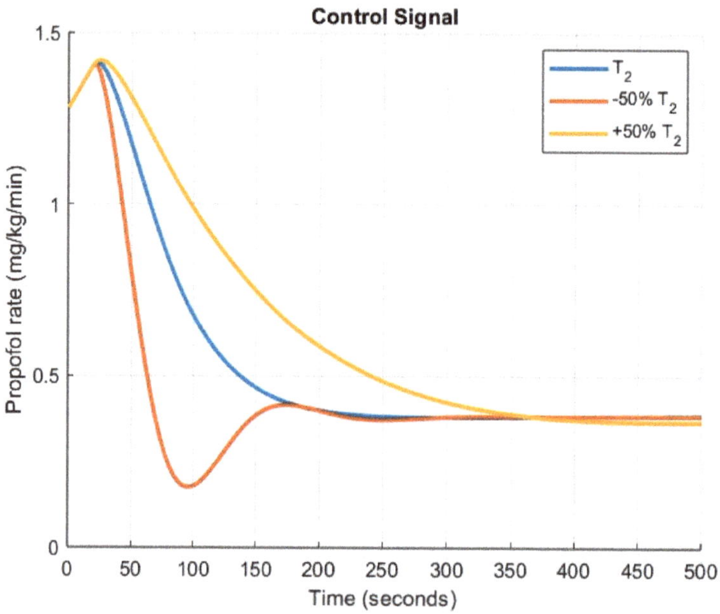

Figure 8. Control signals for BIS control, considering T_2 and $\pm 50\%$ variations.

3.2. Glucose Control for Diabetic Patients Using an FO-PI Controller for Robustness to Time Constant Variations

The proposed design method can also be applied to other processes from biomedical engineering, such as the blood glucose level control for type-I diabetes patients. The Bergman minimal model is used to model the dynamic interaction between the glucose concentration of blood and the administration of insulin for a patient [60,61]. The system response is estimated by a second-order linear transfer function, and it has the following form [62]:

$$P(s) = \frac{\frac{G_b p_3}{n V_1 p_1 p_2}}{\left(\frac{1}{n}s + 1\right)\left(\frac{1}{p_1}s + 1\right)} = \frac{K}{(\tau_1 s + 1)(\tau_2 s + 1)} \tag{30}$$

where G_b is the initial blood glucose concentration, n is the decay rate of plasma insulin, V_1 is the blood volume, and p_1, p_2, p_3 are the pre-calibrated parameters of the blood sample. The numerical values of the parameters for the Bergman minimal model are given in Table 1. These values are given in [45] and are used to compute the transfer function in (30).

Table 1. The parameter values for Bergman minimal model.

Parameter	Value	Unit
p_1	0.0317	min^{-1}
p_2	$12\cdot10^{-3}$	min^{-1}
p_3	$4.92\cdot10^{-6}$	min^{-1}
n	0.2659	min^{-1}
G_b	80	mg/dL
V_1	12	L

Replacing the parameter values of Table 1 in (30), the following transfer function of the process for the glucose–insulin dynamics model is determined as:

$$P(s) = \frac{0.3164}{118.6s^2 + 35.31s + 1} \tag{31}$$

where $k = 0.3164$, $T_1 = 3.7608$, and $T_2 = 31.5457$.

To design an FO-PI controller for blood glucose level control, a gain crossover frequency $\omega_c = 0.11$ rad/s and a phase margin $\varphi_m = 65°$ are imposed as performance criteria. Moreover, the robustness to time constant variations is considered. As a function of fractional order λ, the A values are determined using (22) and (24). Figure 9 shows the resulting values, and the intersection point is given by $\lambda = 0.6028$ and $A = 1.67$. Using (25) and (27), the proportional and integral gains are computed as $k_p = 55.56$ and $k_i = 3.65$. The determined FO-PI controller has the following transfer function:

$$C_2(s) = \left(55.56 + \frac{3.65}{s}\right)^{0.6028} \tag{32}$$

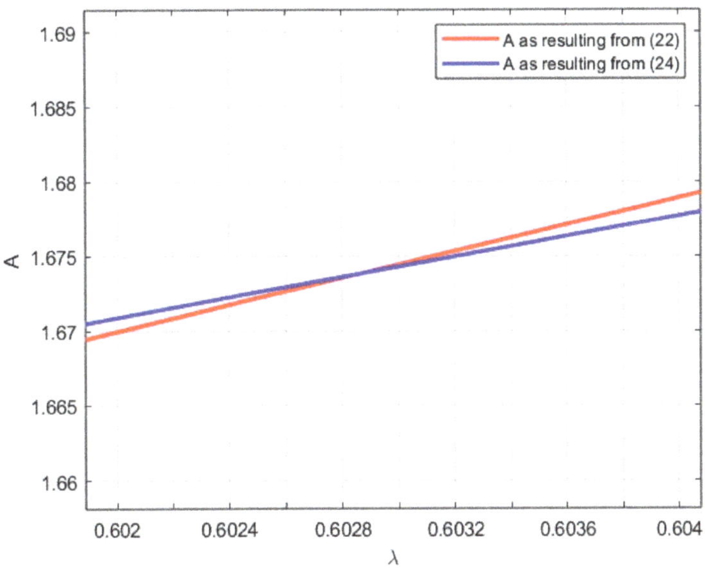

Figure 9. Graphical solution for A as a function of λ for glucose control.

A similar approach to the designed $C_1(s)$ controller in (26) is used to implement the $C_2(s)$ controller. The direct discretization method in [54] is used to produce a discrete-time fourth-order integer transfer function with the sampling period chosen to be $T_s = 0.1$ min. The open-loop Bode diagram is included in Figure 10 and clearly shows that the performance specifications have been met.

The closed-loop responses for the blood glucose level control, considering the time constant T_2 and ±20% variations in T_2 are depicted in Figure 11. The blood glucose level presents an initial state of hyperglycemia (200 mg/dL) and reaches a set-point value of 80 mg/dL. As indicated in this figure, the overshoot remains constant at approximately 4% for these variations, which demonstrates the robustness of the proposed method. The settling time of the system is 225 min for nominal T_2, and for ±20% variations in T_2, it is between 217 and 233 min. According to the scientific literature [45,63,64], the obtained values correspond to the clinical data. The control signals are represented by the insulin infusion rate and can be seen in Figure 12.

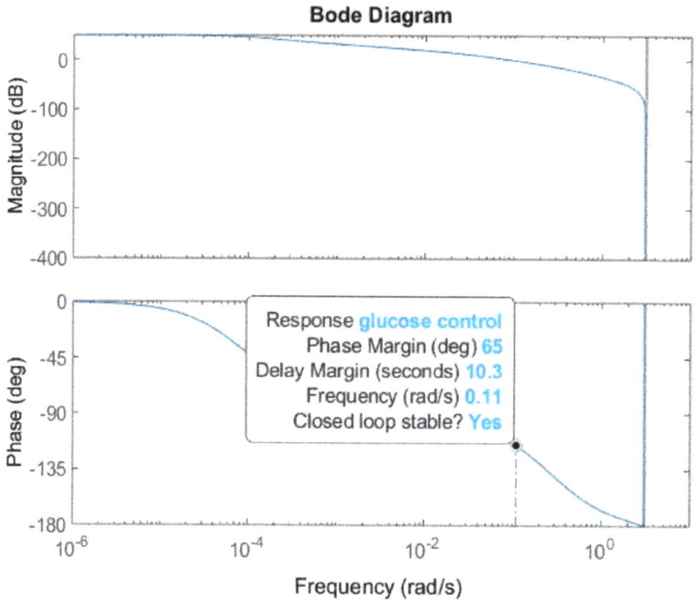

Figure 10. Bode diagram of the open-loop system for glucose control.

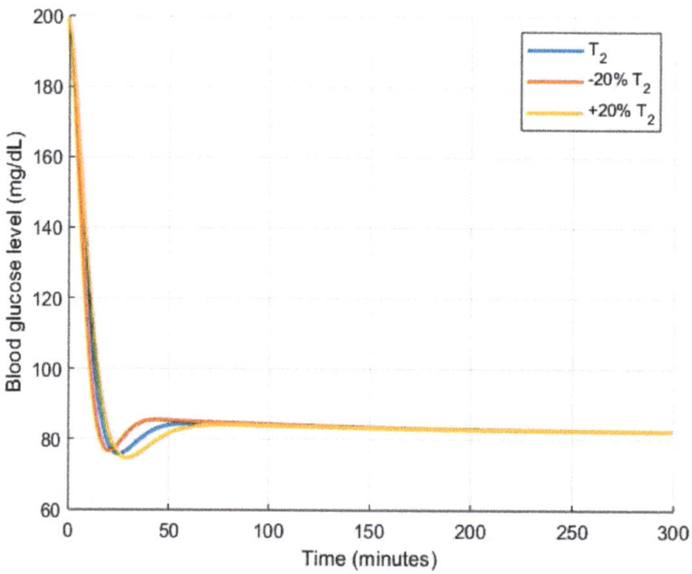

Figure 11. Closed-loop responses for glucose control, considering T_2 and ±20% variations.

The closed-loop system responses for glucose control with ±50% variations in the time constant T_2 are presented in Figure 13. For −50% variation in T_2, the amplitude decreases up to a value of 77, corresponding to 3% overshoot. In the nominal case, the overshoot is 4%. A slight increase in the overshoot is visible for +50% variation, with the amplitude decreasing up to 74, which corresponds to an overshoot of 7.5%. The proposed method manages to maintain the robustness to ±20% time constant variations, as indicated in Figure 11, as well as for −50%, as seen in Figure 13. Some alterations of the robustness occur for significantly larger variations of +50%. In this particular case, the system also exhibits a slower response time. Nevertheless, the obtained results fall within the ranges specified in [45] and meet clinical requirements. The glucose level control signals for ±50% variations in T_2, representing the insulin infusion rate, are shown in Figure 14.

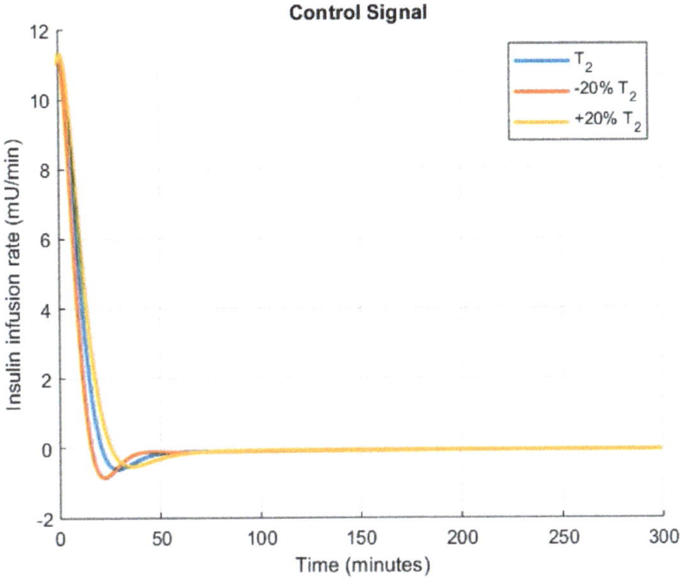

Figure 12. Control signals for glucose control, considering T_2 and ±20% variations.

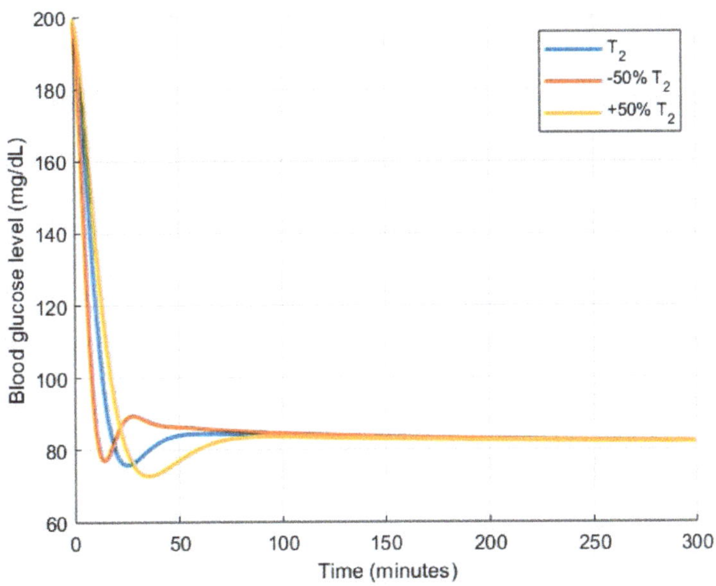

Figure 13. Closed-loop responses for glucose control, considering T_2 and ±50% variations.

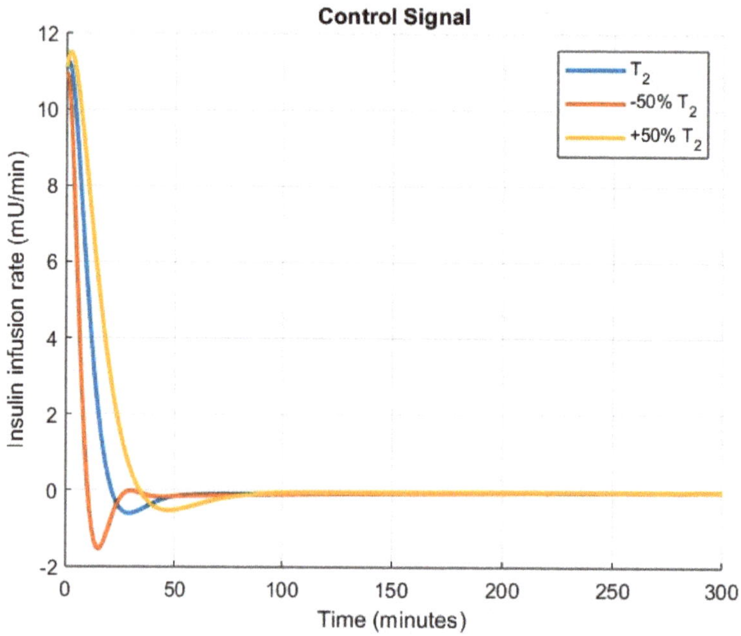

Figure 14. Control signals for glucose control, considering T_2 and $\pm$50% variations.

3.3. Computer-Controlled Chemotherapy Using an FO-PI Controller for Robustness to Time Constant Variations

The proposed design method for the FO-PI controller can also be applied in chemotherapy to control the required drug dose for a patient. One of the chemotherapeutic drugs used in cancer treatment is irinotecan [49]. The mathematical model is represented by the following transfer function:

$$P(s) = \frac{3.15}{(2.99s + 1)(0.1s + 1)} \tag{33}$$

where $k = 3.15$, $T_1 = 0.1$, and $T_2 = 2.99$.

To design an FO-PI controller for automatic control of chemotherapy, the following performance criteria are imposed: $\omega_c = 1.4$ rad/s and $\varphi_m = 60°$. Moreover, the robustness to time constant variations is considered. As a function of fractional order λ, the A values are determined using (22) and (24). Figure 15 shows the resulting values, and the intersection point is given by $\lambda = 0.4159$ and $A = 0.08$. Using (25) and (27), the proportional and integral gains are computed as $k_p = 0.1785$ and $k_i = 3.0246$. The determined FO-PI controller has the following transfer function:

$$C_3(s) = \left(0.1778 + \frac{3.0253}{s}\right)^{0.4158} \tag{34}$$

To implement the controller $C_3(s)$, the direct discrete-time approximation method detailed in [54] is used. The resulting discrete-time integer-order transfer function that approximates the dynamics of the initial fractional-order controller is of the fourth order and was computed using a sampling period of $T_s = 0.01$ s. The open-loop Bode diagram is included in Figure 16 and clearly shows that the performance specifications have been met.

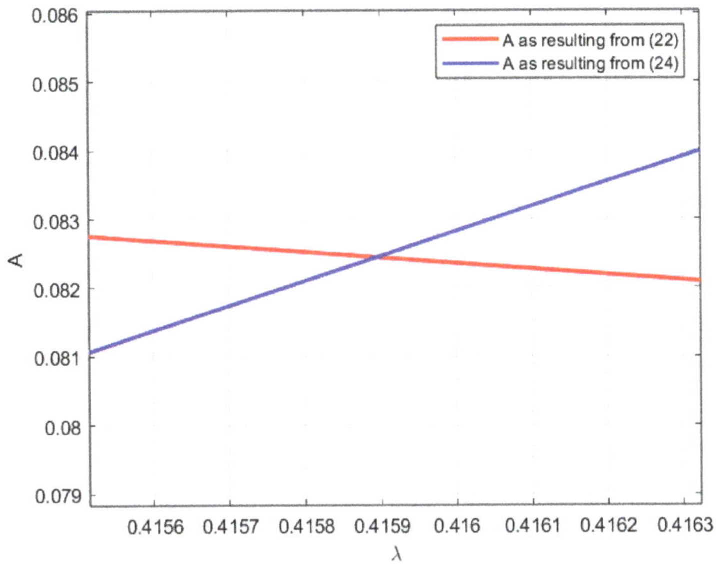

Figure 15. Graphical solution for A as a function of λ for chemotherapy control.

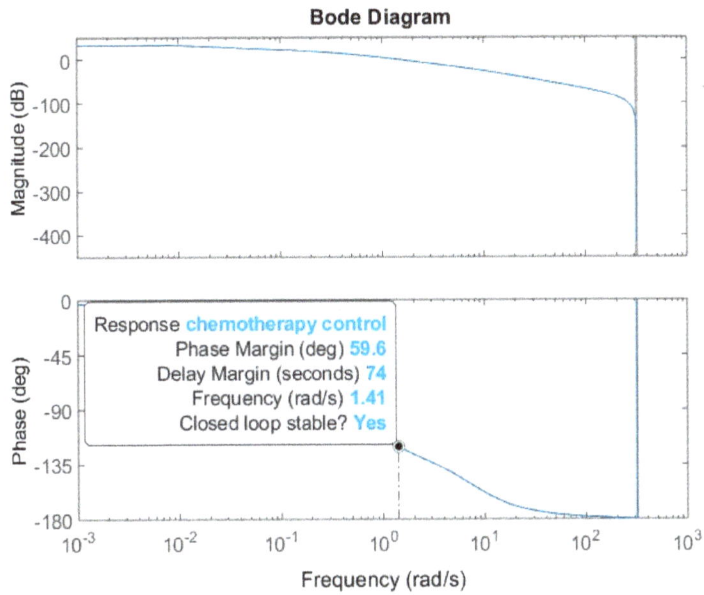

Figure 16. Bode diagram of the open-loop system for chemotherapy control.

The irinotecan concentration used in cancer treatment is approximately 35 mg/dL. The closed-loop simulation results for the chemotherapy control, considering the variable time constant T_2 and $\pm$20% variations in T_2, are shown in Figure 17. The overshoot remains constant at approximately 9%. The obtained results are according to those in [49,65]. The control signals are represented by the drug dose and can be noticed in Figure 18.

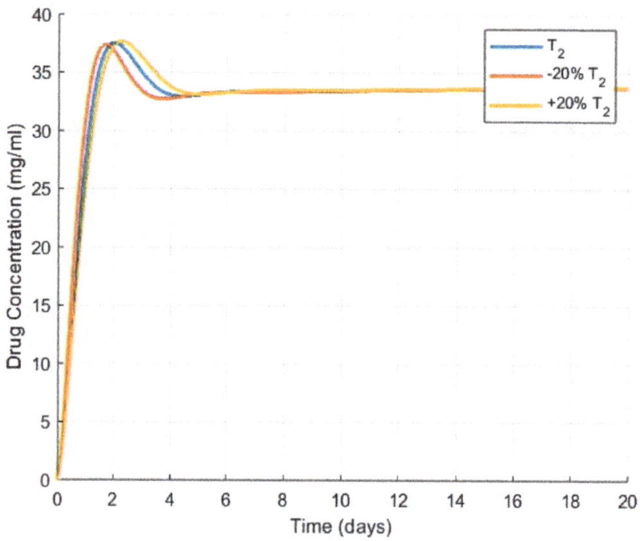

Figure 17. Closed-loop responses for chemotherapy control, considering T_2 and $\pm 20\%$ variations.

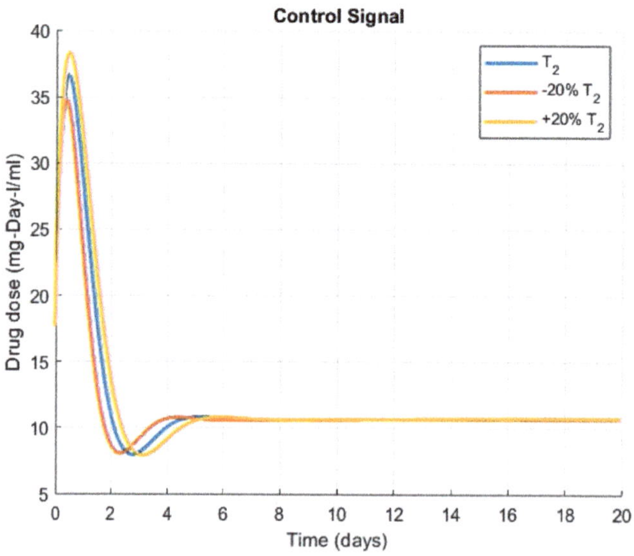

Figure 18. Control signals for chemotherapy control, considering T_2 and $\pm 20\%$ variations.

Figure 19 shows the closed-loop system responses for chemotherapy control with $\pm 50\%$ variations in the time constant T_2. In this case, compared to the nominal case when an overshoot of 9% was obtained, overshoot varies to 8% for -50% variation in T_2 and 10% for the case when the time constant varies by +50%. The obtained results remain within the ranges specified in [49], and the system remains robust under these variations as well. The control signals of the FO-PI controller applied in chemotherapy for $\pm 50\%$ variations in T_2, representing the drug dose, are shown in Figure 20.

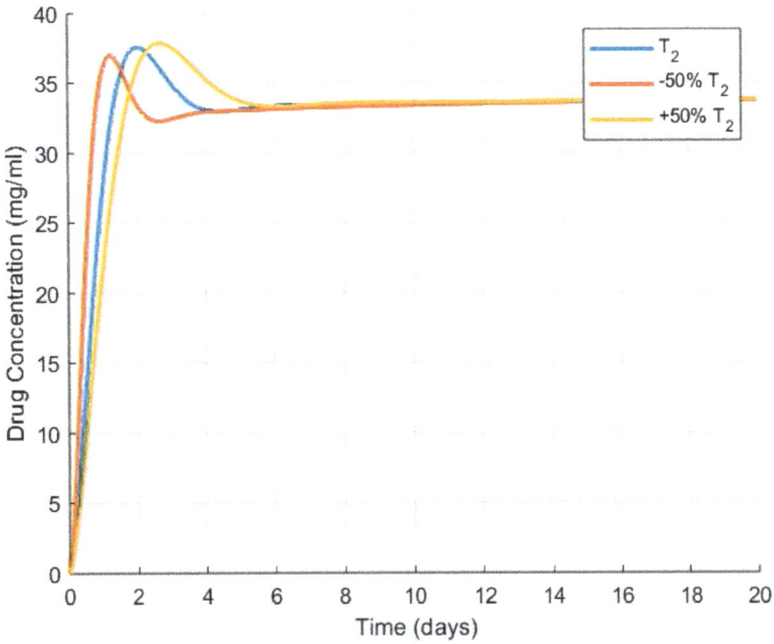

Figure 19. Closed-loop responses for chemotherapy control, considering T_2 and ±50% variations.

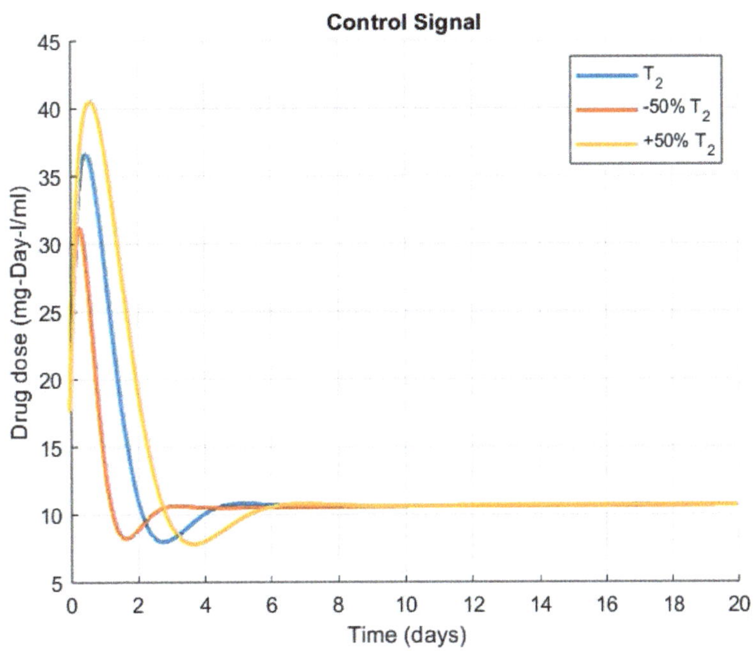

Figure 20. Control signals for chemotherapy control, considering T_2 and ±50% variations.

4. Comparative Results with Traditional PI Control

4.1. BIS Level Control Using a Standard PI Controller

A traditional PI controller is designed for the BIS level to meet the same performance specifications imposed as for the previously presented FO-PI controller, a gain crossover frequency $\omega_c = 0.0135$ rad/s and a phase margin $\varphi_m = 65°$. This controller is used for comparative purposes. By solving (7) and (9) with $\lambda = 1$, the standard PI controller has the following form:

$$C_{PI}(s) = k_p + \frac{k_i}{s} \tag{35}$$

and by computing the controller parameters k_p and k_i using the same algorithm as for the fractional-order controller, the following transfer function of the simple PI controller is obtained:

$$C_4(s) = 0.0259 + \frac{1.32 \cdot 10^{-4}}{s} \tag{36}$$

The closed-loop responses of the BIS level using a standard PI controller are shown in Figure 21, for the time constant T_2 as well as for the ±50% variations in T_2. Figure 22 shows the closed-loop control signals for the BIS level with ±50% variations in T_2. For this controller, the root mean square error (RMSE) was computed to be 18.22 and for the FO-PI controller, it is 16.44. For −50% variation in T_2, the RMSE using the classical PI controller is 16.11, and the RMSE using the FO-PI controller is 14.3. For +50% variation in T_2, the RMSE using the classical PI controller is 20.33, and the RMSE using the FO-PI controller is 18.53. The RMSE results for the BIS level control are presented concisely in Table 2. Compared to the obtained results for the FO-PI controller, larger discrepancies of the undershoot can be noticed in Figure 21 and of the drug doses in Figure 22, when significant variations in the constant T_2 occur. Therefore, the FO-PI controller is more robust than the standard one for BIS level control.

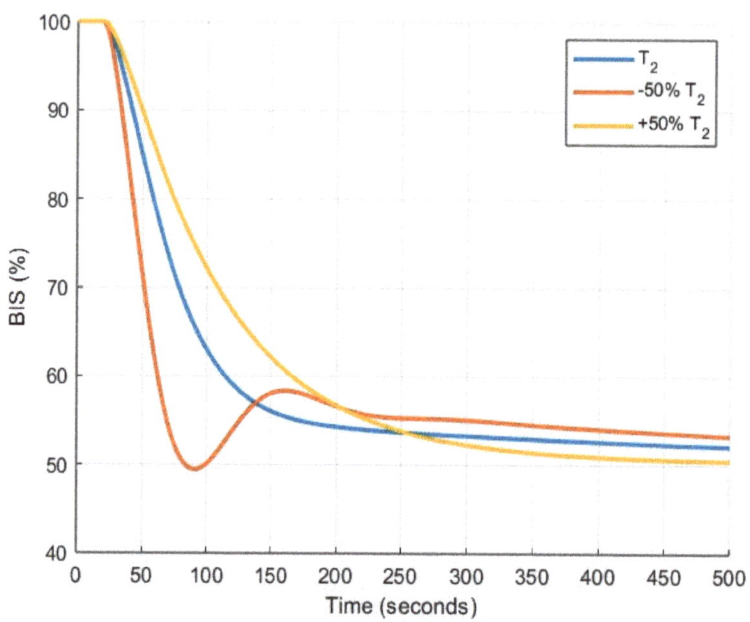

Figure 21. Closed-loop system responses for BIS control, using a traditional PI controller and ±50% variations in T_2.

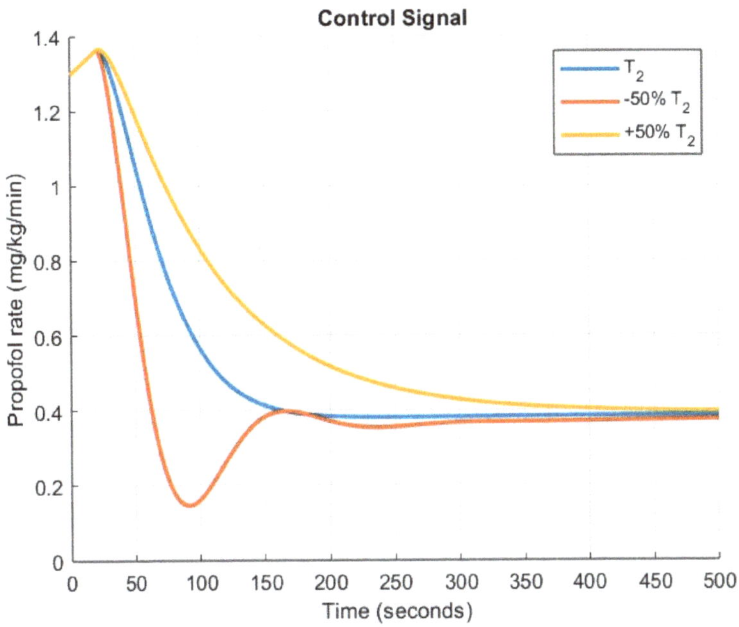

Figure 22. Control signals for BIS control, using a traditional PI controller and ±50% variations in T_2.

Table 2. The RMSE values for all three case studies.

Controllers and Variations	BIS Control	Glucose Control	Chemotherapy Control
FO-PI	16.44	35.74	51.57
Standard PI	18.22	38.18	52.34
−50% for FO-PI	14.3	34.59	41.64
+50% for FO-PI	18.53	36.76	58.79
−50% for PI	16.11	36.99	41.05
+50% for PI	20.33	39.3	61.6

4.2. Glucose Control for Diabetic Patients Using a Standard PI Controller

For the blood glucose level control, a traditional PI controller is tuned using the same performance criteria as for the proposed FO-PI controller, a gain crossover frequency of $\omega_c = 0.11$ rad/s and $\varphi_m = 65°$. By solving (7) and (9) with $\lambda = 1$, the resulting PI controller has the following transfer function:

$$C_5(s) = 11.7063 + \frac{0.4334}{s} \tag{37}$$

The closed-loop responses of the blood glucose level control using a standard PI controller are depicted in Figure 23, considering the time constant T_2 and ±50% variations in T_2. Notice that in this case, there is no actual overshoot, but the dynamics become oscillatory for −50% variation in the time constant. The RMSE of the classical controller was computed to be 38.18, and for the FO-PI controller, it is 35.74. For −50% variation in T_2, the RMSE using the PI controller is 36.99, and the RMSE using the FO-PI controller is 34.59. For +50% variation in T_2, the RMSE using the PI controller is 39.3, and the RMSE using the FO-PI controller is 36.76. The RMSE values demonstrate that better closed-loop control can be achieved with the FO-PI controller despite significant time constant variations. The

RMSE results for glucose level control are presented concisely in Table 2. The closed-loop control signals for the standard PI controller are represented by the insulin infusion rate and are shown in Figure 24.

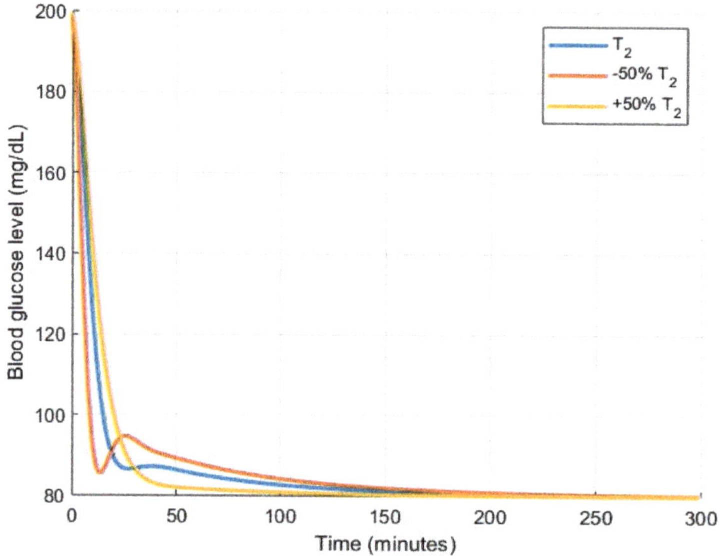

Figure 23. Closed-loop system responses for glucose control, using a traditional PI controller and ±50% variations in T_2.

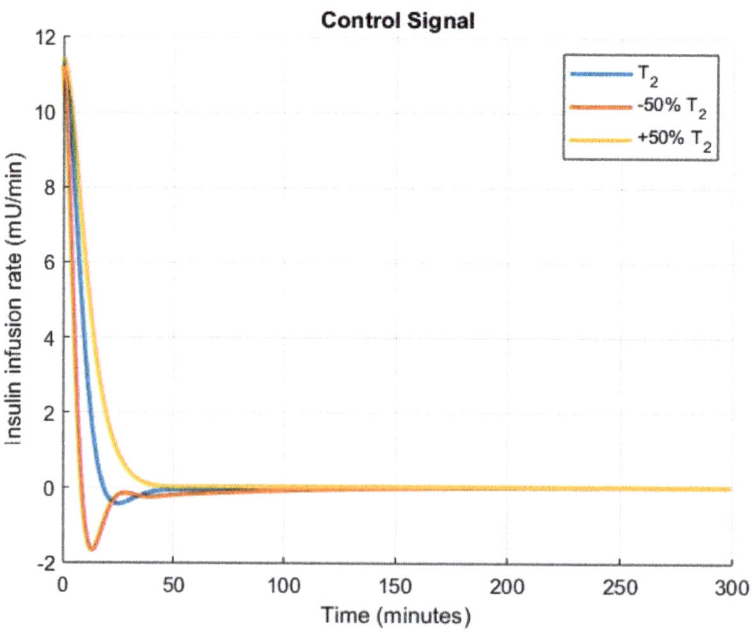

Figure 24. Control signals for glucose control, using a traditional PI controller and ±50% variations in T_2.

4.3. Computer-Controlled Chemotherapy Using a Standard PI Controller

For the chemotherapy control, a standard PI controller is designed for comparative purposes. The same performance criteria as for the FO-PI controller are imposed, including a gain crossover frequency $\omega_c = 1.4$ rad/s and a phase margin $\varphi_m = 60°$. The standard PI controller transfer function is determined using (7) and (9) with $\lambda = 1$:

$$C_6(s) = 1.1236 + \frac{1.1206}{s} \tag{38}$$

The closed-loop responses for the chemotherapy control using a standard PI controller are presented in Figure 25, for the time constant T_2 as well as for the $\pm 50\%$ variations in T_2. For the nominal case, an overshoot of 5% is obtained. This varies to 0% for -50% variation in the time constant and increases to 10% for +50% variation in T_2. This clearly shows that the PI controller cannot maintain a constant overshoot despite the time constant variations. The FO-PI controller on the other hand maintains a quasi-constant overshoot between 8 and 10%, according to Figure 19, and it is therefore more robust than the standard one for the chemotherapy control. The RMSE value of the classical PI controller is 52.34, which is higher than that of the FO-PI controller, which has a value of 51.57. For -50% variation in T_2, the RMSE using the classical PI controller is 41.05, and the RMSE using the FO-PI controller is 41.64. For +50% variation in T_2, the RMSE using the classical PI controller is 61.6, and the RMSE using the FO-PI controller is 58.79. These RMSE values clearly indicate that the FO-PI controller achieves better closed-loop control compared to the standard PI controller. The RMSE results for chemotherapy control are shown concisely in Table 2. The closed-loop control signals for the standard PI controller are represented by the drug dose and can be noticed in Figure 26.

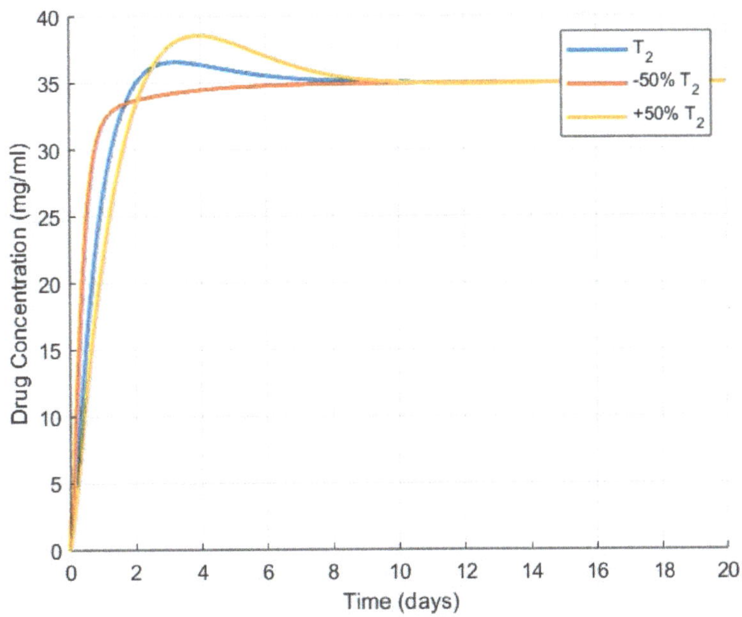

Figure 25. Closed-loop system responses for chemotherapy control, using a traditional PI controller and $\pm 50\%$ variations in T_2.

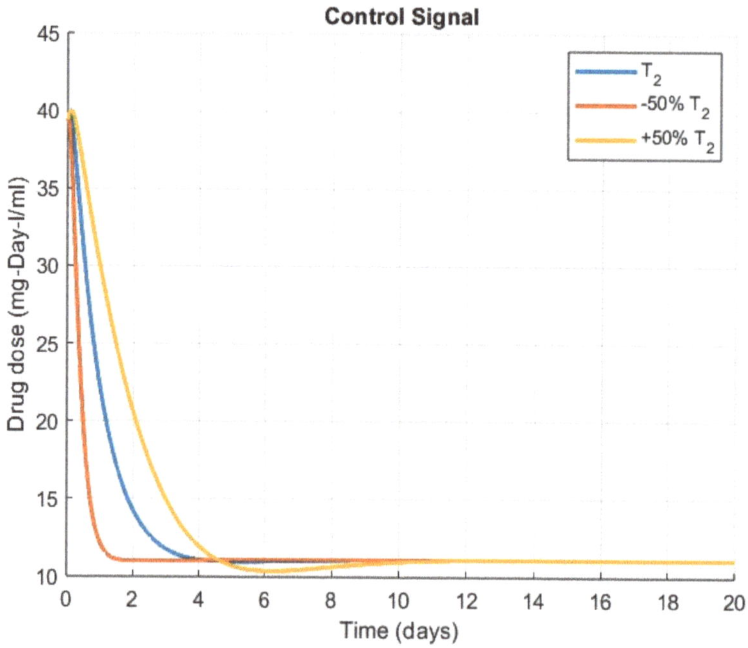

Figure 26. Control signals for chemotherapy control, using a traditional PI controller and ±50% variations in T_2.

5. Insights and Limitations of the Proposed Approach

As indicated in the Introduction section, a limited number of papers cover the design of fractional-order controllers for robustness to time constant variations. The main novelty of this research resides in the direct design of the fractional-order controllers to ensure robustness to time constant variations. The graphical method used in the tuning is by no means better compared to standard optimization routines. These offer the benefit of a higher degree of automation in determining the solution. This is not the case with the current approach, which might be seen as a limitation. However, the graphical approach comes with some important advantages. The main advantage is that such a graphical approach is very simple, straightforward, and easy to understand, without requiring expert knowledge of optimization routines. At the same time, the graphical approach is as efficient in determining the solution compared to optimization routines. Naturally, the step size used in the graphical approach is important, but even a large step size can indicate an approximate range of the solution. Once this approximate range has been estimated choosing a smaller step size implies an increased accuracy in determining the final solution.

The great majority of fractional-order tuning algorithms are exemplified and validated on simple mathematical representations of the processes, such as FOPDT or SOPDT systems. From this point of view, the proposed tuning algorithm is similar to existing methods. The approach can be easily extended to multivariable systems, in a decentralized or decoupled approach, similarly to other types of fractional-order controllers.

The case studies considered in this paper are mathematically represented by simple SOPDT models. These are simplistic representations of biomedical applications that do not cover the complexity of the human body. All these transfer functions are taken from existing research studies, and they have been used in the design of different types of controllers. Such simplified models have been used before to tune controllers that are next validated on complex patient models [49,52,55–59,63–65]. To account for uncertainties and modeling mismatches due to patient variability, the current paper introduces the design of a robust fractional-order controller. The robustness refers to the time constants that govern the patient dynamics, which are different from one patient to another due to different reaction times to the administered drugs. Numerical simulations are used to demonstrate the efficiency and robustness of the proposed approach by varying the time constant of the SOPDT model.

The approach comes with some limitations. First of all, the method does not account for variations that might occur in other parameters of the process. This is however similar to the majority of papers dealing with the design of fractional-order controllers. Secondly, although it accounts for patient variability, the human body is complex and generally characterized by nonlinear dynamics. This might limit the applicability of the proposed approach but nevertheless constitutes an important addition to the current state of the art for designing robust fractional-order controllers. Future research could focus on dealing with nonlinearities. Thirdly, the constraints related to the minimum and maximum values for the input signals are not directly addressed, and this is a key feature in optimal drug dosing. However, most existing research papers do not tackle this issue and prefer to use hard limits rather than include the input constraints in the design of the controller.

6. Conclusions

The number of publications addressing the design of fractional-order controllers has increased over the past two decades. The generalization of the standard PID controller to fractional order has brought a multitude of advantages in system control, thus increasing the interest in this approach. The improved robustness of a fractional-order control system is one of these advantages.

The three main performance criteria in the frequency domain used in most tuning procedures of the controllers are a certain phase margin, a gain crossover frequency, and an iso-damping criterion (usually to ensure the robustness to gain variations). The robustness of fractional-order systems to all possible uncertainties in process parameters is studied in various research manuscripts, but this does not provide a clear approach for controller design. The robustness to gain variations is extended to time constant variations in some recent research papers, also providing a mathematical background. The analytical equations have been derived from integrative first-order systems plus time delay. Using optimization methods, the resulting system of nonlinear equations can only be solved numerically.

However, the most common mathematical representations of the patient dynamics in biomedical engineering are represented by SOPDT transfer functions. This manuscript extends existing tuning methodologies and focuses on the design of robust FO-PI controllers for these types of processes. In order to ensure the robustness to variations in the process time constant, the analytical equations are developed. Using a simple graphical method, the nonlinear system of equations is solved more easily than by applying optimization routines. The efficiency of the proposed approach is demonstrated and validated using three case studies.

The first case study consists of BIS level control in general anesthesia. The closed-loop simulation results for BIS control show that the tuned controller is robust to time constant variations. In the second and third case studies, blood glucose level control for diabetic patients and computer control in chemotherapy are presented. The process transfer functions for these systems are either SOPDT or simply second order without time delay and have been sourced from the literature. The closed-loop step responses for blood glucose level control, as well as automatic control in chemotherapy, show a constant overshoot despite the time constant variations, thereby proving the robustness of the designed controllers. The performance specifications and the results obtained are consistent with those reported in the literature for all three case studies.

For future research, the method studied could be extended to the design of fractional-order controllers that are robust to dead time variations. The control algorithm designed in the current paper could be integrated into a toolbox dedicated to educational applications. The tuned controllers can be reduced to recurrence relations and implemented in dedicated devices such as microcontrollers.

Author Contributions: Conceptualization, N.E.B. and C.I.M.; methodology, N.E.B.; software, N.E.B. and M.D.M.; validation, N.E.B., T.M.P. and C.I.M.; formal analysis, N.E.B.; investigation, N.E.B.; resources, N.E.B.; data curation, I.R.B.; writing—original draft preparation, N.E.B.; writing—review and editing, N.E.B., I.R.B. and C.I.M.; visualization, I.R.B.; supervision, C.I.M.; project administration, C.I.M.; funding acquisition, C.I.M. All authors have read and agreed to the published version of the manuscript.

Funding: This work was in part supported by a grant from the Romanian Ministry of Research, Innovation and Digitization, PNRR-III-C9-2022-I8, grant number 760068/23.05.2023. I. R. Birs acknowledges the support of Flanders Research Foundation, Postdoc grant 1203224N, 2023-2026. I.R.Birs was financed by a grant from the Ministry of Research, Innovation and Digitization, CNCS-UEFISCDI, project number PN-IV-P2-2.1-TE-2023-0831.

Data Availability Statement: The original contributions presented in this study are included in the article. Further inquiries can be directed to the corresponding author.

Conflicts of Interest: The authors declare no conflicts of interest.

Appendix A

In the first phase, the fractional order λ is determined using the graphical method, and then the controller parameters are computed using the resulting value of λ.

```
wc=0.0135; % cutting freq
PM=65*pi/180; % phase margin in rad
data1=[];data2=[];data3=[];
f=2;
for lambda=0:0.01:f
    z1 = wc^2*(T1^2-T1*T2-T2*tau-T1^2*T2*wc^2*tau)
    z2 = wc*T2*lambda*(1+T1^2*wc^2)
    z3 = lambda+T1^2*wc^2+T1^2*wc^2*lambda-T1*T2*wc^2-tau*T2*wc^2-T1^2*T2*tau*wc^4
    % A is computed from the robustness equation
    A1= (-z2+sqrt(z2^2-4*z1*z3))/2/z1;
    A2= (-z2-sqrt(z2^2-4*z1*z3))/2/z1;
    % A is computed from the phase margin condition
    A3= tan((atan(T1*wc)+atan(T2*wc)+tau*wc+lambda*pi/2-pi+PM)/lambda);
    data1=[data1; [A1]];
    data2=[data2; [A2]];
    data3=[data3; [A3]];
end
lambda=0:0.01:f;
figure(1),plot(lambda,data1,'r')
hold on,plot(lambda,data3,'b'),title('A1 vs A3'),grid
figure(2),plot(lambda,data2,'r')
hold on, plot(lambda,data3,'b'),title('A2 vs A3'),grid
```

To compute the FO-PI controller, a function RdK_foc.m is used to approximate a fourth-order discrete-time transfer function of the controller, as detailed in [54].

```
% read from the graph
lambda=0.82
z1 = wc^2*(T1^2-T1*T2-T2*tau-T1^2*T2*wc^2*tau)
z2 = wc*T2*lambda*(1+T1^2*wc^2)
z3 = lambda+T1^2*wc^2+T1^2*wc^2*lambda-T1*T2*wc^2-tau*T2*wc^2-T1^2*T2*tau*wc^4
% A is computed from the robustness equation
A1= (-z2+sqrt(z2^2-4*z1*z3))/2/z1
A2= (-z2-sqrt(z2^2-4*z1*z3))/2/z1
% A is computed from the phase margin condition
A3= tan((atan(T1*wc)+atan(T2*wc)+tau*wc+lambda*pi/2-pi+PM)/lambda)
delta = A3;
Ki = wc*sqrt(((wc^2*T1^2+1)*(wc^2*T2^2+1))/(k^2*(delta^2+1)^lambda))^(1/lambda)
Kp = delta*Ki/wc
Ts=1;
FO_PI_dis = RdK_foc(@Example3,4,1,pi/Ts);
Hdis = c2d(H,Ts,'tustin');
```

The fractional-order system and the controller parameters are specified in an m-file Example3.m presented below.

```
function [FreqResp]=RdK_FreqResp(s)
lambda=0.82; kp=0.011419802079288; ki=7.264824279109768e-05; % PM=65, wc=0.0135
s(1)=0.1*s(2); FreqResp=(kp+ki./s).^lambda; % example FO-TF3 (PID);
% prevent inf at w=0
```

References

1. Tepljakov, A.; Alagoz, B.B.; Yeroglu, C.; Gonzalez, E.A.; Hosseinnia, S.H.; Petlenkov, E.; Ates, A.; Cech, M. Towards Industrialization of FOPID Controllers: A Survey on Milestones of Fractional-Order Control and Pathways for Fu ture Developments. *IEEE Access* **2021**, *9*, 21016–21042. [CrossRef]
2. Shah, P.; Sekhar, R.; Sharma, D.; Penubadi, H.R. Fractional order control: A bibliometric analysis (2000–2022). *Results Control Optim.* **2024**, *14*, 100366. [CrossRef]
3. Petráš, I. Chapter Three- Fractional-order control: New control techniques. In *Emerging Methodologies and Applications in Modelling, Fractional Order Systems*; Radwan, A.G., Khanday, F.A., Said, L.A., Eds.; Academic Press: Cambridge, MA, USA, 2022; Volume 1, pp. 71–106. [CrossRef]
4. Li, X.; Gao, L. Robust Fractional-order PID Tuning Method for a Plant with an Uncertain Parameter. *Int. J. Control Autom. Syst.* **2021**, *19*, 1302–1310. [CrossRef]
5. Luo, Y.; Chen, Y. Stabilizing and robust fractional order PI controller synthesis for first order plus time delay systems. *Automatica* **2012**, *48*, 2159–2167. [CrossRef]
6. Feliu-Batlle, V. Robust isophase margin control of oscillatory systems with large uncertainties in their parameters: A fractional-order control approach. *Int. J. Robust Nonlinear Control* **2017**, *27*, 2145–2164. [CrossRef]
7. Birs, I.; Muresan, C.I.; Nascu, I.; Ionescu, C. A Survey of Recent Advances in Fractional Order Control for Time Delay Systems. *IEEE Access* **2019**, *7*, 30951–30965. [CrossRef]
8. Dastjerdi, A.A.; Vinagre, B.M.; Chen, Y.; Hassan HosseinNia, S. Linear fractional order controllers; A survey in the frequency domain. *Annu. Rev. Control* **2019**, *47*, 51–70. [CrossRef]
9. Ruan, S. Robust Fractional-Order Proportional-Integral Controller Tuning for Load Frequency Control of a Microgrid System with Communication Delay. *Energies* **2023**, *16*, 5418. [CrossRef]
10. Zheng, W.; Luo, Y.; Chen, Y.; Wang, X. A Simplified Fractional Order PID Controller's Optimal Tuning: A Case Study on a PMSM Speed Servo. *Entropy* **2021**, *23*, 130. [CrossRef]
11. Hegedus, E.; Birs, I.; Muresan, C. Fractional order control of the combined anaesthesia-hemodynamic system: A preliminary study. *IFAC-PapersOnLine* **2021**, *54*, 19–24. [CrossRef]
12. Chen, P.; Luo, Y.; Peng, Y.; Chen, Y. Optimal robust fractional order PIλD controller synthesis for first order plus time delay systems. *ISA Trans.* **2021**, *114*, 136–149. [CrossRef] [PubMed]

13. Sánchez, H.S.; Padula, F.; Visioli, A.; Vilanova, R. Tuning rules for robust FOPID controllers based on multi-objective optimization with FOPDT models. *ISA Trans.* **2017**, *66*, 344–361. [CrossRef]
14. Yumuk, E.; Güzelkaya, M.; Eksin, İ. Analytical fractional PID controller design based on Bode's ideal transfer function plus time delay. *ISA Trans.* **2019**, *91*, 196–206. [CrossRef]
15. Liu, L.; Zhang, S. Robust Fractional-Order PID Controller Tuning Based on Bode's Optimal Loop Shaping. *Complexity* **2018**, *2018*, 6570560. [CrossRef]
16. Azarmi, R.; Tavakoli-Kakhki, M.; Sedigh, A.K.; Fatehi, A. Robust fractional order PI controller tuning based on Bode's ideal transfer function. *IFAC-PapersOnLine* **2016**, *49*, 158–163. [CrossRef]
17. Saxena, S.; Hote, Y.V. Design of robust fractional-order controller using the Bode ideal transfer function approach in IMC paradigm. *Nonlinear Dyn.* **2016**, *107*, 983–1001. [CrossRef]
18. Şenol, B.; Demiroğlu, U. Fractional order proportional derivative control for first order plus time delay plants: Achieving phase and gain specifications simultaneously. *Trans. Inst. Meas. Control* **2019**, *41*, 4358–4369. [CrossRef]
19. Monje, C.; Calderon, A.; Vinagre, B.; Chen, Y.; Feliu, V. On Fractional PI^{λ} Controllers: Some Tuning Rules for Robustness to Plant Uncertainties. *Nonlinear Dyn.* **2004**, *38*, 369–381. [CrossRef]
20. Wu, Z.; Li, D.; Xue, Y.; He, T.; Zheng, S. Tuning for fractional order PID controller based on probabilistic robustness. *IFAC-PapersOnLine* **2018**, *51*, 675–680. [CrossRef]
21. Alagoz, B.B.; Yeroglu, C.; Senol, B.; Ates, A. Probabilistic robust stabilization of fractional order systems with interval uncertainty. *ISA Trans.* **2015**, *57*, 101–110. [CrossRef]
22. Kumar, V.; Rana, K.P.S.; Mishra, P. Robust speed control of hybrid electric vehicle using fractional order fuzzy PD and PI controllers in cascade control loop. *J. Frankl. Inst.* **2016**, *353*, 1713–1741. [CrossRef]
23. Pachauri, N.; Thangavel, V.; Suresh, V.; Kantipudi, M.P.; Kotb, H.; Tripathi, R.N.; Bajaj, M. A Robust Fractional-Order Control Scheme for PV-Penetrated Grid-Connected Microgrid. *Mathematics* **2023**, *11*, 1283. [CrossRef]
24. Martins-Gomes, M.C.; Junior, F.A.D.C.A.; da Costa Junior, C.T.; de Bessa, I.V.; Farias, N.J.D.S.; de Medeiros, R.L.; Silva, L.E.; de Lucena Júnior, V.F. Fractional-Order Robust Control Design under parametric uncertain approach. *ISA Trans.* **2024**, *153*, 420–432. [CrossRef] [PubMed]
25. Gao, Z. Robust stabilization criterion of fractional-order controllers for interval fractional-order plants. *Automatica* **2015**, *61*, 9–17. [CrossRef]
26. Lanusse, P.; Malti, R.; Melchior, P. CRONE control system design toolbox for the control engineering community: Tutorial and case study. *Philos. Trans. R. Soc. A Math. Phys. Eng. Sci.* **2013**, *371*, 20120149. [CrossRef] [PubMed]
27. Mseddi, A.; Abid, A.; Naifar, O.; Rhaima, M.; Ben Makhlouf, A.; Mchiri, L. Investigation of the Robust Fractional Order Control Approach Associated with the Online Analytic Unity Magnitude Shaper: The Case of Wind Energy Systems. *Fractal Fract.* **2024**, *8*, 187. [CrossRef]
28. Mihaly, V.; Şuşcă, M.; Dulf, E.H.; Morar, D.; Dobra, P. Fractional Order Robust Controller for Fractional-Order Interval Plants. *IFAC-PapersOnLine* **2022**, *55*, 151–156. [CrossRef]
29. Rhouma, A.; Hafsi, S.; Laabidi, K. Stabilizing and Robust Fractional PID Controller Synthesis for Uncertain First-Order plus Time-Delay Systems. *Math. Probl. Eng.* **2021**, *2021*, 9940634. [CrossRef]
30. Beschi, M.; Padula, F.; Visioli, A. The generalised isodamping approach for robust fractional PID controllers design. *Int. J. Control* **2015**, *90*, 1157–1164. [CrossRef]
31. Jin, Y.; Chen, Y.Q.; Xue, D. Time-constant robust analysis of a fractional order [proportional derivative] controller. *IET Control Theory Appl.* **2011**, *5*, 164–172. [CrossRef]
32. Badri, V.; Tavazoei, M.S. On time-constant robust tuning of fractional order proportional derivative controllers. *IEEE/CAA J. Autom. Sin.* **2019**, *6*, 1179–1186. [CrossRef]
33. Peker, F.; Kaya, I. Maximum sensitivity (Ms)-based I-PD controller design for the control of integrating processes with time delay. *Int. J. Syst. Sci.* **2022**, *54*, 313–332. [CrossRef]
34. Arrieta, O.; Vilanova, R. Simple PID tuning rules with guaranteed Ms robustness achievement. *IFAC Proc. Vol.* **2011**, *44*, 12042–12047. [CrossRef]
35. Padula, F.; Visioli, A. Tuning rules for optimal PID and fractional-order PID controllers. *J. Process Control* **2011**, *21*, 69–81. [CrossRef]
36. Patel, K.D.; Patil, S.L. Non-linear tank level control using fractional PI. In Proceedings of the 2019 3rd International Conference on Trends in Electronics and Informatics (ICOEI), Tirunelveli, India, 23–25 April 2019; pp. 113–116. [CrossRef]
37. Padula, F.; Visioli, A. Optimal tuning rules for proportional-integral-derivative and fractional-order proportional-integral-derivative controllers for integral and unstable processes. *IET Control Theory Appl.* **2012**, *6*, 776–786. [CrossRef]
38. Padula, F.; Visioli, A. Set-point weight tuning rules for fractional-order PID controllers. *Asian J. Control* **2013**, *15*, 678–690. [CrossRef]
39. Muresan, C.I.; De Keyser, R. Revisiting Ziegler–Nichols. A fractional order approach. *ISA Trans.* **2022**, *129*, 287–296. [CrossRef]

40. Gude, J.J.; Kahoraho, E. Modified Ziegler-Nichols method for fractional PI controllers. In Proceedings of the 2010 IEEE 15th Conference on Emerging Technologies & Factory Automation (ETFA 2010), Bilbao, Spain, 13–16 September 2010; pp. 1–5. [CrossRef]
41. Hegedus, E.T.; Birs, I.R.; Ghita, M.; Ionescu, C.M.; De Keyser, R.; Muresan, C.I.; Ghita, M.; Nascu, I. Optimal Fractional Order PID based on a Modified Ziegler-Nichols method. In Proceedings of the 2022 International Conference on Electrical, Computer, Communications and Mechatronics Engineering (ICECCME), Maldives, Maldives, 16–18 November 2022; pp. 1–6. [CrossRef]
42. Marshiana, D.; Thirusakthimurugan, P. Fractional order PI controller for nonlinear systems. In Proceedings of the 2014 International Conference on Control, Instrumentation, Communication and Computational Technologies (ICCICCT), Kanyakumari, India, 10–11 July 2014; pp. 322–326. [CrossRef]
43. Copot, D. (Ed.) *Automated Drug Delivery in Anesthesia*; Elsevier: London, UK; Academic Press: San Diego, CA, USA, 2020; ISBN 978-0-12-815975-0.
44. Mihai, M.D.; Birs, I.R.; Badau, N.E.; Hegedus, E.T.; Ynineb, A.; Muresan, C.I. Personalised Fractional-Order Autotuner for the Maintenance Phase of Anaesthesia Using Sine-Tests. *Fractal Fract.* **2025**, *9*, 317. [CrossRef]
45. Saleem, O.; Iqbal, J. Complex-order PID controller design for enhanced blood-glucose regulation in Type-I diabetes patients. *Meas. Control* **2023**, *56*, 1811–1825. [CrossRef]
46. Kiss, B.; Sápi, J.; Kovács, L. Imaging method for model-based control of tumor diseases. In Proceedings of the 2013 IEEE 11th International Symposium on Intelligent Systems and Informatics (SISY), Subotica, Serbia, 26–28 September 2013; pp. 271–275. [CrossRef]
47. Biro, J.; Neyens, D.M.; Jaruzel, C.; Tobin, C.D.; Alfred, M.; Coppola, S.; Abernathy, J.H.; Catchpole, K.R. "One size" doesn't "fit all": Understanding variability in anesthesia work practices. *Hum. Factors Healthc.* **2022**, *2*, 100026. [CrossRef]
48. Abdulla, S.A.; Wen, P. The Effects of Time-Delay on Feedback Control of Depth of Anesthesia. In Proceedings of the 2012 IEEE EMBS International Conference on Biomedical and Health Informatics, Hong Kong, China, 5–7 January 2012; pp. 956–959.
49. Pachauri, N.; Suresh, V.; Kantipudi, M.P.; Alkanhel, R.; Abdallah, H.A. Multi-Drug Scheduling for Chemotherapy Using Fractional Order Internal Model Controller. *Mathematics* **2023**, *11*, 1779. [CrossRef]
50. Schiff, J.H.; Welker, A.; Fohr, B.; Henn-Beilharz, A.; Bothner, U.; Van Aken, H.; Schleppers, A.; Baldering, H.J.; Heinrichs, W. Major incidents and complications in otherwise healthy patients undergoing elective procedures: Results based on 1.37 million anaesthetic procedures. *BJA Br. J. Anaesth.* **2014**, *113*, 109–121. [CrossRef]
51. Muresan, C.I.; Mihai, M.D.; Hegedus, E.T.; Birs, I.R.; Ionescu, C.M.; De Keyser, R. A Simplified Robust Fractional Order PID for Dead Time Processes. In Proceedings of the 2025 International Conference on Advanced Robotics, Control, and Artificial Intelligence (ARCAI2025), Nadi, Fiji, 23–26 November 2025.
52. Merigo, L.; Beschi, M.; Padula, F.; Latronico, N.; Paltenghi, M.; Visioli, A. Event-Based control of depth of hypnosis in anesthesia. *Comput. Methods Programs Biomed.* **2017**, *147*, 63–83. [CrossRef] [PubMed]
53. Badau, N.; Popescu, T.; Mihai, M.; Birs, I.; Muresan, C. Personalized Control using Fractional Calculus for Patients Experiencing Surgical Stimuli. In Proceedings of the 2025 29th International Conference on System Theory, Control and Computing (ICSTCC), Cluj-Napoca, Romania, 9–11 October 2025.
54. De Keyser, R.; Muresan, C.I.; Ionescu, C.M. An efficient algorithm for low-order direct discrete-time implementation of frac tional order transfer functions. *ISA Trans.* **2018**, *74*, 229–238. [CrossRef] [PubMed]
55. Padula, F.; Ionescu, C.; Latronico, N.; Paltenghi, M.; Visioli, A.; Vivacqua, G. Optimized PID control of depth of hypnosis in anesthesia. *Comput. Methods Programs Biomed.* **2017**, *144*, 21–35. [CrossRef]
56. Pawłowski, A.; Schiavo, M.; Latronico, N.; Paltenghi, M.; Visioli, A. Event-based MPC for propofol administration in anesthesia. *Comput. Methods Programs Biomed.* **2023**, *229*, 107289. [CrossRef]
57. Hegedüs, E.T.; Birs, I.R.; Ionescu, C.M.; Muresan, C.I. A Novel Decentralized–Decoupled Fractional-Order Control Strategy for Complete Anesthesia–Hemodynamic Stabilization in Patients Undergoing Surgical Procedures. *Fractal Fract.* **2024**, *8*, 623. [CrossRef]
58. Merigo, L.; Padula, F.; Latronico, N.; Paltenghi, M.; Visioli, A. Event-based control tuning of propofol and remifentanil coadministration for general anaesthesia. *IET Control Theory Appl.* **2020**, *14*, 2995–3008. [CrossRef]
59. Hegedus, E.; Mihai, M.D.; Birs, I.R.; Farbakhsh, H.; Yumuk, E.; Copot, D.; De Keyser, R.; Ionescu, C.M.; Muresan, C.I. A Decoupled Fractional Order Control Strategy to Increase Patient Safety During Anesthesia-Hemodynamic Interactions. In Proceedings of the 2024 European Control Conference (ECC), Stockholm, Sweden, 25–28 June 2024; pp. 3039–3044. [CrossRef]
60. Dubey, R.S.; Baleanu, D.; Mishra, M.N.; Goswami, P. Solution of modified bergman minimal blood glucose-insulin model using Caputo-Fabrizio fractional derivative. *Comput. Model. Eng. Sci.* **2021**, *128*, 1247–1263.
61. Palumbo, P.; Ditlevsen, S.; Bertuzzi, A.; De Gaetano, A. Mathematical modeling of the glucose–insulin system: A review. *Math. Biosci.* **2013**, *244*, 69–81. [CrossRef]

62. Percival, M.W.; Zisser, H.; Jovanovic, L.; Doyle, F.J. Closed-Loop Control and Advisory Mode Evaluation of an Artificial Pancreatic β Cell: Use of Proportional-Integral-Derivative Equivalent Model-Based Controllers. *J. Diabetes Sci. Technol.* **2008**, *2*, 636–644. [CrossRef] [PubMed]
63. Saravanakumar, K.; Isaac, J.S. IMO-PSO FO-PID controller based insulin infusion system for type 1 diabetes patients during post-operation condition. *Meas. Sens.* **2024**, *33*, 101172. [CrossRef]
64. Pintea, P.; Mihaly, V.; Şuşcă, M.; Dobra, P. Koopman Linearization and Optimal Control of Glucose Level. In Proceedings of the 2024 28th International Conference on System Theory, Control and Computing (ICSTCC), Sinaia, Romania, 10–12 October 2024; pp. 45–50. [CrossRef]
65. Pachauri, N.; Yadav, J.; Rani, A.; Singh, V. Modified fractional order IMC design based drug scheduling for cancer treatment. *Comput. Biol. Med.* **2019**, *109*, 121–137. [CrossRef] [PubMed]